"Susan Ackerman's work on goddesses, Israelite women, and religion in ancient Israel has changed how we understand gender and the past. This collection gathers essays from more than three decades, offering a comprehensive yet highly readable overview of Ackerman's scholarship. Reading the essays together reveals Ackerman's acuity as a historian and a scholar of gender, and her ongoing importance in the field of biblical studies. A highly recommended resource."

—RHIANNON GRAYBILL
Rhodes College

"Any reader wedded to the exegetical quest for biblical origins must read Susan Ackerman's new book. Steeped in comparative historical criticism that regards the Bible 'as a window into ancient Israel's past,' ten essays present fascinating gynocritical reconstructions of women's religious practices on the basis of Ackerman's reconstructive 'magic' with biblical and ancient Near Eastern texts. The book as a whole argues for a differentiated reading of women as worshippers, priests, prophets, or queen mothers. Complex and thorough investigations into the significance of goddesses like the Queen of Heaven, Tiamat, or Asherah propose their popularity among the non-elite Israelite population, especially women, in opposition to the 'minoritarian' views of biblical writers like Isaiah, Jeremiah, Micah, or 'the spokespersons of the Deuteronomistic school.' Yet whether these historical portrayals are not altogether only 'speculative' is an important methodological issue that this collection of essays does not aim to resolve."

—SUSANNE SCHOLZ
Southern Methodist University

Gods, Goddesses, and
the Women Who Serve Them

SUSAN ACKERMAN

WILLIAM B. EERDMANS PUBLISHING COMPANY
GRAND RAPIDS, MICHIGAN

Wm. B. Eerdmans Publishing Co.
4035 Park East Court SE, Grand Rapids, Michigan 49546
www.eerdmans.com

28 27 26 25 24 23 22   1 2 3 4 5 6 7

ISBN 978-0-8028-7956-1

Library of Congress Cataloging-in-Publication Data

A catalog record for this book is available from the Library of Congress.

Contents

꙰

Abbreviations

❧

ABD	*Anchor Bible Dictionary.* Edited by David Noel Freedman. 6 vols. New York: Doubleday, 1992.
AHw	*Akkadisches Handwörterbuch.* Wolfram von Soden. 3 vols. Wiesbaden: Harrassowitz, 1965–1981.
ANEP	*The Ancient Near East in Pictures Relating to the Old Testament.* Edited by James B. Pritchard. Princeton: Princeton University Press, 1954.
ANET	*Ancient Near Eastern Texts Relating to the Old Testament.* Edited by James B. Pritchard. 3rd ed. with supplement. Princeton: Princeton University Press, 1969.
AOAT	Alter Orient und Altes Testament
ARM	Archives royales de Mari
AYB	Anchor Yale Bible
AYBRL	Anchor Yale Bible Reference Library
BA	*Biblical Archaeologist*
BAR	*Biblical Archaeology Review*
BASOR	*Bulletin of the American Schools of Oriental Research*
BDB	Brown, Francis, S. R. Driver, and Charles A. Briggs. *A Hebrew and English Lexicon of the Old Testament.* Oxford: Clarendon, 1907.
Bib	*Biblica*
BJS	Brown Judaic Studies
BN	*Biblische Notizen*
BRev	*Bible Review*
BZAW	Beihefte zur Zeitschrift für die alttestamentliche Wissenschaft
CAD	*The Assyrian Dictionary of the Oriental Institute of the University of Chicago.* Edited by Ignace J. Gelb et al. 21 vols. Chicago: The Oriental Institute, 1956–2010.

CANE	*Civilizations of the Ancient Near East.* Edited by Jack M. Sasson. 4 vols. New York: Scribner, 1995.
CBC	Cambridge Bible Commentary
CBQ	*Catholic Biblical Quarterly*
CBQMS	Catholic Biblical Quarterly Monograph Series
CIS	*Corpus inscriptionum semiticarum*
COS	*The Context of Scripture.* Edited by William W. Hallo and K. Lawson Younger, Jr. 3 vols. Leiden: Brill, 2003.
ErIsr	*Eretz-Israel*
ExpTim	*Expository Times*
FCB	Feminist Companion to the Bible
GKC	*Gesenius' Hebrew Grammar.* Edited by E. Kautzsch. Translated by A. E. Cowley. 2nd ed. Oxford: Clarendon, 1910.
HALOT	Koehler, Ludwig, Walter Baumgartner, and Johann Jakob Stamm. *The Hebrew and Aramaic Lexicon of the Old Testament.* Translated and edited under the supervision of Mervyn E. J. Richardson. 4 vols. Leiden: Brill, 1994–1999.
HAR	*Hebrew Annual Review*
HSM	Harvard Semitic Monographs
HSS	Harvard Semitic Studies
HTR	*Harvard Theological Review*
HUCA	*Hebrew Union College Annual*
ICC	International Critical Commentary
IEJ	*Israel Exploration Journal*
JAOS	*Journal of the American Oriental Society*
JBL	*Journal of Biblical Literature*
JEA	*Journal of Egyptian Archaeology*
JESHO	*Journal of the Economic and Social History of the Orient*
JNES	*Journal of Near Eastern Studies*
JSOT	*Journal for the Study of the Old Testament*
JSOTSup	Journal for the Study of the Old Testament: Supplement Series
KAI	*Kanaanäische und aramäische Inschriften.* Herbert Donner and Wolfgang Röllig. 3 vols. 2nd ed. Wiesbaden: Harrassowitz, 1966–1969.
KAR	*Keilschrifttexte aus Assur religiösen Inhalts.* Erich Ebeling. 2 vols. Leipzig: J. C. Hinrichs, 1919–1922.
KBL	Koehler, Ludwig, and Walter Baumgartner. *Lexicon in Veteris Testamenti libros.* 2nd ed. Leiden: Brill, 1958.

KTU	*Die keilalphabetischen Texte aus Ugarit, Ras Ibn Hani und anderen Orten.* Edited by Manfried Dietrich, Oswald Loretz, and Joaquín Sanmartín. 3rd ed. Münster: Ugarit-Verlag, 2013.
LXX	Septuagint
MT	Masoretic Text
NEA	*Near Eastern Archaeology*
OBO	Orbis biblicus et orientalis
OLP	*Orientalia Lovaniensia Periodica*
Or	*Orientalia*
OTL	Old Testament Library
PRU	*Le palais royal d'Ugarit.* Jean Nougayrol and Charles Virolleaud. Edited by Claude F. A. Schaeffer. 6 vols. Mission de Ras Shamra. Paris: Imprimerie nationale, 1955–1970.
Qad	*Qadmoniot*
RA	*Revue d'assyriologie et d'archéologie orientale*
RB	*Revue biblique*
RES	*Répertoire d'épigraphie sémitique*
RS	Ras Shamra
SBLDS	Society of Biblical Literature Dissertation Series
SBLMS	Society of Biblical Literature Monograph Series
SBLRBS	Society of Biblical Literature Resources for Biblical Studies
SBLWAW	Society of Biblical Literature Writings from the Ancient World
TA	*Tel Aviv*
UF	*Ugarit-Forschungen*
VT	*Vetus Testamentum*
VTSup	Supplements to Vetus Testamentum
WBC	Word Biblical Commentary
WdO	*Die Welt des Orients*
WIS	*Women in Scripture: A Dictionary of Named and Unnamed Women in the Hebrew Bible, the Apocryphal/Deuterocanonical Books, and the New Testament.* Edited by Carol Meyers, with Toni Craven and Ross S. Kraemer. Boston: Houghton Mifflin, 2000.
ZAW	*Zeitschrift für die alttestamentliche Wissenschaft*

Preface

❧

In 1980, when I started graduate school and began seriously to study the Hebrew Bible, I did so with two main interests in mind: a love of ancient history (an iconic moment of my childhood was a family trip to Stonehenge) and my undergraduate major, religion. What appealed to me most about the Bible, it follows, was the way it could serve as a window into ancient Israel's past (as opposed, say, to the way the Bible might speak to modern theological concerns), and especially the way in which the Bible could help illuminate the world of ancient Israelite religion (as opposed, say, to the way it might illuminate ancient Israel's political, social, or economic history). But I also brought a certain feisty streak to my study of the Bible (and to almost everything else, but that's a different story!), and I think it is because of this feistiness that my work in biblical studies came to focus on the outliers and even the renegades of ancient Israelite religion: those ancient Israelites whose religious beliefs and practices the biblical writers either ignored (at best) or, more often than not, denigrated. In my doctoral dissertation, for example, I examined, among other things, biblical denunciations of child sacrifice and certain practices concerning deceased spirits, such as necromancy, and considered why some ancient Israelites might see these ritual acts as legitimate religious undertakings, even as the biblical writers disapproved.

Twice in my dissertation, I also touched on issues of women's religious practice: first, in discussing the prophet Jeremiah's censure of those Israelites, including women, who, in the late seventh and early sixth centuries BCE worshipped a goddess called the Queen of Heaven (Jer 7:16–20; 44:15–19, 25); then, in discussing the prophet Ezekiel's indictment of women who sat in the north gate of Yahweh's temple precinct in Jerusalem "mourning" over Tammuz, a Mesopotamian god of fertility (Ezek 8:14). Issues regarding women and gender had become, moreover, an increasingly important topic within colleges, universities, and other institutions of higher learning at that time. Indeed,

I earned the equivalent of a minor in women's studies as an undergraduate, and after I completed my doctorate in 1987 and began my academic career, I found myself more and more engaged in conversations about women and the religion of ancient Israel. I was often asked to speak or write about issues related to Israelite women's religious lives and experiences, for example, and I also often found myself working on issues regarding women's religious culture without being asked.

The results of this work ended up in many disparate places, some easily obtained (such as my 1998 monograph, *Warrior, Dancer, Seductress, Queen: Women in Judges and Biblical Israel*), some not as readily accessed. It is thus a pleasure to have the opportunity to republish some of my less accessible essays here, in order to make them more available. Even more so, it is a pleasure to offer updated versions of certain aspects of these previously published works. In some cases, this has meant deleting materials about which I no longer feel as confident or with which I no longer agree; in other cases, it has meant updating some key arguments in the text and some key items in the bibliography. In one instance, moreover, I have added a "2022 Postscript," responding to a 2020 challenge to my original article's thesis; in another, I have rewritten a major section of my original essay to reflect my updated thinking. I have also tried to polish my original prose, and I have, in addition, modified systems of citation and other stylistic features used in the original publications to make the essays as presented in this volume harmonious in terms of format.

What has brought me the greatest pleasure, however, in revising these essays for republication is to present them in the form of a narrative that charts the different yet interrelated directions my analyses have taken over the years. In part, this narrative is put forward in the short introductions that I have provided at the beginning of almost every chapter, and so I need not reiterate those ideas here. But it is appropriate that I comment at this point on the ways the narrative that shapes this volume is embedded in the four-part organizational strategy I have deployed.

Part 1 of this volume begins in the same place I began all those years ago, during my doctoral work, with a chapter about the Queen of Heaven, the goddess whose worship by women (among other Israelites) results in Jeremiah's censure in Jer 7:16–20 and 44:15–19, 25. There then follow chapters that concern two other goddesses: Asherah, the great mother goddess of the Canaanite world, and Tiamat, the primordial sea goddess of Mesopotamian mythology. In each of these chapters, I consider how these goddess figures might be associated (explicitly or implicitly) with portrayals of women characters found in the biblical text.

Next, in part 2, I present three chapters regarding the two major types of religious functionaries attested in the biblical record, priests and prophets, exploring first the stories of the few women in the Bible who are designated as prophets (*nĕbî'â*) in order to ask why these designations are so rare, especially when compared to all the men whom the Bible identifies as prophets. Even more urgently, I ask in all three chapters, and especially in the third, why, when compared to other cultures of the ancient Near East, there is no ancient Israelite tradition of women priests. I do maintain, however, that in Israel's Southern Kingdom of Judah, the queen mother (that is, the mother of the reigning king or, as in 1 Kgs 15:9–10, a mother figure who fulfilled this role) played an important role as a religious functionary within the royal court. The two chapters in part 3 of this volume are devoted to that topic, describing, first, the evidence that I suggest supports my contention that the queen mother served as an official religious functionary within the royal court in Jerusalem and exploring, second, evidence regarding the queen mother's religious role elsewhere in biblical tradition and in the ancient Near East.

Finally, in the two chapters in part 4 of this volume, I seek to bring together many of the ideas that I introduce in the chapters in parts 1, 2, and 3, first by looking in tandem at several of the instances of women's goddess worship that I document in earlier chapters, and second by asking what the relationship is between these various instances of women's goddess worship that I have documented and women's engagement in the cult of Israel's national god, Yahweh. Indeed, this volume's final chapter, which considers the cult of Yahweh, goddess worship, and women's participation in both Yahwistic and goddess traditions, aims to bring together the three aspects of Israelite religion that comprise this book's title, *Gods, Goddesses, and the Women Who Serve Them*. As such, the chapter seems a fitting conclusion to this volume and, I hope, a fitting summary of the thirty years of my scholarly work presented in these pages.

PART 1

Goddesses

CHAPTER 1

"And the Women Knead Dough"

THE WORSHIP OF THE QUEEN OF HEAVEN IN SIXTH-CENTURY JUDAH

This chapter is based on the first article I ever published, in 1989. At that time, very little scholarship had been generated about the Queen of Heaven, the goddess who appears in the Bible in Jer 7:16–20 and 44:15–19, 25 and who is said by the prophet Jeremiah to have been worshipped by some of the inhabitants of sixth-century BCE Judah, especially women. Indeed, although short discussions about the Queen of Heaven had appeared in various commentaries on the book of Jeremiah and in standard Bible dictionaries, encyclopedias, and kindred reference works, the goddess had been the subject of only five stand-alone studies (a sixth appeared just as my essay was going to press). My research thus focused on what I took to be a fundamental issue for furthering the nascent scholarly deliberations: Who was the goddess referred to only by the epithet "Queen of Heaven"? Several other scholars have since taken up this question, and while the answers they have proposed have been diverse, I still stand by my original conclusion: that the Queen of Heaven is a goddess who combines characteristics of the East Semitic goddess Ishtar and the West Semitic goddess Astarte.

I also retain my interest in the question that I hoped identifying the Queen of Heaven might help answer: Why was the worship of this goddess especially appealing to Judean women? To be sure, it was not only women who participated in the cult of the Queen of Heaven; rather, according to Jer 7:18, entire families (men, women, and children) contributed to a household ritual of baking bread cakes that were offered to the goddess, and according

An earlier version of this chapter appeared in Peggy L. Day, ed., *Gender and Difference in Ancient Israel* (Minneapolis: Fortress, 1989), 109–24. Used here by permission of Fortress Press.

to Jer 44:17–18, husbands and wives affirmed together their intent to burn incense and pour out libations to the Queen of Heaven, despite Jeremiah's condemnation. Jeremiah 44:17 also identifies Judah's "kings" and "princes" as being among those who had at some point made offerings to the goddess. Still, it is women alone who speak of pouring out libations, burning incense, and baking bread cakes for the Queen of Heaven in Jer 44:19. And while the Hebrew text of Jer 44:25 is grammatically confused, the ancient Greek translation of the Bible (the LXX) makes clear that in this verse, Jeremiah specifically denounces women who have "spoken" and "vowed" to make incense and libation offerings to the Queen of Heaven. In addition, in Jer 7:18, the prophet specifically identifies women as kneading the dough used for the bread cakes that are to be offered to the Queen of Heaven, and, presumably, these women baked the cakes as well—acts that were surely more integral to a family's fulfilling its ritual commitments to the goddess than were the contributions of the children and fathers (gathering wood and kindling fires so the cakes can be baked).

In the concluding paragraphs of my 1989 article, I offered some thoughts about why the worship of the Queen of Heaven might have special appeal for women, and I have returned to that topic with more fully fleshed-out ideas elsewhere: for example, in my 2006 essay "Women and the Worship of Yahweh in Ancient Israel," which is included in this volume as chapter 10. Over the years, I have also become increasingly interested in another matter that I raised only briefly in my original 1989 article: not who the Queen of Heaven was and why her adherents were attracted to her cult but rather where this goddess was worshipped. Again, some of my more developed thoughts on this subject are addressed in this volume's chapter 9, "At Home with the Goddess," which was originally published in 2003.

In short, although this chapter first appeared in print a little over three decades ago, the questions it raises have continued to occupy my (and other scholars') attention, and it is thus a pleasure to re-present my analysis here. I have used this opportunity to polish my original language a little, to augment and refine some of my arguments, and to update key (but by no means all!) bibliographic references. But my continued commitment to my prior convictions means that in most respects, this chapter stands as it was previously published.

The typical historian of ancient Israelite religion, especially the historian of Israelite religion of the so-called preexilic period (ca. 1200–586 BCE), relies heavily, if not exclusively, on the Bible. This is unavoidable, since the Bible is in essence the only written source (and indeed the only significant source of any kind) that describes the religion of preexilic Israel and Judah. Yet it has become increasingly obvious to historians of Israelite religion that the Bible's descriptions of the preexilic cult are highly selective. For example, the biblical materials, which come predominantly from the hands of priests and prophets, present priestly and prophetic religion as normative and orthodox in ancient Israel, while nonpriestly and nonprophetic religious beliefs and practices are condemned as heterodox and deviant. A more nuanced reconstruction of the religion of ancient Israel suggests, however, that despite the biblical witness, neither the priestly nor prophetic cult was normative in the religion of the preexilic period. Rather, a diversity of beliefs and practices thrived and were accepted by the ancient Israelites as legitimate forms of religious expression.

Uncovering this diverse character of ancient Israelite religion requires special methodologies. First, we must train ourselves to supplement continually the biblical picture of Israelite religion by referring to other sources. Archaeological remains from Israel are crucial, as are comparative data from the ancient Near East and from elsewhere in the Mediterranean world. Yet this evidence is often sparse and not easily interpreted. It is thus equally important that we learn to treat our major source, the Bible, differently. We must examine the biblical presentations of the orthodox with an eye to the heterodox, seeking, for example, to look without prejudice at those cultic practices that the biblical writers so harshly condemn. Only when we acknowledge the polemical nature of many biblical texts can we see, underlying their words, evidence of the multifaceted nature of ancient Israelite religion.

This second methodological point especially helps illuminate an often overlooked aspect of ancient Israelite religion: women's religion. The all-male biblical writers treat this issue with, at best, silence and, at worst, hostility; still, a careful reading of the biblical text suggests that the women of Judah and Israel had a rich religious tradition.[1] Some of the women of early sixth-century BCE Judah, for example, devoted themselves to the worship of a goddess called the Queen of Heaven (Jer 7:16–20; 44:15–19, 25). Indeed, although the prophet Jeremiah makes the women of Judah and Jerusalem the objects of his special scorn due to their devotion to the Queen of Heaven (Jer 44:25),[2] the women

---

1. Phyllis Bird's programmatic article, "Place of Women," 397–419, offers a good introduction to this subject.

2. The grammar of this verse is confused. The verbs with which Jeremiah, speaking for God, condemns his audience refer to those who have "spoken" and "vowed" to make

are steadfast in their worship of the goddess: baking bread cakes "in her image" as offerings (Jer 7:18; 44:19) and pouring out libations and burning incense to her (Jer 44:15, 19).[3] This devotion in the face of persecution indicates that the worship of the Queen of Heaven was an important part of at least some women's religious expression in the sixth century BCE. Here, by establishing the identity of the goddess whom the Bible calls the Queen of Heaven,[4] I propose to explore why the women of Judah found this goddess's cult so appealing.

Scholars, unfortunately, have reached no consensus on the identity of the Queen of Heaven. The great East Semitic goddess Ishtar,[5] Ishtar's West Semitic

---

offerings and pour out libations to the Queen of Heaven using *feminine* plural forms, suggesting that Jeremiah's subject is the assembly's women. But when it comes to nouns, the "mouths" with which the assembly has articulated its intentions, the "vows" regarding the offerings and libations to which it has committed, and the "hands" with which these commitments have been fulfilled carry *masculine* suffixes. This has driven the Hebrew text as it has come down to us to direct the words of opprobrium in v. 25 to both "you" (masculine plural; presumably the assembly's husbands) and "your wives," even as the LXX gives priority to the feminine verb forms and so renders the verse as addressed to the assembly's women alone.

3. The grammar in Jer 44:19 is, as in 44:25 (above, n. 2), confused, as the MT does not explicitly identify those who speak of making libation, incense, and bread cake offerings for the Queen of Heaven, although these worshippers use masculine plural verbs to refer to themselves. However, the version of the LXX represented in the Lucianic minuscules (thought to date back to the third century CE and to be based on older traditions still) reads *kai hai gynaikes eipon*, "and the women said," in identifying the verse's speakers, and the reference later in the verse to the speakers' "husbands" makes clear that the Greek reading is necessary for the sense.

4. The consonantal Hebrew text, in describing the deity to whom veneration was offered, reads *lmlkt*, "for the Queen of [Heaven]" (Jer 7:18; 44:17, 18, 19, 25), but the MT vocalizes *limleket*, as if the word were *lml'kt*, "for the work of [heaven]," meaning, presumably, "the heavenly host" that is referred to in Jer 8:2. Many Hebrew manuscripts in fact read *lml'kt* in 7:18 and 44:17, 18, 19, 25, which is supported by the Targum and Peshitta and by the LXX in Jer 7:18 (*tē stratia tou ouranou*, "the army of the heavens"). But as is commonly recognized (see R. P. Gordon, "Aleph Apologeticum," 112), the Masoretic pointing is an attempt to remove any hint that the people of Judah worshipped the Queen of Heaven. The correct reading, *lĕmalkat*, "for the Queen of [Heaven]," is supported by the Greek translations of Aquila, Symmachus, and Theodotion; by the rendering of 44:17, 18, 19, and 25 in the LXX; and by the Latin Vulgate.

5. See, e.g., Bright, *Jeremiah*, 56; Held, "Studies in Biblical Lexicography," 76–77; Pope, *Song*, 149 (but cf. n. 6 below); Rast, "Cakes for the Queen of Heaven," 167–80; Rudolph, *Jeremia*, 55; Weinfeld, "Worship of Molech and the Queen of Heaven," 148–54; and Weiser, *Buch des Propheten Jeremia*, 70. See also the extensive bibliography compiled by Hadley, "Queen of Heaven," 46–47n88.

counterpart, Astarte,[6] the West Semitic goddesses Anat and Asherah,[7] and even the Canaanite goddess Šapšu have been suggested.[8] Other scholars maintain that it is impossible, given the available data, to determine to which goddess of the Semitic world the Queen of Heaven corresponds.[9] Finally, there are some who believe that the Queen of Heaven is not one deity but rather a goddess who combines the characteristics of East Semitic Ishtar and West Semitic Astarte.[10]

My own sympathies lie with this latter position, which sees in the Queen of Heaven characteristics of both West Semitic Astarte and East Semitic Ishtar. The Queen of Heaven as described in the Bible certainly shares with Astarte many features: first, the title of "Queen" or some related epithet. For example,

6. See, e.g., Bresciani and Kamil, *Le lettre aramaiche di Hermopoli*, 400; Culican, "Votive Model from the Sea," 121–22; Fitzmyer, "Phoenician Inscription from Pyrgi," 287–88; Herrmann, "Aštart," 29n67; Holladay, *Jeremiah*, 1:254–55; Mesnil du Buisson, *Études sur les dieux phéniciens*, 126–27; Olyan, "Some Observations Concerning the Identity of the Queen of Heaven," 161–74; Pope, "'Attart, 'Aštart, Astarte," 251 (but cf. above, n. 5); and Silverman, *Religious Values in the Jewish Proper Names at Elephantine*, 225n6. See also the extensive bibliography compiled by Hadley, "Queen of Heaven," 48–49n97.

7. For Anat, see, e.g., Albright, *Yahweh and the Gods of Canaan*, 130; Cogan, *Imperialism and Religion*, 85; Kapelrud, *The Violent Goddess*, 13, 16; McKay, *Religion in Judah under the Assyrians*, 110–11n19; Porten, *Archives from Elephantine*, 165, 177; and van der Toorn, "Goddesses in Early Israelite Religion," 83–88. For Asherah, see, preeminently, Koch, "Aschera als Himmelskönigin," 97–120; see also, for other references, Fidler, "Writing and Rewriting," 155n61; Hadley, "Queen of Heaven," 45n80.

8. For Šapšu, see Dahood, "La Regina del Cielo," 166–68. Other scholarly suggestions include identifying the Queen of Heaven with the Egyptian goddess Hathor (Avaliani, "Egyptian and Canaanite Religious Convergence," 47–51; Avaliani, "Which Goddess Could Be Hidden Behind the Title 'Queen of Heaven?'," 239–48) and identifying the Queen of Heaven as "'part of' the category of Yhwh," so that, while the Queen of Heaven is "not identical to Yhwh, worshipping her is . . . an aspect of worshipping Yhwh" (Ellis, "Jeremiah 44," 482, 486).

9. E.g., Gray, "Queen of Heaven," 975. A somewhat similar position is put forward by Hadley, "Queen of Heaven," 50–51, who suggests the text of Jeremiah deliberately obscures the Queen of Heaven's identity in order that different goddesses might be identified with the Queen of Heaven in different places and/or at different times; see likewise Fidler, "Writing and Rewriting," 156, discussing the views of Houtman, "Queen of Heaven," 678, and of Leuchter, "Cult of Personality," 95–115, esp. 106–7.

10. Note the comments of Fitzmyer, "Phoenician Inscription from Pyrgi," 287, and Rast, "Cakes for the Queen of Heaven," 170; see also Bright, *Jeremiah*, 56. Marvin H. Pope may also indirectly indicate his support for such a thesis, since he identifies the Queen of Heaven as Astarte in "'Attart, 'Aštart, Astarte," 251, but as Ishtar in *Song*, 149 (above, nn. 5–6). Other scholars who evoke both Ishtar and Astarte when proposing an identification for the Queen of Heaven are cited in Hadley, "Queen of Heaven," 46–47n88, 48–49n97.

in texts from the Egyptian New Kingdom (ca. 1539–1075 BCE), Astarte is called "Lady of Heaven."[11] More notably, in the first millennium BCE, Astarte bears the title "Queen." On the obverse face of the fifth-century BCE Kition Tariff inscription, which lists the monthly expenditures for the Phoenician temple of Astarte at Kition, Cyprus, Astarte is referred to as "the holy Queen" and "the Queen."[12] In his *Phoenician History*, Philo of Byblos, citing the hierophant Sakkunyaton, also attests to Astarte's queenly role in first-millennium BCE Phoenicia by describing Astarte as the co-regent of King Zeus Demarous (Canaanite Baal Haddu) and remarking that she wears on her head a bull's head as an emblem of "kingship" (*basileias*).[13]

The biblical Queen of Heaven in addition shares with Astarte an association with the heavens. Astarte's astral features, already indicated in the second millennium BCE by the Egyptian title "Lady of Heaven," are abundantly attested within first-millennium BCE sources. In both the Eshmunazor and the Bodashtart inscriptions from Phoenicia, Astarte's sacred precinct in Sidon is called "the highest heavens."[14] Elsewhere in the Mediterranean world, As-

---

11. Egyptian *nbt pt*. Redford, "New Light on the Asiatic Campaigning of Horemheb," 37, finds this epithet on a stone bowl of the Eighteenth Dynasty (ca. 1539–1292 BCE); the bowl is also discussed by Delcor, "La culte de la 'Reine du Ciel,'" 114. For inscriptions from the Nineteenth Dynasty (ca. 1292–1190 BCE) with the epithet "Lady of Heaven," see Maspero, "Notes de Voyage," 131–32, and Petrie, *Memphis 1*, 19; also Delcor, "La culte de la 'Reine du Ciel,'" 114; Helck, *Die Beziehungen Ägyptiens zu Vorderasien*, 457–58; Leclant, "Astarté à cheval," 10–13 and fig. 1; and Stadelmann, *Syrisch-Palästinensische Göttheitin in Ägypten*, 104, 106.

12. See *CIS* I.86A/*KAI* 37A, *mlkt qdšt* (line 7) and *mlkt* (line 10), following the line numbers of *KAI*; see further Peckham, "Notes on a Fifth-Century Phoenician Inscription from Kition," 304n2. Although Astarte is not mentioned by name in lines 7 and 10, the title "Queen" in an inscription concerned with the cult and temple of Astarte can refer to no other. This is acknowledged by almost all commentators: see as representative Gibson, *Textbook of Syrian Semitic Inscriptions*, 3:128; Healey, "Kition Tariffs," 55; Masson and Sznycer, *Recherches sur les phéniciens*, 44; and Peckham, "Notes on a Fifth-Century Phoenician Inscription from Kition," 312–13. The suggestion of Donner and Röllig (*KAI* 2:55) that *mlkt* is a mistake for *ml'kt*, "service," in line 7 (they do not comment on line 10) is surely not correct, as the scribe demonstrates in line 13 that he knows the proper spelling of *ml'kt*, with an *'alep* (see Masson and Sznycer, *Recherches sur les phéniciens*, 44).

13. Philo of Byblos, *Phoenician History*, as quoted in Eusebius, *Praeparatio evangelica* 1.10.31, trans. Attridge and Oden, *Philo of Byblos*, 55. In addition, in connection with Astarte's royal role according to Phoenician tradition, see the Tyrian "Throne of Astarte" (*KAI* 17) and the inscribed "thrones" like it, as discussed in Milik, "Les papyrus araméens d'Hermoupolis," 572, with references; also, the inscribed throne dedicated to Astarte Ḥor described by Abousamra and Lemaire in "Astarte in Tyre," 155–56.

14. *šmm 'drm* in *KAI* 14 (Eshmunazor), lines 16 and 17; *šmm rmm* in *KAI* 15 (Bodashtart). On these inscriptions, see further Gibson, *Textbook of Syrian Semitic Inscriptions*, 3:112, and

tarte's associations with the heavens are suggested by her identification with Greek Aphrodite, the goddess of Venus, the Morning and Evening Star: as Philo of Byblos writes, "the Phoenicians say that Astarte is Aphrodite."[15] This identification is also made clear also by a fourth-century BCE Greek/Phoenician bilingual inscription from Athens that translates the Phoenician name "'Abd'aštart ['Servant of Astarte'] the Ashkelonite" as "Aphrodisios ['Dedicated to Aphrodite'] the Ashkelonite."[16] Notably, moreover, the Astarte or Aphrodite worshipped by 'Abd'aštart/Aphrodisios and other Ashkelonites is explicitly known as Aphrodite of the *Heavens* (*Aphroditē ourania*), as is made clear by both Herodotus (1.105) and Pausanias (1.14.7), who remark on the cult of Aphrodite of the Heavens in Ashkelon.[17] This correspondence of Astarte with Greek Aphrodite of the Heavens is further confirmed by a second-century BCE inscription from Delos dedicated to "Palestinian Astarte, that is, Aphrodite of the Heavens."[18]

Another datum showing Astarte's association with the heavens comes from Pyrgi, a site on the west coast of Italy about fifty km west-northwest of Rome. The bilingual inscription found there, from ca. 500 BCE, is dedicated in its Phoenician version to Astarte and in its Etruscan form to the goddess Uni. Joseph A. Fitzmyer notes that Etruscan Uni is Roman Juno, and, significantly, that Uni is "closely associated" with "Juno of the Heavens" (*Juno caelestis*) in Roman Africa.[19] Philo of Byblos, too, remarks on Astarte's heavenly associations: "When traveling around the world, she [Astarte] discovered a star which had fallen from the sky. She took it and consecrated it in Tyre, the holy island."[20] Still more evidence comes from Herodian, who, in his second-century CE

Milik, "Les papyrus araméens d'Hermoupolis," 561, 561n2; also 597–98. On *KAI* 14, see also Teixidor, *The Pagan God*, 39; on *KAI* 15, see also Cross, *Canaanite Myth and Hebrew Epic*, 142, and, especially, Eissfeldt, "Schamemrumim 'Hoher Himmel,'" 62–67 (no. 14).

15. Philo of Byblos, *Phoenician History*, as quoted in Eusebius, *Praeparatio evangelica* 1.10.32, trans. Attridge and Oden, *Philo of Byblos*, 55.

16. *KAI* 54. Phoenician *'bd'štrt 'sqlny*; Greek *Aphrodisiou Askalōnitēs*.

17. Note also in Herodotus 1.131; 3.8.

18. *Astartē palaistinē, Aphroditē ourania*. See Roussel and Launey, *Inscriptions de Délos*, no. 2305. Also see inscription no. 1719 and the discussions of Delcor, "La culte de la 'Reine du Ciel,'" 117; Macalister, *The Philistines*, 94; and McKay, *Religion in Judah*, 51.

19. Fitzmyer, "Phoenician Inscription from Pyrgi," 288. The identification of Astarte with Juno, rather than with Etruscan *Turan*, Roman Venus, the usual equivalent of Greek Aphrodite, need not give pause, given the general fluidity of the great Canaanite goddesses in the first millennium BCE.

20. Philo of Byblos, *Phoenician History*, as quoted in Eusebius, *Praeparatio evangelica* 1.10.31, trans. Attridge and Oden, *Philo of Byblos*, 55.

History of the Roman Empire (5.6.4), reports that the Phoenicians referred to Aphrodite of the Heavens (= Astarte) as "Queen of Stars" (*astroarchē*).[21] Also in the second century CE, Apuleius, in his *Metamorphoses* (11.2), calls Caelestis Venus of the Cypriot city of Paphos "Queen of Heaven" (*regina caeli*).[22] Latin *Caelestis Venus* is a simple translation of Greek *Aphroditē ourania*, Aphrodite of the Heavens, whom I have identified with Palestinian Astarte.

A third characteristic Astarte shares with the biblical Queen of Heaven is her close associations with fertility and with war. The fertility aspects of the Queen of Heaven are made clear in Jer 44:17, where the people of Judah claim that when they worshipped the Queen of Heaven, "we had plenty of food, and we prospered." Conversely, "since we stopped worshipping the Queen of Heaven and stopped pouring out libations to her, we have lacked everything and been consumed . . . by famine" (44:18). At the same time, the Queen of Heaven seems to have an association with war: according to her followers as quoted in Jeremiah, her proper worship guaranteed that the people "saw no evil" (44:17), but when her cult was abandoned, "we were consumed by the sword" (44:18).

Astarte, too, has fertility attributes in addition to associations with war. The most striking evidence for Astarte's role as a guarantor of fertility is found in the Hebrew Bible, where the noun *'aštārôt*, which Judith M. Hadley has described as a "de-deification" of the divine name Astarte (*'aštart*), means "increase, progeny" (Deut 7:13; 28:4, 18, 51).[23] As for Astarte's associations with war: an Egyptian New Kingdom stele of Pharaoh Merenptah (r. 1213–1204 BCE) depicts the goddess with shield and spear,[24] and other Egyptian representations of Astarte show her on horseback carrying weapons of war.[25] In addition, Pharaoh Thutmose IV (r. 1400–1390 BCE) is described as being mighty in the chariot like Astarte,[26] and along with Anat, Astarte is called a part of a

21. Pointed out by Delcor, "La culte de la 'Reine du Ciel,'" 115.

22. Pointed out by Teixidor, *The Pagan God*, 36. RES 921, which reads ['š]trt pp[s], confirms that the cult of Palestinian Astarte was known at Paphos. See Dupont-Sommer, "Les Phéniciens à Chypre," 93–94.

23. Hadley, "De-deification of Deities in Deuteronomy," 157–74; Hadley, "Fertility of the Flock?," 115–33.

24. Petrie, *Memphis 1*, 8, and pl. 15 no. 37. See also Leclant, "Astarte à cheval," 10–13, and fig. 1.

25. Leclant, "Astarte à cheval," 1–67. See also the so-called Lady Godiva plaque found at Lachish (Ussishkin, "Excavations at Tel Lachish—1973–1977," 21, and pl. 8), which shows a goddess (Astarte, I would argue) standing astride a horse.

26. Carter and Newberry, *Tomb of Thoutmosis IV*, 27, and pl. 10; also J. A. Wilson, "Egyptians and the Gods of Asia," 250, 250n16.

thirteenth-century BCE king's war chariot.[27] She is also, together with Anat, called a shield to Pharaoh Rameses III (r. 1187–1156 BCE).[28] Furthermore, during the New Kingdom (ca. 1539–1075 BCE), she carries the epithet "Lady of Combat."[29] A millennium later, an Egyptian text from the Ptolemaic period (305–30 BCE) likewise describes her as "Astarte, Mistress of Horses, Lady of the Chariot."[30] In the Canaanite realm, Astarte acts as a war goddess in concert with Ḥoron in Ugaritic mythology,[31] and in later Phoenician tradition, King Esarhaddon of Assyria decrees in a treaty text from 670 BCE that Astarte should "break the bow" of King Baal of Tyre "in the thick of battle" and cause King Baal to "crouch at the feet of your enemy" were he to violate the treaty's terms.[32] Moreover, in the Bible, according to 1 Sam 31:10, the armor of the dead Saul is taken by the Philistines to the temple of Astarte, which may also indicate Astarte's associations with war.

A fourth reason for identifying Astarte with the biblical Queen of Heaven is that the cult of Astarte has as a crucial element the offering of bread cakes, a ritual that also plays an important role in the worship of the Queen of Heaven (Jer 7:18; 44:19). The Kition Tariff inscription cited above is again noteworthy, for line 10 of that inscription mentions "the two bakers who baked the basket of cakes for the Queen";[33] the Queen, I have argued, must be Astarte.[34] In addition, William Culican has drawn attention to a Hellenistic votive model

27. Dawson and Peet, "So-Called Poem on the King's Chariot," 169 (verso, lines 12–14); also J. A. Wilson, "Egyptians and the Gods of Asia," 250, 250n17.

28. Edgerton and J. A. Wilson, *Historical Records of Ramses III*, 75; also J. A. Wilson, "Egyptians and the Gods of Asia," 250, 250n18.

29. Leclant, "Astarte à cheval," 25.

30. Leclant, "Astarte à cheval," 54–58, esp. 57, and pl. 4 (opposite p. 49); also J. A. Wilson, "Egyptians and the Gods of Asia," 250n16.

31. *KTU* 1.2.1.7–8; 1.16.6.54–57. Herrmann, "Aštart," 7–16, has pointed out that the obverse of *PRU* 5.1 (19.39) also describes Ugaritic Astarte as a war goddess; in addition, Schmitt, "Astarte, Mistress of Horses," 215–16, and Smith, *Poetic Heroes*, 195–208, discuss warrior aspects of Ugaritic Astarte.

32. Bloch-Smith, "Archaeological and Inscriptional Evidence for Phoenician Astarte," 192.

33. For the reading *l'pm // 'š'p'yt ṭn' ḥlt* and the translation adopted here, see Peckham, "Notes on a Fifth-Century Phoenician Inscription from Kition," 305–6. Peckham is followed by Gibson, *Textbook of Syrian Semitic Inscriptions*, 3:124–25, and by Masson and Sznycer, *Recherches sur les phéniciens*, 26–27, 28–29. Healey ("Kition Tariffs," 54) offers an alternative reconstruction, *l'pm // 'š'p mntsp' ḥlt lmlkt*, "For the two bakers, who baked choice food, loaves for the Queen."

34. Those who associate the reference in the Kition inscription with the worship of the Queen of Heaven include Culican, "Votive Model from the Sea," 122; Delcor, "La culte de la

found off the Phoenician coast.[35] The model shows six figures positioned around a domed object. Culican identifies four identical seated females as votaresses. Another female figure stands and is pregnant; Culican believes her to be Astarte. This identification cannot be certain, but Astarte's well-attested popularity in the Phoenician and Punic realm in the late first millennium BCE (see below) makes Culican's hypothesis attractive. Culican identifies the sixth figure on the model, a male, as a priest of the goddess. The domed object around which the six figures cluster is interpreted as a beehive oven. Culican proposes the scene is a cake-baking ritual in honor of Astarte. This is a speculative suggestion, but in light of the Kition Tariff inscription and Jer 7:18 and 44:19, it is appealing.

A fifth and final factor that suggests the biblical Queen of Heaven is Astarte is the popularity of the goddess Astarte in the West Semitic realm during the first millennium BCE. Hundreds of Phoenician and Punic personal names incorporate the divine element ʿštrt, Astarte. The goddess's name also appears in many Phoenician and Punic inscriptions, both from the Phoenician mainland and from the Mediterranean world and North Africa; likewise, according to Philo of Byblos, Astarte is an important Phoenician goddess, wife of Kronos, and, as noted above, a co-regent with Zeus Demarous/Baal Haddu.[36] The second- or first-century BCE inscription of Paalaštart from Memphis (*KAI* 48), in addition to other first-millennium BCE Egyptian material cited above, attests to the popularity of Astarte in Egypt. And in Israel, the Deuteronomistic Historians accuse the people of worshipping Astarte in Judg 2:13; 10:6; 1 Sam 7:3–4; 12:10; 1 Kgs 11:5, 33; and 2 Kgs 23:13.[37]

Astarte is thus a worthy candidate for the Queen of Heaven. Yet certain elements of the worship of the Queen of Heaven remain unexplained if we interpret the cult of the Queen of Heaven only as a cult of West Semitic Astarte. For example, the word used in Jer 7:18 and 44:19 for the cakes baked for the Queen, *kawwānîm*, is used nowhere in the extrabiblical materials that pertain to Astarte. Similarly, the biblical reference to baking cakes "in her image" (Jer 44:19) cannot be understood by reference to the worship of West Semitic Astarte. Third, West Semitic evidence attests to no special role for women

---

'Reine du Ciel,'" 110–12; and Peckham, "Notes on a Fifth-Century Phoenician Inscription from Kition," 314–15, 315n2.

35. Culican, "Votive Model from the Sea," 119–23.

36. Philo of Byblos, *Phoenician History*, as quoted in Eusebius, *Praeparatio evangelica* 1.10.22, 24, 31.

37. The LXX, in addition, reads *Astartē* for MT *ʾăšērâ* in 2 Chr 15:16 and *Astartais* for MT *ʾăšērîm* in 2 Chr 24:18.

in the cult of Astarte. However, as we will see, these elements in the worship of the Queen of Heaven can be explained if we examine the cult of the East Semitic goddess, Ishtar.

Certainly Ishtar is a goddess who appropriately bears the title "Queen of Heaven." Indeed, the ancient Sumerian name of Ishtar, Inanna, was thought by the subsequent inhabitants of Mesopotamia, the Akkadians, to mean "Queen of Heaven" (reading [N]IN.AN.NA[K]), and thus the name Inanna is routinely rendered in Akkadian texts as "Queen of Heaven" (*šarrat šamê*) or "Lady of Heaven" (*bēlet šamê*).[38] Ishtar is also called by related epithets: "Queen of Heaven and the Stars," "Queen of Heaven and Earth," "Lady of Heaven and Earth," "Sovereign of Heaven and Earth," and "Ruler of Heaven and Earth."[39] In the west, too, Ishtar is known as "Lady of Heaven." In an Egyptian New Kingdom inscription from Memphis, Ishtar of Nineveh (whom the ancient scribe calls Hurrian Astarte) is given this title.[40] Ishtar has other astral features in addition to her epithets.[41] In Mesopotamia, for example, Ishtar is equated with Sumerian DIL.BAT, the Sumerian name of the planet Venus.

Also, Ishtar is a fertility goddess, as the Mesopotamian stories of Dumuzi/ Tammuz and Inanna/Ishtar show. These stories tell of the young fertility god, Tammuz, a symbol of prosperity and yield, and his courting and wooing of the maiden Ishtar, who represents the communal storehouse in which harvested foodstuffs were kept. Tammuz is successful in his courtship, and the young fertility god and goddess marry. With their sexual union, they guarantee fruitfulness in the land and bounty in the storehouse. This is symbolized in the

38. Edzard, "Inanna, Ištar," 81; Falkenstein, *Inschriften Gudeas von Lagaš* 1: *Einleitung*, 78–79; Helck, *Betrachtungen zur grossen Göttin*, 73; Held, "Studies in Biblical Lexicography," 80n24; Kramer, *Sumerians*, 153.

39. *šarrat šamê u kakkabāni, šarrat šamê u erṣeti, bēlet šamê (u) erṣeti, etellet šamê (u) erṣetim, malkat šamāmī u qaqqari.* See Tallqvist, *Akkadische Götterepitheta*, 39, 64, 129, 239–40; cf. 333–34.

40. On the title Hurrian Astarte, see Albright, *Yahweh and the Gods of Canaan*, 143n88; Cross, "Old Phoenician Inscription from Spain Dedicated to Hurrian Astarte," 192; Helck, *Die Beziehungen Ägyptens zu Vorderasien*, 459–60; Helck, *Betrachtungen zur grossen Göttin*, 213–16; and Stadelmann, *Syrisch-Palästinensische Göttheit in Ägypten*, 107. For the Memphis inscription, see von Bergmann, "Inschriftliche Denkmäler," 196; also see the comments of Culican, "Votive Model from the Sea," 122; Ranke, "Ištar als Heilgöttin," 412–18; Stadelmann, *Syrisch-Palästinensische Göttheit in Ägypten*, 107; and J. A. Wilson, "Egyptians and the Gods of Asia," 250n19. Note, too, a second Memphis inscription in which Hurrian Astarte (= Ishtar of Nineveh) is called Lady of Heaven. See Madsen, "Zwei Inschriften in Kopenhagen," 114, and the comments of Culican, "Votive Model from the Sea," 122.

41. See Edzard, "Inanna, Ištar," 85–86.

myth by the fact that Tammuz, as his wedding gift to Ishtar, brings to Ishtar produce to be placed in her storehouse.[42] The identification of Ishtar with the grain storehouse in these myths and elsewhere demonstrates her role in guaranteeing continual prosperity and preventing famine, an attribute associated with the Queen of Heaven in Jer 44:17–18.

Ishtar also has associations with war. In the epilogue to the eighteenth-century BCE Code of Hammurapi, Hammurapi calls Ishtar "the lady of the battle and of the fight" (col. 50 [rs. 27], 92–93). Her powers on the battlefield are clearly indicated by the curse she is to inflict on Hammurapi's enemy (col. 51 [rs. 28], 2–23):

> May she shatter his weapon at the battle site. May she establish for him confusion (and) rioting. May she cause his warriors to fail. May she give the earth their blood to drink. May she pile up everywhere on the plain heaps of corpses from his army. May she not take pity. As for him, may she give him into the hands of his enemies. May she lead him, bound, to the land of his enemies!

The myth of Inanna and Ebeh, in which Inanna/Ishtar assaults the mountain Ebeh, also attests to Ishtar's warring nature.[43]

Lexicographers generally agree that *kawwānîm*, the word used for the cakes baked for the Queen of Heaven in Jer 7:18 and 44:19, is a loan word from Akkadian *kamānu*, "cake."[44] In Akkadian texts, *kamānu* cakes are often associated with the cult of Ishtar. A hymn to Ishtar reads as follows:

> O Ishtar merciful goddess, I have come to visit you,
> I have prepared for you an offering, pure milk, a pure cake baked
>   in ashes (*kamān tumri*),
> I stood up for you a vessel for libations, hear me and act favorably
>   toward me![45]

---

42. See Jacobsen, *Treasures of Darkness*, 23–73.

43. See Kramer, *Sumerian Mythology*, 83.

44. See as representative *AHw* 1:430, s.v. *kamānu*; *HALOT* 2:466, s.v. *kawwān*; and *KBL*, 428, s.v. *kawwān*. See also Held, "Studies in Biblical Lexicography," 76–77; Jeremias, *Das Alte Testament im Lichte des Alten Orients*, 611–12; and Zimmern, *Akkadische Fremdwörter*, 38.

45. The text can be found in Craig, *Assyrian and Babylonian Religious Texts*, 1:15–16, lines 20–22. For transcription, translation, and notes, see Ebeling, *Quellen zur Kenntnis*, 2:4 (lines 20–22), 12.

Another text describes a healing ritual associated with the Ishtar cult, in which a cake baked in ashes (*kamān tumri*) is prepared in honor of the goddess.[46] Finally, in the Gilgamesh epic (tablet VI, lines 58–60), Gilgamesh describes how Tammuz brought ash cakes (*tumru*) to his lover Ishtar. Although the term *kamānu* is not used in this passage, most commentators assume that the reference to *tumru* is a shorthand expression for *kamān tumri*, "cake baked in ashes," the cake associated with the Ishtar cult in our first two examples.[47]

Scholars who have commented on the biblical cult of the Queen of Heaven are generally puzzled by the phrase "cakes in her image" (*kawwānîm lĕhaʿăṣîbāh*; Jer 44:19).[48] Those holding that the Queen of Heaven is Ishtar sometimes explain what "in her image" means by pointing to several clay molds found at Mari, a site in northwest Mesopotamia. These molds portray a nude female figure who holds her hands cupped under her breasts. Her hips are large and prominent.[49] It has been suggested that the molds represent Ishtar and that they were used to shape cakes baked in the image of the goddess. These cakes were then offered to Ishtar as part of her sacrificial cult.[50] Although there are problems with this suggestion,[51] the proposal to relate the Mari molds to the Bible's *kawwānîm lĕhaʿăṣîbāh* is still worth noting.

Finally, we observe that women seem to have a special place in the Ishtar cult. In Mesopotamian mythology, as noted above, the largest complex of stories about Ishtar deals with her courtship and marriage to the young fertility god Tammuz. In the myths, Tammuz symbolizes the spring season of prosperity and yield, a season when dates and grain were harvested, calves and lambs were born, and milk ran. But when the spring harvest season ended, the mythology perceived that the god Tammuz had died.[52] The death of

---

46. The text can be found in *KAR* 42, line 25. For transcription, translation, and some notes, see Ebeling, *Quellen zur Kenntnis*, 2:22 (line 25), 27.

47. So, for example, *AHw* 3:1370, s.v. *tumru(m)*; Oppenheim, "Mesopotamian Mythology II," 36n6; Saggs, *Greatness That Was Babylon*, 395; Schott and von Soden, *Das Gilgamesch-Epos*, 52; and Speiser, "Epic of Gilgamesh," 84.

48. Reading *lĕhaʿăṣîbāh* for MT *lĕhaʿăṣîbâ*. On suffixal *hē* without *mappiq*, see GKC 56g; cf. 91e.

49. The molds were first published by Parrot, *Mission archéologique de Mari* 2: *Le palais-documents et monuments*, 37–38, and pl. 19. For a readily accessible photograph of the largest and best-preserved mold, see Malamat, "Mari," fig. 9 (p. 21); Pope, *Song*, pl. 1 (opposite p. 360).

50. This is proposed by Pope, *Song*, 379, and by Rast, "Cakes for the Queen of Heaven," 171–74. See also Holladay, *Jeremiah*, 1:254.

51. Vriezen, "Cakes and Figurines," 262.

52. Although seasonal interpretations of ancient Near Eastern myths are often unwar-

Tammuz was an occasion of sorrow for his young bride, Ishtar, and Akkadian mythology preserves many of her laments over her dead lover.[53] And as a woman (Ishtar) laments the death of her lover in myth, it is women (devotees of Ishtar) who lament Tammuz's passing in the rituals of the Mesopotamian Tammuz cult.[54] Indeed, women's role in these lamentation rituals is vividly illustrated in the Bible in Ezek 8:14, where it is women who are specifically identified as those who sit at the gate of the Jerusalem temple's inner court "mourning over Tammuz." I suggest that it is this special place of women in the cult of Tammuz that is reflected in the biblical materials about the Queen of Heaven.

At first glance, it may seem a long jump from the role of women "mourning over Tammuz" to the role of women in baking cakes for the Queen of Heaven. But, in fact, the two are closely related. The *kamānu* cakes associated with the Ishtar cult (*kawwānîm* baked as offerings to the Queen of Heaven) were a staple food of Mesopotamian shepherds,[55] and Tammuz was the prototypical and patron shepherd of Mesopotamia. Moreover, as I noted above, in the Gilgamesh epic (tablet VI, lines 58–60), Gilgamesh describes Tammuz as the one who heaps up ash cakes for his lover, Ishtar. The cult of Tammuz the shepherd is thus closely tied to the Ishtar cult that involves the baking of offering cakes, and the cultic participants who mourned the death of Tammuz are thus the worshippers who baked cakes for Ishtar, the Queen of Heaven. And as women played a crucial role in the ritual mourning over Tammuz, they also played an important role in the cult involving the baking of *kamānu* cakes.

I submit that the Queen of Heaven is a deity whose character incorporates aspects of West Semitic Astarte and East Semitic Ishtar. This synthesis probably occurred early in Canaanite religious history, well before the sixth century BCE. Certainly the people of Judah, in Jer 44:17, and Jeremiah himself, in Jer 44:21, describe the cult as one practiced by past generations. Moreover, we know that the cult of Ishtar of Nineveh is attested in Egypt during the

---

ranted, the myths of Tammuz do seem best understood as having agricultural concerns as their main (but not exclusive) focus.

53. See, for example, the laments collected in Jacobsen, *Treasures of Darkness*, 49–50, 53–54.

54. Although facile equations of myth and ritual must be avoided (see, e.g., Hendel, *Epic of the Patriarch*, 69–71; in addition to Hendel's references, note Burkert, *Homo Necans*, 29–34), it is acknowledged by all commentators that the Mesopotamian myth of Tammuz is to some degree reflective of and at the same time reflected in Mesopotamian ritual and cult.

55. See *CAD* 8:111, s.v. *kamānu*: "Baked in ashes, the *k*.-cake seems to have been a dish of the shepherd"; also note the references listed there.

New Kingdom and as far west as Spain by the eighth century BCE.[56] This would suggest that the cults of Astarte and Ishtar were exposed to each other and began intermingling sometime during the last centuries of the second millennium BCE. This intermingling then continued throughout the first millennium BCE. Indeed, the cult of the Queen of Heaven prospered in the first half of the first millennium BCE, in particular attracting the women of sixth-century BCE Judah and Jerusalem.

But surprisingly, this women's cult did not prosper only in those spheres where we might expect to find women's religious practice, such as the home and the family. To be sure, there is a strong domestic component to the cult, seen especially in Jer 7:18, where "the sons gather wood, the fathers kindle fire, and the women knead dough to make bread cakes for the Queen of Heaven."[57] But if Jer 44:17 is to be taken at all seriously, then the "kings and princes" of Judah are also among those who worshipped the Queen. And if the worship of the Queen of Heaven was a part of the religion of the monarchy, the Queen's cult may also have been at home in what was essentially the monarch's private chapel, the temple. This is certainly suggested by Ezek 8:14, where the women who participate in the related cult of wailing over the Queen's deceased lover, Tammuz, sit at the north gates of the temple's inner court. The presence of a temple dedicated to the Queen of Heaven in fifth-century BCE Egypt, a century after Jeremiah berates the Judahites who have fled to Egypt for their worship of the Queen of Heaven (Jer 44), is also suggestive.

Jo Ann Hackett has argued that women in ancient Israelite society had a higher status and more opportunities to hold public and powerful positions in times of social dysfunction.[58] Certainly, the calamitous years of the late seventh and early sixth centuries BCE, which witnessed the senseless death of King Josiah, the David *revividus*, in 609 BCE, the Babylonian exiles of 597 BCE and 586 BCE, the final destruction of the temple by the Babylonians in 586 BCE, and the simultaneous end of Judahite political independence,

---

56. For the Egyptian materials, see the references cited in n. 40 above; also Helck, *Die Beziehungen Ägyptiens zu Vorderasien*, 458–60; Helck, *Betrachtungen zur grossen Göttin*, 213–16. For Ishtar of Nineveh in Spain, see Cross, "Old Phoenician Inscription from Spain Dedicated to Hurrian Astarte," 189–95.

57. Jeremiah 7:18 is usually translated "the children gather wood," rendering the Hebrew *bānîm* (the plural of *bēn*, "son") as a generic rather than as gender specific. But a comparison with Lam 5:13, a composition closely related to the book of Jeremiah that describes young boys (*nĕʿārîm*) carrying loads of wood, suggests that wood-gathering was a task more typically assigned to males.

58. Hackett, "In the Days of Jael," 15–38.

qualify as a period of severe dysfunction. There is, admittedly, little evidence from this period for women wielding political power. But the biblical data about the Queen of Heaven do suggest that the women of late seventh- and early sixth-century BCE Judah and Jerusalem exercised religious power.[59] They worshipped a goddess whose cult they found particularly appealing and went so far as to introduce the cult's rituals that related to Tammuz lamentation into the temple compound itself.

Since it is winners who write history, the importance of this women's cult in the history of the religion of Israel has been obscured by our sources. The ultimate "winners" in the religion of early sixth-century BCE Judah were men: the Deuteronomistic Historians, the priest-prophet Ezekiel, and the prophet Jeremiah. The biblical texts these men wrote malign non-Deuteronomistic, nonpriestly, and nonprophetic religion, and in the case of the cult of the Queen of Heaven, they malign the religion of women. But fortunately for us, the sources have not completely ignored some women's cults. The losers have not been totally lost. If historians of Israelite religion continue to push beyond biblical polemic, we should hear more and more the voices of the women of Israel witnessing to their religious convictions.

---

59. It is perhaps not coincidental that Hulda, the first woman prophet reported by the biblical writers since the premonarchic period, is active at approximately the same time, the last quarter of the seventh century BCE (2 Kgs 22:14–20).

CHAPTER 2

Asherah, the West Semitic Goddess of Spinning and Weaving?

๖๙

This chapter had its origins in my interest in one verse of the Bible, 2 Kgs 23:7, and its description of women who were housed in the temple compound in Jerusalem in King Josiah's day (ca. 640–609 BCE) "weaving for Asherah." When I started working on this text, my concern was its human subjects. What did the women's task of weaving for Asherah, the great mother goddess of the Canaanite pantheon, entail? What did it mean for these women and for their weaving enterprise when Josiah, as part of his sweeping program of religious reformation, tore down the houses in the Jerusalem temple compound where the women did their work? How did losing their temple workshop affect these women's role as religious functionaries who wove cloth for cultic purposes? I detailed some my answers to these questions in my 2006 article "Women and the Worship of Yahweh in Ancient Israel," which appears in this volume as chapter 10.

But my inquiries regarding the fate of the women weavers of 2 Kgs 23:7 also led me to questions about Asherah, the goddess for whom the women wove. More specifically, in the chapter that follows, I hypothesize that Asherah might play a role in the West Semitic pantheon as the patron deity of spinning and weaving. Paradoxically, though, 2 Kgs 23:7—even though it inspired my questions regarding Asherah's relationship to textile production—does not ultimately provide evidence in support of my thesis. Instead, I conclude that the women's weaving described in 2 Kgs 23:7 was characteristic of the kinds of textile-making activities that could be found in the cults and cultic venues of many ancient Near Eastern gods, not Asherah in particular. Nevertheless, I suggest that texts from the book of Proverbs, as

An earlier version of this chapter appeared in *JNES* 67 (2008): 1–29. Used here by permission.

well as myths from Late Bronze Age Ugarit and the Hittite world and cer-
tain archaeological data from Iron Age Israel, do point to Asherah's role as
the patron goddess of spinning and weaving in the West Semitic world.

   Still, when I originally published "Asherah, the West Semitic Goddess of
Spinning and Weaving?" in 2008, I concluded by commenting on the ques-
tion mark in my title, noting that I had deemed this punctuation appropri-
ate because none of the evidence I had assembled in support of my thesis
was ironclad. Thus, I felt it necessary to signal that my conclusions were
tentative. However, it took over a decade for anyone to push back against
them: Theodore J. Lewis in his 2020 book, The Origin and Character of
God: Ancient Israelite Religion through the Lens of Divinity, *and in a*
2020 article, "Ugaritic Athtartu Šadi, Food Production, and Textiles: More
Data for Reassessing the Biblical Portrayal of Aštart in Context." As the title
of Lewis's article suggests, his aim is to highlight Ugaritic texts that suggest an
association between the Ugaritic goddess Athtartu/Athtart (biblical Aštart/
Astarte) and textile production. Below, in a postscript appended to this chap-
ter, I consider Lewis's arguments, which I propose might augment, yet need
not necessarily contradict, my previously published hypothesis concerning
Asherah. Accordingly, the text of my 2008 article is re-presented here without
any significant revisions except for the 2022 addition that I just noted.

1. Goddesses of Spinning and Weaving in the Ancient Mediterranean World

In *Oikonomikos*, his fourth-century BCE treatise on estate management,
the Greek author Xenophon describes how the fourteen-year-old bride of a
wealthy friend knew nothing of the world other than how to work wool herself—and how to allot woolwork to the maidservants.[1] Scholars of the ancient
Near East might well be reminded of the Sumerian mythological poem that
Thorkild Jacobsen calls "The Bridal Sheets of Inanna," even though this text
is almost two millennia older than Xenophon's work. In it, the young bride-
to-be and goddess Inanna teases back and forth with her brother Utu, the sun
god, about the process of making linens for her marriage bed. Utu begins by
suggesting that he bring Inanna flax to render into cloth, but without telling
her explicitly that she will be producing the bedsheets that will be used on her
wedding night. She, however, seems to sense the purpose for which the cloth is

---

1. Xenophon, *Oikonomikos* 7. This reference was brought to my attention by Barber,
"Peplos of Athena," 104–5.

to be made yet coyly works to prolong the process of revelation by asking Utu repeatedly by whom the various stages of preparing the fabric—the retting, the spinning, the doubling up of the threads, the weaving, and the bleaching—will be performed.[2] For example:

> Brother, when you have brought me the flax,
> who will ret for me, who will ret for me,
> who will ret its fibers for me?[3]

Here, one thinks of the maidservants to whom wool working was to be assigned by the young bride of Xenophon's text, and this despite the millennia and miles that separated ancient Sumer and classical Greece.

Still, it should come as no surprise that these two otherwise disparate texts share the perception that young women were responsible for producing, or at least overseeing the production of, textiles in the home, for domestic fabric-making was a primary task of women in all parts of the ancient world. E. J. W. Barber has written of Greek women, for example, that "spinning and weaving occupied most of women's time in Classical Greece. . . . Properly married Athenian women . . . spent their lives sequestered at home spinning and weaving for the family's needs."[4] Tikva Frymer-Kensky has similarly noted that "producing cloth" was the most "basic economic task" of Mesopotamian

2. In the translation of this poem found in *Inanna, Queen of Heaven and Earth*, 30–31, Diane Wolkstein and Samuel Noah Kramer offer a slightly different list of the stages of cloth production: combing, spinning, braiding the thread, setting the warp, weaving, and bleaching. Here, I have generally followed Jacobsen, *Treasures of Darkness*, 30–31. Yet I cannot agree with Jacobsen that the purpose of Inanna's repeated questioning of her brother is her being "on guard" and "attempting to push" the whole matter of the bedsheets aside, leery that the groom that has been chosen for her will not be the suitor she prefers. Nor do I agree with Tikva Frymer-Kensky that Inanna "declines to ret, spin, dye, weave, or bleach" the raw flax because this headstrong and independently minded goddess rejects women's role in fabric production (*In the Wake of the Goddesses*, 26–27). Rather, as my remarks here suggest, I find Inanna's "spinning out" of the exchange with her brother Utu to be both a marker of her aristocratic status—spinning and weaving is work she expects maidservants to do—and coquettish in character, a coy dialogue leading up to the pronouncement that she eagerly awaits: that she is to be the bride of her beloved Dumuzi. I would also take the lines from a different text that Frymer-Kensky quotes as evidence of Inanna's "gender-bending" rejection of a woman's typical tasks of spinning and weaving—lines in which her husband Dumuzi tells her she shall not weave or spin—as indicating instead Inanna's aristocratic status as a woman whose spinning and weaving will be done by others.

3. Translation by Jacobsen, *Treasures of Darkness*, 31.

4. Barber, "Peplos of Athena," 104.

wives and their "most important and characteristic nonprocreative function."[5] Indeed, in the Greek world, a tuft of wool was customarily placed on the door of a house upon the birth of a baby girl in order to symbolize the critical role that spinning and weaving would play in this child's later life. Likewise, in the ancient Near East, the spindle or distaff served as the characteristic emblem of femininity.[6]

Because of the importance of spinning and weaving in these ancient cultures, it reasonably follows that the various pantheons of the Near East and eastern Mediterranean would include a deity who was patron of the arts of spinning and weaving, and it also follows reasonably enough that because of the almost stereotypical association of women with the domestic arts of spinning and weaving,[7] this patron deity of spinning and weaving would be female. To be sure, gender roles in Near Eastern and eastern Mediterranean pantheons do not invariably follow the gender roles assumed within the human communities of the Near East and eastern Mediterranean.[8] In these communities, for example, the arts of war are most typically associated with men, yet warrior goddesses—Mesopotamian Inanna/Ishtar, Canaanite Anat, and Greek Athena—are well attested. Still, in the case of spinning and weaving,

---

5. Frymer-Kensky, *In the Wake of the Goddesses*, 23.

6. On Greek tradition, see Neils, "Children and Greek Religion," 143; on the ancient Near East, see Hoffner, "Symbols for Masculinity and Femininity," 329; also Bird, "Women (OT)," 954 (this reference was brought to my attention by Yoder, *Wisdom as a Woman of Substance*, 81n43); Holloway, "Distaff, Crutch or Chain Gang," 370–71.

7. While domestic weaving was almost entirely, if not exclusively, the province of women, weaving that was done outside the home was often the work of men. See, e.g., for the Greek world, the data collected by Thompson, "Weaving: A Man's Work," 217–22, and also Scheid and Svenbro, "From the Sixteen Women to the Weaver King," 23, 181n75. In Egypt, the famous Middle Kingdom text "The Satire of the Trades" presents the professional weaver as male—indeed, a male so miserable in his work that he is "worse off than a woman" (translation by Lichtheim, *Ancient Egyptian Literature*, 1:188). Isaiah 19:9–10 also uses masculine grammatical forms in three of its four references to Egyptian textile workers, indicating, at a minimum, that some of the laborers to whom this text refers were men (although, according to the rules of Hebrew grammar, women could be included in the collectives described by this passage's masculine plural forms). Exodus 35:35; 36:14, 35, 37; 38:22–23; 39:27–29; 2 Chr 2:12–13 (in most English translations, 2:13–14); Isa 38:12; and Job 16:15 similarly refer to male textile workers within the Israelite sphere. Moreover, the name of one of the sons of Issachar, Tola (*tôlāʿ*, "[dyed with] scarlet stuff"), can be taken to indicate that this man was the head of a clan of professional dyers (as pointed out by Sheffer, "Needlework and Sewing in Israel," 544n13). On male professional weavers in New Testament times, see Bird, "Spinning and Weaving," 988.

8. See, e.g., the discussion of Lambert, "Goddesses in the Pantheon," 127.

a correlation between women spinners and weavers on earth and a female patron of spinning and weaving in the heavens does seem to hold, as is suggested by evidence from three Near Eastern and eastern Mediterranean societies. In Mesopotamia, the patron deity of spinning and weaving, at least in the Sumerian period, was the goddess Uttu. In Egypt, the divine patron of spinning and weaving was the goddess Tait, or Tayet. In Greece, the deity of spinning and weaving, and indeed of all handicrafts, was the goddess Athena.

Uttu. According to the myth "Enki and Ninhursag," Mesopotamian Uttu comes from a distinguished lineage, as she is the great-granddaughter (or perhaps the great-great-granddaughter) of the Sumerian mother goddess Ninhursag.[9] More important for our purposes, though, is a myth commonly called "Enki and the World Order," which describes how the god Enki, in assigning to the various gods of the pantheon oversight of the main features of both cosmos and civilization (e.g., the regulating of the water flow of the Tigris and Euphrates, the economies of agriculture and herding, and the technologies of the pick-axe and brick-mold), decrees that Uttu will be in charge of "everything pertaining to women," and specifically the weaving of textiles.[10] Frymer-Kensky in addition describes how Uttu is recognized as the patron goddess of weaving in the philosophical disputation "Lahar and Ašnan" ("Ewe and Grain," lines 4–5), as she is also in a bilingual Sumerian and Akkadian book of incantations.[11] In logographic writing, moreover, the same sign that is used for Uttu's name is sometimes used to write the word "spider," probably because of the expertise in weaving that Uttu and the spider shared.[12]

Tait/Tayet. Egyptian Tait, or Tayet, is best known as the goddess who provides the linens used in rituals of embalming and mummification. In the Old Kingdom Pyramid Texts, for example, she is said to be the mother who clothes the dead king and lifts him to the sky.[13] Similarly, in the Middle Kingdom "Story of Sinuhe," the courtier Sinuhe, years after he had left Egypt for an extended exile in the Levant, is urged by the Pharaoh Sen-Usert to return to his homeland, in particular so that proper burial rites can be observed at the time of Sinuhe's death. These include, among other observances, a funeral procession, coffining in a mummy case made of gold, and "a night . . . made

9. On the two versions of this myth, and their different versions of Uttu's genealogy, see Jacobsen, *Treasures of Darkness*, 112–13.

10. Frymer-Kensky, *In the Wake of the Goddesses*, 23; see similarly Kramer, *Sumerians*, 174, and Kramer and Maier, *Myths of Enki*, 53, lines 380–85.

11. Frymer-Kensky, *In the Wake of the Goddesses*, 23.

12. Black and Green, *Gods, Demons, and Symbols*, 182.

13. Wilkinson, *Complete Gods and Goddesses of Ancient Egypt*, 168, citing Pyramid Text 741.

Fig. 2.1. Red-figure calyx-krater showing Athena Ergane in a pottery shop, ca. 450 BCE

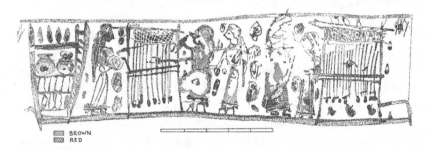

BROWN
RED

Fig. 2.2. Detail of an aryballos painting from ca. 600 BCE showing the weaving contest between Athena and Arachne

for you with ointments and wrappings from the hand of Tait."[14] The Egyptian goddess Neith, too, can be associated with the ointments and wrappings of mummification and so, consequently, with weaving:[15] an inscription from the Ptolemaic temple at Esna, for example, speaks of Neith as "Mistress of the oil of unction as well as the pieces of cloth."[16] There is also a minor Egyptian god,

14. Translation by Lichtheim, *Ancient Egyptian Literature*, 1:229.
15. Bleeker, "The Goddess Neith," 42, 54; el-Saady, "Reflections on the Goddess Tayet," 216.
16. Quoted in Hollis, "Queens and Goddesses in Ancient Egypt," 212.

Fig. 2.3. Loom weight with Athena's characteristic bird, the owl, spinning

Hedjhotep, associated with fabrics and weaving: thus he is described in a New Kingdom papyrus as creating the cord that is attached to an amulet of healing.[17] By the time of the New Kingdom's Nineteenth Dynasty, moreover, Hedjhotep is identified as the consort of Tait, although in some materials from the Late Period of Egyptian history, Hedjhotep appears as a *goddess* in the company of Tait.[18] Still, throughout most of Egyptian history, Tait's place as the patron goddess of weaving seems primary. It is thus Tait who is said to weave the curtain that hangs in the tent of purification where the embalming rituals take place;[19] an Egyptian magical spell further describes linen bandages that are used to prevent hemorrhage as the "land of Tait";[20] and numerous first-millennium BCE images of the goddess show her holding two pieces of cloth.[21]

Athena. Although we may more readily think of Athena as the Greek goddess of wisdom as well as of war, the evidence demonstrating her role in Greek culture as the goddess of spinning and weaving is substantial. At several points, she is identified in Greek tradition as Athena Ergane, or Athena the "Worker Goddess," the goddess of handicrafts (*technai*), and thus the divine patron, for example, of potters (see fig. 2.1), of goldsmiths, and preeminently

17. Zecchi, "The God Hedjhotep," 5, 7.
18. Zecchi, "The God Hedjhotep," 8–9.
19. Hart, *Routledge Dictionary of Egyptian Gods and Goddesses*, 156; Wilkinson, *Complete Gods and Goddesses of Ancient Egypt*, 168.
20. Hart, *Routledge Dictionary of Egyptian Gods and Goddesses*, 156.
21. El-Saady, "Reflections on the Goddess Tayet," 214.

Fig. 2.4. Drawing of fifth-century BCE relief from Scornavacche, Sicily, showing Athena Ergane (?) with distaff in her left hand

of weavers and others involved in the production of textiles.[22] Athena's role as patron of weavers is further illustrated in several literary texts. In Homer's *Odyssey* 7.110–11, it is said that the Phaiakian women "are skilled in weaving," having been "dowered with wisdom bestowed by Athene, to be expert in beautiful work"; later in the epic, Athena is described as the one who instructed the daughters of Pandareos "in glorious handiwork" (20.72).[23] This same sentiment is expressed elsewhere in Homeric tradition in the Homeric Hymn to Aphrodite, lines 10–11, 14–15, in which we read that "pleasure" for Athena lies "in fostering glorious handicrafts," so that she "taught smooth-skinned palace maidens at work in their quarters to weave with bright strands."[24] Athena is also identified in *Iliad* 14.178–79 as having made an elaborately decorated robe for the goddess Hera, and in *Iliad* 5.735, she is similarly described as having made her own elaborate dress. According, moreover, to Hesiod's story of the creation of Pandora found in his *Works and Days*, Athena is charged with teaching Pandora "to weave a complex warp"; Athena in addition, according

22. On Athena as a divine patron of potters, see Neils, "Panathenaia," 21; on Athena as a patron of goldsmiths, see *Odyssey* 6.233, as pointed out by Rose and Robertson, "Athena," 138.

23. Translations by Lattimore, *Odyssey*, 114, 300. These references were brought to my attention by Milanezi, "Headaches and Gnawed *Peplos*," 323n63.

24. Translation by Sargent, *Homeric Hymns*, 46; this reference was brought to my attention by Milanezi, "Headaches and Gnawed *Peplos*," 323n63.

Fig. 2.5. A sixth-century BCE statue of Athena (spinning?), attributed to the sculptor Endoios

Fig. 2.6. A late fifth- or early fourth-century BCE terra-cotta relief plaque of a mortal woman spinning

to a second version of the Pandora story found in Hesiod's *Theogony*, made Pandora's girdle, robe, and veil.[25] We can note as well the story told in Ovid's *Metamorphoses*—but known to be centuries older than Ovid—of the maiden Arachne's challenging Athena to a weaving contest, an act of such utter hubris on Arachne's part, given Athena's expertise in textile production, that it results in Arachne's transformation into a spider, doomed to weave forever.[26]

Scholars know that Ovid's story of the weaving contest of Arachne and Athena is hundreds of years older than Ovid's first-century BCE/first-century CE text because it is found represented on a small Corinthian jug dating from ca. 600 BCE (fig. 2.2). Other iconographic materials that demonstrate Athena's association

25. Hesiod, *Works and Days* 60–65; Hesiod, *Theogony* 573–75; both as quoted in Barber, "Peplos of Athena," 105.

26. Ovid, *Metamorphoses* 6.5–145. This reference was brought to my attention by Barber, "Peplos of Athena," 105–6.

Fig. 2.7. A late fifth- or early fourth-century BCE terra-cotta relief plaque
of Athena, perhaps in the same "spinning" pose as assumed by the
mortal woman of fig. 2.6

Fig. 2.8. The presentation of the peplos to Athena as depicted on the Parthenon frieze

with weaving include the several loom weights that show Athena's characteristic
bird, the owl, spinning wool from a basket that sits in front of her (fig. 2.3) and
the numerous fragments of terra-cotta plaques found on the Athenian Acrop-

olis that depict weaving scenes.[27] Scholars have in addition suggested that at least three sixth- and fifth-century BCE images depict Athena herself as a spinner: a fragmentary fifth-century BCE terra-cotta relief from Sicily (fig. 2.4), a sixth-century BCE statue from the Acropolis (fig. 2.5), and a late fifth- or early-fourth century BCE terra-cotta relief plaque that also comes from the Acropolis and that, while fragmentary, seems to show Athena in the same pose as assumed in a contemporaneous relief by a mortal woman who is spinning (figs. 2.6 and 2.7).[28]

Finally, we must cite in this catalog of Athena's associations with textile production the fact that the central event in the central festival of Athena, the Panathenaia, is the offering of a newly woven peplos, a robe elaborately decorated with images of the cosmogonic battle between the gods and the gigantic Titans that is draped over

Fig. 2.9. A small fifth-century BCE terra-cotta statue of Athena (?), showing what her cult statue with the peplos draped over it may have looked like

Athena's cult statue (figs. 2.8 and 2.9). Indeed, so closely is the weaving of Athena's Panathenaic peplos associated with her role as the goddess of textile production that the actual making of the peplos is inaugurated in October–November, nine months prior to the celebration of the Panathenaia, at a festival known as the Chalkeia, which was held in honor of Athena in her guise as Athena Ergane, Athena the "Worker Goddess," patron of handicrafts.[29]

II. Asherah, the West Semitic Goddess of Spinning and Weaving?

The presence of these goddesses of spinning and weaving in the pantheons of Mesopotamia, Egypt, and Greece suggests that we might well expect to find a goddess patron of spinning and weaving also in the pantheons of the West

27. Barber, "Peplos of Athena," 106.
28. Ridgway, "Images of Athena," 138–39.
29. Neils, "Panathenaia," 17; for the dates of the Chalkeia and Panathenaia, see Scheid and Svenbro, "From the Sixteen Women to the Weaver King," 18–19.

Semitic world. Below, I propose that this is a responsibility assumed by the Canaanite mother goddess Asherah. Three bodies of evidence lend support to this conclusion. They are (1) Late Bronze Age Ugaritic and Hittite mythological texts; (2) first-millennium BCE biblical texts from the book of Proverbs and also, perhaps, 2 Kgs 23:7; and (3) Iron Age archaeological data from the sites of Ta'anach, Tel Miqne-Ekron, and Kuntillet 'Ajrûd.

Ugaritic and Hittite Mythological Texts. In a scene found in tablet 4 of the Ugaritic Baal cycle, the gods Baal and Anat come to the mother of the gods, Asherah, in order to secure her help as they seek permission from the high god of the pantheon, El, to have a palace built for Baal. Baal and Anat find Asherah undertaking domestic chores: setting a pot upon a fire; carrying her robes into the river (presumably to wash them); and holding a spindle (*plk*) in her hand (*KTU* 1.4.2.3–9). According to some translations of the Hittite myth of Elkunirsa, Asherah (Ashertu) also carries a spindle, with which she attempts to stab Baal after he refuses to sleep with her.[30] To be sure, as noted above, the spindle is a typical symbol of femininity in the ancient Near East, and so the fact that Asherah is depicted as holding one in these Ugaritic and Hittite myths may be a marker only of her gender. In addition, as I have just mentioned, only *some* translations of the Hittite myth of Elkunirsa describe Asherah grasping a spindle—this because of lacunae in the crucial passage.[31] Still, the Ugaritic reference to Asherah with a spindle in her hands is secure; moreover, Asherah is the *only* goddess in our rather rich Ugaritic mythological corpus who appears with a spindle. This perhaps indicates that Asherah has a special association in Late Bronze Age mythological tradition with spinning and weaving.

Texts from the Hebrew Bible. Much more suggestive, however, than the Hittite and Ugaritic materials is the portrait of the *'ēšet-ḥayil,* the "woman of valor" or "capable wife," that is found in the biblical tradition in Prov 31:10–31, especially when this text is considered in conjunction with the texts describing Woman Wisdom that are found interspersed in Prov 1–9 (Prov 1:20–33; 3:13–18; 4:1–9; 7:4–5; 8:1–36; 9:1–6). To begin with the latter: several scholars have sug-

30. This text was brought to my attention by Willett, "Women and Household Shrines," 104, who cites Goetze's translation in *ANET,* 519, and Hoffner's translation in "The Elkunirsa Myth Reconsidered," 6–8.

31. In his 1965 article "The Elkunirsa Myth Reconsidered," Hoffner writes that although the reading "spindle" is restored, "there is no reason to doubt" it (7n10). In his 1998 translation of the myth, however, Hoffner marks each of the three possible occurrences of the term "spindle" with empty brackets: see Hoffner, "Canaanite Myth," 90–91.

gested that the Wisdom figure of Prov 1–9 takes over—"in rather unabashed fashion," to use Claudia Camp's words—imagery associated with older ancient Near Eastern goddesses.[32] And although many goddesses have been nominated as Wisdom's primary antecedent (Egyptian Ma'at, Mesopotamian Ishtar, Canaanite Astarte, Canaanite Anat),[33] the most compelling arguments, in my opinion, see Woman Wisdom as a reflex of Canaanite Asherah.[34] Especially notable in this regard is the Prov 8 description of Woman Wisdom as present with and the partner of the Israelite god Yahweh in creation, a tradition that parallels closely both Ugaritic materials that describe Asherah as "creatress" (*qnyt*), the consort of the creator god (*qny*) El,[35] and the biblical and extrabiblical materials that suggest an ancient Israelite belief that Asherah was the consort of Yahweh.[36] In Prov 3:18, moreover, Woman Wisdom is described as a "tree of life" (*'ēṣ-ḥayyîm*), language that recalls not only the tree of life (*'ēṣ-haḥayyîm*) in Gen 3:22 and the associated "tree of the knowledge of good and evil" (Gen 2:9, 17) that so obviously draws on wisdom motifs, but also the stylized pole or tree that is frequently associated with the goddess Asherah in biblical literature and arguably in West Semitic iconographic tradition.[37] That

32. Camp, "Woman Wisdom as Root Metaphor," 61.

33. See Camp, "Woman Wisdom as Root Metaphor," 61; Coogan, "Goddess Wisdom," 203–4; Frymer-Kensky, *In the Wake of the Goddesses*, 179; Hadley, "Wisdom and the Goddess," 235; and (with extensive references) Yoder, *Wisdom as a Woman of Substance*, 4.

34. Coogan, "Canaanite Origins and Lineage," 119–20; Smith, "Myth and Mythmaking in Canaan and Israel," 2039; cf. also Hadley, "Wisdom and the Goddess," 234–43.

35. For Asherah as *qnyt*, see, e.g., *KTU* 1.4.1.23; 1.4.3.26, 30, 35; and 1.4.4.32. For El as *qny*, see *KTU* 1.10.3.6, a reading based on the reconstruction proposed by Ginsberg, "Ba'l and 'Anat," 9.

36. The bibliography is vast. I have described my own position, and listed references in support, in Ackerman, "Women and the Worship of Yahweh in Ancient Israel," 189–90, reprinted in this volume at pp. 210–12; also in Ackerman, "At Home with the Goddess," 455–59, reprinted in this volume at pp. 192–98.

37. Smith, "Myth and Mythmaking in Canaan and Israel," 2039. On the evidence for associating Asherah with a stylized pole or tree in biblical literature, see especially Deut 16:21, which speaks of "planting" (*nāṭa'*) a tree to serve as an *'ăšērâ*, which I, along with most commentators, presume refers to the cult object that represented the goddess Asherah and that is called by her name. Elsewhere in the Bible (e.g., 1 Kgs 14:15, 23; 16:33; 2 Kgs 17:10, 16; 21:3; 2 Chr 33:3), the *'ăšērâ* cult object is described as being "made" (*'āśâ*), "built" (*bānâ*), "stood up" (*'āmad*), or "erected" (*hiṣṣîb*), all terms that well describe a stylized pole or tree, as do the terms that describe what happens to the *'ăšērâ* if it is destroyed: it is "burned" (*bî'ēr* or *śārap*), "cut down" (*kārat*), "hewn down" (*gāda'*), "uprooted" (*nātaš*), or "broken" (*šibbēr*). For the evidence that likewise associates Asherah with sacred trees in

"happiness" accrues to those who hold fast to Woman Wisdom in 3:18 further alludes to her identity as Asherah, as the Hebrew word for "happy" (*'šr*) is a pun on the goddess's name.[38]

Scholars have in addition argued that the *'ēšet-ḥayil* of Prov 31:10–31 is a reflex or personification of Woman Wisdom as depicted in Prov 1–9. Thomas McCreesh has pointed out, for example, that the *'ēšet-ḥayil* is described in Prov 31:10 as more precious that *pĕnînîm*, "variously translated as 'pearls,' 'corals,' or simply 'jewels,'" a description that is also offered of Woman Wisdom in Prov 3:15, which states, "She [Wisdom] is more precious than jewels" (*yĕqārâ hî' mippĕnînîm*, reading with the *qere* for the *ketiv mippĕniyyîm*). Moreover, in the related Prov 8:11, it is said that "Wisdom is better than jewels" (*ṭôbâ ḥokmâ mippĕnînîm*). McCreesh further notes that the husband of the *'ēšet-ḥayil* is said to trust in her (Prov 31:11), as the student of Wisdom is exhorted to "love," "prize" and "embrace" her in Prov 4:6, 8–9, rather than "trust in his own mind" in Prov 28:26.[39] Christine Roy Yoder adds that the noun *saḥar*, which she translates as "merchant profit" (more typically it is rendered "income" or "revenue"), occurs in Proverbs only in Prov 31:18, where the *'ēšet-ḥayil* perceives that her merchandise is profitable, and in Prov 3:14, where Woman Wisdom's income is said to be better than silver. Both the *'ēšet-ḥayil* and Woman Wisdom, Yoder also points out, are difficult to "find" (*māṣā'*, Prov 1:28; 8:17; 31:10). Yoder observes, too, that each has a house (*bayit*, 9:1; 31:15, 21, and 27) and a staff of young women (*na'ărôt*, 9:3; 31:15), and each provides food (*leḥem*) for her companions (9:5; 31:14) and offers a life of security (*bāṭaḥ*, 1:33; 31:11). What's more, according to Yoder, both are known at the city gates (*šĕ'ārîm*, 1:21; 8:3; 31:31), and both stretch out their hand (*yād*) to the needy (1:24; 31:20).[40] Mary Petrina Boyd in addition notes that "as Wisdom rejoiced (*mĕśaḥeqet*) before God at all times" according to Prov 8:30, the *'ēšet-ḥayil* in 31:25 delights (*wattiśḥaq*) in each coming day.[41]

Al Wolters has somewhat similarly argued that the rare participial form of the verb *ṣāpâ*, "to watch over," used to describe the *'ēšet-ḥayil* at the beginning of Prov 31:27 (*ṣôpiyyâ*, instead of the more typical feminine participial form *ṣôpâ*, and also in lieu of the perfect or imperfect verb forms used everywhere else in the poem

---

West Semitic iconographic representations, see Hestrin, "Cult Stand from Ta'anach," 61–77; Hestrin, "Lachish Ewer," 212–23.

38. Smith, "Myth and Mythmaking in Canaan and Israel," 2039.

39. McCreesh, "Wisdom as Wife," 41–42.

40. Yoder, *Wisdom as a Woman of Substance*, 91–92.

41. Boyd, "House That Wisdom Wove," 9n46.

to describe the deeds of the *'ēšet-ḥayil*), was deliberately chosen by the poem's authors as a Hebrew pun on the Greek word *sophia*, "wisdom."[42] This evidence, Wolters writes, lends support to the conclusion that the *'ēšet-ḥayil* is the "personi-fication of wisdom.... The Valiant Woman [the *'ēšet-ḥayil*] represents wisdom in action and ... her deeds are the practical and concrete incarnation of what it means to be wise.... She personifies wisdom in both word and deed."[43] McCreesh likewise concludes, "The remarkable similarities between the portrait of the wife and various descriptions of Wisdom ... indicate that the poem in chapter 31 is the book's final, masterful portrait of Wisdom."[44] Yoder concurs: "The specific nature and extent of [the] parallels suggest that ... the Woman of Substance (31:10–31) and Woman Wisdom (1–9) ... essentially coalesce as one figure."[45]

If McCreesh, Yoder, Wolters, and the several other scholars who have urged this correlation between the *'ēšet-ḥayil* and Woman Wisdom are correct,[46] and if, moreover, it is correct to see Woman Wisdom in Prov 1–9 as a reflex of the goddess Asherah, then it becomes significant for our purposes to note the degree to which the activities associated with textile production dominate in the Prov 31 description of the *'ēšet-ḥayil*. Of the verses in the poem that speak specifically to tasks undertaken by the *'ēšet-ḥayil*, the largest number—fully five and perhaps up to seven—speak to this woman's work in the making of both woolen and linen cloth. She procures the necessary raw materials (wool and flax) according to v. 13; uses a spindle and a related implement (the *kîšôr*, traditionally translated as "distaff") to spin these fibers into thread according to v. 19;[47] and makes clothing for herself and, it seems, for her household as

---

42. Wolters, "*Ṣôpiyyâ* (Prov 31:27)," 577–87; see also Rendsburg, "Bilingual Wordplay in the Bible," 354–55.

43. Wolters, "*Ṣôpiyyâ* (Prov 31:27)," 580–82.

44. McCreesh, "Wisdom as Wife," 46.

45. Yoder, *Wisdom as a Woman of Substance*, 93.

46. For older exegetes (including those dating back to the patristic period) who hold this view, see the catalog assembled by Wolters, "*Ṣôpiyyâ* (Prov 31:27)," 581; for more recent interpretations, see Yoder, *Wisdom as a Woman of Substance*, 91–93, and the references listed there in nn. 78–83.

47. The word *kîšôr* is a *hapax legomenon* in Hebrew. It has traditionally been rendered as "distaff," as translators have assumed that "distaff" is the logical parallel of the *pelek*, "spindle," mentioned in the second colon of Prov 31:19. Wolters has argued, however, that the none of the several spinning technologies of the ancient Near East used a distaff, at least until the Hellenistic period; Wolters further suggests that the grammar of Prov 31:19a, which has the *'ēšet-ḥayil* putting her "hands" (a Hebrew dual form) to the *kîšôr* militates against the meaning "distaff," as a distaff is not normally grasped in this way but is held in one hand

well, according to vv. 21–22. Also, according to v. 24, she makes additional tex-tiles—linen garments and woven sashes—to sell. Verse 18, which describes her merchandise as profitable, may likewise refer to these textiles she produces for commercial purposes, and there is another allusion to her own garments, this one metaphorical, in v. 25: "Strength and dignity are her clothing." Moreover, as befits a woman whose description is derived from the Prov 1–9 portrayal of Woman Wisdom, the fabrics the 'ēšet-ḥayil produces seem to be of the highest quality: the clothes she makes for her household are a richly dyed crimson (v. 21), and some of her own clothing is also colored with a rich purple dye (v. 22). Other of her garments are fine linen rather than being the easier-to-produce and less luxurious garments made of wool (v. 22).

The association of the 'ēšet-ḥayil with so much imagery concerning luxury textile production, when coupled with the 'ēšet-ḥayil's associations with the figure of Woman Wisdom-cum-Asherah, speaks clearly to the hypothesis I have been exploring here: the possibility that Asherah was the West Semitic goddess of spinning and weaving. It is also of interest for my thesis that, like Asherah as represented in the Hittite myth of Elkunirsa, who can be taken (depending on how one translates) to use her spindle to attack Baal,[48] the 'ēšet-ḥayil is described in Prov 31:10–31 not just in conjunction with textile production but also using militaristic imagery. Wolters has catalogued multiple instances of militaristic language in the poem, and Boyd and Bruce K. Waltke have added more.[49] These

---

or stuck into a belt or into a special backstrap (see Barber, *Prehistoric Textiles*, 69). Likewise, Wolters suggests, the translation of "spindle whorl" for *kîšôr* that is sometimes proposed is disallowed, as the technology of spinning does not involve grasping the spindle whorl at all, with either one hand or two. Wolters thus proposes a translation of "grasped spindle," a large type of spindle known to have been used in the ancient Near East, especially for respinning or doubling in order to make two-ply or three-ply yarn out of previously spun thread. (Although not cited by Wolters, the illustrations found in Barber, *Prehistoric Textiles*, 57–58, of a spindle held in two hands are particularly instructive; see figs. 2.18 and 2.21.) For further discussion, see Wolters, "Meaning of *Kîšôr* (Prov 31:19)," 91–104; also Rendsburg, "Double Polysemy in Proverbs 31:19," 267–74, who, although for different reasons than Wolt-ers, similarly advocates for translating *kîšôr* as "spindle." One should be aware, however, regarding Wolters's arguments, that the evidence regarding the ancient Near Eastern use of the "distaff" is not as conclusive as he claims. While there is indeed no evidence of the use of distaffs in Egypt (Barber, *Prehistoric Textiles*, 50), distaffs may have been used in Meso-potamia for spinning as early as the fourth millennium BCE (Barber, *Prehistoric Textiles*, 56–57; Barber, "Textiles of the Neolithic through Iron Ages," 192). Also, a Late Bronze Age distaff was possibly found at Enkomi, on Cyprus (Barber, *Prehistoric Textiles*, 63).

48. See above, n. 31.

49. Boyd, "House That Wisdom Wove," 180–234; Waltke, "Role of the 'Valiant Wife,'" 23–34; and Wolters, "Proverbs XXXI 10–31 as Heroic Hymn," 446–57.

scholars note, for example, that very term *ḥayil* used to describe the poem's subject (v. 10) implies strength and virility; indeed, Wolters proposes that the *'ēšet-ḥayil* should "probably be understood as the female counterpart of the *gibbôr ḥayil*, the title of the 'mighty men of valour' which are often named in David's age."[50] In her PhD dissertation on Prov 31:10–31, Boyd somewhat similarly observes that when *ḥayil* occurs with the masculine *'îš* in the Hebrew Bible, it typically describes a "warrior" or "mighty man," which suggests the conjunction of *ḥayil* with the feminine *'iššâ* should be analogously understood.[51]

A number of other terms in the poem can also be seen as having military connotations. Wolters notes in this regard (1) *'ālâ 'al* in v. 29, typically translated in the Prov 31 context as "to surpass" but used "elsewhere in the sense of going out to do battle against an enemy"; (2) *šālaḥ yād bě*, "to reach out the hand," in v. 19, which "always has an aggressive connotation elsewhere" (most notably for our purposes in Judg 5:26, where it is used [albeit with the preposition *lě* instead of *bě*] to describe Jael's grasping of the weapon [tent-peg, parallel to laborers' hammer] with which she kills the Canaanite war leader Sisera);[52] (3) *tānâ*, "to celebrate in song," used in v. 31 to command the poem's audience to extol the *'ēšet-ḥayil*, but used elsewhere in the context of heroic poetry to describe songs sung in celebration of military triumphs (again, notably, in the Judg 5 "Song of Deborah"; see Judg 5:11); and (4) *šālāl* and *ṭerep* in vv. 11 and 15, typically translated "profit" and "food" in the context of Prov 31, but elsewhere used as "warlike words" meaning "plunder" and "prey."[53] Waltke notes in addition that (1) "'laughs [in victory]' is a war-like term" (v. 25), and (2) "'watching over' (v. 27) glosses the normal Hebrew term for 'to reconnoiter' and 'to spy.'"[54] Both Wolters and Waltke, among others, further point out that the "strength" (Hebrew *'ōz*) with which the woman metaphorically clothes herself in v. 25 carries militaristic connotations, as does the phrase "she girds

50. Wolters, "Proverbs XXXI 10–31 as Heroic Hymn," 453. For *gibbôr ḥayil*, see Judg 6:12; 11:1; 1 Sam 9:1; 16:18; 1 Kgs 11:28; 2 Kgs 5:1; Ruth 2:1; 1 Chr 12:29(28); 28:1; 2 Chr 13:3; 17:16, 17; 25:6; 32:21; and multiple other citations in the plural.

51. Boyd, "House That Wisdom Wove," 4n8, 182–85. For *'îš ḥayil* as a "warrior" or "mighty man," see Judg 3:29; 1 Sam 31:12; 2 Sam 24:9; 1 Chr 10:12; 11:22; cf., however, 1 Kgs 1:42 and 1 Chr 26:8.

52. Repointing in Judg 5:26 to read MT *tišlaḥnâ* as *tišlaḥannâ*, a third-person feminine singular form with energic *nûn*, as first proposed by Burney, *Book of Judges*, 153, and followed in turn by Cross and Freedman, *Studies in Ancient Yahwistic Poetry*, 19n(r), and by Coogan, "Structural and Literary Analysis of the Song of Deborah," 150–51n52.

53. Wolters, "Proverbs XXXI 10–31 as Heroic Hymn," 453–54.

54. Waltke, "Role of the 'Valiant Wife,'" 25.

her loins with strength" (again *ʿōz*) in v. 17a.[55] Yet Boyd has very provocatively suggested that the mention of the woman's strong arms in v. 17b alludes more to the woman's work as weaver, as, "the task of weaving, as she beats the weft into the warp, requires strong arms."[56] If Boyd is correct, then encapsulated in the description of the *ʾēšet-ḥayil* in v. 17a–b is the same motif of weaver/ warrior that may be encapsulated (depending on how one translates) in the Hittite Asherah's use of her spindle as a weapon.[57] This further supports the series of correspondences I have been arguing for here: that the *ʾēšet-ḥayil* of Prov 31 is to be equated with Woman Wisdom-cum-Asherah in Prov 1–9 and so manifests, as I propose does Asherah, an association with the arts of textile production and also, as perhaps does Asherah in Hittite tradition, an association with militaristic imagery.[58]

There is another text in the Hebrew Bible that explicitly associates Asherah with traditions of weaving: this is 2 Kgs 23:7, which alludes to a group of women weavers who were housed in the temple compound in Jerusalem in King Josiah's day (ca. 640–609 BCE). The most typical translation of this verse, and the one that I would in fact advocate,[59] understands these women weavers to be engaged in the process of weaving garments that were draped over the cultic image of Asherah (the *ʾăšērâ*) that stood somewhere within the temple precinct before it was removed and destroyed as a part of Josiah's religious reforms.[60] The Jerusalem Bible perhaps makes this most explicit when

55. Wolters, "Proverbs XXXI 10–31 as Heroic Hymn," 453; Waltke, "Role of the 'Valiant Wife,'" 24–25; Szlos, "Portrait of Power," 102; the Szlos reference was brought to my attention by Boyd, "House That Wisdom Wove," 6n24.

56. Boyd, "House That Wisdom Wove," 6n25.

57. See above, n. 31.

58. Asherah might also be taken to have an association with militaristic imagery at Ugarit, if we are to translate her standard epithet in the Ugaritic mythological corpus, *rbt ʾtrt ym*, as "the Lady who treads on the Sea(-dragon)" (as proposed, for example, by Cross, *Canaanite Myth and Hebrew Epic*, 33) and see reflected in that title a now otherwise lost tradition that described Asherah as playing a role in the cosmogonic battle against the sea god Yamm.

59. Ackerman, "The Queen Mother and the Cult in the Ancient Near East," 193, reprinted in this volume at pp. 181–82; also Ackerman, "Women and the Worship of Yahweh in Ancient Israel," 189, reprinted in this volume at p. 210; Ackerman, "Digging Up Deborah," 180, 182, 182n11.

60. So, e.g., the Jerusalem Bible; the New American Bible; the New American Bible, Revised Edition; the New English Bible; the New Jerusalem Bible; the New Jewish Publication Society *Tanakh*; and the Revised English Bible. Among commentators, see Cogan and Tadmor, *II Kings*, 286; Gray, *I & II Kings*, 664; Montgomery, *Critical and Exegetical Commentary on the Books of Kings*, 531; and J. Robinson, *Second Book of Kings*, 220.

it translates, "He [Josiah] pulled down the house . . . which was in the Temple of Yahweh and where the women wove clothes for Asherah." I would further suggest, as do multiple commentators, that the clothing of Asherah's cult image in this verse is to be understood as correlate with the tradition of clothing cult statues that is well known elsewhere in the ancient Near East and the eastern Mediterranean world[61]—attested in the Bible, for example, in Jer 10:9 and Ezek 16:18 and in extrabiblical texts in Ep Jer 6:9, 11–13, 20, 33, 72.[62] According to this interpretation, there is nothing exceptional about the fact that the women resident in Jerusalem's temple compound were weaving garments for the cult image of *Asherah*, as opposed to the cult image of any other deity, and thus there is no indication of any special association of Asherah with the arts of textile production.

It is possible, however, to translate 2 Kgs 23:7 to read: "He [Josiah] destroyed the houses (*bāttîm*) . . . where the women wove, [namely] the houses (*bāttîm*) for [i.e., "dedicated to"] Asherah."[63] This translation has the advantage of reading the two occurrences of *bāttîm* in 2 Kgs 23:7 as having the same meaning, as opposed to the translation I have previously presented, which emends the second *bāttîm* to a hypothetical form *kuttŏnîm* (for the more usual *kuttŏnôt*), meaning "robes" or "tunics";[64] or to *baddîm*, "white linen garments";[65] or to *battîm*, a hypothetical cognate of Arabic *batt*, meaning "cloak" or more generally "garment."[66] It further, in support of the thesis I am exploring here, would suggest a special association of Asherah with the arts of spinning and weaving, as it is she in particular who has houses dedicated

---

61. See, e.g., for Mesopotamia, Matsushima, "Divine Statues in Ancient Mesopotamia," 209–19; Oppenheim, "Golden Garments of the Gods," 172–93 (pointed out by Cogan and Tadmor, *II Kings*, 286); for Egypt, David, *Religious Ritual at Abydos*, 89; and for Greece, Mansfield, "Robe of Athena," 438, 442–43, 445.

62. Gressman, "Josia und das Deuteronomium," 325–26 and 326n2 (pointed out by Cogan and Tadmor, *II Kings*, 286); to Gressman's references from the Epistle of Jeremiah, add Ep Jer 6:20, 33.

63. Suggested to me by Peter Machinist, personal communication.

64. Gray, *I & II Kings*, 664n(b).

65. According to Dever, "Silence of the Text," 150, this emendation forms the basis of the translation found in the Revised Standard Version (RSV), "vestments." But Dever gives no references in support of this claim, and he seems mistaken, moreover, about the specifics of it, as the RSV in fact reads "hangings." On the RSV translation, see further below, n. 68.

66. This reading was originally proposed by Šanda, *Die Bücher der Könige*, 2:344, and also by Driver, "Supposed Arabisms in the Old Testament," 107 (as pointed out by Cogan and Tadmor, *II Kings*, 286; Day, "Asherah in the Hebrew Bible," 407; and Gray, *I & II Kings*, 664n[b]).

to her within the temple's walls in which weaving is undertaken. Still, despite the support this translation offers for my thesis, I cannot, as I have already indicated, embrace it. This is because, first, the emended reading "garments" or the like that I advocate does find a significant piece of corroboration in the versions, specifically in the Lucianic recension of the LXX, which reads *stolas*, "garment, robe." It is important to note, moreover, that the Lucianic recension of 2 Kings generally seems to offer an earlier and more reliable text than the main tradent of the LXX, which "apparently represents a revision based on a form of the Hebrew text current at a later time."[67] Also important to the note is the fact that the Masoretic accentuation does not support a translation that reads the second *bāttîm* of 2 Kgs 23:7 as the first word of a concluding appositional clause, and such a translation in addition leaves a very awkward *šām* dangling at the end of the main clause.[68] I conclude that, unlike the Proverbs materials we have examined, 2 Kgs 23:7—despite its tantalizing juxtaposition of Asherah and weaving—does not seem to provide evidence that argues in favor of my thesis that Asherah is the patron goddess of textile production in the West Semitic world.

Iron Age Archaeological Data. As I have just intimated, we might reasonably expect textile production to be present at any ancient Near Eastern religious site where a divine image or divine images stood—this because of the well-known ancient Near Eastern tradition of clothing cult statues. In addition, we might just as reasonably expect textile production to be present at religious sites without a cult statue (for example, Israelite religious sites that adhered to the biblical dicta forbidding the making of graven images), as the cult required

67. Allen, "More Cuckoos in the Textual Nest," 70, who cites in support Tov, "Lucian and Proto-Lucian," 101–13, esp. 106.

68. A compromise translation is the one advanced by, for example, the RSV: "And he [Josiah] broke down the houses . . . which were in the house of the Lord, where the women wove hangings for the Asherah." This translation apparently does take the second *bāttîm* of 2 Kgs 23:7 to means "houses" rather than relying on an emended text, although "houses" is rather broadly interpreted to mean "hangings," a reference presumably to a tent-like structure somewhat analogous to the tent shrine that housed the Yahwistic ark of the covenant or to the "colorful shrines" that Jerusalem, envisioned as an apostate harlot, is said to make with her garments in Ezek 16:16. This translation has the advantage of preserving the MT as it stands, and in addition, it does not go against the Masoretic accentuation or leave an awkward dangling *šām*, as opposed to the emendation-free translation I have just presented in the main text. However, it also, as opposed to the emendation-free translation presented in the main text, does not indicate that there is anything distinctive about the women doing weaving for Asherah within the temple compound, as the sort of tent-shrine to which it alludes might also be made for some other deity. Thus it does not suggest any special association of Asherah with the arts of textile production.

fabric for many purposes other than clothing divine images: for example, for priestly vestments; for curtains and other types of draperies that hung in and around cult sanctuaries; and for coverings of things such as the table of the bread of presence in Yahwistic tradition.[69] We should thus not be surprised to learn that evidence for textile production has been found by archaeologists in the excavations of several Levantine sites identified as cultic. Fifteen loom weights were found in Room 204, which the excavators identified as a "kitchen" (perhaps used "for the preparation of ritual meals") that was located just north of Temple 131 in Stratum X (late eleventh/early tenth century BCE) at the Philistine site of Tell Qasile,[70] and eleven more loom weights were found scattered in the various rooms of Building 225, which was just south of the temple.[71] Also, twenty-one loom weights were found in Room 1 of Megaron Building 350 (a Philistine temple) from Stratum V (the first half of the eleventh century BCE) at Tel Miqne-Ekron,[72] and seven loom weights were found in the eleventh-century BCE "Twin" temple complex at Beth-Shean (four in the Northern Temple, one in the Southern Temple, and two in the rooms in between).[73] A single loom weight was found in the Iron Age I Temple Building 30 (Phoenician) at Tell Abu Hawam,[74] and one loom weight was also found in a room north of the inner sanctuary of the so-called Solar Shrine found in postexilic Lachish.[75] Paul W. Lapp in addition reports (unfortunately with no reference) that a cache of loom weights was found in a cultic context at Megiddo.[76] None of these sites, however, has any demonstrable connection with Asherah worship, so none offers any evidence in support of my thesis that posits a special association between Asherah and textile production.

69. Note in this regard the biblical evidence suggesting that textiles were part of the cultic treasury of the temple of Baal in Samaria (2 Kgs 10:22).

70. Mazar, *Excavations at Tell Qasile, Part 1*, 42; see also Mazar, *Excavations at Tell Qasile, Part 2*, 80. The Qasile materials were first brought to my attention by Sheffer and Tidhar, "Textiles and Basketry at Kuntillet 'Ajrud," 22n27; subsequently Sheffer and Tidhar, "Textiles and Basketry," 309n26.

71. Gilmour, "Archaeology of Cult in the Southern Levant," 260. See also Mazar, *Excavations at Tell Qasile, Part 1*, 80, although Mazar's math seems a little confused. In the chart on p. 80, he notes that three loom weights were found in Locus 168 of Building 225, then another three in Locus 171, then five in Locus 187, for a total of eleven; in the text on the same page, however, Mazar writes of the "*10* weights . . . scattered in the various rooms" (emphasis mine).

72. Discussed in Zevit, *Religions of Ancient Israel*, 135.

73. Gilmour, "Archaeology of Cult in the Southern Levant," 260.

74. Gilmour, "Archaeology of Cult in the Southern Levant," 260.

75. Tufnell, *Lachish III*, 143.

76. Lapp mentions these loom weights in "The 1968 Excavations at Tell Ta'annek," 45, but with no citation.

Fig. 2.10. Remains from the storage room of the so-called Cultic Structure at Tell
Taʿanach, showing an eight-handled krater filled with fifty-eight loom weights

Strikingly, though, two of the largest collections of loom weights that have
been found in West Semitic cultic contexts—indeed, loom weight collections
substantially larger than any of those just described—come from sites arguably associated with the worship of Asherah. We begin with remains from
tenth-century BCE Tell Taʿanach discovered in the 1963 excavations of Lapp.
These include artifacts from two rooms of a large building (much of which
had been destroyed by the trenching of Ernst Sellin's earlier excavations),
called by Lapp the "Cultic Structure" because of the arguably cultic nature of
many of the finds: for example, 140 sheep and goat astragali, most likely used
in divination rites; a complete mold of the "figurine-with-a-disk" type; and
three small standing stones or *maṣṣēbôt*.[77] All of these remains were found in
Room 1 of Lapp's "Cultic Structure," in which the objects were, according to
him, so tightly packed that it should be considered a room in which various

---

77. Lapp, "The 1963 Excavation at Taʿannek," 28, actually identified the 140 astragali as
pig, but more recent investigators identify them as sheep and goat: see Zevit, *Religions of
Ancient Israel*, 237.

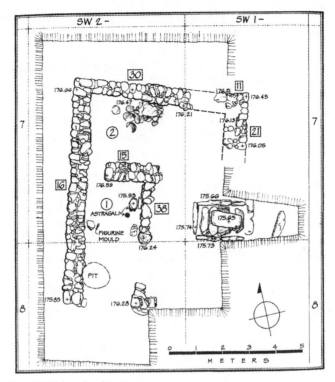

Fig. 2.11. Plan of the Taʿanach cultic structure

cultic paraphernalia were stored.[78] A large assemblage of loom weights (fifty-eight according to Lapp's original publication; sixty-two according to Glenda Friend's 1998 study of Tell Taʿanach's loom weights) was also found as part of this apparent collection of cultic paraphernalia, gathered in an eight-handled krater (figs. 2.10 and 2.11).[79] Friend in addition reports that the Room 1 loom

---

78. Lapp, "The 1963 Excavation at Taʿannek," 28.

79. Lapp, "The 1963 Excavation at Taʿannek," 28 (as pointed out by Sheffer and Tidhar, "Textiles and Basketry at Kuntillet ʿAjrud," 12; subsequently, Sheffer and Tidhar, "Textiles and Basketry," 307); Friend, *Tell Taannek 1963–1968 III/2*:10, 43. It should be noted that in his report on the 1963 season, Lapp indicated he had some doubts about identifying the several dozen doughnut-shaped clay objects he found in the eight-handled krater as loom weights; he used quotation marks around the term *loom weights* when describing them and footnoted an article by Rodney Young raising doubts about identifying a similar hoard of five hundred of these objects at Gordion as loom weights (Young, "The 1961 Campaign at Gordion," 165).

weights were uniform in dimension and weight and that they represent 68 percent of all the Iron Age loom weights found at Taʿanach. Together, these data, in addition to the presence in Room 1 of five bone spatulas that Friend proposes were tools used to pick up threads in order to weave patterned textiles, suggest to her "large-scale" as well as "specialized textile production."[80]

Then, in his 1968 excavations, "within a few meters of the 1963 cultic finds,"[81] Lapp found the most famous of Taʿanach's three cult stands, an impressive rectangular shaped object standing over half a meter tall whose iconography has suggested to many that tenth-century BCE Taʿanach was a site associated with the worship of Asherah (fig. 2.12).[82] In particular, scholars have suggested that the first and third registers of the stand's four registers (counting from the bottom) are replete with Asherah imagery. In the first, a naked woman with a crudely modeled headdress of the Hathor type stands facing frontally, with her arms extended to grasp two lions. All of these aspects (the naked woman facing frontally, the Hathor headdress, and lions) are well known from other iconographic representations of Asherah: for example, on several Late Bronze Age gold and electrum pendants that come from Ugarit and other sites in the northern Levant and that arguably depict Asherah, the goddess is depicted standing atop a lion.[83] In the third register, the lions reappear, this time flanking two caprids that rear up to graze on a stylized tree. As I have mentioned already in discussing Prov 3:18, this sort of "sacred tree" image, like lion imagery, is well known as a part of Asherah iconography, and, indeed, gold and electrum pendants similar to those that show Asherah standing atop a lion depict her with a tree or branch etched in her pubic region.[84] Textual

---

Then, in his report on the 1968 seasons, Lapp raised even more concerns, arguing that the "loom weights" he had found in 1963 within the "Cultic Structure" were unfired and so extremely fragile that they could have hardly served in weaving: see Lapp, "The 1968 Excavations at Tell Taʿannek," 47; also Lapp, "Taanach by the Waters of Megiddo," 25. Avigail Sheffer, however, has demonstrated that such weights, baked only in the sun, function perfectly "to keep the warp threads properly taut during the weaving process" and that the weights are quite durable, sustaining "no damage . . . even when the loom had to be moved from place to place." See Sheffer, "Use of Perforated Clay Balls on the Warp-Weighted Loom," 82–83; also Friend, *Tell Taannek 1963–1968 III/2*:5, who discusses problems with Lapp's analysis of the doughnut-shaped objects as heat absorbers used during sacrificial rituals.

80. Friend, *Tell Taannek 1963–1968 III/2*:10.

81. Lapp, "The 1968 Excavations at Tell Taʿannek," 42.

82. Hestrin, "Cult Stand from Taʿanach," 61–77; Taylor, "Two Earliest Known Representations of Yahweh," 557–66.

83. Hestrin, "Cult Stand from Taʿanach," 68.

84. Hestrin, "Cult Stand from Taʿanach," 71; Hestrin, "Lachish Ewer," 215–17.

Fig. 2.12. Drawing of the Ta'anach cult stand

traditions in addition associate Asherah with lions and with sacred trees: in *KTU* 1.3.5.37; 1.4.1.8; 1.4.2.25–26, for example, the children of Asherah are called her "pride of lions," *ṣbrt ary*, and Deut 16:21 forbids the Israelites to plant a tree representing Asherah beside any altar of Yahweh.[85]

The likely conclusion to be drawn from the evidence of this cult stand is the one I have stated above: that tenth-century BCE Ta'anach was a site associated with the worship of Asherah, probably—whatever the proscriptions articulated in Deut 16:21 and related texts—in conjunction with the Israelite god Yahweh (who is arguably represented on the Ta'anach cult stand's second and fourth registers; this is suggested, for example, by the two representations of cherubim, which are so often associated with Yahweh in biblical tradition, that flank the second register). Less certain, but I believe a probable conclusion based on the other data I have presented, is that the Asherah worship at Ta'anach is to be associated with the rather extraordinary collection of loom weights and other tools of textile production found there. The Ta'anach data, in short, seem to support my thesis that Asherah was the patron deity of spinning and

85. See further n. 37 above and my discussion in Ackerman, *Under Every Green Tree,* 189–91.

weaving in the West Semitic world. Indeed, we might go so far as to suggest that it was *because* Asherah was the patron deity of spinning and weaving in the West Semitic world that she was worshipped at Tell Taʿanach, her cultic presence there an appropriate and perhaps even a necessary part of the large-scale and specialized textile industry to which the Taʿanach artifacts point.

The second Levantine site that has produced a rather extraordinary assemblage of loom weights is Tel Miqne-Ekron, where a large number of loom weights were found in association with the enormous olive-oil production complex of the seventh century BCE (Stratum IC and possibly IB). Seymour Gitin, one of the primary excavators at Ekron, has theorized that the presence of these loom weights intermingled with olive-oil production equipment at Ekron is due to the fact that the olive-oil industry is seasonal, and so the installations for oil production were idle six to ten months a year; during this time, he proposes, Ekron's so-called industrial zone was reconfigured as a textile-production workshop.[86] Gitin has further proposed, based on the discovery of nine horned altars in the "industrial zone," that this seemingly secular manufacturing area should actually be understood as "sacred space."[87] But sacred to whom? Religion as practiced in Ekron was a complex and multi-faceted phenomenon, but the seventh-century BCE data indicate that Asherah was among the deities being worshipped there.[88] Baruch Halpern, moreover, has argued that, of the Ekron deities, Asherah is to be particularly associated with the "industrial zone,"[89] as is suggested by the fact that the two store jars found at Ekron that were inscribed with Asherah's name were specifically used for storing oil.[90] To be sure, this evidence might seem more to point to Asherah's association with oil production than the making of textiles,[91] but the presence

---

86. Gitin, "Tel Miqne-Ekron," 50; see also Dothan and Gitin, "Miqne, Tel (Ekron)," 1058.

87. Gitin, "The Four-Horned Altar and Sacred Space," 113.

88. Gitin, "Seventh Century B.C.E. Cultic Elements at Ekron," 250, and fig. 2a on p. 251; Gitin, "Israelite and Philistine Cult," 280; Gitin, Dothan, and Naveh, "Royal Dedicatory Inscription from Ekron," 13.

89. Halpern, "The Baal (and the Asherah) in Seventh-Century Judah," 137.

90. Gitin and Cogan, "New Type of Dedicatory Inscription from Ekron," 196.

91. Halpern's suggestion that Asherah is the deity particularly associated with the industrial zone hinges, in fact, on his supposition that Asherah is specially associated with the oil production facilities there—this because of Asherah's well-known association with trees (above, nn. 37, 85), including, Halpern seems to imply, the sort of tree iconography we know better from Egyptian tradition, which depicts an Asherah-like tree goddess/mother goddess giving suck to the pharaoh. This evidently suggests to Halpern (although he does not say so explicitly) a more general association of Asherah with the production of liquids from trees,

of textile production along with oil production in the Ekron industrial zone's "sacred space," in conjunction with some of the other evidence I have cited, could be taken to indicate that, in addition to being associated with oil production, Asherah was also considered to be the patron deity of spinning and weaving at Ekron. Indeed, as at Taʿanach, we might suggest that it was due to Asherah's role as the patron deity of spinning and weaving in the West Semitic world that her cult was present in the industrial zone at Ekron, as the goddess could have been revered there because of the divine blessings she could provide the site's textile workers.

The evidence from Taʿanach and Ekron, moreover, might lead us to suggest that two other cultic sites at which major textile-production complexes were found are to be associated with Asherah worship: these are Tell el-Ḥammah, located at the southern end of the Beth-Shean valley, and Tel ʿAmal, which lies three km west of Beth-Shean.[92] Tell el-Ḥammah was excavated most recently (in 1985, 1987, and 1988) by Jane M. Cahill, David Tarler, and Gary Lipton (Lipovich) on behalf of the Institute of Archaeology at the Hebrew University of Jerusalem. Artifacts suggesting a spinning and weaving center—including wood spindles and spindle whorls, remains of thread wrapped around spindle fragments, stone and clay loom weights, and textile scraps—were found in two adjoining rooms that were part of one of the two building complexes of the tenth-century BCE layer.[93] The other building complex, which lay across a courtyard from the first, also consisted of at least two adjoining rooms, one room of which contained artifacts that seemed to the excavators cultic in character (for example, a kernos with five projectiles; a zoomorphic vessel; and a multi-handled krater with horned animal appliqués).[94] Also found in this room were the upper half of a female plaque figurine, a large quantity of astragali, and perhaps a faience amulet.[95]

---

such as the oil from olive trees produced in such vast quantities at Tel Miqne-Ekron. See Halpern, "The Baal (and the Asherah) in Seventh-Century Judah," 137.

92. These sites brought to my attention by Nakhai, *Archaeology and the Religions of Canaan and Israel*, 180–81.

93. Cahill, Lipton (Lipovich), and Tarler, "Tell el-Ḥammah, 1985–1987," 280–83; Cahill, Tarler, and Lipton (Lipovich), "Tell el-Ḥammah in the Tenth Century B.C.E.," 36; and Cahill and Tarler, "Ḥammah, Tell el-," 562. See also, on the artifacts suggesting a spinning and weaving center at Tell el-Ḥammah, Nakhai, *Archaeology and the Religions of Canaan and Israel*, 180–81.

94. Cahill, Lipton (Lipovich), and Tarler, "Tell el-Ḥammah, 1988," 193; Cahill and Tarler, "Ḥammah, Tell el-," 562. See also Nakhai, *Archaeology and the Religions of Canaan and Israel*, 181.

95. Cahill, Lipton (Lipovich), and Tarler, "Tell el-Ḥammah, 1988," 193; Gilmour, "Ar-

Some similar objects were found in the textile-production complex as well.[96] In his PhD dissertation on cultic sites from the southern Levant, Garth Hugh Gilmour suggests that the cultic activities implied by these finds may be related to the Tell el-Ḥammah's textile industry,[97] and I would then ask, in the light of the thesis I have advanced here, whether we might suggest the cultic activities were thus associated with the goddess Asherah in her role as the West Semitic patron goddess of spinning and weaving? I would also ask the same question of Tel ʿAmal, where excavations revealed a three-room building from the period of the tenth and ninth centuries BCE in which both textile production and cult activities took place (cultic remains include votive vessels, a decorated bowl, chalices, a figurine holding a disk, a fenestrated ceramic stand, a cup-and-saucer lamp, and stone cultic stands).[98]

Because, however, none of the cultic remains from either Tell el-Ḥammah or Tel ʿAmal can be connected explicitly with the worship of Asherah, any conclusions regarding these sites remain tenuous; also tenuous, although somewhat less so, are any conclusions we might draw regarding the final site I will discuss here, the early eighth-century BCE site of Kuntillet ʿAjrûd, in the northern Sinai. As is well known, both epigraphic evidence and also (according to some) iconographic data found at Kuntillet ʿAjrûd suggest that Asherah was worshipped—probably, as at Tell Taʿanach, in conjunction with the Israelite god Yahweh—as a part of whatever cultic activities took place at the site:[99] particularly critical are the inscription that reads, "I bless you by Yahweh of Samaria and by his Asherah/asherah," and the three inscriptions that mention "Yahweh of Teman and his Asherah/asherah."[100] What is somewhat

---

chaeology of Cult in the Southern Levant," 94; Nakhai, *Archaeology and the Religions of Canaan and Israel*, 181.

96. Nakhai, *Archaeology and the Religions of Canaan and Israel*, 181.

97. Gilmour, "Archaeology of Cult in the Southern Levant," 95.

98. Gilmour, "Archaeology of Cult in the Southern Levant," 95; Levy and Edelstein, "Cinq années de fouilles à Tel ʿAmal," 331–44; and Nakhai, *Archaeology and the Religions of Canaan and Israel*, 181.

99. The bibliography is vast. Key references include the 2012 publication volume, Meshel, *Kuntillet ʿAjrud*; as well as Becking, ed., *Only One God?*; Dever, "Asherah, Consort of Yahweh?," 21–37; Dever, *Did God Have a Wife?*, 160–67, 197–208; Dever, "Recent Archaeological Confirmation of the Cult of Asherah," 37–43; Hadley, *Cult of Asherah*; Lemaire, "Date et origine des inscriptiones hébraiques et pheniciennes de Kuntillet ʿAjrud," 131–43; Lemaire, "Who or What Was Yahweh's Asherah?," 42–51; and Olyan, *Asherah and the Cult of Yahweh*.

100. See Aḥituv, Eshel, and Meshel, "The Inscriptions," 86–91, 94–100, 105–7. The translations here are my own.

Fig. 2.13. Rolled hem from textiles at Kuntillet 'Ajrûd

Fig. 2.14. Linen with colored wool decoration from Kuntillet 'Ajrûd

less well known is that a large assemblage of textile fragments (approximately one hundred and twenty), mostly linen with only eleven pieces of woolen fabric, was also found at Kuntillet 'Ajrûd, along with wooden beams that may have belonged to a loom and two groups of loom weights.[101]

The quality of many of the textiles found at Kuntillet 'Ajrûd, moreover, is extremely high: fragments exhibit, for example, complicated and meticulously executed sewing techniques (fig. 2.13), in addition to the use of some colored threads for decoration (blue and, in one example, red; see fig. 2.14). In fact, the quality of the fabrics found at Kuntillet 'Ajrûd is so high that the scholar who has written most extensively on the site's textiles, Avigail Sheffer, has suggested that their excellence should be related to cultic activities at the site.[102] Similarly, Sheffer and Amalia Tidhar have argued that the overwhelming predominance of *linen* textiles at Kuntillet 'Ajrûd may also be due to cultic activities that oc-

101. See Sheffer and Tidhar, "Textiles and Basketry," 289, 305–7; originally published as Sheffer and Tidhar, "Textiles and Basketry at Kuntillet 'Ajrud," 1, 11–12.

102. Sheffer, "Needlework and Sewing in Israel," 547–50.

curred at the site, given that linen is the fabric known from the Bible (and from elsewhere in the ancient Near East) to be preferred for priestly vestments and other cultic cloth;[103] note also that the presence of so many linen fragments at Kuntillet ʿAjrûd can otherwise be difficult to explain, as the site's proximity to the sheep-herding region of the Negev, and its distance from flax-growing regions such as the Jezreel and Beth-Shean valleys, should mean that woolen textiles would be far more prevalent.[104] Sheffer and Tidhar have in addition suggested a religious explanation for the three pieces of fabric at ʿAjrûd that mix wool and linen fibers, something that is generally forbidden to the ancient Israelites according to Lev 19:19 and Deut 22:11 but is prescribed for priestly vestments in Exod 28:4–8 and 39:2–5, 24, 27–29.[105]

If Sheffer and Tidhar are correct regarding any or all of these various assessments of the Kuntillet ʿAjrûd fabrics as cultic, then their analysis could be taken to suggest a relationship between textile production and a cult incorporating the worship of Asherah as practiced at the ʿAjrûd site. However, as in our discussion of loom weights above, we must recall that textiles would presumably have been present at any ancient Near Eastern cultic site, and so the presence of arguably cultic textile fragments at Kuntillet ʿAjrûd need not be specifically related to the cult of Asherah that is seemingly represented there. Moreover, while the high concentration of loom weights found in conjunction with Asherah worship at the sites of Taʿanach and Tel Miqne-Ekron *did* suggest a correlation between textile production and the goddess's cult, the high concentration of textile fragments found at Kuntillet ʿAjrûd in conjunction with Asherah worship cannot as definitely indicate a special association between Asherah and the arts of spinning and weaving—this because Kuntillet ʿAjrûd is a desert site, and thus the high concentration of textile fragments found at this location, as opposed to other cultic locales, may be due only to climatological factors, the aridity of the eastern Sinai allowing for the preservation of textile

103. See, e.g., in biblical tradition, Exod 26:1, 36; 27:9; 28:4–5; and for the East Semitic world, the comments of Potts, *Mesopotamia*, 119.

104. Sheffer and Tidhar, "Textiles and Basketry at Kuntillet ʿAjrud," 3, 11, 12, 14; subsequently, Sheffer and Tidhar, "Textiles and Basketry," 290, 305, 307. Sheffer elsewhere has explained that the reason flax-growing is centered in the north, especially in the Beth-Shean region of the Jordan Valley, is because of the fairly significant amount of water required for growing this crop (Sheffer, "Use of Perforated Clay Balls on the Warp-Weighted Loom," 82).

105. Sheffer, "Needlework and Sewing in Israel," 547n16; Sheffer and Tidhar, "Textiles and Basketry at Kuntillet ʿAjrud," 12; subsequently, Sheffer and Tidhar, "Textiles and Basketry," 307.

remains over the millennia. Similar preservation would not have happened at other, more humid religious sites.[106] Moreover, the overall corpus of remains from Kuntillet ʿAjrûd, in addition to indicating cultic activity, demonstrates that the site was a caravanserai, meaning we cannot dismiss the possibility that at least some of the textile fragments found at ʿAjrûd were a part of the trading stock brought by merchants traveling from the textile-producing arenas of the Jezreel and Beth-Shean valleys (e.g., the sites of Tell el-Ḥammah and Tel ʿAmal discussed above) into the Arabian peninsula and were *not* a part of the site's cultic paraphernalia.

Still, the remains from Kuntillet ʿAjrûd do include, as I have already noted, loom parts (worked wooden beams and loom weights) and a bundle of flax fibers, spun yarn, and twisted thread, indicating that some textile production did take place at the site, presumably in order to fabricate materials for use at Kuntillet ʿAjrûd itself and not for trade. Moreover, at least some of the cloth being produced at Kuntillet ʿAjrûd was linen (as evidenced by the presence of bundled flax fibers), even though wool was the only raw material for fabric production locally available. This suggests that at least some of the fabrics being produced at ʿAjrûd were for some sort of special use. That the special use in question is religious is strongly indicated both by the cultic remains otherwise attested at the site and by Sheffer's and Tidhar's reminder that linen is the fabric known from throughout the ancient Near East to be preferred for cultic purposes. That the fabrics produced at ʿAjrûd are specifically to be associated with the worship of Asherah that is seemingly attested there is less sure, but I believe the ʿAjrûd data, when considered in conjunction with the other data suggesting an association between Asherah and the arts of spinning and weaving I have presented, are highly suggestive.

III. Conclusions

I have titled this chapter "Asherah, the West Semitic Goddess of Spinning and Weaving?" with a question mark at its end because I readily admit that none of the evidence I have assembled here is secure. Nevertheless, as I noted above, the comparative evidence available to us from Mesopotamia, Egypt, and Greece seems to indicate that, as in these cultures, there should be a patron goddess of spinning and weaving in West Semitic pantheons. While the data

106. Sheffer, "Needlework and Sewing in Israel," 527, 547.

that Asherah is this patron goddess is not ironclad, I believe a better case can be made for her than for any other West Semitic goddess. I therefore tentatively propose that Asherah, among her many other roles in the West Semitic pantheon, served as the goddess of spinning and weaving in the Late Bronze Age and Iron Age West Semitic world.

2022 Postscript

As I noted above, in my introductory comments to this chapter, Theodore J. Lewis has recently pushed back against my 2008 suggestion regarding Asherah as the West Semitic goddess of spinning and weaving, both in his book *The Origin and Character of God: Ancient Israelite Religion through the Lens of Divinity* and in an article titled "Ugaritic Athtartu Šadi, Food Production, and Textiles: More Data for Reassessing the Biblical Portrayal of Aštart in Context."[107] More specifically, and as I also noted in my comments above, Lewis has suggested—as the title of his article particularly indicates—that Ugaritic evidence demonstrates an association between the Ugaritic goddess Athtartu/Athtart (known in the Bible as Aštart/Astarte) and textile production.

In making this argument, Lewis relies particularly on two ritual and economic texts from Ugarit, both of which speak of Athtartu/Athtart as Athtart-Šad, "Athtart of the Field" or "Athtart of the Steppe Land." Lewis notes, for example, that in *KTU* 4.182, an economic text, Athtart-Šad is mentioned twice, in lines that can be taken to follow a list of various textile products, such as bolts of fabric, different types of garments, and seven hundred and fifty units of wool, including units of wool that have apparently been dyed red or blue (literally "lapis"). This text also mentions a "weaver" (*mḥṣ*), in line 56, in close conjunction with the two references to Athtart-Šad in lines 55 and 58, although the fragmentary nature of this part of the tablet makes it difficult to know whether these lines actually assert an association of Athtart-Šad with weaving. It is also difficult to know how, precisely, the two references to Athtart-Šad in lines 55 and 58 relate to the list of textile products found elsewhere in the text, in lines 2–40, given that only a few letters in the intervening lines, lines 41–54, are preserved. Perhaps, if we are to follow David M. Clemens, who understands

---

107. Lewis, *Origin and Character of God*, 675–96, esp. 690–91; Lewis, "Ugaritic Athtartu Šadi," 138–59, esp. 150–51.

the text as listing textile products that are distributed to multiple gods, we are to take Athtart-Šad as among the divine recipients of these offerings.[108]

Fortunately, in *KTU* 1.148, lines 18–22, a ritual text, things are clearer: there, Athtart-Šad is said to receive offerings that include three hundred units of wool and fifteen garments of four different types, as well as specially processed agricultural products (perfumed oil, balsam, and honey).[109] Lewis suggests these offerings are given to Athtart-Šad because, as the patron goddess of both the cultivated fields and the steppe land (both of which can be referred to as *šadu*), she appropriately receives offerings that represent the fields' and steppe lands' bounty: agricultural products primarily associated with cultivated fields and wool products derived from the sheep and goat pastoralism that predominated in the drier steppes.[110] Regarding the fragmentary *KTU* 4.182, Lewis is appropriately more circumspect: he suggests only that *KTU* 4.182, when coupled with *KTU* 1.148 and with evidence that more generally indicates the "vital importance of *šadu* for agriculture, textiles, and the overall economy,"[111] demonstrates that Athtart-Šad had an important presence among the cultic activities associated with the agro-pastoral products of Ugarit's cultivated fields and steppes, including textile products such as wool.[112]

But what, exactly, Lewis takes this evidence to mean regarding my conclusions about Asherah is less clear to me. In *The Origin and Character of God*, he chides me for being "reductionist," and while his discussion briefly cites my analyses of the archaeological materials from Taʿanach, Kuntillet ʿAjrûd, and Tel Miqne-Ekron, his critique, if I am reading Lewis correctly, particularly concerns my use of the Ugaritic materials, given my reliance only on the mythological text found in the Baal Cycle (*KTU* 1.4.2.3–9) without taking into account "different information" from "different genres" (the Ugaritic ritual and economic texts that Lewis considers).[113] I *think* this focus on "difference" means that Lewis proposes to identify a different goddess—not Asherah, but Athtart-Šad—as the patron goddess of the Ugaritic textile industry, and the

---

108. Clemens, *Sources for Ugaritic Ritual and Sacrifice*, 357–58. For a translation of *KTU* 4.182, see McGeough, *Ugaritic Economic Tablets*, 130–33; for Lewis's discussion, see Lewis, *Origin and Character of God*, 682–83, and Lewis, "Ugaritic Athtartu Šadi," 148–49.

109. Lewis, *Origin and Character of God*, 682; Lewis, "Ugaritic Athtartu Šadi," 148–49. For a translation of *KTU* 1.148, see Pardee, *Ritual and Cult at Ugarit*, 48.

110. Lewis, *Origin and Character of God*, 681–83; Lewis, "Ugaritic Athtartu Šadi," 146–48.

111. Lewis, "Ugaritic Athtartu Šadi," 147.

112. Lewis, *Origin and Character of God*, 683; Lewis, "Ugaritic Athtartu Šadi," 149.

113. Lewis, *Origin and Character of God*, 691.

fact that Lewis couples his discussion of Ugaritic Athtart-Šad with comments regarding biblical Aštart/Astarte suggests he also wishes to identify Aštart/Astarte, and not Asherah, as the patron goddess of the textile industry in Israel.[114] Indeed, Lewis, following on those (including me) who identify the biblical Queen of Heaven as Aštart/Astarte (or a syncretism of West Semitic Aštart and East Semitic Ishtar),[115] uses Jer 44:17–18 (as have I), as well as Deut 7:13; 28:4, 18, 51; and Jer 7:20, to argue that the cult of biblical Aštart, at least in the Southern Kingdom of Judah, "had agrarian concerns that included fecund humans and animals as well as agricultural bounty." This biblical material, he goes on to say, "finds an analogue with the Ugaritic cult surrounding ʿAthtartu of the Field/Steppe Land,"[116] suggesting again that not only does Lewis want to identify Athtart-Šad, and not Asherah, as the patron goddess of textile production in Ugarit; he also wants to identify biblical Aštart/Astarte, and not Asherah, as the patron goddess of textile production in Israel (or at least in Judah).

Still, in "Ugaritic Athtartu Šadi," Lewis concludes the part of his discussion titled "A Goddess of Weaving"—which he begins by briefly summarizing my proposal regarding Asherah—by stating, "Our data are limited, but they suggest that [Ugaritic] Athtart was *also* a prominent deity associated with textile production and commerce" (emphasis mine).[117] As my italics suggest, the force of the "also" attracts my attention here: to me, it most obviously suggests that in this article, Lewis is not rejecting my arguments that associate Asherah with the arts of spinning and weaving but augmenting them by suggesting that, along with Asherah, Ugaritic Athtart has associations with textile production. It is, in addition, surely obvious that this approach to the materials regarding Ugaritic Athtart (and also, by extension, biblical Aštart/Astarte) is more amenable to me than the "Athtart instead of Asherah" argument that I think Lewis is putting forward in *The Origin and Character of God*. More im-

---

114. Note in this regard that in a paper given at the 2018 Annual Meeting of the Society of Biblical Literature, "Ugaritic Athtartu," which I take to be a precursor to his discussions in *Origin and Character of God* and in "Ugaritic Athtartu Šadi," Lewis seems clearly to propose that his interpretation is "different" from mine. More specifically, in the abstract of that paper, he writes that he will "argue that Athtartu is a better fit for a goddess associated with the textile industry (in contrast to Asherah as argued by Ackerman)."

115. Lewis, *Origin and Character of God*, 677; Lewis, "Ugaritic Athtartu Šadi," 141. Lewis specifically cites my work on the Queen of Heaven in *Origin and Character of God*, 899n8, and in "Ugaritic Athtartu Šadi," 141n7; see in particular my essay "'And the Women Knead Dough,'" 109–24, reprinted in this volume at pp. 3–18.

116. Lewis, *Origin and Character of God*, 677, 695; see similarly Lewis, "Ugaritic Athtartu Šadi," 140–41, 153.

117. Lewis, "Ugaritic Athtartu Šadi," 151.

portant, I would suggest that the interpretation "Athtart along with Asherah" better coheres with our evidence from elsewhere in the Near East and eastern Mediterranean. For example, as I noted in part 1 of this chapter, it is not unknown for ancient Near Eastern cultures to have multiple goddesses who are associated with the textile arts, as in Egypt, where, by the Late and Ptolemaic periods, Tait, Neith, and Hedjhotep were all associated with textile production. Somewhat similarly, while I documented in part 1 of this chapter multiple traditions that associate the Greek goddess Athena with spinning, one might add that one of the Greek verbs for spinning, *klōthein*, is the basis of the name Klōthō, the Fate responsible for spinning the threads of humans' destiny.[118]

The Sumerian evidence I cited in part 1 also invites us to consider textile production as a multi-dimensional phenomenon, as in the mythic material found in "The Bridal Sheets of Inanna," where the flax Utu proposes to bring to Inanna to be processed must be retted, spun, and then respun with its threads doubled-up, before it can be woven and, finally, bleached. Likewise, wool must be washed, combed, stretched, and spun before it can be twisted into yarn to be woven; then, after weaving, it is sent to a fuller before it is sewn. In addition, either before or after spinning or before or after weaving, wool is dyed.[119] And preceding all this is the securing and preparation of the raw materials: harvesting, drying, and removing the seeds from the flax stalks that will be used to produce linen; collecting wool fibers by plucking them off molting sheep or, as technologies developed by the time of the Iron Age, by shearing.[120]

Mesopotamian evidence suggests, moreover, that different deities can oversee these different domains of textile production: thus, while Uttu is identified within Sumerian tradition as the patron goddess of weaving, it is her great-grandmother (or great-great-grandmother) Ninhursag who is identified as "the tender mother of herd animals" in a Babylonian liturgical text.[121] Even more telling is the Sumerian myth "Enki and the World Order," in which the god Enki, as part of his work in organizing both cosmos and civilization, specifically assigns oversight of the weaving of textiles to Uttu in lines 380–85, even as the responsibility for herds and herd animals is assigned to the god Dumuzi just a few lines prior (in lines 357–66).[122] Dumuzi is also called "herdsman" and

118. Barber, *Prehistoric Textiles*, 263.

119. Barber, *Prehistoric Textiles*, 262–63, 274–75; Matoïan and Vita, "Wool Production and Economy at Ugarit," 316, citing Breniquet, *Essai sur le tissage en Mésopotamie*.

120. Barber, *Prehistoric Textiles*, 261.

121. Jacobsen, *Treasures of Darkness*, 106; on the different renderings of Uttu's ancestry, see pp. 112–13 (as in n. 9 above).

122. Jacobsen, *Treasures of Darkness*, 115; Kramer and Maier, *Myths of Enki*, 52.

"shepherd" in various Sumerian texts that recount his marriage to the goddess Inanna,[123] although a different Sumerian myth still—the story of "Lahar and Ašnan," or "Ewe and Grain"—describes Lahar as the female archetype of wool-bearing animals, created by the gods in a gesture of magnanimity so that the theretofore naked humans might have clothes. Nevertheless, at several points, this text differentiates Lahar from Uttu so that, for example, Lahar takes responsibility for the fecundity of sheep and goats, and their "twin lambs" and "triplet kids" in lines 6–9, while spun yarn and the loom for weaving are said to be the province of Uttu in lines 4–5.[124]

Might this Sumerian evidence help illuminate the Ugaritic and Israelite materials to which Lewis has pointed us by suggesting that Ugaritic Athtartu/Athtart—or, more specifically, Ugaritic Athtart-Šad, "Athtart of the Field" or "Athtart of the Steppe Land"—as well as biblical Aštart/Astarte, was more associated with the herd animals who grazed, especially, on the steppe, while Asherah was more associated with the technological processes of spinning and weaving that rendered these herd animals' wool into yarn and then cloth? Note particularly in this regard the biblical idiom *'aštĕrōt ṣō'nekâ*, found in Deut 7:13; 28:4, 18, and 51, where (in Lewis's words) "a personalized Aštart [the goddess]" is turned into "a common noun, 'the *fecundity* ['*aštĕrōt*] of your flock.'"[125] As Lewis's italics make clear, his interest in this phrase is the biblical writers' association of Aštart/Astarte with agricultural fertility, as this helps support his conclusion that I quoted above regarding the "agrarian concerns" of the biblical Astarte's cult, which "included fecund humans and animals as well as agricultural bounty."[126] If we focus, though, on the idiom's reference to *flocks*—meaning overwhelmingly in ancient Israel (as in the Middle East still today) flocks of sheep and goats—we can suggest that the specific responsibility assigned to Astarte within the multiple stages of textile fabrication is the production of the raw wool and goat hair with which the whole process of textile production begins.

To put the matter another way: in discussing the ritual and economic texts from Ugarit that concern Athtart-Šad, "Athtart of the Field" or "Athtart of the Steppe Land," Lewis's focus is on the bounty that the *šadu* can yield, including the textile products that ultimately result from sheep and goat pastoralism. But

123. Jacobsen, *Treasures of Darkness*, 35, 45.

124. Alster and Vanstiphout, "Lahar and Ashnan," 14–15; Vanstiphout, "The Disputation Between Ewe and Wheat," 575.

125. Lewis, *Origin and Character of God*, 677; Lewis, "Ugaritic Athtartu Šadi," 140.

126. See above, n. 116.

the epithet Athtart-Šad invites us equally to focus on the *šadu* as a location that is Athtart's appropriate domain. Thus, she is appropriately characterized as the patron of the specific aspects of textile production that took place in the *šadu*, where sheep grew their woolly fleeces and goats their hair. Indeed, Lewis prefaces his discussion of Ugaritic Athtart-Šad with a discussion of Ugaritic Athtart's prowess as a "huntress" within the lands of the outback or steppe,[127] and while Lewis's point—especially in his article—is to segue from his observations regarding hunting to a broader consideration of Athtart-Šad's role in securing other foodstuffs and agricultural products (including the wool and hair that comes from sheep and goat pastoralism), the line of reasoning I am pursuing here suggests we might use the traditions regarding Ugaritic Athtart's prowess as a huntress, coupled with her epithet Athtart-Šad, in order to understand the steppe lands (*šadu*), as well as the kindred cultivated lands (also *šadu*), as Athtart's natural "home." Conversely, while I cannot claim that I was this careful in my thinking when I published my original article in 2008, that article's title did promote Asherah's associations with *spinning* and *weaving*, that is, with aspects of the textile production process that took place in the household or (in more industrialized contexts) in weaving workshops—or, generally speaking, in indoor spaces. Moreover, the Ugaritic text I cited to support my identification of Asherah as the West Semitic goddess of spinning and weaving (*KTU* 1.4.2.3–9) describes Asherah engaging generally in household labors: laundry and (perhaps) cooking. Again, then, I might propose that Ugaritic Athtartu/Athtart—or, more specifically, Ugaritic Athtart-Šad, "Athtart of the Field" or "Athtart of the Steppe Land"—as well as biblical Aštart/Astarte, was more associated with the aspects of textile production that took place in outdoor expanses, whereas Asherah was more associated with the aspects of textile production whose locus was the domestic and industrialized sphere.

In 2014, Catherine Breniquet and Céline Michel published an edited volume titled *Wool Economy in the Ancient Near East and the Aegean: From the Beginnings of Sheep Husbandry to Institutional Textile Industry*. As their subtitle implies, their interest is a chronology of the *longue durée*, from the initial breeding of sheep for wool production in Mesopotamia in the late fifth and fourth millennia BCE to the establishment of professional centers of textile production beginning in the second half of the third millennium BCE and continuing through the rest of ancient Near Eastern history (and, of course, beyond).[128] But Breniquet's and Michel's evocations of sheep husbandry and

127. Lewis, *Origin and Character of God*, 681; Lewis, "Ugaritic Athtartu Šadi," 145–46.
128. Breniquet and Michel, "Wool Economy in the Ancient Near East," 2–3.

textile production also can imply the shorter time span that all woolen fabrics require in order to come into being: from the harvesting of a sheep's wool through the processes of washing, combing, stretching, dying, spinning, twisting, weaving, fulling, and sewing that must take place before, say, a garment is ready to be worn or a curtain is ready to be hung. I am not ready to let go of my hypothesis that in the West Semitic world, Asherah is associated with the technologies of spinning and weaving that are found in the latter part of this list. But inspired by Lewis's work, I am prepared to add that Ugaritic Athtart, especially in her guise as Athtart-Šad, and biblical Astarte, especially when identified with the fecundity of the flocks, exercised dominion over the pastoralist domain where the whole process of textile production begins.

CHAPTER 3

The Women of the Bible
and of Ancient Near Eastern Myth

THE CASE OF THE LEVITE'S *PÎLEGEŠ*

❧

This chapter is very different from the two that precede it in this volume in that the goddess on which it focuses—the Mesopotamian goddess Tiamat—is, unlike Jeremiah's Queen of Heaven or the West Semitic goddess Asherah, not a deity whom any ancient Near Easterner, man or woman, would typically worship. This is because in Mesopotamian mythology, and especially in the Mesopotamian creation epic known as the Enuma Elish, Tiamat represents the primeval waters that must be defeated by the warrior god Marduk in order that the world be created. As such, she personifies eminently undesirable traits, such as cosmic disorder and even chaos, and this ominous symbolism is reinforced in the Enuma Elish and elsewhere by evocations of the monstrous beings—snake dragons and the like—that she creates to abet her in her primordial battle against Marduk. Yet however ferocious her allies, their help is of no avail, as Marduk harnesses fearsome storm winds to roil Tiamat's watery body and, ultimately, to inflate her belly so that he can shoot an arrow into her midst and pierce her through. He then uses her dismembered body to create the cosmos. For example, Mesopotamia's two great rivers, the Tigris and Euphrates, well up from her eyes. Many scholars have argued, moreover, that these rivers' annual spring floods, when they are filled with run-off waters from the melting snows of the Armenian highlands, were

---

An earlier version of this chapter appeared in John J. Collins, T. M. Lemos, and Saul M. Olyan, eds., *Worship, Women, and War: Essays in Honor of Susan Niditch*, BJS 357 (Atlanta: Society of Biblical Literature, 2015), 215–26. Used here by permission of Brown Judaic Studies.

understood by the ancient Mesopotamians to be a sign that Tiamat's chaotic nature, although subdued, still lurked just below the surface of Marduk's orderly cosmos. Her monstrous allies also lived on as demonic beings in ancient Mesopotamian understanding. No wonder no one worshipped her!

Still, in the same way that chapter 1, "And the Women Knead Dough,'" and chapter 2, "Asherah, the West Semitic Goddess of Spinning and Weaving?," considered ways in which the Bible's accounts of ancient Israelite women intersected with ancient Near Eastern traditions concerning the goddesses Astarte, Ishtar, and Asherah, so too does this chapter take up the issue of a biblical portrayal of a human woman—the Levite's pîlegeš, or concubine, in Judg 19—and ways in which she might be associated with Tiamat as a divine counterpart. To be sure, the specific ways in which biblical women might be associated with Near Eastern goddesses vary significantly. For example, I take the women who made bread cakes for the Queen of Heaven according to Jer 7:16–20 and 44:15–19, 25 to be historically realistic figures who produced their cakes as part of the ritual devotions they offered to the goddess. Conversely, in "Asherah, the West Semitic Goddess of Spinning and Weaving?," I suggested that the 'ēšet-ḥayil, or "woman of valor," of Prov 31:10–31 represents an idealized (i.e., an ahistorical) human manifestation of the divine figure of Woman Wisdom who appears in Prov 1–9 and who is arguably, in turn, to be understood as a reflex of the goddess Asherah. The Levite's pîlegeš, I argue in this chapter, is something different still, as I do not take her story in Judg 19 to be a realistic depiction of a historical event, like the stories of the Queen of Heaven's devotees, or even a realistic depiction of an event that, even if not historical, might have happened during an ancient Israelite woman's lifetime. Yet neither is the pîlegeš the sort of idealized character we encounter in the Proverbs description of the 'ēšet-ḥayil. Moreover, as I have already intimated, the pîlegeš, unlike, say, the women who bake cakes for the Queen of Heaven, is not a devotee of Tiamat, the goddess with whom I associate her, nor do I want to suggest that, as the 'ēšet-ḥayil is a reflex of Asherah, the pîlegeš is a reflex of Tiamat.

Rather, in what follows, I propose that the Levite's pîlegeš and Tiamat are of a "type," in that both are female characters whose stories present an object lesson to their audiences regarding proper gender behavior. More specifically, I discuss the ways in which the story of the Levite's pîlegeš ends as badly for her as does Tiamat's combat with Marduk. I furthermore argue that in both cases, these unhappy endings result because the stories' female characters act contrary to, and even in defiance of, the norms that ancient Near Eastern tradition required of women. Reading the story of the Levite's pîlegeš in tandem with Mesopotamian mythological traditions about Tiamat thus brings into greater relief the way narrative traditions that focus on female characters—whether human or divine—can be deployed to enforce ancient Near Eastern gender expectations.

Scholars have often noted the close parallels between the stories of Gen 19, where divine emissaries lodge overnight in Sodom in the house of Abraham's nephew Lot, and Judg 19, where a Levite sojourner from Ephraim and his entourage lodge overnight in Gibeah with another Ephraimite who is temporarily resident in this Benjaminite town.[1] Especially of note is the violent episode that happens once the evening proceeds in both tales: men from Sodom, in Gen 19:4–5, and Benjaminites from Gibeah, in Judg 19:22, come to the residences where the visitors are housed in order to demand that the divine emissaries (in Gen 19) and the Levite (in Judg 19) be sent forth "so that we might know them/him." The language here draws on the Bible's well-known use of the verb "to know" (*yādaʿ*) as a sexual euphemism, meaning that what the Sodomites and Benjaminites each seek is to assert their dominance over the strangers in their midst by subjecting them to homosexual rape. This symbolically renders the male strangers as females and thus, according to the patriarchal norms of ancient Israelite society, as subordinate.[2] In both stories, however, the strangers' hosts resist this gross assault on their male guests by offering female alternatives.[3] Lot offers the Sodomites his two daughters who "have not known a man," and the Ephraimite likewise offers the Benjaminites his daughter who is unmarried, yet of marriageable age.[4] The Ephraimite also offers the Benjaminites the female companion of the Levite, called at multiple

1. See, e.g., Lasine, "Guest and Host in Judges 19," 37–59; Niditch, "The 'Sodomite' Theme in Judges 19–20," 365–78.

2. For a particularly trenchant analysis of the sexual dynamics at play in Judg 19 (and, by extension, in Gen 19), see K. Stone, "Gender and Homosexuality in Judges 19," 87–107, esp., regarding my point here, 96–99.

3. As in n. 2 above, K. Stone, "Gender and Homosexuality in Judges 19," 92–93, 99–101, offers a particularly trenchant analysis of Lot's and the Ephraimite's proposals to substitute female victims for their male guests and demonstrates why, from an Israelite perspective, offering up females is a "better" (albeit still bad) alternative.

4. That the term used of the Ephraimite's daughter, *bĕtûlâ*, designates a stage in life, "a young woman" (and more specifically, a young woman who has entered into puberty and so is of marriageable age), rather than the more usual "virgin," has been preeminently demonstrated by Wenham, "*Betûlāh*," 326–48. See also Pressler, *View of Women*, 25–28, with multiple references.

points in the story his *pîlegeš*, a term usually translated as "concubine" but probably better rendered as "secondary wife."[5]

In both cases, the Sodomites and the Benjaminites reject this offer and press on with their threats against Lot and (seemingly) the Levite's Ephraimite host. (This is not stated explicitly in Judg 19, but it seems clearly implied.) But as the action continues, the stories rather dramatically diverge. In Gen 19, the divine emissaries step in to avert the Sodomites' violent intentions and, ultimately, to save the lives of Lot and his family as Sodom is destroyed. In Judg 19, conversely, the Levite thrusts his *pîlegeš* out of the Ephraimite's door, where she is subjected to a brutal gang rape, enacted by the Benjaminites, "all the night" (Judg 19:25). Then, the next morning, when the Levite finds her on the Ephraimite's doorstep (dead? more on this below), he throws her body over the back of his donkey (Judg 19:27–28). Next, once he arrives back at his home in Ephraim, the Levite dismembers the *pîlegeš*'s body and cuts it into twelve pieces (Judg 19:29). These he then sends throughout Israel, hoping that by drawing the Israelites' attention to the Gibeahites' crime, he will cause his countrymen, according to Judg 19:30, to "set your minds upon it, take counsel, and speak out" against their Gibeahite compatriots.

Most typically, commentators compare this dismemberment of the *pîlegeš* in Judg 19:29 to 1 Sam 11:7, in which Saul, after hearing of an attack by the Ammonites upon the Israelite village of Jabesh-Gilead, takes a yoke of oxen, cuts them into pieces, and sends these pieces to the various tribes of Israel in order to summon the Israelites to do battle against Ammon. Indeed, already in his 1895 International Critical Commentary volume on Judges, George Foot Moore wrote of Judg 19:29 that "just so Saul cut up a yoke of oxen at Gibeah, and sent the pieces by messengers *throughout all the territory of Israel* [*běkol-gěbûl yiśrā'ēl*, the same phrase used in Judg 19:29] . . . to raise the Israelites for the relief of Jabesh Gilead."[6] More recently, James D. Martin, in his 1975 contribution to the Cambridge Bible Commentary, notes, "The action described in this verse [Judg 19:29] is paralleled by that taken by Saul to summon the Israelites to war against the Ammonites in 1 Sam 11:7,"[7] and this parallel was cited as well in 1975

---

5. In the Bible, the term "concubine" can mean either a woman who is a part of a man's household and one of his sexual partners but is not one of his actual wives (2 Sam 5:13; 15:16; 19:6 [in most English translations, 19:5]; 1 Chr 3:9; 2 Chr 11:21; Cant 6:8, 9; Esth 2:14) or a woman who is married to a man as a secondary wife. In Judg 19, the meaning "secondary wife" is surely intended, given that we are told in 19:3 that the Levite is the woman's husband (*'îšāh*) and in 19:4, 7, and 9 that the woman's father is the Levite's father-in-law (*ḥōtěnô*). See further Fewell, "Judges," 81.

6. Moore, *Critical and Exegetical Commentary on Judges*, 420.

7. Martin, *Book of Judges*, 206.

by Robert G. Boling in his Anchor Bible Judges commentary.[8] More recently still, we can quote Victor H. Matthews, from his 2004 New Cambridge Bible Commentary: "There are clear parallels between this action [in Judg 19:29] and Saul's call to arms in 1 Sam 11:7";[9] Marc Zvi Brettler, in his 2002 contribution to the series Old Testament Readings: "There is . . . a connection between the end of the chapter [Judg 19] and 1 Sam 11:7";[10] and Susan Niditch, in her 2008 Old Testament Library commentary on Judges: "The image of dividing the woman's corpse into twelve pieces . . . is a macabre parallel to Saul's divvying up of his father's oxen and sending the pieces abroad to the territories of Israel."[11]

Commentators whose interest in Judg 19 is driven by an explicitly feminist agenda have also cited 1 Sam 11:7 in relation to Judg 19:29. For example, Gale A. Yee, in the volume she edited, *Judges and Method: New Approaches in Biblical Studies*, states, "Undoubtedly, the Deuteronomist intends that the Levite's act be contrasted with 1 Sam 11, where Saul, under the power of God's spirit, hacks a yoke of oxen to pieces."[12] And similarly, J. Cheryl Exum, in her book *Fragmented Women: Feminist (Sub)versions of Biblical Narratives*, writes, "I am prepared to grant that the dismemberment [of the Levite's *pîlegeš*] is a morbid parody of Saul's cutting into pieces a yoke of oxen and sending the parts throughout Israel to muster the people to battle."[13] I too find the 1 Sam 11:7 parallel useful for illuminating Judg 19:29, especially because the notice in Judg 19:29 that the body of the *pîlegeš* was cut into *twelve* pieces otherwise makes no sense within the Judg 19 tale, as the point in Judg 19 is *not*, as in 1 Sam 11:7, to assemble all twelve tribes to fight against Ammon, an enemy of Israel, but to assemble *eleven* of Israel's tribes to take action against Benjamin, the tribe cast in the story as a renegade twelfth. The cutting of the *pîlegeš*'s body into *twelve* pieces, that is, seems clearly to be a detail in Judg 19:29 that is part and parcel with the 1 Sam 11:7 story—so much so that I would be willing to support a suggestion originally made (as far as I know) by Julius Wellhausen and most recently championed (again, as far as I know) by Brettler that the author(s) or redactor(s) of Judg 19:29 were influenced by the 1 Sam 11 text.[14]

Still, one must admit, as do almost all the commentators who cite 1 Sam 11:7 in explicating Judg 19:29, that the parallel does not hold perfectly, in that the

8. Boling, *Judges*, 276.

9. Matthews, *Judges and Ruth*, 190.

10. Brettler, *Book of Judges*, 86.

11. Niditch, *Judges*, 193.

12. Yee, "Ideological Criticism," 155.

13. Exum, *Fragmented Women*, 180.

14. Wellhausen, in *Die Composition des Hexateuchs*, as cited by Brettler, *Book of Judges*, 86, and by Moore, *Critical and Exegetical Commentary on Judges*, 421.

stated purpose of the dismemberment in 1 Sam 11:7 is *not* the stated purpose of the dismemberment in Judg 19:29. Among feminist commentators, this point has best been made by Koala Jones-Warsaw: "Some have compared this dismemberment of the concubine to Saul's dismemberment of an oxen (1 Sam. 11.7), for the purpose of threatening those who did not assemble for war with a similar fate. But the Levite did not have the military might, nor the political authority to make such a threat."[15] Similarly, from the standard commentaries, we can quote again Martin: "In the incident in 1 Samuel the act is explained; the same fate of being cut up will befall the cattle of all who fail to obey the summons to battle. Here [in Judg 19:29], the action is clearly intended to arouse the horror and indignation of all against those who had perpetrated such an outrage."[16] More forceful are the comments of J. Alberto Soggin:

> In 1 Sam 11.5ff., Saul dismembers his oxen under the power of the spirit of God, whereas here [in Judg 19:29] the only motive force seems to be the desire to inform the others and to arouse a healthy horror for the crime that has been committed. Despite the formal similarity, the substance of the message here [in Judg 19:29] is different . . . from 1 Sam. 11.[17]

Soggin, however, is unable to explain what, exactly, the message of Judg 19:29 to which he alludes might be: the "macabre gesture," he writes, "does not . . . seem to serve a useful purpose."[18] Exum, moreover, who brought this Soggin quote to my attention, argues that most other commentators are likewise at a loss to explain the symbolic value of the Judg 19:29 dismemberment.[19]

Exum, however, does not find herself so stymied, nor does the feminist scholarly enterprise of which she is a part, because the feminist enterprise has at its heart the articulation of another juncture where the parallel between Judg 19:29 and 1 Sam 11:7 breaks down: over the issue of gender. As Exum writes, "Commentators are at a loss to explain . . . [the] symbolic value [of the

---

15. Jones-Warsaw, "Toward a Womanist Hermeneutic: A Reading of Judges 19–21," 178n2.

16. Martin, *Book of Judges*, 206.

17. Soggin, *Judges*, 289.

18. Soggin, *Judges*, 282.

19. Exum, *Fragmented Women*, 180. In addition to the references cited by Exum, see (among commentators who have written since her work was published) Brettler, *Book of Judges*, 86, who writes, "The action of butchering the woman is highly unusual and unnatural, and certainly is not the typical way of mustering the army"; likewise, Amit, "Literature in the Service of Politics: Studies in Judges 19–21," 34, who states, "The Levite's action is strange: what could be understood from receiving the severed hand of a woman?"

Judg 19:29 dismemberment] . . . because they have looked elsewhere than the gender code for its meaning." But, she continues, "if we seek the meaning of the act in the gender code, we discover that an implicit message about sexual behavior is being given to women."[20] More specifically, Exum argues that the narrative of Judg 19 seeks to punish the *pîlegeš* "in the most extreme form" possible because of her acts in the beginning of the story,[21] when she is said, according to the Hebrew of Judg 19:2, to have "prostituted herself against" or "fornicated against" or even "whored against" the Levite (*wattizneh ʿālâw pîlagšô*) and to have left him to go to her father's house in Judah. To be sure, how to take this notice of prostitution or fornication is a matter of some debate, since the Greek tradition offers a different reading entirely (*wattiznaḥ*, "she spurned him") and since "the literal sense" of the MT's *wattizneh* (to suppose that the *pîlegeš* actually had illicit sex with another man or other men) "presents interpretive problems": "Why would her father accept such a shameless daughter?" Yee asks. "Why would her husband [as the story goes on] expend the time and effort to bring her back?"[22] Both Exum and Yee thus propose that (in Yee's words), "A stronger case can be made for considering her [the *pîlegeš*'s] act figuratively":[23] that by leaving her husband, the woman "whores" by asserting her sexual autonomy, removing herself from her husband's sexual purview and sexual control.[24] But this act of self-assertion so violates gender norms, Exum argues, that the narrative requires the woman to be punished for her transgression to the fullest possible extent: she must be destroyed and the threat she poses diffused by her body being cut into pieces and scattered. As Exum writes:

> By leaving her husband the woman makes a gesture of sexual autonomy so threatening to patriarchal ideology that it requires her to be punished sexually in the most extreme form. The symbolic significance of dismem-

20. Exum, *Fragmented Women*, 180–81.

21. Exum, *Fragmented Women*, 181.

22. Yee, "Ideological Criticism," 152; the same questions are raised by Fewell and Gunn, *Gender, Power, and Promise*, 133.

23. Yee, "Ideological Criticism," 153.

24. See similarly Fewell and Gunn, *Gender, Power, and Promise*, 133; Müllner, "Lethal Differences: Sexual Violence as Violence against Others in Judges 19," 138, who writes, "The Levite's wife's behavior falls into the category of 'sexual misconduct' (i.e., socially inappropriate) *because* she has left him" (emphasis mine); and Niditch, *Judges*, 191, who comments, "The woman's departure in accordance with her own decision could be regarded as an act of defiance."

bering the woman's body lies in its intent to de-sexualize her. . . . "If the female body offends you, cut it up" might be the motto.[25]

I very much agree with Exum that the seeming excess of violence perpetrated on the *pîlegeš* in Judg 19:22–29—not only her dismemberment, but the gang rape she suffers and her subsequent demise, perhaps (as the LXX would have it) as a result of the night of abuse but perhaps (as the Hebrew text could allow) some time later, at the hands of her Levite husband after he returned home and began to cut her body into pieces[26]—can be read as a response generally to her act of self-assertion in v. 2 and more specifically as a response to her failure to abide by the ancient Israelite gender codes that granted control of her sexuality to her husband. I also think that this conclusion has been strengthened by Karla Bohmbach's 1999 article on Judg 19, in which Bohmbach points out yet another insult the text heaps upon the *pîlegeš*: the fact that the final act of brutality she suffers—the dismemberment—takes place within her own home, "a space" that "normally . . . assumed connotations of safety and security" for women. "Thus the place," Bohmbach writes, "that is expected to serve as the secure center of a woman's life (and the locus of whatever authority she might have), [sic] becomes for this woman, [sic] the site where her husband finally and most horrifically, [sic] destroys her."[27] Nevertheless, I think Exum's conclusion could be strengthened still further by reference to another story from ancient Near East literature in which a woman is murdered and her body then cut apart: this is the story of the slaying and partitioning of the goddess Tiamat found in the Mesopotamian Enuma Elish.

Before I explore this thesis in more detail, however, let me just say parenthetically that I am not the only commentator who has suggested that we might look for parallels to Judg 19:29 elsewhere in the ancient Near East: Gerhard Wallis, and later Boling, have argued, for example, that a Mari text reporting how one "Bahdi-Lim suggested to Zimri-Lim that a prisoner be slain and his head paraded throughout the Hanean territory in order to stimulate enthusiasm for sending in the requested quota of troops" (ARM 2:48) is similar to the Levite's strategy in sending the cut-up pieces of the *pîlegeš*'s body throughout

---

25. Exum, *Fragmented Women*, 181.

26. This ambiguity in the Hebrew text has been best and most profoundly explored by Trible, "An Unnamed Woman," 79.

27. Bohmbach, "Conventions/Contraventions: The Meanings of Public and Private for the Judges 19 Concubine," 96.

Israel.[28] But Soggin has rightly labeled this Mari parallel as "remote," since there is no dismemberment of a full body but only a beheading;[29] somewhat more germane, therefore, is the Hittite and Greek evidence that Theodore H. Gaster has put forward regarding twelve-piece sacrifices: during funerary rituals and rituals of healing and exorcism in the Hittite cases and in funerary ritual and sacrificial ritual generally in the case of the Greeks.[30] Gaster, however, as with those commentators who refer to 1 Sam 11:7 to illuminate Judg 19:29, seems to have focused only on the detail of the *twelve* pieces of the *pîlegeš*'s mutilated body rather than considering gender as a possible point of comparison; regarding this issue, the most germane parallel is again a Mari text, from the Rimaḥ archives, most recently discussed by Jack M. Sasson. In it, a woman, Iltani, opens a letter to her husband by quoting his threat to cut her into twelve pieces because of some questionable business dealings in which she has (at least seemingly, in his opinion) engaged.[31] Yet Sasson deems this ultimately to be a "hollow threat," even part of the "playfulness in some of the [other] exchanges between husband and wife,"[32] which is hardly how we can characterize the Levite's actual dismemberment of his *pîlegeš* in Judg 19:29. Hence my proposal that we look to the Enuma Elish to see how issues of the slaying of a female character and the cutting up of her body are played out in that text.

The critical scene in the Enuma Elish comes in tablet IV, lines 93–122, in which Marduk, who has been declared king of the gods, engages Tiamat, the gods' mother (tablet I, line 112, and many other places)—or, more literally, according to the myth's logic, Marduk's great-great-great-grandmother—in single-handed combat. Marduk, who previously in the myth has been given a gift of the fourfold winds (tablet I, lines 105–106), uses these natural forces to confine Tiamat's watery body so nothing of her could escape (tablet IV, lines 41–44, 95); then he sends forth the wind of the *imḫullu* storm, which he has created (tablet IV, line 45), to force open her mouth and, as Tiamat is compelled to swallow, to distend her belly (tablet IV, lines 96–100). Next, he shoots an arrow down her wide-open mouth and into her stomach, killing her (tablet IV, lines 101–102); finally, after subduing those allied with her, he

28. Boling, *Judges*, 277 (from whom the quote here is taken); Wallis, "Eine Parallel zu Richter 19:29ff," 57–61. Both references were brought to my attention by Soggin, *Judges*, 289.

29. Soggin, *Judges*, 289.

30. Gaster, *Myth, Legend, and Custom*, 444, 538n4.

31. Sasson, "Vile Threat," 924–25.

32. Sasson, "Vile Threat," 936.

returns to her body, and "divided the monstrous shape" (tablet IV, line 136).[33]
More specifically, he "broke her in two like a shellfish" (tablet IV, line 137) and
used half of her to make the heavens above and half to make the earth below.
Subsequently, he heaps up mountains upon her head (tablet V, line 53)[34] and
forms others either at or from her udder (tablet V, line 57); he drills holes
through her carcass for springs and wells (tablet V, line 54); and he pokes
out her eyes so that the Tigris and Euphrates Rivers can rise through them
(tablet V, line 55). He also stops up her nostrils for a purpose that is unclear
(the text is fragmentary) and twists up her tail to fasten her lower body to the
heavens (tablet V, lines 56, 59).

Now, obviously, at some level, this splitting and subsequent mutilation of
Tiamat's body serves a far different purpose—the process of cosmogony—than
does the dismemberment of the Levite's *pîlegeš*, which is done, to quote again
Judg 19:30, so that the Israelites who see her cut-up body might "set your minds
upon it, take counsel, and speak out" against the Benjaminites of Gibeah. But
at another level, which pertains to the issues of gender ideology and proper
gender roles that Exum has brought to our attention, the fate of Tiamat and
the fate of the Levite's *pîlegeš* are profoundly parallel. Regarding the Enuma
Elish, let us consider, first what got us to the murder of Tiamat and the mutilation of her body in the first place: it was a domestic conflict between the
younger generation of the gods, who were inclined, like the young generally,
toward rowdy play, and the pantheon's older generation, and especially its
oldest, Apsu, the gods' "progenitor" (tablet I, line 3), and his consort Tiamat,
who valued their peace and quiet. In Judg 19, although the battle lines are not
specifically the same, so too is the precipitating event that culminates in the
murder and dismemberment of the *pîlegeš* a matter of domestic conflict, with
the woman deciding to up and leave her Levite husband in Ephraim to return
to the house of her father in Judah.

More precisely still, though, what leads to Tiamat's demise and subsequent
mutilation in the Enuma Elish is the fact that she shifts, at the end of the
Enuma Elish's tablet I and the beginning of tablet II, from enacting the behaviors that ancient Near Eastern gender ideologies expected of mother figures to
enacting behaviors that violated the culture's definitions of maternal norms.
Throughout most of tablet I, that is, although Apsu and Tiamat are both disturbed by the play of the younger gods, Tiamat urges forbearance and even
compassion while Apsu rages: "Their behavior really is quite irritating," she

---

33. As translated by Dalley, *Myths from Mesopotamia*, 255.
34. Restored on the basis of tablet VII, line 71.

admits to him, "but let us be kind and patient" (tablet I, line 46). Thus it is only Apsu, in the middle of tablet I, who acts to subdue the younger gods (by killing them off); unfortunately for him, however, his plan is thwarted, and it is he who ends up killed (tablet I, line 69), by the god Ea (the father of the yet unborn Marduk). Ea further strips from Apsu his royal diadem and takes it as his own (tablet I, lines 67–68); he and his wife Damkina then give birth to Marduk (tablet I, lines 80–84). Subsequently, Marduk receives from his grandfather Anu the gift of the fourfold winds (tablet I, lines 105–106). The roiling waves he raises with them churn within Tiamat (tablet I, lines 108–109), who is envisioned as a goddess of waters, and thus the whole crisis of the younger gods disturbing the older gods begins anew.

This time, however, Tiamat does not endure the youngsters' disruptive behavior patiently; rather, she plots evil against her descendants (tablet I, lines 125–128), and they in turn repeatedly report this news to one another (Ea to his grandfather Anshar; Anshar to his vizier Gaga; and Gaga, on Anshar's behalf, to Anshar's father and mother, Laḫmu and Laḫamu). The texts that document these various recitals (tablet II, lines 5–48; tablet III, lines 1–66, 67–124) are highly repetitive and so cannot be taken as independent indictments of Tiamat. Nevertheless, it is striking that, in them, Tiamat's position as a mother is stressed, yet stressed in a way that positions her as having failed in that role. Each report begins, for example, with the claim that "Tiamat, our mother, *hates us*" (tablet II, line 11; tablet III, lines 15, 73; emphasis mine), although surely what is expected of a mother is that she dispenses love to her children. In each of these reports, moreover, Tiamat is described using the epithet "Mother Ḫubur" (tablet II, line 19; tablet III, lines 23, 81),[35] as she is described also in tablet I, line 133, just following the lines where she voices her decision to do battle against the disruptive younger gods. In all four instances, the epithet "Mother Ḫubur" is glossed by a description of Tiamat/Mother Ḫubur as the

35. In Mesopotamian tradition, "Ḫubur" appears most commonly as the name of the river that runs through the netherworld (see, e.g., line 17 of "The Babylonian Theodicy," as found in Foster, *Before the Muses*, 2:807). But most commentators take "Mother Ḫubur" in the Enuma Elish as an epithet of Tiamat: see, for example, *CAD* 6:219, s.v. *ḫubur* A(c), and also Michalowski, "Presence at the Creation," 385–86. Michalowski construes "Mother Ḫubur" in the Enuma Elish as "Mother Noise" (relying on the wordplay suggested by *ḫubur*, "river," and *ḫubūru*, "hubbub," on which see also Dalley, *Myths from Mesopotamia*, 274n8) and argues that because "throughout the text [of the Enuma Elish], and in other Mesopotamian literary compositions, noise [is a] . . . symbol of action," Tiamat is called "Mother Noise" at the point in the Enuma Elish when she "springs into action" to engage in battle with Marduk. For further discussion, with additional references, see Foster, *Before the Muses*, 1:358n2.

one who "creates all things." But according to all four, what Mother Ḥubur in fact gives birth to are "monster serpents" who are to cause the younger gods to perish. As Mother Ḥubur, that is, Tiamat again defies cultural expectations about the proper maternal role, for while she bears offspring, as mothers are expected to do, she bears agents who position "Mother Ḥubur" in the role of a destroyer rather than as a female who exemplifies the typical maternal attributes of life-giver and life-sustainer.

Also striking is the fact that the text creates a scenario for Tiamat whereby the "good mother" game is one she just cannot win. In tablet I, lines 111–124, for example, some contingent among her descendants who share the frustrations of their now deceased progenitor Apsu come to her to complain about those others among the pantheon who are disturbing their rest. In issuing this complaint, moreover, they quite explicitly call into question Tiamat's performance *as a mother*: "You are no mother," they say, "you rock and roll" (a reference to the way Marduk's fourfold winds are roiling Tiamat's watery body, in which they dwell), "and we, your sleepless children," they continue, "*you show us no love*" (tablet I, lines 119–120; emphasis mine). Mother Tiamat, that is, stands accused here of withholding love from this branch of her descendants. Yet once she resolves to act on their behalf, she is almost immediately—a scant 50 or so lines later (in tablet II, line 11)—accused of being the "mother" who "hates" the other branch. To accommodate some offspring is to alienate others, that is, and so I repeat: the "good mother" game is one Tiamat just cannot win. Indeed, when the term "mother" is used in the Enuma Elish to describe Tiamat, it is always used to describe *faults* in Tiamat's mothering skills.

Tiamat, in short, has failed according to the gender codes of ancient Near Eastern tradition, and thus, I would argue, as Exum argues for Judg 19, she is punished by the narrative "in the most extreme form": by being killed and afterward suffering bodily partition and mutilation. Important to contrast in this regard is the myth's treatment of Apsu. Even though he aims in the middle of tablet I to accomplish exactly the same goal that Tiamat undertakes by the tablet's end—to kill off the rowdy gods of the younger generation—he does not suffer the same excess of violence as does his consort. Thus, while, like Tiamat, Apsu is slain, he is not the subject of the same sort of postmortem abuse she endures. To be sure, he is stripped of his crown, and Ea does build himself a palace atop Apsu's watery abyss (Apsu, like Tiamat, is envisioned in the mythological tradition as god of waters). Still, Apsu's body remains whole while Tiamat's does not. Apsu does not, that is, have to suffer a doubly gruesome fate, death *plus* dismemberment, for his transgression, as the myth would have it, is only to threaten the future of his divine descendants. Tiamat, however, ultimately threatens both those descendants' future and her culture's code of gender behavior; she therefore must be doubly subdued, just as the Levite's *pîlegeš*, by threatening her culture's gender codes, is repeatedly punished.

It is interesting to consider in this regard vv. 22–24 of Judg 19. Here, when the Benjaminite men first come to the house of the Ephraimite sojourner who gives shelter to the Levite and his *pîlegeš* in Gibeah and demand that the Levite be sent forth "so that we may know him" (i.e., so that he might be subjected to homosexual rape), the Ephraimite offers to give them both the Levite's *pîlegeš* and his own unmarried daughter instead. Ultimately, though, the daughter stays within the house and only the *pîlegeš* ends up on the street, just as, ultimately, in the kindred episode in Gen 19, Lot's unmarried daughters are not sent out to the rapacious Sodomites. Why? Because neither the Ephraimite's daughter nor Lot's daughters have violated the gender codes that govern their culture, and so neither needs, to paraphrase Exum, to be raped by the narrator's pen.[36] Conversely, the transgressive *pîlegeš*, who has defied her culture's expectations regarding female submissiveness, must, like Tiamat, who transgresses cultural expectations regarding motherhood, be made victim to the punishments inflicted—not coincidentally—by *male* authorities.

In conclusion, let me be clear that it is not my intent to claim here that the Enuma Elish influenced Judg 19 directly and that we should read the dismemberment of the Levite's *pîlegeš* as some demythologized recounting of the splitting and subsequent mutilating of Tiamat's body. In fact, it is obvious that, in many respects, the tale of Tiamat's fate in the Enuma Elish is not at all parallel to the tale of the Levite's *pîlegeš* we find in Judg 19: in Judg 19, for example, it is unclear (as I noted above) exactly when and how the *pîlegeš* actually dies, whereas the Enuma Elish recounts the moment and means of Tiamat's murder in great detail. Tiamat, moreover, whatever her ultimate fate, is cast in the Enuma Elish as a very powerful character and formidable presence while she still lives, whereas the Levite's *pîlegeš*, subsequent to her initial act of self-assertion—leaving her husband's home—never again acts in her story with authority or autonomy. Indeed, unlike Tiamat, she is unnamed;[37]

36. "Raped by the Pen" is the title of the chapter in *Fragmented Women* in which Exum discusses the Judg 19 story.

37. On the issue of being named versus nameless in the Hebrew Bible, and on issues concerning women's anonymity, especially women's anonymity in the book of Judges, see Bal, *Death and Dissymmetry*, 43–93; Brenner, "Introduction," 10–14; Exum, "Feminist Criticism," 75–86; and Meyers, "Hannah Narrative," 120–22 (= "Hannah and Her Sacrifice," 96–99). But cf. the important cautions offered by Reinhartz, *"Why Ask My Name?"*

unlike Tiamat, she never speaks;[38] and unlike Tiamat, who is abetted in her war against the younger gods by the various serpents she has created as well as by other supporters, the *pîlegeš* is utterly without allies. Rather she is, to quote Phyllis Trible's pathbreaking study of the Judg 19 story, "alone in a world of men."[39] Nevertheless, despite these many differences between the Enuma Elish and Judg 19, I still wish to claim that aspects within Judg 19—the role of gender and themes concerning gender expectations—are illuminated by the process of comparing the Mesopotamian myth, allowing us to see that in both stories, although the cut-up woman is not the only character threatened by or subject to horrific violence (there is Apsu, and in Judg 19 there is the Levite, threatened with homosexual rape, and the Ephraimite's unmarried daughter), ultimately, it is *only* the woman character who acts out with respect to ancient Near Eastern gender norms who becomes victim to the greatest terrors the stories' authors and/or redactors can find to offer up.

38. Fewell, "Judges," 75; Lasine, "Guest and Host in Judges 19," 47; Trible, "An Unnamed Woman," 66.

39. Trible, "An Unnamed Woman," 80.

PART 2

Priests and Prophets

CHAPTER 4

Why Is Miriam Also among the Prophets?
(And Is Zipporah among the Priests?)

I wrote the article on which this chapter is based in 2002, in response to questions that had arisen in my mind while I was working on my 1998 book Warrior, Dancer, Seductress, Queen: Women in Judges and Biblical Israel. *In that book, as its subtitle implies, I was interested in the truly remarkable collection of women characters who appear in the biblical book of Judges, and more specifically, as the book's main title perhaps suggests, I was interested in the multitude of roles these women characters could assume within Judges' narrative accounts. In particular, I was interested in roles that transcended the more common biblical depictions of women as mothers, daughters, sisters, and wives. One such role, ascribed to Deborah in Judg 4:4, is to serve as a prophetic intermediary who brings the words of Yahweh to the people of Israel—something I took to be rather extraordinary, given that elsewhere in the Bible, this religious function is undertaken almost exclusively by men.*

In Warrior, Dancer, Seductress, Queen, *I sought to explain Deborah's role as a prophet through what I described as "a sociological investigation of the ancient Israelite understanding of religious status," which I used to suggest that in historical periods when certain social conditions were manifest, ancient Israelite tradition could more readily conceive of women exercising religious (as well as other types) of power and authority. One such period within ancient Israelite history, I proposed, was the late seventh century BCE, which was also the period during which (in my understanding) the text of Judg 4, with its depiction of Deborah as a prophet, was promulgated.*

An earlier version of this chapter appeared in *JBL* 121 (2002): 47–80. Used here by permission of the Society of Biblical Literature.

Thus, I argued that even though Deborah, according the Bible's chronology, lived five or so centuries before Judg 4 was written (or, at least, assumed its final form), it was the social environment of the late seventh century BCE that encouraged Judg 4's authors, and their audience, to embrace a portrayal of Deborah as a prophet. Nor was it coincidental, I proposed, that another of the Bible's women prophets, Hulda, was portrayed in the biblical text as exercising significant religious power and authority in exactly this same period.

Yet my focus on Judg 4 in Warrior, Dancer, Seductress, Queen *meant I gave only short shrift (a one-paragraph discussion) to the intimations of Deborah's prophetic status that are found in Judg 5:1–31, a text that is closely related to Judg 4 but which arguably dates from many centuries prior. Likewise, because my focus in* Warrior, Dancer, Seductress, Queen *was women in the book of Judges, I allotted only one paragraph to Hulda (whose story appears in 2 Kgs 22), and I did not mention at all the three other women assigned the title "prophet" in biblical tradition: Miriam, Isaiah's wife, and Noadiah. This meant I did not address the fact that the sociological analysis I had deployed to discuss Deborah's and Hulda's prophetic roles would not work to explain Miriam's prophetic status, given that the exodus accounts in which Miriam's story appears cannot be taken to depict actual moments within Israelite history and so cannot be taken to reflect real social conditions that might, or might not, facilitate women's ability to exercise prophetic authority.*

So why is Miriam among the prophets? And what about Noadiah and Isaiah's wife? Also, could more be said about Deborah in Judg 5:1–31 and Hulda in 2 Kgs 22? Finally, were there female religious functionaries in ancient Israel other than prophets whose cultic roles might be explained by a more detailed study of the Bible's women prophets? "Why Is Miriam Also among the Prophets? (And Is Zipporah among the Priests?)" was written to address these questions. As time went on, moreover, my answer to the first of these queries—Why is Miriam also among the prophets?—continued to provoke my thinking, as is reflected in publications as diverse as my 2005 book, When Heroes Love: The Ambiguity of Eros in the Stories of Gilgamesh and David, *and two 2014 essays, "Moses' Death" and "Women's Rites of Passage in Ancient Israel: Three Case Studies (Birth, Coming of Age, and Death)." I'm thus very pleased to present an updated version of my original discussion about Miriam here, reflecting the growth and development of my work on this issue. I have also added a few updated comments regarding Deborah and Hulda.*

1. The Bible's Women Prophets

Without doubt, the feminist revolution that swept through the academic world beginning in the late 1960s has had an enormous impact upon Hebrew Bible studies, as questions regarding the roles and status of women in ancient Israel assumed a dominant place within the biblical field during the last quarter of the twentieth century.[1] Yet equally without doubt is the fact that for biblical scholars who have sought to uncover indications of positive roles and an elevated status for women within ancient Israelite society, the results of their research have been somewhat mixed.[2]

Certainly, this is true for scholars whose primary interest is the place of women within ancient Israelite religion. On the one hand, such scholars have been able to bring to the fore evidence of women's religious observances that were basically equivalent to those of men and have even been able to isolate certain cult functions that seem to have been the exclusive or at least principal responsibility of Israelite women. Women, for example, seem to have held the exclusive responsibility for singing victory songs after an Israelite triumph in holy war and appear to have assumed a principal position as ritual musicians upon occasions of lament.[3] On the other hand, our examinations have revealed

1. By no means did discussions regarding gender and the place of women in ancient Israel emerge only in the last quarter of the twentieth century: see, for example, Milne, "Feminist Interpretations of the Bible," 38–43, 52–55, for a survey of 150 years' worth of feminist biblical scholarship; also, Bellis, "Feminist Biblical Scholarship," 24–32, esp. 24–25. But I highlight the works that appeared beginning in the last quarter of the twentieth century because it was at that quarter's inception that two landmark articles were published that, in my opinion, launched the twentieth and twenty-first centuries' enterprise of feminist biblical research: Bird, "Images of Women in the Old Testament," 41–88, and Trible, "Depatriarchalizing in Biblical Interpretation," 30–48.

2. In my mind, no example illustrates this "mixed-bag" phenomenon better than J. Cheryl Exum's two companion articles on women in the birth story of Moses. In the first, "'You Shall Let Every Daughter Live,'" 63–82, Exum offers a reading of Exod 1:8–2:10 that celebrates a positive role for women in this text, with depictions of "women as defiers of oppression, women as givers of life, women as wise and resourceful in situations where a discerning mind and keen practical judgment are essential for a propitious outcome" (82). However, in the second article, "Second Thoughts about Secondary Characters," Exum repudiates her earlier interpretation and instead derides the way "that the narrative quickly and thoroughly moves from a women's story to a men's story" (76). She also notes how even "the positive portrayal of women in Exod 1:8–2:10 nevertheless serves male interests" (78), given that the text restricts women to traditionally female activities, especially motherly activities focused on children (81).

3. On women's responsibility for singing victory songs in ancient Israel, see especially Poethig, "Victory Song Tradition," and Burns, *Has the Lord Indeed Spoken Only through*

manifold ways in which Israelite religion excluded or marginalized women. For example, while a woman, like a man, could dedicate herself as a Nazirite to God (Num 6:2), her vow, according to Num 30:4–16 (in most English translations, 30:3–15) could be nullified by her father (if she was yet unmarried) or by her husband (if she had wed). Likewise, although a woman, like a man, could participate in the great pilgrimage festivals of Passover/Maṣṣot, Shavuʿot, and Sukkot (as does Hannah, for example, in 1 Sam 1),[4] it was only men, according to Exod 23:17; 34:23; and Deut 16:16, who were *required* to make these pilgrimages central to the Israelite festal calendar.

Another manifestation of this same "on the one hand"/"on the other hand" phenomenon is the role women could play as prophets within Israelite religion. Five women bear the title *nĕbîʾâ*, the feminine form of *nābîʾ*, "prophet," in the Hebrew Bible: (1) Miriam, the sister of Moses, in Exod 15:20; (2) Deborah, said also to be "judging Israel" (*šōpĕṭâ ʾet-yiśrāʾēl*), in Judg 4:4; (3) the unnamed wife of the prophet Isaiah in Isa 8:3; (4) Hulda, the prophet who verified the validity of the recently discovered "book of the law" for King Josiah, in 2 Kgs 22:14 (paralleled in 2 Chr 34:22); and (5) Noadiah, who seems to have opposed the restoration projects of Nehemiah in some way, in Neh 6:14. In many respects, this register provides important evidence for modern scholars who seek attestations of positive roles and positions of elevated status for women within Israelite religion. Indeed, a positive role and an elevated status for these women prophets seem especially indicated given how dominant a place prophetic narratives and the prophetic books hold in the biblical tradition, at least as it has come down to us.

Still, we should express reservations. First, we must resist characterizing Isaiah's wife as a prophet in the vein of Miriam, Deborah, Hulda, and Noadiah. Unlike these women, Isaiah's wife did not engage in a typical prophetic ministry, making proclamations about matters of public interest and participating directly in public affairs. Rather, the sole action attributed to Isaiah's wife is a domestically based enterprise in which almost all ancient Israelite women engaged: conceiving by her husband and bearing their child. It is also important to note that alone of the Bible's five women prophets, Isaiah's wife is not given a name. This is significant, for the giving of names in the Bible—especially the giving of

Moses?, 11–40, although I would note my disagreement with many of the specifics of Burns's interpretation, especially her differentiation of "cultic" and "secular" victory songs. On women's responsibilities as singers of lament, see especially Bird, "Israelite Religion," 106; Bird, "Women's Religion in Ancient Israel," 295–96.

4. See Bird, "Women's Religion in Ancient Israel," 292–94.

names to women—is often an important marker of those women's autonomy and authority.[5] The nameless status of Isaiah's wife, conversely, suggests relative powerlessness. In fact, I would argue that Isaiah's wife is assigned the title "prophet" only as an honorific by virtue of her marriage to the male prophet Isaiah, in much the same way, say, that Esther is assigned the title "queen" by virtue of her marriage to Ahasuerus, despite the fact that Esther is not of royal birth.

Furthermore, we must acknowledge that the same biblical tradition that recognizes four women as prophets (excepting, now, Isaiah's wife) assigns the title *nābî'* to no less than twenty-nine men,[6] and if we assume, as I do, that the members of the various companies or bands of prophets mentioned in the Bible, such as the four hundred prophets of Ahab (1 Kgs 22:6),[7] were exclusively (or at least almost exclusively) male, then the number of men designated as "prophet" in the biblical account soars into the triple and even quadruple digits.[8] We should add to this soaring total, moreover, the names of the books attributed to eight additional men who, while not explicitly given the title *nābî'* in the biblical text, were certainly assumed by its redactors to be prophets: they are Amos, Hosea, Joel, Micah, Nahum, Obadiah, Zephaniah, and the anonymous Malachi. Most modern biblical scholars would add as well Sec-

---

5. See Meyers, "Hannah Narrative in Feminist Perspective," 120–122 (= "Hannah and Her Sacrifice," 96–99), but cf. the important cautions offered by Reinhartz, *"Why Ask My Name?"*

6. These are (in alphabetical order) Aaron, Abraham, Ahijah, Elijah, Elisha, Ezekiel, Gad, Habakkuk, Haggai, Hananiah, Iddo, Isaiah, Jehu, Jeremiah, Jonah, Micaiah, Moses, Nathan, Oded, Samuel, Shemiah, Zechariah, and the anonymous, but clearly male, prophets of Judg 6:8; 1 Kgs 13:11, 18; 20:13, 38; 2 Kgs 9:4; and 2 Chr 25:15. This list counts, moreover, only men whom the biblical record labels *nābî'*; if we were to include those men who bear the kindred titles of "seer," "man of God," and the like, our total would be still higher.

7. The "king of Israel" of the Micaiah story in 1 Kgs 22 is in fact only identified by the name Ahab in v. 20, and thus some commentators have suggested that the narrative is not actually to be associated with this king. Discussion can be found in DeVries, *Prophet against Prophet*, 5; McKenzie, *The Trouble with Kings*, 88–93; and Pitard, *Ancient Damascus*, 114–22; see also the further references catalogued by Pitard, 115n48.

8. Ezekiel does speak of "the daughters of your people who prophesy" (Ezek 13:17), but whether this implies a company of female prophets, analogous to the companies or bands attested elsewhere in the biblical text, is unclear. Bowen, "Daughters of Your People," 417–33, who provides the fullest analysis of this text, suggests, using comparative material, that Ezekiel's female prophets assisted women at childbirth and also helped Israelite women deal with other issues they might have had relating to pregnancy and delivery. This very compelling analysis, however, while it does suggest some sort of a professional community of female prophets, does not necessarily imply the sort of company or band of prophets that lived and traveled together, as is described, for example, in the Elijah-Elisha narratives.

ond (and possibly Third) Isaiah and the anonymous author(s) of Zech 9–14. The Protestant and Roman Catholic communities would include Daniel, and the Catholic tradition would also admit Baruch. Yet however one tallies up the specifics, any examination of the Bible's prophetic literature makes clear that the prophetic words and deeds that dominate in the tradition are the prophetic words and deeds of men.

Such extensive documentation of the male-dominated character of the prophetic community, as well as the sorts of data mentioned above that more generally intimate women's marginalization or exclusion from Israel's cultic life, calls into question the degree to which the women named as "prophet" in the Bible can be considered examples of a positive role for women within Israelite religion. Instead, what becomes noteworthy about these women is how few of them there are compared to the number of men who were assigned the prophetic designation throughout Israel's history. Miriam, Deborah, Hulda, and Noadiah, that is, ultimately appear to be not so much exemplars as anomalies, their role as prophets exceptional rather than acceptable within Israelite religion.

My intent in this chapter is to explore the anomalous position of these four women prophets within Israelite religion, asking in particular how *any* women could have come to be considered prophets given the overwhelmingly male character of the Bible's prophetic tradition. In undertaking this enterprise, I will draw, at least initially, on explanatory models offered (in somewhat variant forms) by Jo Ann Hackett and Carol Meyers.[9] Both these scholars rely on the sorts of "theoretical formulations . . . the social sciences provide"[10] to suggest that the amount of status and power that could be accorded to women in ancient Israel varied over time in relation to the social and political organization that distinguished a particular era. Meyers, for example, in her book-length study *Discovering Eve: Ancient Israelite Women in Context*, argues that throughout Israel's premonarchic period (ca. 1200–1000 BCE), women experienced relatively high status and an increased potential for the exercise of power because of the predominantly domestic orientation of premonarchic society. More precisely, Meyers suggests that Israelite women of the premonarchic era could have been integrally involved in their community's economic, social, political, and cultural affairs, because in premonarchic Israel, the household was "the central institution for most economic, social, political, and cultural

9. Hackett, "In the Days of Jael," 15–38; Hackett, "Women's Studies," 141–64; Meyers, *Discovering Eve*.

10. Meyers, *Discovering Eve*, 19–20.

aspects of human existence" and because "ethnographic evidence specifically indicates the vital and active roles that females play in societies in which the household is the base unit of production and consumption."[11] Consequently, Meyers concludes, women of the premonarchic period would have been "accorded prestige and experience[d] self-esteem."[12]

Conversely, Meyers suggests that during periods of Israelite history when economic, social, political, and cultural matters were dealt with in a more public realm, an arena separated and differentiated from the domestic sphere, women's status and potential for the exercise of power declined. Meyers associates this shift with the emergence of the monarchy. "State formation created hierarchical relationships and robbed females of their customary equality and interdependence with men. . . . The rise of a public world dichotomized the social structure and led to male preeminence."[13] Nevertheless, Meyers believes that even during the monarchic period, there were opportunities for women to experience some of the same elevated status and increased potential for the exercise of power that had characterized the lives of their premonarchic foremothers. She proposes, for example, that monarchic-era women who lived in a rural as opposed to an urban setting would have had more opportunities for status elevation and the exercise of power, given that the sort of self-sufficient household in which the amount of status and power accorded to women is relatively high remained typical of Israel's village landscape throughout much of the monarchic period.[14] Meyers further suggests that during the exilic and postexilic eras, Israelite culture experienced a "pioneer" period of extensive rebuilding that was not unlike the "pioneer" period associated with the development of new hill-country settlements in premonarchic times. Such "pioneer" periods, Meyers goes on to claim, can also accord women higher status and opportunities to exert power because, during such times, a society needs and consequently assigns value to the labor of all its members, including women.[15]

In her two articles on basically this same topic—the ways in which certain types of Israelite social and political organization affected the amount of status

---

11. Meyers, *Discovering Eve*, 139, 145.

12. Meyers, *Discovering Eve*, 173.

13. Meyers, *Discovering Eve*, 190.

14. Meyers, *Discovering Eve*, 191–92. In subsequent publications, Meyers has pursued this line of thought aggressively: see, e.g., Meyers, "Material Remains and Social Relations," 425–44; Meyers, "From Field Crops to Food," 67–84; and Meyers's comments on the developments in her thinking in *Rediscovering Eve*, ix.

15. Meyers, *Discovering Eve*, 50–63, 196; see also Eskenazi, "Out of the Shadows," 33.

and power that could be accorded to women—Hackett puts forward many
similar formulations. For example, like Meyers, Hackett suggests that a domestically oriented form of social and political organization is a significant factor
in making possible a relatively high degree of social and political status for
women. Thus, she writes, "Studies have shown that women tend to have more
status within a society when the public and domestic spheres are not widely
separated, that is, when important decision making is done within or near
the home." Also like Meyers, Hackett argues that the emergence of more for-
mal and public decision-making systems corresponds to a decline in women's
ability to exert power: "Hierarchical and centrally structured institutions have
been less open to participation by women than have local and nonhierarchical
institutions."[16] Hackett further, like Meyers, notes the relatively higher status
and opportunities for the exercise of power that are available to rural women
as opposed to women who live in urban contexts,[17] and along with Meyers,
Hackett believes that the premonarchic era is the period of Israelite history
that best exemplifies the sort of rural, nonhierarchical, decentralized, and domestically based environment in which women can most easily be accorded
high status and attain positions of power.

In addition, Hackett calls our attention to two other factors that need to
be taken into account when detailing the societal and political conditions
that determine the amount of status and power available to women: first, the
importance of class. Class, of course, implies a hierarchical society and, consequently, according to both Hackett and Meyers, a society characterized by the
relative disempowerment of women in general. Nevertheless, as Hackett points
out, even within an otherwise male-dominated society, upper-class women,
because of their families' associations with the power structures of their community, can find themselves able to exert power and achieve a relatively high
degree of status.[18] Second, Hackett speaks persuasively of the potential for
an elevation in the amount of status and power available to women during
times of social dysfunction—during times of war, for example. Americans
know this as the "Rosie-the-Riveter" phenomenon: how, during World War II,
because American men were away fighting, American women were able to
move out of a relatively disempowered position in the home and into a much
more acclaimed and appreciated role in the workplace. Hackett further notes
that during such times of social dysfunction, hierarchical structures can break

16. Hackett, "In the Days of Jael," 17–18.
17. Hackett, "In the Days of Jael," 19; Hackett, "Women's Studies," 151.
18. Hackett, "In the Days of Jael," 18–19; Hackett, "Women's Studies," 149.

down to some degree, and centralized institutions can give way to more local-ized control.[19] As already discussed, these sorts of nonhierarchical and decen-tralized conditions can in turn foster opportunities for an elevation in women's status and for an increase in their ability to exercise power.

To be sure, both Hackett and Meyers are concerned only with the general status and amount of power accorded to women in ancient Israelite society and not with my more particular focus, the degree of status and power assigned to the women prophets of Israelite religion. Both Hackett and Meyers, moreover, examine primarily the village- and domestically based social and political organization of premonarchic Israel as a test case for their theses and do not describe in extensive detail the variations that can be found in Israel's first-millennium BCE social and political organization and the consequent varia-tions we would expect to find in the amount of status and power assigned to women throughout that period. My examination of Israel's women prophets, however, is interested in the points where women prophets appear through-out the course of Israelite history, including points during the premonarchic, monarchic, and postexilic eras. Yet despite their more general focus on the amount of status and power available to all sorts of ancient Israelite women, and despite their limited chronological concentration, I do think Hackett and Meyers set out theoretical approaches that can be profitably used to explore why at least some of the Bible's women prophets appear anomalously at certain points in Israelite history.[20] I thus draw upon their insights to consider each of the women recognized as a prophet in the Hebrew Bible. As we will see, however, Hackett's and Meyers's approaches, while very useful in considering Deborah, Hulda, and Noadiah, are less applicable in analyzing Miriam. Hence, although Miriam is the prophet who appears first in the biblical text, she will appear last in my discussion, in part 2 of this chapter. In the remaining pages of part 1, I will present the Bible's other three women prophets.

Before I begin that presentation, though, a caveat concerning the order in which the rest of part 1 will proceed: considering first Noadiah, then Hulda, and finally Deborah. Although somewhat unusual, I adopt this reverse chronolog-ical order for two reasons. First, and less significantly, it is in keeping with the "first will be last" structure that defers the discussion of Miriam until this chap-

19. Hackett, "In the Days of Jael," 19; Hackett, "Women's Studies," 149–51.

20. The only other scholar I know of who addresses this question is Bird, "Place of Women," 405, 407–8. Bird's remarks are very brief, but she does explore some of the same issues that interest me here, in particular by noting the restricted number of religious roles available to women as "centralization, specialization, and power (at least in Judah) under a royally sanctioned Zadokite priesthood" increased over time (405).

ter's part 2. The second and more important reason concerns issues of the biblical text and history. As will be discussed more thoroughly below, the crucial problem in using the theories of Hackett and Meyers to analyze Miriam's prophetic role is the historical unreliability of the Bible's exodus account. Historical unreliability on the part of the biblical text is also a significant (although I believe surmountable) problem in analyzing the prophetic role of Deborah.

I am more confident, however, of the historical reliability of the Bible's accounts that describe Hulda and Noadiah (although I would certainly resist any literalistic reading of these narratives). My confidence stems from the texts' dates of composition. While it is difficult, for example, to attribute historical reliability to the Deuteronomistic account in Judg 4 depicting Deborah, since it postdates the events it purports to describe by five hundred or more years, I believe the Deuteronomists' account in Kings depicting Hulda must be reasonably accurate, at least in its broad outline. This is because this Kings' account, in my opinion, was written at a time roughly contemporary with the period of Hulda's ministry.[21] Thus, its authors would have been compelled to present their story in a way believable to an audience that was already generally familiar with the period's social world and major events. The date of the Nehemiah accounts is less secure, but according to multiple commentators, the text postdates the time of Ezra and Nehemiah by only a few decades, and its place of composition was Jerusalem, or at least Palestine.[22] Like Kings, then, the book of Nehemiah would have needed to present its story in a way that generally rang true to an audience already familiar with its basic premises. Again, this is not to say the Kings and Nehemiah accounts are correct in all their details, even including, perhaps, all the details these texts offer regarding their women prophets. Still, I consider these sources' overall portrayal of Hulda's and Noadiah's social worlds basically reliable—especially, in Hulda's case, Kings' portrayal of the Josianic reform and its major objectives, and, in Noadiah's case, Nehemiah's portrayal of Jerusalem's civil and cultic affairs in the mid- to late-fifth century BCE. As we will see, moreover, it is this sort of general information about Hulda's and Noadiah's social worlds that is most crucial to my argument. I thus begin my examination with this more trustworthy material before turning to the less secure accounts of Deborah and, finally, Miriam.

21. On the dating of the Deuteronomistic History to the last quarter of the seventh century BCE, see Cross, *Canaanite Myth and Hebrew Epic*, 274–89, esp. 284, 287; Friedman, *Exile and Biblical Narrative*, 1–26; and Nelson, *Double Redaction of the Deuteronomistic History*, passim, but esp. 13–28, 119–28.

22. E.g., Japhet, "Sheshbazzar and Zerubbabel," 89n55; Throntveit, *Ezra-Nehemiah*, 9–10; van Wijk-Bos, *Ezra, Nehemiah, and Esther*, 14; and Williamson, *Ezra, Nehemiah*, xxxvi.

Noadiah. All we know from the account of Noadiah found in Neh 6:14 is that she was active during Nehemiah's attempts to rebuild the walls of Jerusalem that began in 445 BCE[23] and that she somehow stood in opposition to this project.[24] Still, however vague the specifics concerning Noadiah's ministry, the very facts, first, that the walls of Jerusalem were in need of restoration during her day; second, that these walls were presumably in need of repair because of some recent destruction they had suffered;[25] and third, that Nehemiah faced dissent in regard to his rebuilding endeavors suggest a period of tumult and disquiet within Judah. Passages elsewhere in Nehemiah's memoirs also speak of this time as one of social unrest and upheaval. Nehemiah 1:3, for example, describes how Jerusalemites during the time of Nehemiah's wall-rebuilding project found themselves living "in great trouble and shame" (*běrā'â gědōlâ ûbḥerpâ*), and Neh 5:1–5 elaborates by indicating that at least some of the Jerusalemites' troubles stemmed from their experiences of famine and a heavy debt load. This debt load, indeed, is described as being so heavy that some of the people found it necessary to mortgage their fields, vineyards, and houses, while others were forced to sell their children into debt slavery. This sort of devastating poverty, and the unwanted breakup of families and households

---

23. While the date of Ezra's mission to postexilic Jerusalem and that mission's chronological relationship to the missions of Nehemiah are much debated among scholars (see, perhaps most thoroughly, the various positions summarized in Clines, *Ezra, Nehemiah, Esther,* 16–24, and in Kellermann, "Erwägungen zum Problem der Esradatierung," 55–87), there is almost unanimous agreement that Nehemiah's initial mission should be dated to 445–433 BCE and his second mission to sometime before 424 BCE. Cf. only Saley, "The Date of Nehemiah Reconsidered," 151–65.

24. Along with most commentators, I take Noadiah in Neh 6:14 to be a woman prophet (*nĕbî'â*) who was associated with a larger community of prophets (*hannĕbî'îm*) who wanted to make Nehemiah afraid (*mĕyārĕ'îm*). The Greek tradition, however, reads a masculine form, *tō prophētē,* for Hebrew *nĕbî'â,* and Codices Vaticanus and Sinaiticus read *hiereōn,* "priests," for *hannĕbî'îm.* The Lucianic tradition, moreover, reads *enouthetoun,* "warned," reflecting Hebrew *mbynym,* for *mĕyārĕ'îm,* suggesting Noadiah was an ally rather than an opponent of Nehemiah.

25. It is often assumed that the description of Jerusalem's breached walls and burned gates (Neh 1:3) refers to the Babylonian destruction of 586 BCE, but as many commentators have pointed out, such an interpretation fails to explain why hearing what would be 150-year-old news distresses Nehemiah (Neh 1:4). Batten, *Critical and Exegetical Commentary on the Books of Ezra and Nehemiah,* 184, thus suggests that Nehemiah is distressed because he learns that the wall-rebuilding efforts of Ezra 4:7–24 have failed; most other commentators, however, argue that there was some serious disturbance in and attack on Jerusalem shortly before the time of Nehemiah's wall-rebuilding mission. Blenkinsopp, *Ezra-Nehemiah,* 204, offers a particularly good discussion.

that resulted, surely speaks of a society in crisis. Another significant contrib-
utor to the society's sense of disorder must have been the well-known tensions
that existed between Nehemiah and the leaders of the neighboring communities of Samaria, Ammon, Ashdod, and Edom (Neh 2:10, 19; 4:1–3, 7–8, 11;
6:1–14). These tensions appear to have been so heated that they culminated
with threats to kill Nehemiah because of the specter of militarization that his
wall-rebuilding project implied (Neh 6:10–14).

We should, moreover, take note of some of the major objectives of Nehemiah's second mission, which took place at some point after the wall-rebuilding
project had been completed but before 424 BCE.[26] These objectives included
the attempt to remove the civil official Tobiah from an apartment that had
been provided for him in the temple compound; the attempt to guarantee that
the Levitical priests were receiving their proper tithes; the attempt to ensure
proper Sabbath observance; and the attempt to dissolve mixed marriages
(Neh 13:4–31). These endeavors were all religious in nature, which suggests
that the overall period of Nehemiah's ministry was characterized by cultic
turmoil as well as by the sorts of civil disorder evidenced during the time of
the wall-rebuilding project. In the portion of his memoirs that describes his
second mission, Nehemiah in fact is pictured as being at odds with some of
the major religious leaders of Jerusalem. For example, Nehemiah opposed
the presence of an apartment for Tobiah within the temple compound, although it had been sanctioned by Eliashib, the priest who was in charge of
the temple's chambers (Neh 13:4–5), and one of the targets of Nehemiah's
attacks on mixed marriages was the grandson of a different (?) priest Eliashib
(Neh 13:28).[27] The textual tradition indicates, in short, a significant degree
of disagreement among the community's leaders as to how its religious affairs should be managed. This in turn intimates, as already suggested, that
religious tensions were present in Jerusalem in the mid-fifth century BCE
alongside the civil discord that manifested itself during the time of Nehemiah's
wall-rebuilding endeavors.[28]

26. See above, n. 23.

27. It is probably best to understand Neh 13:4–5 and 13:28 as referring to two different
Eliashibs, given that the high priest, the title conferred upon the Eliashib of 13:28, is not
likely also to have held the more minor role of "the one appointed over the chambers of the
house of our God," which is the title assigned to the Eliashib of 13:4–5.

28. See also Albertz, *History of Israelite Religion in the Old Testament Period*, 2:497–99,
who suggests another source of religious tensions in the community: namely, that the economic crisis of, especially, Jerusalem's lower classes had led to a religious split among the
community's elite concerning the degree to which Yahwism demanded of them a commit-

All of this evidence of cultic and civil disarray is, of course, indicative of precisely the sort of unstable social and political situation in which, according especially to Hackett's theoretical formulations, women are more likely to achieve higher status and have more opportunities for the exercise of power. We should recall, moreover, that Meyers specifically suggests that Israelite society during the postexilic period exhibits some of the pioneer-like conditions that can occasion an upsurge in the positions of power available to women. I thus propose, based on these models of Hackett and Meyers, that we see Noadiah's prophetic ministry as an example of the sorts of power a woman could assert in such a destabilized society. I further propose that because at least some of the instabilities that characterized the period in question were religious in nature, it is significant that the position of power in which Noadiah is said to assert herself is a religious position. Noadiah, that is, is a woman able to gain recognition as a religious functionary because the relatively destabilized religious organization of Jerusalem during her lifetime had room for women prophets in a way that the cult in more stabilized periods did not.

Hulda. The major events of Hulda's ministry—that she is called upon by King Josiah (r. 640–609 BCE) to validate and in essence to enshrine a newly revealed version of Israel's covenant code and, consequently, to set in motion Josiah's massive program of religious reforms—already suggest that she is active as a prophet in a period marked by at least some degree of religious upheaval. Of further importance in this regard are the biblical texts describing the reigns of Josiah's predecessors, Manasseh (r. 687–642 BCE) and Amon (r. 642–640 BCE), as these accounts also suggest certain religious instabilities that existed within Judah and Jerusalem during the mid- to late seventh century BCE. Granted, the accounts of Manasseh's and Amon's reigns have been so heavily shaped by their Deuteronomistic redactors that they cannot indicate definitively the precise nature of any cultic disorder. Still, we can say with confidence that during the reigns of Manasseh and Amon, Jerusalem and the Southern Kingdom of Judah found themselves under Assyrian hegemony, and even though the notion that the Assyrians imposed their own religious practices on their vassals has been discounted,[29] it is nonetheless the case that Judah and Jerusalem would have experienced at least some degree of contact with the religious ideologies and practices of their suzerain. Mordechai Cogan,

---

ment to reform exploitative financial systems within their society and even to eliminate them (especially systems relating to credit and interest).

29. Cogan, *Imperialism and Religion*; Cogan, "Judah under Assyrian Hegemony," 403–14; McKay, *Religion in Judah under the Assyrians.*

for example, speaks of "the *voluntary* adoption by Judah's ruling classes of the prevailing Assyro-Aramaean culture" (emphasis mine).[30] The result was surely some disruption of Judah's and Jerusalem's traditional religious routine. Can it be coincidence that Hulda is described as playing a major role in her community's cultic life in conjunction with this period of religious disarray? Again, the theoretical formulations put forward by, especially, Hackett would argue no, suggesting instead that like Noadiah's, Hulda's prophetic role is directly linked to the period of religious destabilization during which she lived.

Hackett's study also suggests a second explanation for Hulda's preeminence: class. Hulda, we are told, is the wife of Shallum, the keeper of the king's wardrobe (2 Kgs 22:14; 2 Chr 34:22). Unfortunately, neither this position nor this particular Shallum is mentioned elsewhere in the Bible, and thus the specifics of Shallum's place in Judahite society and the responsibilities of his station are basically unknown to us.[31] Surely, however, the keeper of the wardrobe was an official of at least some rank and status within the royal bureaucracy.[32] Shallum, to put the matter another way, must have been a member of his society's upper classes, and according to Hackett, women who are a part of this kind of upper-class household may, by virtue of the power available to their families, be accorded opportunities to exert power as individuals, even if they live during a time when the overall possibilities for women's exercise of power are constrained.

Hackett's work, along with Meyers's, puts forward a third explanation for Hulda's preeminence: that Hulda's prophetic ministry was conducted in an environment where certain aspects of the domestic and public spheres were not widely separated. Note in this regard that 2 Kgs 22:14 and 2 Chr 34:22 describe how King Josiah's emissaries, Hilkiah, Ahikam, Achbor, Shaphan, and Asiah, went to Hulda's house in Jerusalem's Second Quarter (the Mishneh) in order to consult with her. It is precisely this sort of situation, where decision-making is done in or near the home, that, according to Hackett and Meyers, allows women greater potential for the exercise of power. In addition, we can note that Hulda's home is—at least in terms of the biblical text's silence—atypical in Israelite tradition, in that no mention is made of Hulda having children. This is

30. Cogan, *Imperialism and Religion*, 113.

31. According to Yeivin, "Families and Parties in the Kingdom of Judah," 261, Hulda's husband Shallum is the same Shallum identified in Jer 35:4 as the father of Maaseiah, a keeper of the temple threshold. This reference was brought to my attention by Cogan and Tadmor, *II Kings*, 283.

32. Cf. the temple bureaucrat "in charge of the vestments" of the Baal temple in Samaria (2 Kgs 10:22).

significant, for, as Esther Hamori has particularly demonstrated, childlessness is another factor that facilitates women's ability to gain recognition as prophets. More specifically, Hamori has shown that in many different cultures, and at many different points in history (ancient, medieval, and modern), there is an "association" between "unusual access to the spirit world" and a "nonnormative social position" and that for women, this "nonnormative social position" is "often expressed through unconventional family structures," including "the lack of children."[33] Hamori suggests this is due, cross-culturally, to an ideological preference for the male body and the authority that comes with male embodiment, meaning that female sexuality, including female sexuality as revealed through childbearing, needs to be effaced in order for women to assume positions as prophets (and also positions as other types of visionaries—for example, shamans—who mediate between the divine and human realms).[34] In particular, regarding biblical tradition, Hamori writes, "Divine favor to a woman is commonly manifested through her becoming a mother," while for women such as Hulda, who are divinely favored with the gift of prophetic insight, motherhood seems precluded.[35]

As we read on in the biblical account of Hulda's prophetic work, we find one final aspect of her ministry that Hackett's and Meyers's theories might allow us to explain: the way in which Hulda disappears from the biblical text as soon as the descriptions of Josiah's reforms begin. To be sure, Hulda's absence from the biblical text at this point may be coincidental, completely unrelated to the endeavors Josiah had begun to undertake. But the specific nature of Josiah's reforms may suggest otherwise. As described in the biblical text, these reforms had cult centralization as a major priority, so that the shrines and "high places" of the Judean countryside and of the old Northern Kingdom were destroyed (2 Kgs 23:8, 10, 13, 15, 19) and the priests of the towns of Judah were brought to Jerusalem (2 Kgs 23:8).[36] Centralization, of course, is one of the factors that both Hackett and Meyers describe as detrimental for women who seek to assume power within their society. Hulda may therefore have

33. Hamori, "Childless Female Diviners," 178; see also Hamori, "The Prophet and the Necromancer," 829n9.

34. Hamori, "Childless Female Diviners," 182, 190–91.

35. Hamori, "Childless Female Diviners," 170.

36. Because Josiah's reforms are described in 2 Kgs 23 as being so extensive, some scholars have raised doubts concerning the text's historical reliability. See, for example, Lohfink, "Cult Reform of Josiah of Judah," 459–75, and the references collected in Albertz, *History of Israelite Religion in the Old Testament Period*, 1:345n5. For a generally positive evaluation, see Dever, "Silence of the Text," 143–68.

vanished from the tradition at precisely the moment Josiah's reforms began because Josiah's program of increasing centralization and institutionalization made it difficult and perhaps impossible for her to maintain her position of prophetic authority.

Deborah. For both Hackett and Meyers, Deborah presents one of the best test cases for their theories (if not the best), given that the twelfth and eleventh centuries BCE, the period in which biblical tradition locates Deborah, is the period that each scholar explores as generally having the richest possibilities for women exercising power and attaining a relatively high status. For both Hackett and Meyers, this is because the premonarchic period represents a time of major decentralization and deinstitutionalization, during which the public sphere was not widely separated from the domestic sphere and during which leadership was generally ad hoc rather than being hierarchically structured. Also, both Meyers and Hackett stress the predominantly domestic orientation and rural demographic that characterized premonarchic Israel. Meyers further draws attention to the period's pioneer quality, and Hackett to the era's relative instability and features of turmoil.

Meyers probably has the better of Hackett with regard to this final point and, indeed, with regard to her overall argument concerning the premonarchic era—this due to the primary evidence on which each relies. Hackett's primary data for describing the premonarchic period as a time of turmoil are the biblical accounts found in Judges.[37] In making this claim, Hackett recognizes and forthrightly acknowledges the problem with using Judges as a historical source. Nevertheless, she maintains that it is possible to extract useful historical information from Judges. This may be somewhat the case regarding the arguably archaic poem found in Judg 5:1–31 (see further below),[38] but according to Hackett, even Judges' seventh-century BCE Deuteronomistic redaction contains some "information that seems to me relatively free of editorial reworking" and thus contains information, especially regarding "social data," that is historically authentic.[39]

I am less sanguine regarding this assessment of Judges' historical authenticity. I am more confident, however, regarding the archaeological evidence upon which Meyers relies. In particular, Meyers relies upon the excavations

37. See, e.g., Hackett, "In the Days of Jael," 25–26.

38. On the date of Judg 5, see Freedman, "Divine Names and Titles in Early Hebrew Poetry," 83–85; Halpern, "Resourceful Israelite Historian," 379n2; Halpern, *First Historians*, 102–3n36; Stager, "Archaeology, Ecology and Social History," 224; and Stager, "Song of Deborah," 64n1.

39. Hackett, "In the Days of Jael," 37n34.

and regional surveys that have indicated an explosion of one-period sites in the previously unoccupied hill country of Canaan in the late thirteenth, twelfth, and eleventh centuries BCE.[40] Like many scholars, Meyers understands this new hill-country population to be Israelite (or at least "proto-Israelite"),[41] and also like many scholars, she proposes to describe early Israelite society using the hill-country data. These data indicate, first, that the primary demographic of Israel in the Iron Age I period (ca. 1200–1000 BCE) was rural or village-based, which is, of course, precisely the sort of setting that Meyers's analysis identifies as being most conducive for generating positions of elevated status for women and the increased potential for the exercise of power. Because the hill-country villages, moreover, contain no remains of palaces or large residences, no public or administrative structures, and no sanctuaries or temples, Meyers, like others, posits a relatively undifferentiated and unstratified social order, with no political or religious elite and no civil bureaucracy. Similarly, because the hill-country remains indicate a primarily agrarian society, with only minimal evidence of manufacturing, mostly small-scale in nature (what we might call cottage industry), Meyers, like others, reconstructs an economy in which each household seems basically a self-sufficient unit, producing only what it needs for its own consumption but not any excess for sale or trade. In short, according to Meyers, the archaeological evidence reveals a rural, nonhierarchical, decentralized, and domestically based society—the sort in which, according to her social-scientific model, a woman like Deborah could assume a position of leadership.

Meyers, however, and also Hackett focus primarily on the possibility of Deborah assuming a role as a military leader in early Israelite society, as is intimated in the archaic poem of Judg 5:1–31, and not on the religious role of prophet assigned to Deborah in the Deuteronomistic-era redaction of Judg 4:4.[42] Yet even though Deborah is not specifically labeled as a prophet

---

40. See, e.g., I. Finkelstein, *Archaeology of the Israelite Settlement*; I. Finkelstein, *'Izbet Ṣarṭah*; Gal, *Lower Galilee*; Kochavi, "Israelite Settlement in Canaan," 54–60; Zertal, "Settlement of the Tribes of Israel in the Manasseh Region"; see also, for earlier materials, Stager, "Archaeology of the Family," 1–35, and the works of Campbell, Kochavi et al., and Sapin cited there.

41. For the term "proto-Israelite," see Dever, "Cultural Continuity," 24*; Dever, "How to Tell a Canaanite from an Israelite," 55; Dever, *Recent Archaeological Discoveries*, 78; Dever, "Unresolved Issues in the Early History of Israel," 206; Gottwald, "Method and Hypothesis," 77*; and Malamat, "Proto-History of Israel," 303–13, esp. 303–4.

42. See, e.g., Meyers, *Discovering Eve*, 174; Hackett, "In the Days of Jael," 26–28; Hackett, "Women's Studies," 156.

in Judg 5, there are manifold indications in that text that she is to be regarded as a prophetic functionary. Certainly Deborah is "called" in Judg 5:1–31 in much the same way the root meanings of *nābî'* and *nĕbî'â* suggest a prophet is "called," summoned by God to "Awake!" (Judg 5:12) and muster the Israelite tribes for battle against Sisera. Moreover, as is implicit within this call to arms and explicit elsewhere in the Judg 5 poem (see especially vv. 4–5, 19–21), the battle to which Deborah summons the Israelites is a holy war, in which God sanctions the combat and even goes forth to fight at Israel's side. To verify that a battle is an actual holy war of God is, of course, a major role assumed by prophets elsewhere in biblical tradition (see, e.g., 1 Kgs 20:13; 22:6; 2 Kgs 3:11), suggesting again Deborah's role as a prophetic functionary in Judg 5. Some scholars have further argued that the title "mother in Israel" assigned to Deborah in Judg 5:7 is a marker of her prophetic role, the counterpart of the title "father" assigned to male prophets such as Elijah and Elisha elsewhere in the Hebrew Bible (2 Kgs 2:12 and 13:14).[43] Yet even if this specific interpretation is questioned, it is noteworthy that Judg 5 does not suggest that the epithet "mother in Israel" refers to Deborah as a childbearer. Instead, just as Hamori's work on women prophets suggests, Deborah seems to derive at least some measure of her prophetic authority from her nonnormative family status. Finally, note that, as Baruch Halpern has definitively shown, the prose account of Deborah's exploits found in Judg 4 is literarily dependent on the poetic narrative found in Judg 5.[44] This suggests that the prose derived its explicit designation of Deborah as a prophet in Judg 4:4 from indications found in the Judg 5 poem—presumably the same sorts of markers I have just located.

Yet this is not to say, we should be clear, that there actually was a prophet Deborah: because of the historical unreliability of all of the premonarchic era's textual sources, including Judg 5:1–31, this remains unknown. What we can say, rather, is that the early Israelites generated a piece of literature, Judg 5:1–31, in which a woman was portrayed as a significant actor in the religious (and military) functioning of her society. I propose, following Hackett and Meyers, that what makes such a portrayal possible is that premonarchic Israel was a rural, nonhierarchical, decentralized, and domestically based society in which positions of power could be held by women. The authors of Judg 5:1–31

43. See Boling, *Judges*, 257; Hackett, "In the Days of Jael," 28; and Meyers, *Discovering Eve*, 159–60.

44. Halpern, "The Resourceful Israelite Historian," 379–401; Halpern, *First Historians*, 76–103.

were thus able to envision a woman like Deborah acting as a prophetic functionary. Indeed, although I am, as I have previously stated, more confident of the historical reliability of 2 Kgs 22 and of the Nehemiah memoirs, including Neh 6:14, and thus more confident of the actual existence of Hulda and Noadiah as women prophets, I would, if pushed, insist only on the same claim regarding these two women: that the periods in which they are depicted as active are periods in Israelite history characterized by the destabilized context—especially the destabilized religious context—that makes it possible for the biblical authors to imagine that women could act as prophets.

Miriam. However challenging the problems faced by the historian who would consider the Bible's portrayals of Noadiah, Hulda, and especially Deborah as prophets, significantly more problematic is a discussion of Miriam's prophetic role. This is because, increasingly, biblical scholars have come to doubt the historicity not just of the Bible's exodus accounts but of the entire exodus event. In particular, models that locate the origins of Israel within Canaan have called into question the notion of any Israelite immigration from outside the "promised land," and even those contemporary scholars who do still admit the possibility of an exodus event now tend to describe the group involved as numerically insignificant.[45] What all this means is that we cannot speak in any meaningful way of an "Israel" that existed before the premonarchic period, and certainly not of an "Israel" large enough to have a describable social and political organization. Consequently, we cannot assess whether that social and political organization was of the sort that would have allowed a depiction of a woman like Miriam achieving a relatively high status within her community and stepping forward in the exercise of power.

45. The thesis that the Israelites emerged from within the context of Canaanite culture rather than entering the "promised land" from without was originally associated with the work of Gottwald, *Tribes of Yahweh*, and Mendenhall, "Hebrew Conquest of Palestine," 66–87. It now has several spokespersons, perhaps the most ardent among them being William G. Dever, who has written on the topic repeatedly. See, for example, Dever, "Archaeological Data on the Israelite Settlement," 77–90; Dever, "Archaeology and Israelite Origins," 89–95; Dever, "Cultural Continuity," 22*–33*; Dever, "How to Tell a Canaanite from an Israelite," 27–56; Dever, "Is There Any Archaeological Evidence for the Exodus?," 67–86; Dever, "Israel, History of," 545–58; Dever, *Recent Archaeological Discoveries*, 37–84; Dever, "Unresolved Issues in the Early History of Israel," 195–208; and, preeminently, Dever, *Who Were the Early Israelites?* Dever in turn cites as his primary influences certain parts of the work of I. Finkelstein, *Archaeology of the Israelite Settlement*; aspects of the "symbiosis" model developed by Fritz, "Conquest or Settlement?," 84–100; and, although he criticizes him for being too cautious (in "Cultural Continuity," 30*), the excavation reports of Mazar, "Giloh," 1–36, and Mazar, "Iron Age I and II Towers at Giloh," 77–101.

To put the matter another way: the model used by Hackett and Meyers depends on historically describable societies. With the exodus narrative, we leave history behind. To discuss Miriam's role as a prophet in Exod 15:20, therefore, we must leave the Hackett-Meyers analytical model behind in favor of another methodological approach.

11. Why Is Miriam Also among the Prophets?

When the French ethnographer and folklorist Arnold van Gennep published his groundbreaking book *Les rites de passage* in 1909,[46] his intent was primarily to define a tripartite structure of (1) separation, (2) margin or *limen* (from the Latin meaning "threshold"), and (3) reaggregation or reincorporation that he proposed characterized birth rites, puberty rites, marital rites, and, indeed, almost all life-cycle rituals across cultures. Yet within that same volume, van Gennep also suggested that his tripartite model of separation/ liminality/reincorporation could be applied to the cross-cultural analysis of rituals other than life-cycle rituals—passage rites related to seasonal and calendrical change, for example.[47] Other scholars, pushing even further, subsequently argued that van Gennep's rites-of-passage model might apply to elements within religious systems beyond those in which ritual was an explicit concern. For example, in *The Myth of the Eternal Return*, Mircea Eliade proposed that because it is "a consecration, an initiation," a movement from "the profane to the sacred," any journey to the "center" is a rite of passage, whether that journey be a pilgrimage to a sacred place (Mecca, Hardwar, Jerusalem), a heroic expedition in search of some legendary object (the Golden Fleece, the Golden Apples, the Herb of Life), or a quest for "self," for the center of one's being.[48] Eliade's sense that the rites-of-passage model helps structure stories of heroic adventure is also found in Joseph Campbell's *The Hero with a Thousand Faces*; he writes, "The standard path of the mythological adventure of the hero is a magnification of the formula represented in the rites of passage: *separation—initiation—return*."[49]

46. An English translation, *The Rites of Passage*, was published in 1960 and in a second edition in 2019.

47. Discussed in Bell, *Ritual*, 37.

48. Eliade, *Myth of the Eternal Return*, 18. Eliade's discussion was brought to my attention by Elliott, *Roads to Paradise*, 171.

49. Campbell, *Hero with a Thousand Faces*, 30. Campbell goes on to describe this rites-of-passage structure as the "nuclear unit" of his notion of "monomyth," a psychologically

Perhaps, however, the boldest and most thorough attempt to apply van Gennep's rites-of-passage model beyond the confines of that which is explicitly ritual is found in the work of the anthropologist Victor Turner and of his followers. To be sure, Turner, like van Gennep, began his career by seeking to describe ritual, especially the rituals of the Ndembu, a tribal people of Zambia among whom Turner did his primary field work. Turner argued that within Ndembu society, "conflict was rife" and "manifested itself in public episodes of tensional irruption I called 'social dramas.'"[50] These social dramas, Turner went on to propose, were highly structured ritual events comprised of four parts: (1) an initial "*breach* of regular, norm-governed social relations"; (2) a "phase of mounting *crisis*"; (3) an attempt at "*redressive action*" (which, if unsuccessful, could be followed by a return to the crisis stage and then further attempts at redress); and (4) either "the *reintegration* of the disturbed social group or . . . the social recognition and legitimization of irreparable schism between the contesting parties."[51] As commentators have often pointed out, Turner's sense here of an "underlying temporal structure within social processes" is highly reminiscent of the three-part movement of van Gennep's rites-of-passage model,[52] so much so that Turner himself often seemed to use his description of the four parts of the social drama interchangeably with van Gennep's description of the tripartite structure of rites of passage.[53] This is especially true in Turner's discussion of the crisis phase of his social drama, which he saw as characterized by the same sorts of threshold or liminal experiences that van Gennep had earlier described for the middle phase of his rites of passage.[54] Turner too, like van Gennep, saw his social drama model as applying to ritual events across cultures.

Turner further contended, especially in his later writings, that his model of social drama underlies not only ritual events across cultures but narratives as well. His fullest exposition of this thesis is found in his essay "Social Dramas

---

based—more specifically, a Jungian-based—understanding of mythology with which I am not in sympathy. See the particularly trenchant critiques of Lefkowitz, "The Myth of Joseph Campbell," 429–34, and Doniger, "Origins of Myth-Making Man"; Doniger parenthetically raises some important criticisms of the Jungian tendencies of Mircea Eliade (above, n. 48) as well. Also in critique of Campbell, see Manganaro, "Joseph Campbell," 151–85, esp. the references cited on 165–67, and Segal, *Joseph Campbell*, esp. the conclusion, 136–40.

50. Turner, *Dramas, Fields, and Metaphors*, 33.

51. Turner, *Dramas, Fields, and Metaphors*, 38–41.

52. Bell, *Ritual*, 40.

53. As pointed out, for example, by Bynum, "Women's Stories, Women's Symbols," 307n13.

54. Turner, *Dramas, Fields, and Metaphors*, 39; for Turner's most complete discussion of liminality, see "Betwixt and Between," 93–111, and "Liminality and Communitas," 94–130.

and the Stories about Them," originally published in 1980 in a special issue of *Critical Inquiry* and later reprinted (1981) in a collected volume titled *On Narrative*. There he writes, "The social drama, then, I regard as the experiential matrix from which the many genres of cultural performance, beginning with redressive ritual and juridical procedures and eventually including oral and literary narrative, have been generated."[55] This insight about the social drama and its reflection in narrative, especially religious narrative, has subsequently been appropriated by scholars such as Alison Goddard Elliott in her study of the hagiographies of early Christian saints (pre-1000 CE),[56] and André Droogers, in his study of the biographies of several religious leaders (Jesus; the medieval merchant-cum-mendicant and lay preacher, Waldes; the founder of the Salvation Army, William Booth; a Zaire prophet, Kimbongu; the Buddha; and Mohammad).[57] In particular, both Elliott and Droogers focus on various features of liminality and marginality that are present in their subjects' life stories.

Robert L. Cohn, Alfred Haldar, Ronald S. Hendel, William H. C. Propp, and Shemaryahu Talmon have suggested, moreover, that biblical scholars push beyond a rites-of-passage analysis that focuses on stories of individual religious heroes in order to see the exodus story of the Israelite people, and especially that story's description of the people's journey from Egypt to Canaan, as an exemplar of Turner's rites-of-passage model.[58] Most typically, these scholars see the tripartite pattern beginning to manifest itself in Exod 12–15, when the Israelites perform a special blood ritual, the Pesach, and then, by leaving Egypt, separate themselves from their previous geographical home and their previous social status of slavery. Cohn writes, for example, "The crossing of the Red Sea marks the final break."[59] Propp offers an important corrective, however, by pointing out that in the typical rite of passage, the participant returns to his starting point: "He, not his home, has changed." Propp therefore argues that "to fit the initiation pattern as defined by van Gennep and Turner, we should

---

55. Turner, "Social Dramas and the Stories about Them," 154.

56. Elliott, *Roads to Paradise*; see esp. chapter 7, "The Saint as Liminal Hero," 168–80.

57. Droogers, "Symbols of Marginality," 105–21; this reference was brought to my attention by Elliott, *Roads to Paradise*, 171.

58. Cohn, *Shape of Sacred Space*, 7–23; Haldar, *Notion of the Desert*, 5; Hendel, "Sacrifice as a Cultural System," 375; Propp, *Exodus 1–18*, 35–36; and Talmon, "'Desert Motif,'" 50, 54. The Cohn, Haldar, Hendel, and Talmon references were all brought to my attention by Propp, *Exodus 1–18*, 35.

59. Cohn, *Shape of Sacred Space*, 13; see similarly Hendel, "Sacrifice as a Cultural System," 375.

consider Israel's entire absence from Canaan, from Joseph to Joshua, as their liminal period."[60] As I will discuss further in part 4 of this chapter, I disagree somewhat with Propp regarding the end of Israel's liminal period, but I agree wholly with him that it begins already with Israel's descent into Egypt; in Propp's words, "No less than the wilderness, Egypt is the crucible in which Israel is refined (Deut 4:20; 1 Kgs 8:51; Jer 11:4), from which it emerges a great people (Exod 1:7, 8, 12)."[61] It is further my contention that focusing on certain aspects of liminality as found within the Egypt and wilderness sections of the exodus narrative illuminates the assigning of the role of prophet to Miriam in Exod 15:20.

According to Turner, the most defining characteristic of the liminal state or the liminal persona is ambiguity; in Turner's classic formulation, to be liminal is to be "betwixt and between." "Liminal entities," Turner writes, "are neither here nor there; they are betwixt and between the conventions assigned and arrayed by law, custom, convention, and ceremonial. . . . Thus liminality is frequently likened to death, to being in the womb, to invisibility, to darkness, to bisexuality, to the wilderness, and to an eclipse of the sun or moon." Liminal persons, Turner goes on to state, are often represented "as possessing nothing . . . to demonstrate that as liminal beings they have no status, property, insignia, secular clothing indicating rank or role, position in a kinship system." Indeed, so absent are marks of rank or distinction that Turner labels the liminal community as "egalitarian."[62] But, as Turner makes clear (at least in his earlier writings),[63] this liminal experience of egalitarianism and of what he calls communitas, a feeling of "intense social togetherness"[64] and "of union with one's fellow human beings,"[65] is not a wholly idealized experience: the statusless, and even passive and humble participants in an initiation ritual, for example, typically find themselves required to submit to the general authority of ritual elders who impose upon the initiates numerous tests and trials (fasting, seclusion, sexual continence, poverty, homelessness, silence, etc.). Yet these same ritual elders also often reveal to initiates knowledge relating to

60. Propp, *Exodus 1–18*, 35.

61. Propp, *Exodus 1–18*, 35.

62. Turner, "Liminality and Communitas," 95.

63. Michael Taussig, "Transgression," 350, writes of how the depictions of liminality in the later Turner "became increasingly balmy and innocent, with erotic, obscene, sadistic, cruel, and licentious features bleached out."

64. This description comes from Leach, "Anthropological Approaches to the Study of the Bible," 24.

65. This description comes from Bynum, "Women's Stories, Women's Symbols," 30.

the new privileges and responsibilities they are soon to assume within their society, especially the *sacra*, or knowledge relating to things divine.

The degree to which these many markers of liminality are present in the Egypt and wilderness sections of the exodus narrative is striking. As the story of the Egyptian enslavement begins in the first chapters of Exodus, for example, we are introduced to the Israelites as aliens, a people living in a land that is not their own and a people who, increasingly, are perceived as threatening by that land's indigenous inhabitants. We are also told that these Israelites are forced to undergo experiences of trial. First, they are conscripted to build the pharaoh's store cities (Exod 1:11); then they are forced to labor in other construction projects and in agricultural work (Exod 1:14); next, they are required to kill their baby boys at birth (Exod 1:16); finally, when the midwives who attend the Hebrew women circumvent the murderous command of Pharaoh, the Israelites are told to throw their boy children into the Nile to drown (Exod 1:22). As the narrative continues, moreover, the trials of the Israelites continue and even intensify. In Exod 5:7, the pharaoh, in denying Moses's and Aaron's demands that the Israelites be let go to journey three days into the wilderness to sacrifice, orders that the Israelites shall now be forced to make bricks without straw; when the people fail to maintain their daily quota under these oppressive conditions, their supervisors are beaten (Exod 5:14). Especially important to note here is the role of Moses and Aaron in instigating this increase in the Israelites' persecutions, for while it could be argued that the people's trials in Exod 1, imposed upon them by the pharaoh alone, are not really typical of a liminal experience (given that it is more usually the ritual elders of a community who are responsible for the liminal persons' ordeals), by Exod 5, the people's suffering is being brought about by their ritual leaders, Aaron and Moses, and the God for whom those leaders speak. The text indeed makes clear that the people perceive the matter in this way; thus, they cry out to Moses and Aaron, "*You* have made us odious in the eyes of Pharaoh and in the eyes of his officials and have put a sword in their hand to kill us" (Exod 5:21, emphasis mine). More significant still is God's deliberate hardening of Pharaoh's heart throughout the plague cycle (Exod 4:21; 7:3; 9:12; 10:1, 20, 27; 11:10) and the concomitant prolonging of Israel's suffering that this hardening occasions.[66]

Finally, however, the Israelites are able to leave Egypt. But this hardly means their trials are at an end. They are pursued by the Egyptians, who change their

---

66. This "hardening of the heart" motif has been much discussed in the literature: see, e.g., Chisholm, "Divine Hardening in the Old Testament," 410–34; Gunn, "'Hardening of Pharaoh's Heart,'" 72–96; and R. R. Wilson, "Hardening of Pharaoh's Heart," 18–36.

minds about letting the people leave (Exod 14:1–18); they thirst at Marah, where there is only bitter water to drink (Exod 15:22–26), and again at Massah-Meribah, where there is no water at all (Exod 17:1–7). They hunger in the wilderness of Sin, where there is nothing to eat (Exod 16:1–36), and they find themselves under Amalekite attack at Rephidim (the same location as Massah-Meribah, Exod 17:8–16). God's role in bringing about this suffering, moreover, is again a significant feature of the narrative. It is God, for example, who once more hardened the heart of pharaoh (Exod 14:4, 8), and the hearts of Egyptians as well (Exod 14:17), and so laid the foundations for the Israelites' ordeal at the Reed Sea. It is also God who put the Israelites to the test (*nissāhû*) when they thirsted at Marah (Exod 15:25)[67] and again at Massah-Meribah (the very name Massah as given in Exod 17:7 comes from the root *nsh*, "to test").[68] And it is again God who tested the people (*'ănassennû*) when they hungered in the wilderness of Sin (Exod 16:4). All of this—the sustained tests and trials and the role of the deity in giving rise to these ordeals—points to a continuing experience of liminality for the Israelites. The specific trial of hunger—given that fasting is so characteristic of liminality—is particularly important here.

Other specific features of liminality are also readily apparent at this point in the narrative. The Israelites are homeless, and homeless in a way that very literally marks them as "betwixt and between," as they wander between the land of Egypt from which they have escaped and their "promised land" to which they go. "Wandering," moreover, implies there is a quality of aimlessness in the Israelites' movement (see especially in this regard Exod 14:3), which suggests further the sort of ambiguity that characterizes liminality. Then there is the place in which the Israelites are wandering, the wilderness, which, for liminality generally and for the Bible in particular, is *the* paradigmatic liminal space. Edmund Leach, for example, writes of the biblical wilderness as "a 'betwixt and between' locality . . . which is neither fully in This World nor

---

67. The Hebrew *nissāhû*, "he tested him," is in fact ambiguous regarding the identity of the tester and the tested at Marah. I follow most translations and commentators in assuming God as the subject and Israel as the object. For further discussion, see Propp, *Exodus 1–18*, 577–79; Propp, *Water in the Wilderness*, 52–53, 72–73n24.

68. On God's role as "tester" at Massah-Meribah, see similarly Deut 33:8 (*nissîtô*) and Ps 81:8(7) (*'ebḥānĕkâ*). However, in Exod 17:2, 7, and also in Deut 6:16 and Ps 95:8–9, it is the Israelites who are said to test Yahweh at Massah-Meribah. As my argument makes obvious, it is my inclination to take God's identity as the "tester" as the primary tradition. Certainly, the identification of God as "tester" in Exod 15:22–26 and 16:1–36, the two pericopes that immediately precede and stand generally parallel to Exod 17:1–7, suggests this. Further discussion (although not necessarily agreement) can be found in Propp, *Exodus 1–18*, 577–79, 601–6; Propp, *Water in the Wilderness*, 53–61.

in The Other."[69] Leach further points out that in the Bible, the wilderness as liminal space gives rise to the characteristically liminal experience of divine inspiration and revelation, given that the wilderness's position "at the boundaries between This World and The Other . . . [is an] appropriate place for a meeting between the natural and the supernatural."[70] Certainly this is true for the exodus narrative, which devotes Exod 20:1 through Num 10:11 to the story of Israel's encounter with Yahweh at the wilderness mountain of Sinai and the revelation there of the *sacra* or *tôrâ*.

There is one final feature of liminal periods in general and of Israel's liminal experiences in particular that is necessary to discuss here: Turner's description of liminality as a time of "antistructure," during which, among other things, the social identities that have previously defined liminal entities dissolve. For Turner, this dissolution is most often manifested by a temporary inversion or reversal of the liminal entities' previous social stature. A political authority is debased, for example, or a person of wealth assumes a stance of poverty.[71] Yet in a trenchant review of Turner, titled "Women's Stories, Women's Symbols: A Critique of Victor Turner's Theory of Liminality," the noted historian of medieval Christianity Caroline Walker Bynum observes that this temporary debasement that Turner defines as characteristic of liminal persons needs to be more carefully parsed in terms of gender, given that "at many points" in Turner's writings, "he suggests women are liminal or . . . marginals" not just temporarily, during key moments within certain ritual transitions, but as part of the *normal* course of their existence.[72] While Turner, for example, described liminal entities as deprived temporarily of "property, insignia, secular clothing indicating rank or role, position in a kinship system" during the course of a rite of passage,[73] women, during many periods in history and in many cultures, have been unable to hold property as part of the *normal* course of their existence. They have also, as part of the *normal* course of their existence, been deemed peripheral or irrelevant in the delineation of kinship systems, and they have often, in the *normal* course of their existence, been without rank or role, especially rank or role independent of some male in their life. Instead, they

69. Leach, "Anthropological Approaches to the Study of the Bible," 16; this quote was brought to my attention by Elliott, *Roads to Paradise*, 173.

70. Leach, "Why Did Moses Have a Sister?," 37.

71. For example, in "Liminality and Communitas," 100–106, Turner discusses how the Ndembu chief-to-be is debased and humiliated as part of his initiation ritual.

72. Bynum, "Women's Stories, Women's Symbols," 33. As examples, Bynum cites Turner, "Liminality and Communitas," 99–105, and Turner, *Process, Performance, and Pilgrimage*, 104–5.

73. Turner, "Liminality and Communitas," 95.

have been required to submit passively and humbly to the demands of fathers, husbands, brothers, and/or other male authorities.

So what happens, Bynum asks, when women, so associated with liminal features, characteristics, and symbols as part of their *normal* course of existence, participate in a rite of passage whose very structure, as van Gennep and Turner would have it, requires a movement *into* liminality as a central and constitutive part? In particular, as the shortened title of Bynum's article, "Women's *Stories*" (emphasis mine), makes clear, Bynum asks what happens to women in narrative accounts that are structured around a rites-of-passage pattern? Bynum's answer—based on narratives from the medieval period about the lives of that era's saints—considers authorship, for she argues that male authors tell rites-of-passage stories in a very distinctive way. More specifically, Bynum argues that when male biographers of the European Middle Ages tell stories of women who pursue a spiritual vocation, these biographers shape the women's stories according to men's typical experiences during rites of passage and rites-of-passage types of events, whereby men undergo profound reversals and inversions with regard to the positions of status and authority they normally hold. In his journey of spiritual transformation, for example, St. Francis of Assisi began by enthusiastically embracing every luxury and all sorts of frivolous pursuits, until he came, as a result of a religious calling, to renounce not only the riches but even the garb bestowed upon him by his wealthy cloth-merchant father. Thereby he enacted a dramatic separation from his previous existence, giving up every possible marker of his opulent past in order to live thereafter as a mendicant and an ascetic.

So too, according to Bynum, medieval men who are writing about women assume that women within their communities who are pursuing a religious vocation "flip-flop" by repudiating their previous identity and renouncing all markers of it. But while men are said to "flip-flop" by *giving up* markers of status, power, wealth, and authority as they enter into a rite of passage's liminal phase, Bynum argues that the male biographers of women saints describe these women as *taking on* the markers of status, power, wealth, and authority that they normally lack as they move into a period of liminality. The medieval women Bynum studies can be said by their biographers, for example, to "disguis[e] themselves as men" in order to "flee the world and join monasteries," thereby temporarily becoming—during this liminal phase of transition—higher-status males. "To men," Bynum writes, "women reverse images and 'become men' in renouncing the world."[74]

74. Bynum, "Women's Stories, Women's Symbols," 38.

Needless to say, medieval Europe is not ancient Israel, nor are the Bible's prophets analogs of medieval Europe's saints. Nevertheless, Bynum's analysis regarding the rites-of-passage pattern as it is manifest in male-authored narratives about medieval saints offers insight regarding the Bible's exodus account, a narrative that arguably follows van Gennep's rites-of-passage pattern and that also considers women but that I take to be authored by men (as, in my opinion, are all biblical texts).[75] According to these male authors, Miriam could be identified and even embraced as a prophet in Exod 15:20, at a point during the liminal phase of the exodus narrative, because in such liminal periods, women's empowerment and ability to accrue status are possible. Indeed, according to the paradigms of inversion and reversal that male narrators see as crucial motifs during the liminal phase of a rite of passage, this enhancing of a woman's normally debased status is *required*. To paraphrase Bynum: in the exodus narrative's liminal phase, Miriam "reverses image" and "becomes" a high-status prophet.

In answer, then, to the question that I posed as the main title of this chapter, "Why is Miriam also among the prophets?" it is my contention that Miriam is assigned the prophetic role in Exod 15:20 because in male-authored depictions of liminality, the gender conventions that more usually restrict women from holding positions of religious leadership can be suspended. Therefore, Miriam can be described as occupying a position as a prophetic functionary that, outside of liminal time and space, women are generally denied.

III. Is Zipporah among the Priests?

In considering the structure of the exodus narrative, many commentators have noted that the story of Moses as an individual presents in microcosm much of what the story of Israel as a community presents in macrocosm. For example, in his study of Exod 1–4, Michael Fishbane speaks of the ways in which "the

---

75. I have documented several attempts to identify female authors within the Hebrew Bible in Ackerman, *Warrior, Dancer, Seductress, Queen*, 23n34. But this scholarship is so speculative that it has convinced few. In addition, as Phyllis Bird observes in "Women's Religion in Ancient Israel," 285–86n8, the smattering of compositions that the Hebrew Bible does put in the mouths of women (e.g., Judg 5:1–31; 1 Sam 2:1–10) "have all been transmitted to us in the compositions of scribal guilds, which I would view as male associations." Hence, Bird writes, "I believe that we have no *direct* or *unmediated* access to the words or lives of women in the Hebrew scriptures." See similarly Bird, "Women in the Ancient Mediterranean World," 32.

opening chapters of the Book of Exodus (1–4) . . . foreshadow the events and scenarios of chapters 5–19."[76] It thus follows that the reading I have adopted of the Israelites' exodus story—a narrative filled with liminal markers—can also illuminate the life story of Moses. Note, for example, that as the story of Israel in Egypt begins in the book of Exodus by describing the Israelites as aliens, inhabitants of a place that is not their own, so too is Moses quickly characterized in his life story as an alien, a Hebrew slave who is living in an Egyptian palace that is not his own. He is thus residing, to use once more Turner's evocative description of liminality, "betwixt and between" identities.

The text takes care to mark his liminality in other ways as well. In Exod 2:10, for example, Pharaoh's daughter gives her newfound child the very "betwixt and between" name of Moses (*mōšeh*). To be sure, an ancient Israelite audience might not have understood one aspect of this name's liminality that modern scholars do: the linguistic ambiguities that, despite the Hebrew etymology proposed in Exod 2:10 for *mōšeh*, just as plausibly allow us to understand the name as etymologically related to Egyptian *ms(w)*, "to beget," as found in names such as Thutmose or Rameses.[77] Yet even for an ancient audience, the name Moses, because it is derived by an *Egyptian* princess from a *Hebrew* verb (*māšâ*, "to draw out"), carries within it connotations of a "mixing up" of tongues, which in turn implies for Moses a "mixed-up" or liminal identity. Within the narrative tradition, Moses's "mixed-up" identity further manifests itself after he has grown up. He kills an Egyptian one day because he sees him beating a Hebrew (Exod 2:11), suggesting that by this point in the story, Moses's allegiances have come to lie with the Hebrew part of his identity.[78] Yet the very next day, two Hebrews question Moses's right to interfere in their affairs (Exod 2:13–14), which implies that they identify Moses not as "one of us" (the Hebrews) but as "one of them" (the Egyptians). He thus continues to be caught between worlds.

As Israel's liminal experiences in Egypt finally come to an end, however, after the tenth plague, so too do Moses's, as he flees from the pharaoh who seeks to kill him because of the Egyptian taskmaster's death (Exod 2:15). Yet as Israel fled the liminality of Egypt only to encounter more experiences of liminality in the wilderness, so too does Moses. Despite, for example, his ef-

76. Fishbane, "Exodus 1–4," 64. See also Greenberg, *Understanding Exodus*, 117–19; Fretheim, *Exodus*, 79; and Propp, *Exodus 1–18*, 242.

77. See Griffiths, "The Egyptian Derivation of the Name Moses," 225–31.

78. Although there has been much speculation in, especially, the rabbinical tradition, the biblical text is in fact silent on the questions of how and when Moses learns of his Hebrew heritage.

forts at marriage and at beginning a family once he has settled in the land of
Midian, he still seems to perceive himself as an outsider within this community. Thus he names his firstborn son Gershom, from the Hebrew *gēr*, "alien,"
because, he says, "I have been an alien residing in a foreign land" (Exod 2:22).
Like the Israelites, moreover, Moses receives a typically liminal revelation of
divine knowledge, or *sacra*, while in the wilderness (Exod 3:1–4:17), at the very
mountain, indeed, where God subsequently speaks to the Israelites en masse.
Finally, like the Israelites, Moses's wilderness experience is characterized by
liminal-like testing, and testing that is instigated, as is usual in liminality, by
a spiritual elder—in both Israel's and Moses's case, God. In Moses's case, this
testing manifests itself as Moses journeys back to Egypt to take up his divinely
appointed role as the Israelites' redeemer, when "at a lodging place along the
way, Yahweh met him and sought to kill him" (Exod 4:24).[79]

As many commentators have pointed out, the "him" to which Exod 4:24
refers is in fact unclear, and some thus see Yahweh's intended victim as Gershom, Moses's son.[80] But because Gershom has not previously been mentioned
in the pericope, I agree with the ancient versions and with the vast majority
of commentators that the intended victim of Yahweh's attack is Moses.[81] I further agree, again with the vast majority of commentators, that after Zipporah,
Moses's wife, moves in Exod 4:25 to avert Yahweh's attack by circumcising
Gershom, her son by Moses, the "feet" she is next said to touch are Moses's
(although the text again uses a pronoun referent that does not make this totally clear). Finally, I agree, still with the majority of commentators, that the
reference to Moses's "feet" in the text is to be taken as a euphemism for his gen-
italia and that what Zipporah is doing with her touching is either actually or
symbolically circumcising Moses. She then addresses Moses with what seems
to be liturgically laden language: "You are surely a bridegroom of blood [or

79. The enigmatic passage found in Exod 4:24–26 has occasioned much discussion.
Along with the standard commentaries, add to the exhaustive bibliography collected by
Childs, *Book of Exodus*, 90, the following works: Ashby, "Bloody Bridegroom," 203–5; Beltz,
"Religionsgeschichtliche Marginalie zu Ex 4:24–26," 209–11; R. and E. Blum, "Zippora und
ihr *ḥtn dmym*," 41–54; Frolov, "Hero as Bloody Bridegroom," 520–23; Gelernter, "Tsipporah's
Bloodgroom," 46–57; Houtman, "Exodus 4:24–26," 81–105; Kaplan, "'And the Lord Sought to
Kill Him,'" 65–74; Kunin, "Bridegroom of Blood," 3–16; Propp, "That Bloody Bridegroom,"
495–518; Richter, "Gab es einen 'Blutbräutigam?,'" 433–41; B. P. Robinson, "Zipporah to the
Rescue," 447–61; and Römer, "De l'archaique au subversif," 1–12.

80. So, for example, Blau, "Ḥatan Dāmîm," 1–3; Greenberg, *Understanding Exodus*,
113–14, 116; Kosmala, "'Bloody Husband,'" 20–23; and Morgenstern, "'Bloody Husband,'" 45.

81. For further discussion, see Kaplan, "'And the Lord Sought to Kill Him,'" 65–74.

a "bloody bridegroom"] to me" (Exod 4:25).[82] What all this suggests is that Zipporah, in performing an actual circumcision of Gershom, in performing some sort of circumcision, whether actual or symbolic of Moses, and in giving voice to a highly formalized and even formulaic pronouncement after these acts, is characterized in this passage as some sort of ritual specialist.

As to what sort of ritual specialist Zipporah might be, Bernard P. Robinson gives us a clue. He writes: "By undertaking the circumcision of her son, a male role, Zipporah has taken the place of her father Jethro. Henceforth she is not only Moses's wife, but also his surrogate father-in-law."[83] Propp similarly suggests Zipporah may be "usurping the role of father-in-law. For, if Moses is her *ḥātān* 'bridegroom/son-in-law/circumcised,' she is conversely his *ḥōtēn* 'father-in-law/circumciser.'"[84] Moses's actual father-in-law, however, is pictured throughout the exodus tradition not just as the potential circumciser of his son-in-law, but also as a priest (Exod 2:16; 3:1; 18:1).[85] We are thus led to ask, as I do in the second half of this chapter's title: If Zipporah is to be seen as assuming her father's role as circumciser, should she also be seen as assuming in certain ways his role as priest? Note in this regard that in the exodus tradition, the blood offering of circumcision is closely associated with the offering of blood sacrifice,[86] and, while we must grant that the biblical authors do not necessarily regard the offering of sacrifice as the prerogative of priests alone,[87] the exodus account does ultimately insist on sacrifice as

82. Kosmala's etymology of *ḥtn*, "to circumcise," based on a cognate in Arabic, and his resulting translation of *ḥatan-dāmîm* as "the blood-circumcised one" (Kosmala, "'Bloody Husband,'" 25–27) have generally been rejected by biblical scholars. See Childs, *Book of Exodus*, 97–98.

83. B. P. Robinson, "Zipporah to the Rescue," 458. See similarly Morgenstern, "'Bloody Husband,'" 67, 69–70, who sees Zipporah as acting in Exod 4:24–26 on behalf of her brother.

84. Propp, *Exodus 1–18*, 240.

85. The name of Moses's father-in-law is a matter of some confusion in the biblical text. The dominant tradition, in Exod 3:1; 4:18; and 18:1–27, identifies the father-in-law as Jethro. But in Exod 2:16–22, the father-in-law is assigned the name Reuel, and, although the Hebrew is ambiguous, Num 10:29–32 seems to take the father-in-law's name to be Reuel as well. That text further mentions Hobab, identified as Reuel's son. But in Judg 1:16 and 4:11, Hobab is the name given Moses's father-in-law! Still, despite these ambiguities, the tradition is practically unanimous regarding the salient point for my argument here: that Moses's father-in-law was a priest.

86. See especially the association of circumcision and the Pesach sacrifice in Exod 12:1–27, 43–49 and the more general association of circumcision and the keeping of Passover in Josh 5:2–12.

87. I think, for example, of the sacrifices said to be offered by various patriarchs in Genesis and the sacrifices offered in the book of Judges by Gideon (6:26–27) and by Ma-

an exclusively priestly franchise. Thus, by presenting Zipporah as making a sacrificial-like offering that we normally would have expected to have been made by her priestly father, Exod 4:24–26 provocatively hints at the notion of Zipporah assuming a priestlike role.

Yet everywhere else in biblical tradition, the priesthood is characterized as the province of males alone. How, then, to explain the language hinting at Zipporah's priestlike status? I would again turn to Bynum's analysis to suggest that as Miriam could be imagined as holding the otherwise typically male position of prophet during the story of the liminal sojourn of the people of Israel in the wilderness, so too can Zipporah be depicted as if she occupies the otherwise exclusively male position of priest during the story of the liminal sojourn of Israel's spiritual leader and microcosmic representative, Moses.[88] Indeed, the site of Zipporah's priestlike actions—some unnamed lodging place at some unspecified point on Moses's journey back to Egypt—could hardly be more ambiguously (that is, liminally) described. Thus, I conclude that as liminal space and time in the life story of Israel made possible the character-ization of Miriam as a prophet, so too have liminal space and time in the life story of Moses made possible a priestlike role for Zipporah that is otherwise difficult (if not impossible) to imagine within the organizational structure of Israelite religion.

IV. Concluding Thoughts on the Conclusion of Liminality

As I noted above, in part 2 of this chapter, Turner's notion of social drama, as derived from van Gennep's rites-of-passage model, assumes an underlying temporal structure and, consequently, change. Liminality, to put the matter somewhat more bluntly, does not last forever. It is succeeded, in van Gen-nep's terms, by reaggregation/reincorporation or, in Turner's terminology, by reintegration. In the story of Moses's life, this moment of reintegration is dramatically suggested in Exod 4:27, when Aaron, sent out into the wilder-ness by Yahweh to rendezvous with Moses, meets him and kisses him (hence reuniting Moses with his rightful family), and in Exod 4:29–31, when Moses, through Aaron, tells the Israelites of all Yahweh has said to him, and "the people believed" (hence reuniting Moses with his rightful community and

---

noah (13:19–20). On Gideon's claim to priestly authority, however, see Halpern, "Rise of Abimelek," 85–88.

88. See, similarly, Kunin, "Bridegroom of Blood," 9–10.

reuniting him in such a way that affirms his newly designated identity as the people's leader and redeemer). Not coincidentally, these episodes take place immediately after Moses survives Yahweh's murderous threat in Exod 4:24–26. It is almost as if, having passed liminality's final test, Moses can instantly find himself accepted back into the bosoms of his birth family and his people. Also, not coincidentally, it is at this point that Zipporah essentially disappears from the text, as there seems to be no place in the life of the reintegrated Moses for such a liminally depicted (that is, priestlike and foreign) wife. Gershom, the alien son, essentially disappears at this point in the story as well, his liminally depicted character likewise deemed by the tradition to be an element inappropriate to the narrative's reaggregated phase.[89]

Miriam, I would argue, is similarly a character who belongs only to the liminal phase of the life story in which she is found, the life story of Israel as a community. Unfortunately, however, the story of the Israelite community does not mark as clearly the concluding moments of Israel's liminal life as the Moses narrative marks the end of Moses's liminality. According to most who have previously commented on this issue, Israel's liminality continues throughout the entire course of the exodus tradition, ending only with the conclusion of the community's forty years of wandering, at the moment in Josh 3–5 when the people celebrate Passover after finally having entered into the promised land.[90] There is much that can be said on behalf of this interpretation: during the forty years of wandering, the Israelites' lives are filled with experiences

89. To be sure, Zipporah, along with Gershom, does return briefly to the exodus tale in Exod 18:1–6 (accompanied by Moses's second son, Eliezer, who, if anything, is even more invisible in the text than his mother and elder brother; prior to Exod 18:3–4, see only Exod 4:20). But the reappearance of Zipporah and Moses's children in Exod 18:1–6 should not be seen as signaling their reincorporation into the narrative but rather serves only to underscore the marginal position they occupy in the life story of the reincorporated Moses. This is evidenced by the fact that we are told, in Exod 18:2, that it was Moses himself who had brought about their disappearance in his life by sending them back to his father-in-law at some point after the Exod 4:24–26 episode; also by the fact that there is no indication anywhere in the Exod 18 text that Moses proposes to take Zipporah or his offspring back. As I understand it, this is because the alien and liminal Zipporah, along with her alien sons, belongs only to the alienated or liminal phase of Moses's life story. When that liminality ends, beginning in Exod 4:27, so too does any place for Zipporah in the text. Some commentators, however, do believe Zipporah rejoined Moses at Sinai. Milgrom, *Numbers*, 93, suggests, for example, that the reason Aaron and Miriam speak out against Moses's Cushite wife (whom Milgrom presumes to be Zipporah) only in Num 12:1, long after the original marriage, is because she has just become affiliated with the Israelite community, having joined them at Sinai after having been separated from Moses during his efforts in bringing the people out of Egypt.

90. Cohn, *Shape of Sacred Space*, 13; Propp, *Exodus 1–18*, 35; Talmon, "'Desert Motif,'" 54.

we have come to understand as liminal, such as trials and ordeals and the revelation of sacred knowledge. Throughout the forty years, moreover, the Israelites sojourn in the wilderness, which for the Bible, as we have seen, is the prototypical liminal space. The generally aimless quality of the Israelites' wandering I have also characterized as typical of liminal movement.

Hendel, however, interprets somewhat differently, arguing that "the liminal stage is represented by the encounter with Yahweh at the holy mountain, Sinai/Horeb" and that the Israelites' subsequent sojourn in the wilderness and entry into Canaan belongs to the "third and final stage of reaggregation."[91] In support of this view, Hendel points out that it is at Sinai that Israel's new social and religious identity is forged and consecrated.[92] Thus it is at Sinai that the antistructural status that has previously characterized Israel's liminality disappears, and by extension, it is at Sinai that liminality more generally comes to an end. I agree with Hendel on this point and, indeed, would adduce even more evidence to suggest that the making of the covenant at Sinai marks the conclusion of Israel's liminal period. Note, first, that while the Israelites do continue to experience liminal-like ordeals after leaving Sinai, these ordeals are not depicted in the same way as were the ordeals the Israelites experienced before Sinai, which, as is typical in liminality, were tests imposed upon the community by its spiritual authorities (Moses, Aaron, and God). Rather, the post-Sinai ordeals are construed as examples of the people putting Yahweh on trial, demanding more and greater assurances of God's power and presence. For example, in Num 11:4–35, we find a story about the Israelites' experiencing hunger in the post-Sinai period that parallels in certain respects the pre-Sinai story of how the Israelites hungered in the wilderness of Sin (Exod 16:1–36). But while the Exod 16 account is full of liminal features—the characteristically liminal ordeal of fasting; the suggestion that Yahweh is testing the Israelites within the context of this ordeal (*'ănassennû*, Exod 16:4)—the Num 11 narrative has a very different sense. The people in Num 11:4–6 hunger not because they lack food, as in Exod 16, but because they are tired of eating the same food, the manna God causes to fall from the heavens day in and day out. They are not suffering because of a characteristically liminal ordeal, that is; they are suffering because of an ingrate and churlish nature. For Moses, moreover, this seems to suggest the community is testing Yahweh and has found the deity

91. Hendel, "Sacrifice as a Cultural System," 375.
92. This is effected especially through Moses's offering of sacrifice and his throwing of the collected bowls of blood on God's altar and on the congregation in Exod 24:3–8. See further my discussion below.

wanting (hence the people are said to have rejected Yahweh in Num 11:20), and Yahweh is similarly described as regarding this incident and several other post-Sinai instances of complaining as tests the people have imposed upon the deity (*waynassû 'ōtî,* Num 14:22).

It is also the case that while there is some of the revelation of sacred knowledge characteristic of liminality in the post-Sinai parts of the exodus narrative, there is not much compared to the massive amount of revelation associated with the Sinai event.[93] Furthermore, it is not clear how much liminal-like wandering the authors of the exodus tradition envision as being a part of Israel's post-Sinai experience. Rather, the people are depicted as spending the bulk of their time at one location, Kadesh Barnea. Kadesh Barnea, moreover, is not a particularly good exemplar of the typically liminal space of wilderness, given that it is an oasis location with three major springs. Finally, it is important to note that one of the major themes of the Bible's post-Sinai exodus account concerns the killing off of the original exodus generation (see, e.g., Num 14:26–35; 26:63–65) and not the reaggregation or reintegration of this previously liminal community.

Hence my agreement with Hendel that we locate the Israelites' movement out of liminality at the time of their departure from Sinai.[94] Like Hendel, moreover, I would identify the ritual of Exod 24:3–8—when Moses offers sacrifice and then throws the collected bowls of blood on God's altar and on the congregation—as crucial in effecting Israel's transition from a liminal to a reaggregated state. I would further point out the degree to which this sacrificial act parallels Zipporah's act of circumcision in Exod 4:24–26, which is also a ritualized moment involving blood sacrifice that propels the previously liminal Moses into his reaggregated identity as the leader who will bring his people out of bondage.[95] More significantly, I would argue that the Sinai account seems to offer a parallel to Zipporah's disappearance within the Moses narrative im-

93. See only the materials found in Num 15, 18–19, 28–30, 34–35, as compared to the materials of Exod 20:1–17; 20:22–23:33; 25:1–31:17; 34:10–26; 40:1–15; Lev 1:1–27:33; Num 1:1–16; 2:1–31; 3:5–4:33; 5:1–6:27; 8:1–9:14; 10:1–10.

94. This position, on my part as well as Hendel's, might seem to stand in contradiction to the claim of Propp I earlier embraced: that in the typical rite of passage, the participant returns to his starting point, which, as Propp understands it, means that Israel's rite of passage begins with the people's descent into Egypt at the end of Genesis and concludes with their return to Canaan in the first chapters of Joshua. As Propp himself notes, however, the trek to Sinai is "a return to Canaan in miniature" (*Exodus 1–18,* 35n14). Thus, Israel can metaphorically be said to have returned "home" at Sinai, and the expected rites-of-passage pattern can be understood as fulfilled. See further Smith and Bloch-Smith, *Pilgrimage Pattern in Exodus.*

95. Fretheim, *Exodus,* 79, also notes a possible parallel between Exod 4:24–26 and 24:3–8.

mediately following the reintegration of Moses in Exod 4:27–31: to wit, Miriam being deposed from a position of elevated status almost immediately after the newly reaggregated Israelites leave God's holy mountain in Num 10:12.

The crucial text is found in Num 12, a story set in terms of chronology only a short time after the Israelites' departure from Sinai (according to Num 10:33, there is an initial three-day journey from Sinai to a place eventually named Kibroth-hattaavah, and then a subsequent march of unknown duration to the site of the Num 12 account, Hazeroth). At Hazeroth, Miriam and Aaron are said to challenge Moses's position of authority within their community. As commentators have often pointed out, the difficulties in interpretation associated with this challenge are legion.[96] For example, two different reasons are given to account for Miriam's and Aaron's defiance: first, Miriam and Aaron speak against Moses because of his "Cushite wife" (Num 12:1); second, they question Moses's right to serve as Yahweh's sole spokesperson within the Israelite community. "Has not," they ask, "he [Yahweh] spoken through us also?" (Num 12:2). As the text continues, however, the initial concern that was expressed about Moses's marriage seems to be forgotten, and the focus becomes the question of Yahweh's appropriate spokespersons. According to Num 12:6–8, God addresses this issue directly, signaling Moses out as unique because Moses alone speaks with God "mouth to mouth" (*peh 'el-peh*). Then, according to Num 12:9, "the anger of Yahweh was kindled against *them* [Miriam and Aaron]" (emphasis mine) because of their affront. But as God's anger manifests itself, in Num 12:10–16, only Miriam is punished, afflicted with ṣāra'at, some sort of skin disease, and then shut out of the Israelite camp for seven days. Aaron, conversely, remains unharmed and is not rebuked; indeed, he seems to retain the authority to speak out as an intercessor (Num 12:11). This inconstancy has been another major point of confusion for interpreters of the passage.[97] It is particularly disturbing for those who see *Aaron* as the primary

96. The bibliography is extensive. In addition to the standard commentaries, see the following analyses: Anderson, "Miriam's Challenge," 16, 55; Burns, *Has the Lord Indeed Spoken Only through Moses?*, 41–79; Coats, "Humility and Honor," 97–107; Cross, *Canaanite Myth and Hebrew Epic*, 203–4; Culley, "Five Tales of Punishment," 25–34; Jobling, "Structural Analysis of Numbers 11–12," 31–65; Trible, "Bringing Miriam Out of the Shadows," 14–25, 34; Trible, "Eve and Miriam," 15–24; and R. R. Wilson, *Prophecy and Society*, 155–56.

97. Milgrom, for example, in *Numbers*, 93, suggests that only Miriam is punished because, according to the verb form in Num 12:1 (*wattĕdabbēr*), only Miriam spoke out against Moses's wife (see similarly Cross, *Canaanite Myth and Hebrew Epic*, 204). Yet Milgrom simultaneously wishes to claim that the real challenge of the Num 12 pericope is the challenge to Moses's sole leadership mounted by Miriam and Aaron *together* in v. 2. If this is so, then the question of why both were not punished remains. Alternatively, R. R. Wilson, *Prophecy*

instigator of the Num 12:2–9 confrontation, a reading based on the fact that Aaron's name comes before Miriam's in Num 12:4 and 5.[98]

If, though, we understand this passage as occurring at a point in the exodus narrative after Israel's period of liminality has ended and during a period of reaggregation, then the punishing of Miriam alone—even the punishing of Miriam alone despite the possible role of Aaron as the incident's principal instigator—is not so hard to understand. Both Miriam and Aaron have indeed previously been assigned the label "prophet" that in certain respects designates them as spokespersons for God: Aaron in Exod 7:1 and Miriam in Exod 15:20. But in Miriam's case, that label was assigned only within the context of liminal antistructure, during a point in the narrative when she, although a woman, could assume an otherwise almost exclusively male role. Now, in Num 12, when liminality has come to an end, Miriam's claims about her prophetic stature within a reaggregated community are perceived as presumptuous, and far more presumptuous than are Aaron's, for while he has only misconstrued the nature of his relationship to God as compared to Moses's, she both has been guilty of this misconstruing *and* has overstepped the bounds of gender.[99] It is for this double transgression that Miriam is so harshly punished, and it is because he is less reprobate within Turner's logic of rites of passage that Aaron emerges from this episode essentially unscathed. In fact, throughout the subsequent chapters of Numbers, Aaron appears again and again alongside Moses in a position of leadership among the people, indicating that his mounting of the Num 12 challenge has done him no apparent harm.[100] The now-disempowered Miriam, conversely, appears only once more in the exodus story, in Num 20:1, to die.

The Bible thus does admit the possibility that women could assume the role of prophet within Israelite society and, in the case of Zipporah, may even inti-

---

and Society, 155, considers the role ascribed to Aaron in mounting a challenge against Moses to be secondary, which he claims explains why Aaron is absent from the punishment section of the story. Unfortunately, however, Wilson's argument here suffers from circularity, given that one of Wilson's primary pieces of evidence for considering Aaron to be secondary in the Num 12 narrative is that he is absent from the punishment episode.

98. Codices Vaticanus and Alexandrinus, however, place Miriam's name first in 12:4. This was brought to my attention by Burns, *Has the Lord Indeed Spoken Only through Moses?*, 65n66.

99. Although her overall analysis differs from mine, it is interesting to note that Exum, "Second Thoughts about Secondary Characters," 86, also speaks of Miriam's overstepping of gender boundaries in Num 12 in order to explain why only she, and not Aaron, is punished.

100. E.g., Num 13:26; 14:2, 5, 26; 15:33; 16:3, 11, 16–22; 17:1–5(16:36–40), 6–15(16:41–50), 16–26(17:1–11); 18:1–7; 19:1; 20:2, 6, 8, 10.

mate the possibility of a woman taking on priestlike functions. But the biblical record also suggests that the Israelites could only imagine women as occupying these sorts of roles within the context of some very specific conditions. Historically, the conditions required were the kind of period of destabilization or decentralization during which women can generally achieve a more elevated status and find opportunities for a greater exercise of power. Literarily, the conditions required were a narrative containing a liminal phase in which the characteristically liminal experience of antistructure allowed women to be depicted as holding positions within their communities that in the reaggregated sections of the text they would otherwise be denied.

CHAPTER 5

The Mother of Eshmunazor, Priest of Astarte

A STUDY OF HER CULTIC ROLE

In the previous chapter that appears in this volume, "Why Is Miriam Also among the Prophets? (And Is Zipporah among the Priests?)," I considered the two major types of religious functionaries attested in the biblical record: priests and prophets. More specifically, concerning priests: in part 3 of that chapter, I suggested that Moses's wife, Zipporah, performs some ritual functions that might more logically be performed by her father, who it just so happens is also a priest. Thus, while I tried to be very cautious in the language I used (and so shied away from explicitly identifying Zipporah as a priest), and while I in addition tried to signal caution through my use of a question mark when referring to Zipporah in the chapter's title ("Is Zipporah among the Priests?"), I still associated Zipporah with what would have been, in her family, priestly responsibilities.

In the same chapter, I further suggested that even the very understated depiction of Zipporah as a priestlike character that I identified was dependent on a particular set of structural features that defined the exodus pericope in which she most notably appears (Exod 4:24–26). Because, moreover, those structural features were only temporarily present in the exodus story, I argued that Zipporah's ability to enact what were, for her family, priestlike functions was likewise temporary and nigh-on unique, given that elsewhere in biblical tradition, the priesthood is the province of males alone.

But it is a curious feature of ancient Israelite religion—or at least of ancient Israelite religion as depicted in the Bible—that we have no significant

---

An earlier version of this chapter appeared in *WdO* 43 (2013): 158–78. Used here by permission of Vandenhoeck & Ruprecht.

evidence for priestesses, for we have significant evidence for priestesses and related female religious functionaries from "right next door" to ancient Israel, so to speak: both from ancient Phoenicia, just north of the Israelite border, as well as some fragmentary data from late ninth- or early eighth-century BCE plaster inscriptions that come from the site of Deir ʿAlla, just a few kilometers east of the Jordan River.

In its lack of evidence for priestesses, Israel is thus an outlier in its own "neighborhood." And while there are other Near Eastern cultures for which evidence for priestesses is lacking (for example, the Late Bronze Age city-state of Ugarit), attestations of priestesses in the Near East and within the greater Mediterranean basin are generally robust. In articles I published in 2012 and 2013, I set out to explore and (more importantly) to try to explain these cultural variations, and those two articles are re-presented here. The first, "The Mother of Eshmunazor, Priest of Astarte: A Study of Her Cultic Role," concentrates especially on the evidence for priestesses from Phoenicia that I mentioned just above, as well as documenting the lack of Ugaritic materials concerning priestesses that I also just noted. The second, "Priestesses, Purity, and Parturition," which follows immediately after the conclusion of "The Mother of Eshmunazor, Priest of Astarte," begins by broadening this survey of comparative evidence to include, for example, Mesopotamia and Egypt. Yet that chapter's focus narrows, in its latter half, to consider ancient Israelite religion and propose a reason why Israelite tradition turned away from including priestesses among its religious functionaries when the majority of Israel's neighbors did not.

On the fifth-century BCE sarcophagus inscription of Eshmunazor II, king of the Phoenician city-state of Sidon, the dead king's mother is identified as a *khnt*, or priestess, of the goddess Astarte (*KAI* 14, line 15). Moreover, this is only one among several inscriptions from the Phoenician world in which the term *khnt* is used to identify a woman priest. The oldest of these Phoenician attestations may, like the sarcophagus inscription of Eshmunazor II, have its origins in Sidon. Or at least this was hypothesized by Émile Puech, in his 1994 editio princeps of said inscription, which appears on a funerary crater that comes from the antiquities market.[1] A Sidonian provenance for the inscription was likewise proposed by Corrine Bonnet, in her 1996 monograph *Astarté*, although Bonnet also indicated that the crater might come from Tyre.[2] More

1. Puech, "Un cratère phénicien inscrit," 47–73.
2. Bonnet, *Astarté*, 31.

recently, Gaby Abousamra and André Lemaire have argued emphatically for the crater's Tyrian origins, and they also argue for a somewhat later date than had been put forward by Bonnet: "the inscription arguably dates to *ca.* 700 (or more generally in the seventh century BCE.),"[3] as opposed to the eighth-century BCE date that Bonnet had proposed (which was based on the eighth-century BCE date of what Bonnet saw as a kindred funerary urn that came from the Sidonian necropolis of Tambourit).[4] Yet whatever disagreements these various commentators voice regarding provenance and date, on the issue of the inscription's text, they all concur: it identifies the crater as holding the (cremated) remains of one Gerat-milk, "priestess [*kh<n>t*] of Astarte Hor."[5]

Other instances of women identified as priestesses, or *khnt*, in Phoenician tradition are found in Punic and Neo-Punic texts from the western Mediterranean. For example, a grave inscription from Avignon that dates from the end of the third century BCE (*KAI* 70) describes its honorand as a *khnt* of a goddess who is called *rbt*, or "the Great Lady" (line 1), but who is not further identified, due to the fact that portion of the inscription that immediately follows is damaged.[6] A similar gravestone from Djebel Mansour, in modern-day Tunisia (*KAI* 140), has carved upon it a bilingual inscription in Neo-Punic and Latin that also describes its honorand as a priestess (using the Neo-Punic spelling *knt*; line 2). This inscription further describes the priestess as responsible for the building of a temple.[7] Elsewhere from modern-day Tunisia, more specifically, from the site of Henchir Maktar, comes a long dedicatory text (*KAI* 145) that includes the name of one R'g't', the son of "the *khnt*" (line 45). Other *khnt* are found on grave inscriptions from Carthage (for example, *KAI* 93, line 1);[8] these include, most remarkably, the grave inscription of Batba'al, the "head" (*rb*) of the *khnm* (*KAI* 95), and the two separate grave inscriptions of Hld and Hnb'l, who are both memorialized in their epitaphs as *rb khnt*, or the "chief priestess."[9]

---

3. Abousamra and Lemaire, "Astarte in Tyre," 156.

4. Bonnet, *Astarté*, 30; see similarly Puech, "Un cratère phénicien inscrit," 61–65, who proposes a date for the crater in the second half of the eighth century BCE.

5. For the most recent discussion and bibliography concerning the epithet Hor, see Abousamra and Lemaire, "Astarte in Tyre," 156, 156nn27–28; Kerr, "Notre-Dame-de-la-Huronie?," 206–12.

6. For the inscription's date, see Donner and Röllig, *KAI* 2:83, 87.

7. For discussion, see, most recently, Jongeling and Kerr, eds., *Late Punic Epigraphy*, 31–32.

8. For other examples of Carthage *khnt* grave inscriptions, see Tomback, *Comparative Semitic Lexicon*, s.v. KHNT (a), (b).

9. For the Hld inscription, see Tomback, *Comparative Semitic Lexicon*, s.v. KHNT (f).

In all, I am aware of at least fourteen inscriptions from Phoenicia and the Phoenician colonies that identify a female *khn*.[10] This textual evidence, moreover, can be supplemented by iconographic data. First, we can note an engraved cow scapula from the seventh or early sixth century BCE that was found during the 1993 excavation season at Tel Dor. The scene on the scapula shows a woman wearing an Egyptian-style headdress and holding a libation bowl in her upraised right hand as she stands, seemingly in some sort of doorway or gate, facing a docked sailing vessel. According to the director of the Dor excavations, Ephraim Stern, this image is to be interpreted as a depiction of a priestess standing in a harbor gateway—perhaps the gateway of a harbor shrine—bestowing a blessing upon the soon-to-depart boat and its crew. Stern, moreover, takes the image to be Phoenician in provenance—from which it follows, under the terms of Stern's analysis, that the priestess should be understood as a Phoenician *khnt*.[11]

More significant for our purposes, though, are engravings found on the interiors of several of the bronze and silver Phoenician bowls that have been found at various locations around the Mediterranean basin and even beyond (Crete, Etruria, Greece, Cyprus, the Levant, Turkey, Iraq, and Iran) and that date from the latter half of the ninth century or the first half of the eighth century BCE (for the earliest bowls) through the second and third quarters of the seventh century BCE (for the latest).[12] In his 1985 study of all the eighty-plus bowls and bowl fragments then known in this corpus (minus the distinctive collection of bowls from Nimrud),[13] Glenn Markoe describes several stock images—for example, a sphinx, a griffin, a cow suckling a calf—that could be used in these bowls' decorations. Markoe also notes several stock scenes—for exam-

For the grave inscription of Ḥnbʿl, see Gubel and Bordreuil, eds., "Bulletin d'antiquités archéologiques du Levant," 486 (inscription I.7).

10. In addition to the two inscriptions from the Phoenician mainland and the nine Punic and Neo-Punic inscriptions I have documented in my text and in n. 8 above, see Krahmalkov, *Phoenician-Punic Dictionary*, s.v. *KHNT*; Tomback, *Comparative Semitic Lexicon*, s.v. *KHNT* (d), (e). Note also lines 1–2 of *KAI* 136 (a grave marker from Ain Zakkar, in Tunisia), which have been read as identifying the stone's honorand as a priestess. But the reading is difficult and disputed: for discussion, see, most recently, Jongeling and Kerr, eds., *Late Punic Epigraphy*, 28–29.

11. Stern, "Cypro-Phoenician Dedicatory Offering," 34–38; Stern, "Phoenician-Cypriote Votive Scapula from Tel Dor," 1–12; Stern, "Priestly Blessing of a Voyage," 51–55. My thanks to Christian Frevel for bringing these references to my attention.

12. Markoe, *Phoenician Bronze and Silver Bowls*, 1, 155–56.

13. Markoe, *Phoenician Bronze and Silver Bowls*, 1–2; Karageorghis, "Cypriot Silver Bowl Reconsidered," 13.

Fig. 5.1. Bronze bowl in the collection of the Metropolitan Museum of Art (74.51.5700), from Idalion, Cyprus, dating to ca. 850–750 BCE; diameter: 13.1 cm. Depicted is an enthroned goddess being attended by a priestess and by a procession of female musicians and dancers.

ple, a chariot hunt or a military procession—that could be depicted in frieze-like fashion around the bowls' inner perimeters. He furthermore describes the key elements of one of these frieze-like scenes, what he called the "votive procession toward an enthroned goddess" scene, as follows: (1) "a seated or enthroned goddess . . . holding a lotus and a phiale or pomegranate, situated before a tripodic offering table or altar"; (2) a priestess alone or at the head of a procession of offering bearers"; (3) "a file of musicians approaching the goddess from behind"; and (4) "a chain of dancers with hands linked." "Sometimes," Markoe continues, "there is [also] a secondary four-legged table with vessels upon it."[14]

For instance, engraved around the central medallion of a bronze bowl dating from ca. 850–750 BCE from Idalion, Cyprus,[15] which was discovered in a tomb in 1869 (fig. 5.1), we see a scene of (1) an enthroned goddess, who holds a pomegranate in her left hand and a lotus flower in her right hand, seated before a tripodic offering table atop of which sits a bowl of fruits. On the other side of this table stands (2) a priestess, who holds a fan in her right hand and what Markoe has tentatively interpreted as a wine ladle in her left. Behind the goddess, we see (3) a procession of three female musicians who are playing, respectively, a double flute, a lyre, and a frame drum. Following the musicians, although looking in the opposite direction (i.e., toward the goddess's face, rather than her back), there appears (4) a chain of six female dancers with

14. Markoe, *Phoenician Bronze and Silver Bowls*, 56.
15. Markoe, *Phoenician Bronze and Silver Bowls*, 156.

Fig. 5.2. Bronze bowl in the collection of the Louvre (AO 4702), reportedly from Sparta and dating to the second half of the eighth century BCE; diameter: 19.5 cm. Depicted in the outermost band of decoration is an enthroned goddess who is presumably being attended by a priestess and by other female attendants (although the bowl is heavily damaged). The goddess is also attended by a procession of female musicians and dancers.

hands joined. In front of these dancers, and immediately behind the priestess, there is a four-legged table that holds two pottery vessels.[16]

Similarly, engraved around the central medallion and inner frieze of a bronze bowl that dates from the second half of the eighth century BCE,[17] reportedly from Sparta (fig. 5.2), there is depicted (1) an enthroned goddess, seated before an altar or table heaped with offerings. In front of this altar/offering table stands a figure who must, given the parallel examples, be taken as (2) a priestess, although not much else can be said about her, as the bowl is unfortunately damaged at this point. Still, it seems clear that behind the priestess, there is a second altar or offering table, which three female votaries carrying food offerings approach. Once more, the damage to the bowl means it is impossible to identify precisely what offerings the women carry, but parallels with other bowls suggest they bear fruit, cakes, and/or various forms of game. The depictions of four other women who stand behind the goddess, are, conversely, quite well preserved: rendered here are (3) four female musicians, three who play the lyre and one who plays the frame drum. Behind them are (4) seven female dancers, hands joined, who, as in the Idalion example, face away from the musicians and toward the goddess's face.[18]

16. This is Bowl Cy[prus] 3 in Markoe's catalog in *Phoenician Bronze and Silver Bowls*; my description here is derived from his account on pp. 171–72.

17. Markoe, *Phoenician Bronze and Silver Bowls*, 156.

18. This is Bowl G[reece] 8 in Markoe's catalog in *Phoenician Bronze and Silver Bowls*; my description here is derived from his account on pp. 207–8.

Fig. 5.3. Unprovenanced bronze bowl in the collection of the Iran Bastan Museum (Inv. No. 15198), probably dating to ca. 850–750 BCE; diameter: 16.7 cm. Depicted is an enthroned goddess being attended by two priestesses, by two other female attendants, and by a procession of female musicians.

Yet another example of this same scene is found on a bowl that is unfortunately unprovenanced, but that Markoe dates as coming from ca. 850–750 BCE on stylistic grounds (fig. 5.3).[19] It again shows (1) an enthroned goddess, who holds a pomegranate in her left hand and a lotus flower in her right, seated in front of an offering table with a basket of fruit. To the left of the table stand (2) two female priestesses; then, to their left, there is depicted another table that holds a jug and amphora. This table is flanked by two female attendants who carry jugs. On the opposite side of the bowl, standing behind the goddess, is the expected procession of (3) female musicians, one who plays a double flute, two who play the lyre, and one who performs on a frame drum. Following them is a votary carrying a duck, but not a chain of dancers, which in this rendering of the "votive procession toward an enthroned goddess" scene is missing.[20]

In all, Markoe identified somewhere between nine and twelve variants of this same scene depicting an enthroned goddess, served by a priestess or priestesses and other female votaries and servitors, among the corpus of Phoenician bowls (the exact number of renditions of the scene depends on how, precisely, one counts and just how much variation for which one allows). This gives us a striking iconographical complement to the inscriptions from the Phoenician mainland and colonies I detailed above that refer to individual

19. Markoe, *Phoenician Bronze and Silver Bowls*, 156.

20. This is Bowl U[nprovenanced] 6 in Markoe's catalog in *Phoenician Bronze and Silver Bowls*; my description here is derived from his account on p. 217.

women priests or to women as heads of priestly cohorts—and especially a striking iconographical complement to those texts within the Phoenician, Punic, and Neo-Punic inscriptional corpus (such as the sarcophagus inscription of Eshmunazor II) that refer to priestesses who serve female deities. Yet it is equally striking that elsewhere in the Canaanite world,[21] evidence for women holding sacerdotal positions is almost entirely lacking. From among our various Canaanite inscriptional collections, for example, we can cite only one reference to a woman priest: in the Deir 'Alla plaster inscription, Combination I,[22] where a woman priest (khnh) is listed in conjunction with two other female cult servitors: "a perfumer of myrrh" (rqḥt mr) and "a responder," or "an answerer" (that is, "a diviner," 'nyh).[23] Nowhere, however, among the vast corpus of texts from Ugarit, and nowhere among the books of the Hebrew Bible, does the feminine form of khn, "priest," appear.

Moreover, it is difficult to identify within either the Ugaritic or Hebrew Bible corpora a woman, or women, who might be said to fulfill a priestly role or assume priestly obligations, although some commentators have put forward such suggestions. At Ugarit, for example, Loren R. Fisher and F. Brent Knutson interpret the mythological text RS 24.245/KTU 1.101, which speaks of the enthronement of the storm god Baal on Mount Saphon, attended by Anat, as a liturgy for the ritual of the sacred marriage, where "'Anat is the prototype for the Canaanite temple priestess."[24] Edward Lipiński likewise has proposed that KTU 1.23, the mythological text describing the birth of the "gracious gods," is a sacred marriage liturgy where, during a cultic enactment of the text, the role of the two young women who are said in the text to mate with the god El was played by "the queen and a high priestess" or by "young hierodules . . . who entered the cloister upon reaching their puberty [and] were regarded as the wives of their god."[25] Also, in their interpretation of a text from the corpus of Ugaritic ritual documents, RS 24.260/KTU 1.115, Joshua Blau and Jonas C. Greenfield suggest that the reference to "the woman" (aṯt) in line 8 who may partake of the sacrifice that, according to the previous lines, the king offers within the temple of il bt (the deity Ilu-Bêti, the tutelary deity of the royal pal-

21. "Phoenicians were the Canaanites of Tyre, Sidon, and Byblos": so Peckham, "Phoenicians and Aramaeans," 20, citing Baurain, Bonnet, and Krings, eds., Phoinikeia grammata; Moscati, "Nuovi studi sull'identità fenicia," 15–28, 67–68; and Salles, "Phénicie."

22. On the language of the Deir 'Alla texts as more representative of a South Canaanite dialect than of Aramaic, see Hackett, Balaam Text from Deir 'Allā, 109–24.

23. Levine, "Deir 'Alla Plaster Inscriptions," 143n19.

24. L. R. Fisher and Knutson, "Enthronement Ritual at Ugarit," 166.

25. Lipiński, "Fertility Cult in Ancient Ugarit," 212.

ace, according to Dennis Pardee; two common nouns in construct, meaning "the god of the palace," according to Gregorio del Olmo Lete)[26] could refer to a priestess.[27] Other commentators, however, translate the form *aṯt* not as "the woman" (singular), but as "the women" (plural), which might compromise Blau's and Greenfield's interpretation; more damaging to their interpretation still, however, is the fact that most commentators who read *aṯt* in the singular presume that the woman referred to is the king's wife.[28]

Still, might the king's wife function as a priestess in the Ugaritic cult? Some have suggested that this is indicated in yet another ritual text, RS 1.002/*KTU* 1.40, based on an interpretation that understands the *aṯt* ("woman, wife") of line 36 of this text as identical to the *bt ugrt* ("the daughter of Ugarit") of line 35 and that further understands both the "woman" and the "daughter of Ugarit" in question as referring to the Ugaritic queen.[29] In addition, so this interpretation goes, the queen is to be understood as an *officiant* in the ritual of the expiation of sin and of divine/human reconciliation that RS 1.002/*KTU* 1.40 describes.[30] A role for the Ugaritic queen as a cultic official has also been inferred from *KTU* 1.170, line 1, which reads [*d*]*bḥ m*[*l*]*kt*, presumably "the sacrifices of the queen" (which are then listed in the text's succeeding lines).[31]

26. Pardee, *Ritual and Cult at Ugarit*, 66, 280; Pardee, *Les Textes Rituels*, 1:644–45, 648; del Olmo Lete, *Canaanite Religion*, 266. For the reading "the god of the palace," or "the (royal) house," see also Merlo and Xella, "Ugaritic Cultic Texts," 293.

27. Blau and Greenfield, "Ugaritic Glosses," 15. This possibility is also noted by Dietrich, Loretz, and Sanmartín, "Notizen zum offertext RS 24.260," 544; Janowski, "Erwägungen zur vorgeschichte des israelitischen *šĕlamîm*-Opfers," 247n103; and de Tarragon, *Le Culte à Ugarit*, 88–89, among others.

28. For example, Marsman, *Women in Ugarit and Israel*, 532, with references at 532n293; see also Levine, *In the Presence of the Lord*, 10; de Moor, "Studies in the New Alphabetic Texts from Ras Shamra II," 317; de Tarragon, "Les rituels," 202n178; and (as noted by Blau and Greenfield, "Ugaritic Glosses," 15, and Pardee, *Les Textes Rituels*, 1:648n23), Virolleaud in the editio princeps, "Les nouveaux textes mythologiques et liturgiques," 586.

29. Numerous studies have been published of this important text and the four (unfortunately fragmentary) versions of it (RS 1.034 + 1.045/*KTU* 1.54; RS 17.100 [A] and [B]/*KTU* 1.84; RS 24.270 [A]/*KTU* 1.121; RS 24.270 [B]/*KTU* 1.122). For bibliography through 1992, see Pardee, *Les Textes Rituels*, 1:92, 447; del Olmo Lete, *Canaanite Religion*, 145n198; de Tarragon, "Les rituels," 144; and Wyatt, *Religious Texts from Ugarit*, 342. Important subsequent studies include Pardee, *Les Textes Rituels*, 1:92–142, 446–56; Pardee, *Ritual and Cult at Ugarit*, 77–83; del Olmo Lete, *Canaanite Religion*, 144–60; Shedletsky and Levine, "The *mšr* of the Sons and Daughters of Ugarit," 321–44; and Wyatt, *Religious Texts from Ugarit*, 342–47.

30. This position and the scholarship that supports it are well documented in Marsman, *Women in Ugarit and Israel*, 531–32.

31. As in n. 30 above, this position and the scholarship that supports it are documented

But note that both the *d* of *dbḥ*, "sacrifices," and the *l* of *mlkt*, "queen," are re-stored in *KTU* 1.170, line 1, and the following lines are, if anything, even more fragmentary. This renders any interpretation of this text uncertain. The best reading of RS 1.002/*KTU* 1.40, moreover, seems to understand the *aṯt*, even if she is to be taken as the queen, as a *recipient* of the expiation and of the divine-human reconciliation the ritual is meant to effect, alongside the male and female recipients of expiation/reconciliation who come from the various other social groups at Ugarit that are mentioned in the text.[32] These may in-clude the *bnt ugrt*, "the daughters of Ugarit," an emendation often proposed for *bt ugrt* in line 35.[33]

None of the evidence for Ugaritic priestesses, in sum, appears to be partic-ularly secure, and the same should be said about Hebrew tradition and also—moving somewhat further afield—Aramaean tradition, where the feminine form of *kōmer*, "priest," only shows up late, in one Hatran text,[34] or as a loan-word in Assyrian texts, to describe a priestess of Dilbat, a goddess (or city?) of the northwestern Arabian peninsula, on the outermost fringes of the Assyrian empire.[35] Since, moreover, this priestess of Dilbat is a queen as well, what seems reflected in the Assyrian record is the eighth- and seventh century BCE North Arabian tradition of queen-priestesses as opposed to indigenous Ara-maean practice.[36] Phoenician tradition therefore appears to be—if not wholly unique, given the reference to a "priestess" at Deir 'Alla—distinctive within the Canaanite and larger Northwest Semitic world in terms of allowing for the cultic service of female priests. The question that naturally follows is: what factor or factors might give rise to this distinctively Phoenician position?

One such factor, we might suggest, has to do with cultural influences. Commercial interactions between Egypt and the Phoenicians, for example, were longstanding; indeed, commercial transactions between Egypt and the denizens of what became the Phoenician coast well predate the existence of

---

in Marsman, *Women in Ugarit and Israel*, 533; see also (as cited by Marsman, 519n218) Merlo and Xella, "Ugaritic Cultic Texts," 300.

32. This is the general understanding put forward by del Olmo Lete, *Canaanite Religion*, 151–54, 156–60, even as he notes "the distribution of subjects and beneficiaries is not very clear" (145; similarly 151).

33. Adopted, for example, by del Olmo Lete, *Canaanite Religion*, 149 (but cf. 150); by Shedletsky and Levine, "The *mṣr* of the Sons and Daughters of Ugarit," 341; and also (seem-ingly) by Wyatt, *Religious Texts from Ugarit*, 346.

34. Dijkstra, *Life and Loyalty*, 224.

35. *CAD* 8:532–33, s.v. *kumirtu*; Teppo, "Women and their Agency in the Neo-Assyrian Empire," 49–50.

36. Abbot, "Pre-Islamic Arab Queens," 1–22, as cited by Lipiński, *Aramaeans*, 78n8.

Phoenicia's constituent city-states. Equally well attested is the influence of Egyptian religious tradition within Phoenicia: most famously, we can cite the ways in which the Phoenician understanding of the goddess Baalat Gubul, or the "Lady of Byblos," was shaped by Egyptian traditions regarding Hathor and Isis.[37] Perhaps we should posit as well that Egyptian religious influence manifested itself in Phoenicia—first in the mainland and then in the colonies—with regard to women priests. Certainly, Egypt had a robust tradition of women clergy.[38] This is especially the case within regions of Egypt whose principal deity was female, but as Joachim Friedrich Quack writes, "even in male-dominated cults, there was always one specific office for a woman. . . . The best known of these was the 'god's wife of Amun.'"[39]

Or perhaps, given that the bulk of the textual and iconographic evidence I cited above regarding Phoenician priestesses comes from the western Mediterranean, we might posit that the Phoenicians and their Punic and Neo-Punic successors were influenced by Greek tradition regarding the disposition of religious personnel. After all, "from the earliest representation of Greek thought onward," Simon R. F. Price has noted, "Greek religious personnel . . . consisted equally of men and women."[40] That said, arguments based on cultural influence are tricky things. The Late Bronze Age city-state of Ugarit experienced sustained contact with Egypt and also with Mesopotamia, where there was—as in Egypt—a rich tradition of female priests and other female cult functionaries.[41] Yet Ugarit, as I have noted, does not seem to have assimilated a custom of priestesses in the course of these interactions.

37. Bordreuil, "Astarté, la dame de Byblos," 1156.
38. Bergman, "*kōhēn*: Egypt," 61–62.
39. Quack, "Religious Personnel: Egypt," 290.
40. Price, "Religious Personnel: Greece," 303.
41. Many women cult functionaries are known from third- and second-millennium BCE Mesopotamia: see, e.g., the catalogs assembled by Harris, "Independent Women in Ancient Mesopotamia?," 150, and by Roth, *Law Collections from Mesopotamia and Asia Minor*, 73. Best known of these, perhaps, are the *entu*-priestesses who served the moon god Nanna at Ur in the third millennium BCE, of whom the most famous is Enheduanna, the daughter of Sargon the Great of Akkad (r. 2340–2284 BCE). The bibliography on Mesopotamian *entu* priestesses in general and on the *entu* priestess Enheduanna in particular is extensive. See as representative Bahrani, *Women of Babylon*, 113–17; Collon, "Depictions of Priests and Priestesses in the Ancient Near East," 20–21; Falkenstein, "Enheduanna," 129–31; Hallo, "Women of Sumer," 29–30, 32–33; Hallo and van Dijk, *Exaltation of Inanna*, 1–11; Harris, "Independent Women in Ancient Mesopotamia?," 149; Henshaw, *Female and Male*, 45–51; McHale-Moore, "The Mystery of Enheduanna's Disk," 69–74; Renger, "Untersuchungen zum Priestertum in der altbabylonischen Zeit," 114–39; Weadock, "*Giparu* at Ur," especially 101–5,

Another factor that may therefore be in play regarding the Phoenician evidence is to suggest that there may be something in particular about the Astarte cult that facilitates women's priestly engagement. In the texts from Late Bronze Age Emar, for example, the Sumerian logogram for priestess, NIN.DINGIR, is used to speak of an Astarte priestess of the city (although the goddess's name is usually rendered, under Mesopotamian influence, as $^dI\check{s}_8$-tár or ^{d}INANNA, rather than Aštart/Astarte).[42] The Emar texts also speak of the *maš'artu* priestess in the cult of Aštart/$^dI\check{s}_8$-tár/^{d}INANNA. This servitor's main role was "as a priestess for battle-preparation and military success."[43]

Likewise, we can note just how many of the women priestesses that we know of from Phoenician, Punic, and Neo-Punic inscriptions were associated with Astarte traditions. Granted, this is not exclusively the case, as there is at least one Punic grave inscription (*CIS* I.5987) that identifies its honorand as the priestess of *krw'*, or the Greek goddess Kore. Still, both of the women priestesses whom we know from the Phoenician mainland, Gerat-milk and the mother of Eshmunazor II, are specifically identified as priestesses of Astarte, and Eshmunazor II's mother also carries the goddess's name in her own (which is perhaps to be vocalized Ummi-Ashtart, "My [Divine] Mother is Ashtart/Astarte,"[44] or perhaps as Amoashtart, meaning the "Maidservant of Ashtart/Astarte," with the final *t* of **amot* [Hebrew *'āmâ*] either assimilated or dropped).[45]

To be sure, these data from the Phoenician mainland associating women priestesses especially with Astarte might not seem so extraordinary if we recall that Astarte was the chief goddess of both Sidon and Tyre. Yet in the colonies, too, an association between Astarte and women priestesses is frequently attested. I noted above, for example, that the grave inscription of the woman priest from Avignon (*KAI* 70) denoted her as a priestess of the "Great Lady," *rbt*, an epithet that is well known to be used elsewhere of Astarte (for instance, in the sarcophagus inscription of Eshmunazor II [*KAI* 14, line 15]). Somewhat similarly, one of the priestess grave inscriptions from Carthage

---

112–13, 127–28; Westenholz, "Enheduanna, En-Priestess," 539–56; and I. Winter, "Women in Public: The Disk of Enheduanna," 190–93, 195–96, 198, 200–201. See also, concerning the royal priestess Enheduanna, the related material from Ebla concerning the royal priestesses of the god Idabal, as discussed, e.g., in Archi, "High Priestess, dam-dingir, at Ebla," 43–53.

42. Fleming, *Installation of Baal's High Priestess at Emar*, 83, 98, 124, 196, 221, 238; Fleming, "More Help from Syria," 184.

43. Fleming, *Installation of Baal's High Priestess at Emar*, 211; see also 98–99.

44. McCarter, "Sarcophagus Inscription of 'Eshmunʿazor," 183n9.

45. Gibson, *Textbook of Syrian Semitic Inscriptions*, 3:112.

(*KAI* 93) denotes its honorand as coming from a priestly family (her husband and her husband's father are both designated in the inscription as *rb khnm*), and a priestly family that seems, moreover, to have been affiliated in some way with the cult of Astarte (given that at the end of the inscription, the husband is assigned the title *mtrh 'štrny*, which is usually translated as "the bridegroom" or the "the espoused" of Astronoë [= Astarte]).[46] Moreover, Markoe, albeit tentatively, identifies the enthroned goddess who is served by a priestess, or priestesses, as well as by other female cult servitors on the Phoenician bronze and silver bowls, as Cypriote Aphrodite, or Astarte.[47] Perhaps we are therefore to conclude, as I suggested above, that there is something in particular about the Astarte cult that facilitates women's priestly engagement.

We might in addition ask whether there is something about the Astarte cult that especially facilitates *aristocratic* women's priestly engagement. It is striking in this regard just how many of Astarte's cult servitors come from an aristocratic background. For example, King Eshmunazor II's mother is, obviously, a member of the Sidonian royal court; indeed, it turns out that she had been a part of the royal family all of her life, as she was the daughter of King Eshmunazor I, Eshmunazor II's grandfather, as well as the half-sister of King Tabnit, Eshmunazor II's father. Somewhat similarly, Batbaʿal of Carthage, who according to her grave inscription (*KAI* 95) holds the title *rb khnm*,[48] was the daughter of a man, Ḥmlkt, whose title is, simply, *rb*, "Chief" or "Lord." Astarte, as I have noted above, frequently is identified using the feminine form of *rb*, *rbt*; she also is frequently given the epithet *malkat*, "queen" (again, for instance, in the sarcophagus inscription of Eshmunazor II [*KAI* 14, line 15]).[49] Is it more

---

46. Donner and Röllig, *KAI* 2:62; Tomback, *Comparative Semitic Lexicon*, s.v. *MTRḤ*; cf. Krahmalkov, *Phoenician-Punic Dictionary*, s.v. ʿŠTRNY.

47. Markoe, *Phoenician Bronze and Silver Bowls*, 56.

48. Donner and Röllig, *KAI* 2:105, propose that Batbaʿal holds the title *rb*, rather than the expected *rbt*, to avoid confusion with *rbt* as used elsewhere as an epithet of Astarte.

49. For other instances of Astarte being referred to as "queen," see Sakkunyaton's descriptions of Astarte as the co-regent of King Zeus Demarous (= Baal Haddu) and his remarks that she wears on her head a bull's head as an emblem of kingship (Philo of Byblos, *Phoenician History*, as quoted in Eusebius, *Praeparatio evangelica* 1.10.31), and, from further afield, note Plutarch's reference to Queen Astarte (*Isis and Osiris* 15 [357 B]). Also in connection with Astarte's royalty, note the Tyrian "Throne of Astarte" (*KAI* 17) and the "thrones" like it (see Milik, "Les papyrus araméens d'Hermoupolis," 572, and the bibliography listed there, as well as the inscribed throne dedicated to Astarte Ḥor described by Abousamra and Lemaire in "Astarte in Tyre," 155–56). Finally, note the obverse face of the Kition Tariff inscription (*CIS* I.86A; *KAI* 37A), which lists the monthly expenditures for the temple of Astarte at Kition. There, Astarte is referred to as *mlkt qdšt*, "the holy Queen" or "the Queen, the Holy

than a coincidence, then, that her priestesses can likewise be queens (like Esh-munazor II's mother) or great ladies (like Batba'al of Carthage)? Markoe writes that "in general, the priesthood appears to have been a hereditary institution drawn from the ranks of the . . . aristocracy."[50]

Note here, moreover, Markoe's stress on heredity, which leads me to ask whether Batba'al of Carthage (*KAI* 95) came into her title of *rb khnm* by virtue of her father's position as *rb*. The mother of Eshmunazor II might likewise be assumed to have come into her title as a "priestess of Astarte" through hered-itary means, given that the sarcophagus inscription of her husband and half-brother King Tabnit (*KAI* 13) identifies their common father, King Eshmun-azor I, as a "priest of Astarte" (*khn 'štrt*). Yet because this same sarcophagus inscription also identifies Tabnit as a "priest of Astarte," it could be suggested that Eshmunazor II's mother did not come into her title by inheriting it from her father Eshmunazor I; rather, we might presume that, as is typical of the patrilineal societies of the Near Eastern and eastern Mediterranean worlds, the line of inheritance—in this case, inheritance of the priestly office—passed from the father, Eshmunazor I, to the son, Tabnit. Under the terms of this interpre-tation, Tabnit's wife and Eshmunazor II's mother would have come into the title "priestess" by virtue of her marriage to the "priest," Tabnit. The priestess Batba'al of Carthage (*KAI* 95) is similarly identified on her grave inscription not only as the daughter of Ḥmlkt, the *rb*, but also as the wife of Ḥn', a *špṭ* and a *rb khnm*, who was himself, incidentally, the son of a *špṭ* and a *rb khnm*. Thus we may see here aristocratic positions—the offices of *špṭ* and *rb khnm*—passing across generations through patrilineal descent, whereas within generations, priestly positions might be passed on, by virtue of marriage, from a husband to his wife. Marriage ties might somewhat similarly explain how the priestess known from the Avignon grave inscription (*KAI* 70) came into her title. This

---

One" (line 7), and as *mlkt*, "the Queen" (line 10, following here the line numbers of *KAI* and most commentators; on this issue, see Peckham, "Notes on a Fifth-Century Phoenician Inscription from Kition," 304n2). To be sure, Astarte is not mentioned by name in lines 7 and 10 of the Kition Tariff inscription, but the title "queen" in this inscription, concerned as it is with the cult and temple of Astarte, can refer to no other (as is acknowledged by almost all the commentators: see as representative Gibson, *Textbook of Syrian Semitic Inscriptions*, 3:128; Healey, "Kition Tariffs," 55; Masson and Sznycer, *Recherches sur les phéniciens*, 44; and Peckham, "Notes on a Fifth-Century Phoenician Inscription from Kition," 312–13). The suggestion of Donner and Röllig (*KAI* 2:55) that *mlkt* is a mistake for *ml'kt*, "service," in line 7 (they do not comment on line 10) surely is not correct, as the scribe demonstrates in line 13 that he knows the proper spelling of *ml'kt*—that is, with an *'ālep*. See Masson and Sznycer, *Recherches sur les phéniciens*, 44.

50. Markoe, *Phoenicians*, 120.

is because this inscription not only identifies her as being a priestess but also as the wife of a *mqm 'lm*,[51] a cultic functionary sometimes understood to serve as an "awakener of the [dying and rising] god(s)" who are common figures within Phoenician religion.[52]

Yet whatever the role that heredity and/or marriage may play in facilitating a woman's assuming the title of priestess, I think the wealth of our evidence concerning priestesses in the Phoenician, Punic, and Neo-Punic worlds shows that Phyllis Bird must be wrong when she writes that "*khnt* in the Eshmunazar sarcophagus inscription (*KAI* 14.15) does not represent a class of priestesses, but is the title of a royal widow who has assumed the headship of the national cult as well as the state."[53] That is, Bird takes Eshmunazor II's mother's position as priestess to be one that she assumes under idiosyncratic circumstances, because—the inscription tells us—her husband, Tabnit, had died when Eshmunazor II was quite young (maybe even before he was born)[54] and so the mother had to assume a role as regent—both royal and priestly—on behalf of her son, until he, too, died, tragically while still a minor, at fourteen years of age (*KAI* 14, lines 1–3).[55] Presumably, though, under the terms of Bird's interpretation, the mother, had her son lived to his majority, would have relinquished her priestly office in his favor.

As I have already indicated, however, I think the wealth of our evidence concerning priestesses in the Phoenician, Punic, and Neo-Punic worlds renders Bird's interpretation unlikely, for it seems to me improbable that all of the women who are assigned the title "priestess" in Phoenician, Punic, and Neo-Punic texts, or who are represented as priestesses in Phoenician iconography, hold priestly office only because the male in their families who should properly serve as priest is either dead or has not yet come of age. Still, Bird's focus on the complex circumstances that attend to Eshmunazor II's reign and his mother's regency is helpful in drawing our attention to certain factors regarding the female life cycle that may come into play in relation to women's sacerdotal service. More specifically: however distinctive Phoenicia may be in relation

---

51. For discussion of and bibliography concerning the term *mqm 'lm*, see Smith, *Early History of God*, 68n14; Smith, *Origins of Biblical Monotheism*, 114; and Tomback, *Comparative Semitic Lexicon*, s.v. MQM II.

52. Markoe, *Phoenicians*, 117.

53. Bird, "End of the Male Cult Prostitute," 45n28; see similarly Bird, "Place of Women," 416–17n35.

54. Gibson, *Textbook of Syrian Semitic Inscriptions*, 3:110; McCarter, "Sarcophagus Inscription of 'Eshmun'azor," 182n6.

55. Similarly Bonnet, *Astarté*, 33.

to larger Canaanite tradition when it comes to priestesses, I find it difficult to assume that when it came to childbirth impurity, Phoenician culture differed from Canaanite culture (at least as we know it from the Hebrew Bible), as well as from the cultures of the rest of the Near East and eastern Mediterranean (Mesopotamia, Egypt, Hatti, and Greece). Rather, I assume that in Phoenicia, as in every other Near Eastern and eastern Mediterranean culture from which we have evidence, childbirth rendered a woman impure for some set period of time and that, as a result of that impurity, the postparturient woman was unable to enter sanctuary space, much less—in the case of our Phoenician, Punic, and Neo-Punic priestesses—to participate in cultic service. Therefore: while the sarcophagus inscription of Eshmunazor II logically focuses on sacerdotal service that his mother the priestess rendered during Eshmunazor II's lifetime (and, in the language of the inscription, in conjunction with her son), it may also be that the mother was able to engage more readily in her priestly office because her husband was dead, and thus she was immune from the impurities that might result if he were still alive to impregnate her.

It is also worth noting that in its description of what the mother's priestly service entailed, the Eshmunazor II inscription remarks only on the mother's joining with her son in building temples: (1) a temple to Astarte, in a region of Sidon called "Sidon-Land-of-the-Sea"; (2) a temple to Eshmun, who was Sidon's chief god, as Astarte was the city's chief goddess, at the "spring of YDLL," somewhere in Sidon's environs; (3) a temple for Baal of Sidon, the Lord, that is, of the city and a "divine embodiment of Sidon itself";[56] and (4) a temple for Astarte-Name-of-Baal, who was the Baal of Sidon's consort and "a personification of his cultically available presence."[57] In the one other inscription we have where a priestess's duties are described, the bilingual Neo-Punic and Latin gravestone from Djebel Mansour (*KAI* 140), the focus is also temple building.

Yet Phoenician priestesses also, if our Phoenician bowl collection is any guide, supervise the giving of food offerings and of music-making in service of Cypriot Aphrodite/Astarte. But it is worth noting that the food offerings—which are conveyed into the priestesses' presence by female votaries—are restricted in the representations available to us to fruits, cakes, libations, trussed birds, and fishes. Conversely, in a kindred but not wholly parallel scene (fig. 5.4), in which the enthroned goddess receives offerings of animal sacrifice, the procession to

---

56. McCarter, "Sarcophagus Inscription of 'Eshmun'azor," 183n17.
57. McCarter, "Sarcophagus Inscription of 'Eshmun'azor," 183n18.

her altar consists of two *males* carrying four-legged animals (a calf and what appears to be a ram or a kid), preceded by a third *male* leading a stubborn animal to an altar. The altar, moreover, is attended by two more *males*: one kneeling; one prostrate. Behind the altar is the enthroned goddess, with two additional *male* attendants.[58] And while another kindred scene (fig. 5.5) does show a *female* bearing two legs of sheep or goat,[59] the recipient in this version of the processional vignette is human, a queen who reclines on a couch.[60]

Fig. 5.4. Bronze bowl from Cyprus, dating to ca. 675–625 BCE; diameter: 15.3 cm. Depicted in the second band inward from the perimeter, on the left-hand side, are two men carrying sacrificial animals and a third tugging at another animal's halter as they approach (toward the bottom of the bowl) an altar, behind which sits an enthroned goddess. Four other male attendants are depicted in the enthronement vignette, two in front of the altar and two behind the seated goddess.

Based on these data, I infer that however distinctive among their Canaanite peers the Phoenicians and their Punic and Neo-Punic heirs may be when it comes to allowing women to hold priestly office, Phoenician tradition nevertheless assigns only to men the responsibility for the blood sacrifices that parallels from elsewhere in the Levant and that data from the Phoenician site of Kition suggest were central to Phoenician ritual.[61] Indeed, although Nancy Jay did not consider Phoenicia as one of her case studies, this is precisely what is predicted by her famous hypothesis that blood sacrifice within patrilineally structured societies such

58. Markoe, *Phoenician Bronze and Silver Bowls*, 181 (this is Bowl Cy[prus] 13 in Markoe's catalog).

59. Karageorghis, "Cypriot Silver Bowl Reconsidered," 17.

60. Karageorghis, "Cypriot Silver Bowl Reconsidered," 15, 18, 19.

61. Karageorghis, *Kition*, 105; Markoe, *Phoenicians*, 121; del Olmo Lete, "Religious Personnel: Syria-Canaan," 296.

Fig. 5.5. Fragmentary silver bowl from Cyprus, dating to ca. 710–675 BCE; diameter: 17.5 cm. Depicted is a queen with an Egyptian wig reclining on a couch. Approaching her are three female musicians, another female attendant, and, behind a large amphora and a table with vases and ladles, three women bearing foodstuffs, including one who bears two legs of sheep or goat.

as Phoenicia and its colonies was an exclusively male rite, meant to forge male-male solidarity among and across generations, in place of the mother-son bond that the blood let during birth occasioned.[62] Jay therefore speaks of an opposition between social reproduction of patrilineally structured kinship groups through the blood shed during animal sacrifice and sexual reproduction through the blood shed during birth, or more bluntly, of "oppositions between blood sacrificial religions and childbearing women."[63] Consequently, it is no wonder, Jay's hypothesis suggests, that Eshmunazor II's mother—as I proposed above—might be said to have come into her own as a priestess only after her husband had died and the possibility of her becoming pregnant and giving birth had ceased. It is likewise no wonder that, even then, the mother,

62. Jay, *Throughout Your Generations Forever.*
63. Jay, *Throughout Your Generations Forever,* 148.

apparently like other Phoenician, Punic, and Neo-Punic priestesses, engaged in cult acts *other* than rites of blood sacrifice.

With this paradigm in mind, it is intriguing to consider the one other community of female cult functionaries for whom we have evidence from the Phoenician world. These are the two groups of *'lmt* mentioned in line 9 of the reverse side of the Kition Tariff inscription: first, a group described only as the *'lmt*, with no other qualifications, and then another twenty-two *'lmt* who do something in conjunction with the sacrifice (*bzbḥ*). What exactly these twenty-two *'lmt* do is, however, unclear, although I have just suggested what it is they do not do: they do not perform rituals of blood sacrifice. J. Brian Peckham, in his study of the Kition Tariff inscription, suggests that the twenty-two *'lmt* are musicians,[64] and Richard S. Tomback, in his *Comparative Lexicon of the Phoenician and Punic Languages*, similarly takes the twenty-two *'lmt* to be singers.[65] What inspires this suggestion, according to Peckham, is the parallel found in Ps 68:26 (in most English translations, 68:25),[66] where a group of *'ălāmôt* participate in a procession comprised of singers and musicians that enters into Yahweh's *qōdeš*, or sanctuary[67]—most probably (although not definitively) to be identified as God's temple compound in Jerusalem (the temple is mentioned specifically in v. 30[29] of the following stanza, but v. 30[29] is part of a stanza that may not have originally been associated with vv. 25–26[24–25]).[68]

Still, in Ps 68:26(25), the *'ălāmôt* are not identified as singers nor generically as musicians but specifically as playing frame drums. It is tempting, then, to suggest that the *'lmt* of the Kition Tariff inscription should also be identified specifically as frame-drum players, especially given that women playing frame drums are represented in multiple exemplars of the "votive procession toward an enthroned goddess" scene on the Phoenician bronze and silver bowls. Even more so, it is tempting to wonder if the designation of both the drumming women of Ps 68:25–26(24–25) and of the female temple servitors of the Kition

64. Peckham, "Notes on a Fifth-Century Phoenician Inscription from Kition," 323, 323n5.

65. Tomback, *Comparative Semitic Lexicon*, s.v. *'LMT*.

66. Peckham, "Notes on a Fifth-Century Phoenician Inscription from Kition," 323n5; the same parallel is also noted by Gibson, *Textbook of Syrian Semitic Inscriptions*, 3:127.

67. Cf., however, Dahood, *Psalms II*, 147, who proposes to vocalize the Hebrew as *běqodšô* and to translate so that it is God who marches "*from* his sanctuary" (emphasis mine).

68. The classic presentation of this "disassociated" reading of the stanzas of Ps 68 is Albright, "Catalogue of Early Hebrew Lyric Poems," 1–39. Recall also that Dahood, *Psalms II*, 147, as noted above (n. 67), takes the *qōdeš* of v. 25(24) as a reference to the holy habitation *from which* God marches. This holy habitation is, moreover, "either Sinai . . . or heaven" in Dahood's interpretation, meaning that even if Ps 68:25–26(24–25) were to be associated with 68:30(29), the psalm as Dahood would read it does not speak of the Jerusalem temple.

Tariff inscription as *'lmt*, "young maids," is meant to identify these cult actors as young women who are prepubescent. If so, they would be immune from the pollution of childbirth that otherwise can compromise women's cultic service. In addition, they would be immune from the polluting factor that alongside childbirth is said periodically to restrict at least Israelite women's access to sanctuary space: menstrual impurity.

We may therefore need to conclude our survey of Phoenician, Punic, and Neo-Punic priestesses of Astarte (and other deities) with an "on the one hand . . . on the other hand" assessment. On the one hand, Phoenician, Punic, and Neo-Punic women seem to have had available to them opportunities to hold sacerdotal office that women of other Canaanite cultures did not. On the other hand, these opportunities may have been extended only to Phoenician, Punic, and Neo-Punic women who were born and/or married into priestly families, and even then, the functions of priestly office that these women were allowed to assume may have been limited. In particular, they appear to have been precluded from rendering service during the rite of blood sacrifice so central to Canaanite cult.[69]

69. See similarly Neils, *Women in the Ancient World*, 160: "Recent feminist-driven investigations have perhaps overstated the power and independence of female priestesses."

CHAPTER 6

Priestesses, Purity, and Parturition

❧

1. Priestesses in the Ancient Near East

As I have noted elsewhere, the evidence for priestesses in the Northwest Semitic world is mixed.[1] For example, priestesses are well attested in textual and iconographic materials from the Phoenician world, both in materials from the Phoenician mainland and the Phoenicians' eastern Mediterranean colonies and also in Punic and Neo-Punic texts from the Mediterranean west. Conversely, none of the proposals various commentators have put forward regarding the presence of priestesses at the Late Bronze Age city-state of Ugarit, just 125 km north of the territory that defined Iron Age Phoenicia, is particularly convincing.

Still, as we move further east from Ugarit, into northern Syria and Mesopotamia, attestations of priestesses become more common. At the thirteenth-century BCE city-state of Emar, about 200 km east of Ugarit, there were women priests who served at the temple of the storm god (rendered at Emar using the Sumerian logogram dIM and probably called, as elsewhere in Late Bronze Age

An earlier version of this chapter was published as pages 270–80 in "Women and the Religious Culture of the State Temples of the Ancient Levant, Or: Priestesses, Purity, and Parturition," in *Temple Building and Temple Cult: Architecture and Cultic Paraphernalia of Temples in the Levant (2.-1. Mill. B.C.E.). Proceedings of a Conference on the Occasion of the 50th Anniversary of the Institute of Biblical Archaeology at the University of Tübingen (28–30 May 2010)*, edited by Jens Kamlah and Henrike Michelau, Abhandlungen des Deutschen Palästina-Vereins 41 (Wiesbaden: Harrassowitz, 2012), 259–89. Used here by permission of the German Association for the Exploration of Palestine/Deutschen Palästina-Vereins.

1. Ackerman, "Mother of Eshmunazor, Priest of Astarte," 158–68. Reprinted in this volume at pp. 111–30.

Semitic idiom, Baal).[2] Indeed, one of the most remarkable texts discovered at Emar describes a nine-day ritual that marks the selection and installation of the storm god's high priestess,[3] who is identified using the Sumerian logograms NIN.DINGIR, for Akkadian *entu*, "priestess" (which was probably pronounced *ittu* in the local dialect).[4] Emar texts also speak of other NIN.DINGIR priestesses: for example, the NIN.DINGIR priestess of the god Dagan from the nearby town of Šumi and, from Emar, the NIN.DINGIR priestess of the goddess Aštart/^{d}Iš$_8$-tár.[5] Second in rank in Emar's religious hierarchy behind its NIN.DINGIR priestesses, moreover, is a different priestess:[6] the *maš'artu*, a priestess in the cult of Aštart/^{d}Iš$_8$-tár, whose main role was "as a priestess for battle-preparation and military success."[7] In his book *The Installation of Baal's High Priestess at Emar*, Daniel E. Fleming in addition identifies among the cultic specialists at Emar a woman called the *nugagtu*, or in Fleming's words, a lamentation priestess, who gives special cries at a particular moment on the third day of the installation of the storm god's NIN.DINGIR priestess and who also plays a role in the installation of the *maš'artu* priestess and in one other ritual text.[8]

Others who play a role in the installation ceremony of the storm god's NIN.DINGIR priestess include the "singers," both male and female, who lead ritual processions and perform hymns for specific gods. Indeed, in the three-way division of the sacrificial meat that is part of the NIN.DINGIR priestess's installation ritual, it is the singers, including the female singers, who take one of the portions (the other two go to the king and to the diviner who has a central role in the installation rite). The singers also get a gift of silver for their participation in the installation.[9] Still another group of female cult servitors is attested at four different points elsewhere in the Emar archives:[10] these are the *munabbiātu* of the goddess Išḫara. Fleming takes these to be the counterparts

2. Fleming, *Installation of Baal's High Priestess at Emar*, 4n6.

3. Arnaud, *Recherches au pays d'Aštata*, no. 369; Dietrich, "Das Einsetzungsritual der Entu von Emar," 47–100; and Fleming, *Installation of Baal's High Priestess at Emar*.

4. Beckman, review of *Installation of Baal's High Priestess at Emar*, 88; Fleming, *Installation of Baal's High Priestess at Emar*, 80–82; Postgate, review of *Installation of Baal's High Priestess at Emar*, 285.

5. Fleming, *Installation of Baal's High Priestess at Emar*, 83, 98, 124, 196, 238; Fleming, "More Help from Syria," 184.

6. Fleming, *Installation of Baal's High Priestess at Emar*, 98.

7. Fleming, *Installation of Baal's High Priestess at Emar*, 211; see also 98–99.

8. Fleming, *Installation of Baal's High Priestess at Emar*, 173; see also 104.

9. Fleming, *Installation of Baal's High Priestess at Emar*, 93.

10. Fleming, "*Nābû and Munabbiātu*," 175–77.

of the male *nābû* of Išḫara and understands both the *nābû* and *munabbiātu* to be "invocation-specialists."[11] More specifically, he describes them as "those who invoke the gods in prayer, blessing, or divinatory/oracular inquiry."[12]

The presence of these many different women cult functionaries at Emar is reminiscent of the situation in Mesopotamia, and, indeed, Fleming, while characterizing the religious cult at Emar broadly as West Semitic (although not Canaanite),[13] describes the position of the Emar NIN.DINGIR priestesses as deriving from the office of the *entu* priestesses of Mesopotamia.[14] Best known of these priestesses, perhaps, are the *entu* priestesses who served the moon god Nanna at Ur in the third millennium BCE, of whom the most famous is Enheduanna, the daughter of Sargon the Great of Akkad (r. 2340–2284 BCE).[15] But the office of the *entu* priestess is attested also in the second millennium BCE, during the Old Babylonian period, as are many other female cult functionaries: the *ugbabtu*, the *kulmašītu*, the *qadištu*, the *ištaritu*, the *sekretu*, the *šugītu*, and the *nadītu*.[16] Of these, the *nadītu* is perhaps the best studied, especially by Rivkah Harris,[17] whose work particularly considers the community (or what Harris calls the cloister, *gagûm*) of *nadītu* women who were dedicated to the sun god Shamash at the city of Sippar. (To be clear, there were other *nadītu* communities elsewhere, dedicated to other gods—for example, to the warrior god Ninurta at the city of Nippur and to the storm god Marduk at both Sippar and Babylon[18]—but "the *gagû* of Sippar was apparently the most

11. Fleming, "*Nābû* and *Munabbiātu*," 182.

12. Fleming, "More Help from Syria," 145.

13. Fleming, *Installation of Baal's High Priestess at Emar*, 1.

14. Fleming, *Installation of Baal's High Priestess at Emar*, 283.

15. The bibliography on Mesopotamian *entu* priestesses in general and on the *entu* priestess Enheduanna in particular is extensive. I have catalogued a representative bibliography in Ackerman, "Mother of Eshmunazor, Priest of Astarte," 169n46, reprinted in this volume at pp. 121–22n41. See also the related material from Ebla concerning the royal priestesses of the god Idabal, as discussed, e.g., in Archi, "High Priestess, dam-dingir, at Ebla," 43–53.

16. Harris, "Independent Women in Ancient Mesopotamia?," 150; Roth, *Law Collections from Mesopotamia and Asia Minor*, 73.

17. Harris, *Ancient Sippar*, 188–99, 302–12, 315–23; Harris, "Biographical Notes on the *nadītu* Women," 1–12; Harris, "Hierodulen," 391–93; Harris, "The *nadītu* Laws of the Code of Hammurapi," 163–69; Harris, "The *nadītu* Woman," 106–35; Harris, "Notes on the Babylonian Cloister and Hearth," 133–45; and Harris, "Organization and Administration of the Cloister in Ancient Babylonia," 121–57. See also Henshaw, *Female and Male*, 192–95; Jeyes, "The *Nadītu* Women of Sippar," 260–72; Renger, "Untersuchungen zum Priestertum in der altbabylonischen Zeit," 149–76; Stol, *Women in the Ancient Near East*, 587–607; and E. C. Stone, "Social Role of the *Nadītu* Women," 50–70.

18. Harris, *Ancient Sippar*, 303, 315–23; Harris, "Hierodulen," 391–93; Harris, "Organi-

prestigious of all the cloisters of Mesopotamia."[19]) These *nadītu* women were sexually chaste (the term *nadītu* seems to come from the verb *nadû*, "to leave fallow"),[20] although the *nadītu* of Marduk at Babylon could marry.[21] The *nadītu* women also came, quite often, from wealthy families and, especially at Sippar, from wealthy families throughout Babylonia.[22] Indeed, the community at Sippar included princesses from the royal families of other major Babylonian cities, such as Mari, located on the middle Euphrates, and Babylon itself.[23]

Because of this, Babylonia's *nadītu* women have sometimes been compared to the Egyptian women who held the office of the "God's Wife of Amun."[24] This position of the "God's Wife" (without specifying the divine name Amun) is first attested during the Egyptian Middle Kingdom (ca. 1975–1640 BCE),[25] but the office took on real prominence only in the New Kingdom era (ca. 1539–1075 BCE), during the reign of the founder of the Eighteenth Dynasty, Ahmose (r. 1539–1514 BCE). For example, on most of her monuments, Ahmose's wife Ahmose-Nefertari is called by the title "God's Wife of Amun" (the god Amun likewise having come to prominence in the Eighteenth Dynasty).[26] Another

---

zation and Administration of the Cloister in Ancient Babylonia," 122; Jeyes, "The *Nadītu* Women of Sippar," 263; and Renger, "Untersuchungen zum Priestertum in der altbabylonischen Zeit," 175–76.

19. Harris, "Independent Women in Ancient Mesopotamia?," 151; see similarly Harris, *Ancient Sippar*, 306.

20. Harris, "Hierodulen," 392; Harris, "Independent Women in Ancient Mesopotamia?," 151; Harris, "The *nadītu* Woman," 108; Harris, "Organization and Administration of the Cloister in Ancient Babylonia," 121, 121n1; Henshaw, *Female and Male*, 192; Jeyes, "The *Nadītu* Women of Sippar," 260, 266; and Renger, "Untersuchungen zum Priestertum in der altbabylonischen Zeit," 150. On the anomalous text that has been taken to speak of a Nippur *nadītu* and her "sons," see E. C. Stone, "Social Role of the *Nadītu* Women," 55–56n15.

21. Harris, *Ancient Sippar*, 303, 315, 317; Harris, "Hierodulen," 391–92; Harris, "Independent Women in Ancient Mesopotamia?," 151, 160; Harris, "The *nadītu* Woman," 108, 108n14; Harris, "Notes on the Babylonian Cloister and Hearth," 133; and Henshaw, *Female and Male*, 194.

22. Harris, "Hierodulen," 392–93; Harris, "Independent Women in Ancient Mesopotamia?," 152; Harris, "The *nadītu* Woman," 123–24, 131–32; and Jeyes, "The *Nadītu* Women of Sippar," 263.

23. Harris, "Independent Women in Ancient Mesopotamia?," 151.

24. See, e.g., Lesko, ed., "Responses to Prof. Harris's Paper," 165.

25. Ayad, *God's Wife, God's Servant*, 4; Capel, "Statue of Amenirdas I," 115; and Robins, "God's Wife of Amun," 70.

26. See Ayad, *God's Wife, God's Servant*, 4, 6; Bryan, "In Women Good and Bad Fortune Are on Earth," 31; Graves-Brown, *Dancing for Hathor*, 87; Robins, "God's Wife of Amun," 70, 72–73; Robins, *Women in Ancient Egypt*, 43–44, 150; and Yoyotte, "Divine Adoratrices of Amun," 174.

famous Eighteenth Dynasty "God's Wife of Amun" was Hatshepsut,[27] although once Hatshepsut claimed the Egyptian throne for herself (in about the seventh year of the reign of her young son, Thutmose III), the title of "God's Wife of Amun" passed to her daughter Nefrure.[28] Note here that like some of the Babylonian *nadītu* women, the "God's Wives of Amun" could come from their society's royal family; also like the *nadītu* women, these "God's Wives" were devoted to the service of a particular god (in their case, Amun, the chief god of the royal city of Thebes). Moreover, as the role of the "God's Wife" developed during Third Intermediate Period and early Late Period of Egyptian history (ca. 1075–525 BCE), and especially during the office's heyday during the Twenty-Fifth and Twenty-Sixth Dynasties (ca. 715–525 BCE),[29] the "God's Wives of Amun"—like the Babylonian *nadītu* women of Sippar and Nippur— were, according to most scholars, expected to remain celibate.[30] This tradition may actually extend back into the late New Kingdom period, to the reign of Rameses VI (r. 1145–1137 BCE),[31] and it extends forward into the Ptolemaic period (305–30 BCE).

Yet whatever the relationship of the Babylonian *nadītu* women and the Egyptian "God's Wives of Amun," our move to discuss these "God's Wives" has brought us back from the East Semitic world and somewhat more proximate

27. Bryan, "In Women Good and Bad Fortune Are on Earth," 31–32; Robins, "God's Wife of Amun," 73–75; Robins, *Women in Ancient Egypt*, 44–46, 150.

28. Bryan, "In Women Good and Bad Fortune Are on Earth," 32; Graves-Brown, *Dancing for Hathor*, 87; Robins, "God's Wife of Amun," 74–75; Robins, *Women in Ancient Egypt*, 46, 48, 150; and Yoyotte, "Divine Adoratrices of Amun," 174.

29. Dodson, "Problem of Amenirdis II," 179; Onstine, "Gender and the Religion of Ancient Egypt," 8.

30. Ayad, *God's Wife, God's Servant*, 15, 28, 152; Bryan, "In Women Good and Bad Fortune Are on Earth," 43; Robins, *Women in Ancient Egypt*, 153–54; and Yoyotte, "Divine Adoratrices of Amun," 182. Note, however, that Teeter, "Celibacy and Adoption among God's Wives of Amun," 405–14, has called the assumption that the Twenty-Fifth and Twenty-Sixth Dynasty "God's Wives of Amun" were to remain celibate into question, although not because she produces concrete evidence to the contrary, but only because she finds the evidence that others have cited to be less conclusive than has been claimed. See similarly Bryan, "In Women Good and Bad Fortune Are on Earth," 43, and Graves-Brown, *Dancing for Hathor*, 88.

31. Ayad, *God's Wife, God's Servant*, 9; Capel, "Statue of Amenirdas I," 203n5; Graves-Brown, *Dancing for Hathor*, 88; Robins, *Women in Ancient Egypt*, 153; and Yoyotte, "Divine Adoratrices of Amun," 177. To be sure, past scholars have suggested there may be one childbearing "God's Wife of Amun" from the Twenty-First Dynasty (Princess Maatkare), but this is now discounted: for discussion, see Ayad, *God's Wife, God's Servant*, 146; Bryan, "In Women Good and Bad Fortune Are on Earth," 43; Graves-Brown, *Dancing for Hathor*, 88; and Ritner, "Fictive Adoptions or Celibate Priestesses?," 90.

to the world of the Levant that will be my focus for the rest of this chapter; it has also brought us, in considering the Egyptian Third Intermediate and Late Periods, to the first millennium BCE. We can move, moreover, fully back into the Levant and into the first millennium BCE by considering two last bodies of material concerning female cultic servitors, from Transjordanian Deir ʿAlla and from Phoenicia. In the Deir ʿAlla plaster inscriptions, Combination I, three woman cult practitioners are listed, a "diviner" (literally, a "responder" or an "answerer," ʿnyh), "a perfumer of myrrh" (rqḥt mr), and a "priestess" (khnh), although the enigmatic and fragmentary nature of the text makes it difficult to say much more about these servitors' precise roles.[32]

Regarding the Phoenician data, both iconographic evidence from the ninth and eighth centuries BCE and epigraphic evidence from ca. 500 BCE are crucial. To begin with the latter: in *KAI* 14, which is the sarcophagus inscription of King Eshmunazor II of Sidon, Eshmunazor's mother, Amoashtart—who seems to have served as regent during the reign of her son, who came to the throne as an infant or as a very young child and died fourteen years later, apparently before reaching his majority—is described as a priestess (khnt) of the goddess Astarte (line 15).[33] Although some centuries older, the iconographic evidence of Phoenician metal bowls and ivory pyxides dating to the ninth and eighth centuries BCE may give us some impression of such a priestess's duties on Astarte's behalf, as we see depicted on these various bowls and pyxides an image of an enthroned goddess, typically holding a lotus blossom and a phiale or pomegranate and seated behind an offering table, in front of which stands a priestess (see figs. 5.1, 5.2, and 5.3).[34] Behind this priestess extends a procession of female music-makers, some of whom play instruments—the lyre, the double flute, and the frame drum—while others, shown with linked hands, can be presumed to be dancing and also, perhaps, singing. Indeed, we might suggest that illustrated on these several bowls and pyxides are not only images of Phoenician priestesses, like Amoashtart, but—at least in part—an image of Ps 68:25–26 (in most English translations, 68:24–25), where a proces-

32. Levine, "Deir ʿAlla Plaster Inscriptions," 143n19.

33. Note similarly the Phoenician inscription of Gerat-milk, "priestess [kh<n>t] of Astarte Ḥor" (Abousamra and Lemaire, "Astarte in Tyre," 156) and Punic and Neo-Punic inscriptional evidence for priestesses that comes from various Phoenician colonies: from France (*KAI* 70, line 1); from Carthage (*KAI* 93, line 1); and from elsewhere in Tunisia (*KAI* 140, line 2; *KAI* 145, line 45). See also Ackerman, "Mother of Eshmunazor, Priest of Astarte," 158–60, reprinted in this volume at pp. 112–14.

34. Markoe, *Phoenician Bronze and Silver Bowls*, 56–59; Tubb, "Phoenician Dance," 122–23.

sion of singers, musicians, and, between them, frame-drumming young maids
assemble in honor of the Israelite God Yahweh:

> Behold your processions, O God,
> the processions of my God, my king, into the sanctuary (*qōdeš*)—
> the singers in front, the musicians last,
> between [them] frame-drumming young maids (*ʿălāmôt tôpēpôt*).[35]

11. Priestesses in Ancient Israel

Yet whatever the similarities we can identify between the representations on
the Phoenician metal bowls and ivory pyxides, on the one hand, and the text of
Ps 68:25–26(24–25), on the other, there is an obvious difference: the lack of any
women explicitly identified as priestesses within the biblical tradition—and
this as opposed not only to Phoenicia, but also to Syria (Emar), Mesopotamia,
and Egypt. I suggest that the reason for this is revealed within biblical texts
from Leviticus, which dictate that in order to preserve cultic purity, Israelite
women must be excluded from sanctuary space at frequent intervals during
their reproductive years.

More specifically, Lev 15:19–30 deems women to be impure for seven days
at the time of their menses and states, in addition, that women who suffer vaginal discharges of blood during times other than their menstrual periods and
women whose menstrual discharges last longer than the seven days prescribed
for a typical menstrual flow are impure for the duration of those discharges
and then for seven days afterwards. According to Lev 12:1–8, postpartum discharges from the uterus similarly rendered women who had recently given
birth impure:[36] initially for seven days if the woman had borne a male child
and for fourteen days if the child was female. There then followed for the

35. Hebrew *tōp* is more commonly translated as "timbrel" or "tambourine," but as Carol
Meyers has documented in multiple publications, this translation is anachronistic, as the
"timbrel" or "tambourine," an instrument that adds jingles to a frame drum, was not in-
vented until after the biblical period. For Meyers's original presentations of this argument,
see Meyers, "Of Drums and Damsels," 18, and Meyers, "Terracotta at the Harvard Semitic
Museum," 120.

36. On postpartum uterine discharges as the source of impurity for a woman who has
recently delivered, see Burnette-Bletsch, "Women after Childbirth," 204; Whitekettle, "Leviticus 12," 397, 405–8; and Wright and Jones, "Discharge," 205.

postpartum woman a second period of impurity: thirty-three days long if her newborn child was male and sixty-six days if the child was female.

Leviticus 12:4, moreover, defines explicitly the constraints her impurity imposed on the postpartum woman, as well as the constraints imposed on the menstruant or a woman with an irregular vaginal flow: such a woman was not allowed to touch anything "holy" (*běkol-qōdeš lō'-tiggāʿ*)—an offering bowl, say, or a libation vessel or sacrificial implement consecrated to cultic service—nor was she allowed to enter "holy" space (*'el-hammiqdāš lō' tābōʾ*). The latter restriction is of preeminent importance: as Saul M. Olyan writes, "*The primary objective* of purity systems in the Syro-Canaanite cultural context is to protect the sanctity of a deity's space from any sort of defilement. . . . That which is polluted is kept out" (emphasis mine).[37] This means, as Olyan elsewhere observes, that "women subject to [purity rules] would have spent a substantial amount of time cut off from cultic . . . settings."[38]

To be sure, this "substantial amount of time" may not have been as extensive as it might first seem, as menstruation probably occurred less often among ancient Israelite women than it does within many developed societies today, because of less adequate standards of nutrition and poorer health overall.[39] Ancient Israelite women's menstrual flow would have also been suppressed during their frequent pregnancies and during at least part of the subsequent period of nursing (which may have lasted as long as three years).[40] Still, Israelite women must have contracted impurity on account of menstruation and childbirth relatively frequently during their reproductive years and so, to quote again Olyan, "would have spent a substantial amount of time cut off from cultic . . . settings."[41]

To be cut off from cultic settings is, of course, to be cut off from cultic service: which is to say, cut off from service as a priestess or as any other sort of sanctuary-based religious functionary. As a result, Israelite women, or at least Israelite women of childbearing age—subject so often to ritual im-

---

37. Olyan, "Sin, Pollution, and Purity," 502.

38. Olyan, *Rites and Rank*, 57.

39. On this issue, see Beʿer, "Blood Discharge," 158; Milgrom, *Leviticus 1–16*, 953; also Exum, *Fragmented Women*, 138, 138n78; Gruber, "Women in the Cult," 67n40; Marsman, *Women in Ugarit and Israel*, 543; and Olyan, *Rites and Rank*, 57, 150n79.

40. See 2 Macc 7:27 and, among many modern commentators, Gruber, "Breast-Feeding Practices in Biblical Israel," 72 (citing Granqvist, *Child Problems among the Arabs*, 79); Stol, *Birth in Babylonia and the Bible*, 181; and Stol, *Women in the Ancient Near East*, 376. See also the references assembled by Berlinerblau, *Vow*, 109n37.

41. Above, n. 38.

purity—would seem precluded from roles as cultic servitors and especially from the position of cultic service par excellence: the position of priest as the chief servitor of the Israelite god Yahweh.[42] Yet were women not subject to purity restrictions elsewhere in the ancient Near East that would also have constrained their ability to render cultic service? The answer is yes, but "yes, modified," in that data from elsewhere in the ancient Near East suggest that it is *only* women's impurity as a result of parturition, and not menstrual impurity, that is of concern. In Mesopotamia, for example, "delivery caused serious impurity,"[43] and so, Karel van der Toorn writes, "both the mothers and their babies were kept separate from the other inhabitants of the house,"[44] perhaps until the tenth day after birth during the Old Babylonian period (ca. 1894–1595 BCE),[45] or, according to a Seleucid-era text (ca. 312–63 BCE), for a period of thirty days.[46] Likewise in Egypt, women could be separated from their households and the society at large at birth so that the delivery might take place "in a specially built arbor or hut outside the house,"[47] and then the mother and her newly delivered baby remained secluded there for two weeks until the ritual pollution associated with delivery was dispelled.[48] Similarly, second-millennium BCE Hittite tradition mandated that a newly delivered child was impure and so was presumably separated from the community for a prolonged period postpartum—three months for a boy and four months

42. See similarly Bird, "Images of Women in the Old Testament," 54: "The frequent and regular recurrence of this cultically proscribed state [of impurity] in women of childbearing age must have seriously affected their ability to function in the cult." This quote was brought to my attention by Gruber "Women in the Cult," 67n40.

43. Van der Toorn, *From Her Cradle to Her Grave*, 84.

44. Van der Toorn, *Family Religion*, 123; van der Toorn, "Magic at the Cradle," 142.

45. This is how Moran, "Atrahasis," 58–59n3, would interpret the Epic of Atrahasis, tablet I, lines 299–300, where the newly delivered woman and her husband seem to resume sexual relations on the tenth day after she gives birth, having first purified themselves—she from the ritual pollution she incurred in the process of delivery and he from any pollution he incurred through contact with her.

46. Van der Toorn, *Family Religion*, 123; van der Toorn, "Magic at the Cradle," 142; also van der Toorn, *From Her Cradle to Her Grave*, 92 (with a reference there to the original publication of this text, by Thureau-Dangin, "Rituel et Amulettes Contre Labartu," 161–71).

47. Pinch, "Private Life in Ancient Egypt," 376; see also Pinch, "Childbirth and Female Figurines," 405, 414; Galpaz-Feller, "Pregnancy and Birth in the Bible and Ancient Egypt," 51; R. M. Janssen and J. J. Janssen, *Growing Up in Ancient Egypt*, 4–6; Kemp, "Wall Paintings from the Workmen's Village at el-'Amarna," 51–53; and Ritner, "Household Religion in Ancient Egypt," 179.

48. Pinch, "Private Life in Ancient Egypt," 376. Cf., however, Lesko, "Household and Domestic Religion in Ancient Egypt," 205.

for a girl—and many commentators logically assume that the newly delivered mother would have been sequestered during this time as well. In his book *Hittite Birth Rituals*, for example, noted Hittitologist Gary M. Beckman suggests that after the three- or four-month period of impurity, "*mother and child* would (re-)enter into normal relations with the *rest of their community*," and another well-known Hittitologist, Billie Jean Collins, likewise writes of the "*reentry into the community*" that took place "for *mother and child* after three months for a boy and four months for a girl" (emphases in both these quotes are mine).[49] In Greece too, a newly delivered mother's ritual pollution was registered after birth: first, a "general household pollution," which may have lasted five days after delivery, and then the more serious pollution of the mother herself, which may have extended for forty days.[50]

In none of these cultures, however, is there anywhere near as rich a body of evidence that indicates menstruating women were considered ritually impure. Regarding Mesopotamia: although a rather vast corpus of written materials, spanning over 2000 years, is available to us, scholars have been able to cite only a handful of texts that might speak to a Mesopotamian tradition of menstrual impurity[51]—and I stress "might," as the texts in this "handful" are often oblique. They include, for example, a Sumerian proverb that "hints," in the words of van der Toorn, that a menstruating woman is prohibited from engaging in the typically female task of bread making;[52] a Middle Assyrian (thirteenth century BCE) dictum forbidding "a [harem] woman . . . who should not be approached" from entering into the presence of the king at the time of sacrifices;[53] and *KAR* 300, rev. 6, which categorizes a man as impure for six days if he accidentally touches a passing woman who is "under taboo."[54] Note, however, that among these examples, the Sumerian proverb only "hints" at a

49. Beckman, *Hittite Birth Rituals*, 160; Collins, "Rites of Passage: Anatolia," 444. See also, on the Hittite text that specifies the duration of postpartum impurity, Bachvarova, "Hurro-Hittite Stories," 291, §§10–11; Beckman, *Hittite Birth Rituals*, text K, §§10–11 (pp. 134–37), §§28–29 (pp. 142–43); and Pringle, "Hittite Birth Rituals," 139.

50. Boedeker, "Family Matters," 241.

51. Van der Toorn, *Family Religion*, 129–30; van der Toorn, *From Her Cradle to Her Grave*, 51–52; van der Toorn, *Sin and Sanction*, 31.

52. Van der Toorn, *From Her Cradle to Her Grave*, 52, 52n9, and van der Toorn, *Sin and Sanction*, 31, 170n283, in both cases citing Jacobsen, "Notes on Selected Sayings," 457 (on l. 40).

53. Van der Toorn, *From Her Cradle to Her Grave*, 51, 51n7, and van der Toorn, *Sin and Sanction*, 31, 170n282, in both cases citing Weidner, "Hof- und Harems-Erlasse assyrischer Könige," 276 (text 7, line 47).

54. Van der Toorn, *Family Religion*, 129–30; van der Toorn, *Sin and Sanction*, 31, 170n281.

Mesopotamian tradition of menstrual taboo; indeed, the item that the proverb actually labels as "defiling"[55] or "unclean"[56] (*ú-zug$_x$*) is not a menstruating woman, nor in fact a woman of any sort, but "food"[57] or "bread"[58] (*ninda*), which the great Assyriologist Thorkild Jacobsen can only most hypothetically understand (note Jacobsen's reliance on parenthetical interpolations) as "bread (made by an) unclean (woman)."[59] Only by hypothesizing further, moreover, does the hypothetically "unclean (woman)" of this Sumerian proverb become unclean "during periods of menstruation," as Jacobsen would have it,[60] as opposed, say, to being rendered unclean through childbirth.

Somewhat similarly, even though the Middle Assyrian dictum regarding the "[harem] woman . . . who should not be approached" does specify a woman subject, it lacks language that explicitly indicates that the woman is unapproachable because of menstrual impurity. Equally inexplicit is the language of *KAR* 300, rev. 6, that categorizes a man as impure for six days if he accidentally touches a passing woman who is "under taboo." This is because the term used to describe the woman in question, *musukkatu*, "is a rather general term" that can refer to multiple manifestations of female impurity—for example, a woman's impurity postparturition or the impurity of a woman who had not washed after sexual intercourse[61]—as well as possibly, although not necessarily, a woman's menstrual impurity.[62] Moreover, a critical part of *KAR* 300, rev. 6, is reconstructed (the text reads, "[When a man] touches a passing *musukkatu*: for six days he [will] not [be pure]").[63] Thereby its significance is rendered even more unclear.

It is also unclear, at least to me, whether Marten Stol is right so emphatically to claim that it is "*undoubtedly* due to her menstrual period" (emphasis mine)

55. E. I. Gordon, *Sumerian Proverbs*, 60.

56. Jacobsen, "Notes on Selected Sayings," 457.

57. E. I. Gordon, *Sumerian Proverbs*, 60.

58. Jacobsen, "Notes on Selected Sayings," 457.

59. Jacobsen, "Notes on Selected Sayings," 457; cf. E. I. Gordon, *Sumerian Proverbs*, 60: "The translation of this proverb is very uncertain."

60. Jacobsen, "Notes on Selected Sayings," 457.

61. Van der Toorn, *Sin and Sanction*, 31.

62. This is how I, at least, would interpret the force of the "may" in the second half of this sentence from *CAD* 10:240, s.v. *musukku*: "The term *musukku* refers to a woman in the period after she has given birth . . . when she is in tabooed state until she has taken a ritual bath; it *may* also refer to a menstruating woman" (emphasis mine). Note similarly the tentativeness of *CAD* 20:248, s.v. *urruštu*: "filthy, unclean (menstruating?) woman."

63. Van der Toorn, *Sin and Sanction*, 170n281.

that a woman, according to Sumerian texts from the Ur III period,[64] could not work for six days per month,[65] although far more problematic is the expanded claim of Bertrand Lafont that in these same Ur III texts, "le nombre de journées mensuelles d'absence . . . etait . . . tenant sans doute compte du cycle menstruel, *avec les notions d' 'impurité' qui y étaient liées*" (emphasis mine).[66] It is problematic for Lafont to assume, for example, that notions of impurity are associated with menstruation in Sumer specifically or Mesopotamia more generally, given the lack, as noted above, of any definitive documentation concerning menstrual impurity elsewhere in Mesopotamian sources. Indeed, Lafont can cite as Mesopotamian parallels only an Old Babylonian text from Mari about a woman retiring "chez elle" for five to six days a month. Yet like the Ur III text in question, the Mari text, even as it may suggest a tradition of women withdrawing from public life during their menses, contains no explicit indication that a woman's *impurity* is the reason for that withdrawing. Likewise, in his recent study of letters from Mari, Jack M. Sasson writes that it is "debated" whether a fragmentary letter that speaks of a king's maidservant purifying herself does so because she has experienced a discharge of blood from her vagina. Moreover, even if the woman had been discharging vaginal blood, it is unclear whether the discharge was due to menstruation, or childbirth, or was an irregular discharge due to ill-health.[67]

The Hittite data regarding menstruation are also debated. According to Ada Taggar-Cohen, who has written a book on the Hittite priesthood, "In Hittite society . . . the menstrual state . . . rendered women ritually impure,"[68] but according to Collins, "There is no indication that the Hittites feared menstruation or imbued it with supernatural significance." "Nor," Collins goes on to say, "is there any evidence that they [the Hittites] required a complex set of purificatory rituals to cleanse the woman [after her menses] or anyone with whom she had had contact."[69] Somewhat similarly, in the case of Egypt, there is debate about attitudes regarding the menstruant. According to Gay Robins, "There is little mention of menstruation in surviving documentation"[70]—so

---

64. Waetzoldt, "Die Situation der Frauen und Kinder," 37.

65. Stol, "Women in Mesopotamia," 137.

66. Lafont, "À propos de l'absence cyclique des femmes"; see similarly Stol, "Private Life in Ancient Mesopotamia," 490, who describes women not only as "not hav[ing] to work" but also as "unclean" during their menstrual period.

67. Sasson, *From the Mari Archives*, 318.

68. Taggar-Cohen, "Why Are There No Israelite Priestesses?"

69. Collins, "Sin, Pollution, and Purity: Anatolia," 505.

70. Robins, *Women in Ancient Egypt*, 78.

little that both Annette Depla and Terry G. Wilfong have concluded, in separate studies, that there is no evidence of an Egyptian tradition regarding women's impurity during their menses.[71] Robins is not quite so doctrinaire,[72] but nevertheless, she can cite only one demotic text from the Late Period (ca. 715–332 BCE) that seems to allude to menstrual impurity. In it, a woman subject is said to refrain from purificatory acts that she normally undertook "at the time of my purification" because she had become pregnant, meaning, presumably, that this woman refrained from the rites she normally undertook to counteract the impurity incurred at the time of her menses because, due to her pregnancy, she was no longer menstruating.[73] Wilfong, however, has called into question even this one example (reading instead, "When the time of my menstruation arrived, I did not menstruate," without any reference to purification),[74] concluding that "an explicit interdiction against menstruating women does not appear in Egyptian texts until the Graeco-Roman period" (ca. 332 BCE–395 CE).[75]

Furthermore, while some scholars cite New Kingdom texts that date from ca. 1200 BCE and that come from the village of Deir el-Medina as pointing to an earlier Egyptian tradition of a menstrual taboo, according to which the village's laborers stayed away from their work if their wives or daughters were menstruating, it is not so clear that this set of records points to a general Egyptian tradition of menstrual impurity. For example, Jac. J. Janssen argues that the more logical reading of the Deir el-Medina data, and especially the texts' infrequent and irregular attestation of these wife- and daughter-related absences, suggests that the men's absence was due to impurity after their wives and/or daughters had given birth.[76] Alternatively, the Danish Egyptologist Paul John Frandsen has suggested that the concerns about women's menstruation in Deir el-Medina were directly linked to the specific work undertaken by the village's laborers, which was to build the royal tombs of Egypt's famous Valley of the Kings. More specifically, Frandsen theorizes that the royal tombs were "regarded as a uterus where the mysterious process of rebirth takes place," which was "on a par with the process that takes place inside women"; yet, for whatever reason, the Egyptians felt "the two forms of creation should be kept

---

71. Depla, "Women in Ancient Egyptian Wisdom Literature," 42; Wilfong, "Menstrual Synchrony and the 'Place of Women,'" 431.

72. See also Pinch, "Private Life in Ancient Egypt," 379.

73. Robins, *Women in Ancient Egypt*, 78.

74. Wilfong, "Menstrual Synchrony and the 'Place of Women,'" 422–23.

75. Wilfong, "Menstrual Synchrony and the 'Place of Women,'" 431.

76. J. J. Janssen, "Absence from Work by the Necropolis Workmen," 141–43.

strictly separate."[77] Menstruation, in other words, "was not . . . propitious for work at the tomb" in Frandsen's view,[78] but he cautions that we cannot extrapolate from this a wide scale Egyptian belief in menstrual impurity that would affect, say, women's ability to serve as priests and render temple service.[79]

In ancient Greece, similarly, "any strong fear of menstrual blood as a polluting force" in Greek tradition is lacking.[80] Rather, the notion of "purity from menstrual contamination . . . as a condition for entering a temple" appears only in historically late materials, and even then restrictions concerning menstruating women's access to sacred space are documented only in laws pertaining to non-Greek cults.[81] Conversely, in Israel, evidence suggesting a concern with women's menstrual impurity is widespread, manifest not only in the Priestly, or P, accounts of Lev 12:1–8 (see especially v. 2) and Lev 15:19–30 that I have previously cited, but also in the JE materials within the Pentateuch, in the Deuteronomistic History, and in the prophetic corpus. Within the Pentateuch's JE corpus, for example, the Genesis story of Rachel's theft of her father Laban's těrāpîm indicates that concerns regarding menstrual impurity were held not only by the P authors of Lev 12:2 and 15:19–30 but also by the nonpriestly author(s), redactor(s), and audience of this Genesis account, as it is only the conviction that menstrual discharges were both impure and potentially contaminating that can explain why, in the Gen 31:19–35 narrative, Laban refuses to approach Rachel and search her belongings for his missing těrāpîm once she has told him she is menstruating. Within Deuteronomistic tradition, 2 Sam 11:1–5 seems to put forward presumptions regarding menstrual impurity as well,[82] as the most logical interpretation of v. 4 of that text is to understand Bathsheba as "sanctifying" or "purifying" herself (hî' mitqadešet) from the impurity brought on by her menses,[83] given that shortly afterwards, she ovulates and becomes pregnant by David. Within prophetic and related literature, menstruation is treated as defiling or polluting in Isa 30:22 (although the Hebrew here is difficult and potentially corrupt); in Lam 1:8–9 and 17; and in Ezek 18:6;

77. Frandsen, "Menstrual 'Taboo' in Ancient Egypt," 103.

78. Frandsen, "Menstrual 'Taboo' in Ancient Egypt," 100.

79. See further the discussions of Graves-Brown, *Dancing for Hathor*, 55–56, and Wilfong, "Menstrual Synchrony and the 'Place of Women,'" 422–23.

80. R. Parker, *Miasma*, 101.

81. R. Parker, *Miasma*, 101–2, 353–54.

82. See, e.g., the discussions in McCarter, *I Samuel*, 286, and Wright, "David Autem Remansit in Hierusalem," 218, 218n10.

83. On this translation, see Olyan, *Rites and Rank*, 137n71, 146n29; also Wright, "David Autem Remansit in Hierusalem," 218n9.

22:10; and 36:17. All of this suggests, as van der Toorn writes, that "the train of thought" that lay behind an ideology of menstrual impurity "is deeply rooted in the Israelite experience."[84]

To overlay women's menstrual impurity atop their childbirth impurity, I conclude, may be a feature distinctive—albeit not necessarily unique—to Israelite religion (our data are too limited definitively to make a claim of uniqueness), with the effect being that Israelite women of childbearing age were much more often rendered impure than were others among their Levantine and ancient Near Eastern counterparts. As a result, Israelite women would have been much more restricted during their reproductive years in terms of their ability to enter cultic settings—and so serve as cultic servitors—than would women of reproductive age elsewhere in the ancient Levant and in the ancient Near East. We should note, moreover, that many of the female cultic servitors of Levantine and ancient Near Eastern communities that I have mentioned in my earlier comments were required to remain childless: the NIN.DINGIR priestess of Emar was taken into the storm god's service while still an unmarried woman resident in her father's house, for example, and throughout the Emar archives, "there is no indication that the NIN.DINGIR had a human husband."[85] Nor is there any mention at Emar "of any NIN.DINGIR's child."[86]

Somewhat similarly, in Mesopotamia during the Old Babylonian period and continuing into the first millennium BCE, it seems that the norm for a NIN.DINGIR/*entu* priestess was to have been childless. This is mandated, for example, in an Old Babylonian myth (the Epic of Atrahasis, tablet III, col. vii, lines 6–9) and presumed in a first-millennium BCE legend (the Birth Story of Sargon of Akkad, line 5),[87] and there are accordingly only occasional mentions of an *entu*'s offspring in Mesopotamian administrative and related documents.[88] Likewise, according again to Atrahasis, tablet III, col. vii, lines 6–9, the *ugbabtu* and *igiṣītu* were Mesopotamian women cult functionaries who were to

---

84. Van der Toorn, *From Her Cradle to Her Grave*, 53.

85. Fleming, *Installation of Baal's High Priestess at Emar*, 83.

86. Fleming, *Installation of Baal's High Priestess at Emar*, 83. The *maš'artu* priestess at Emar was, however, allowed to have children; see Fleming, *Installation of Baal's High Priestess at Emar*, 99.

87. For Atrahasis, see Jeyes, "The *Nadītu* Women of Sippar," 266, citing J. J. Finkelstein, "Review Article: On Some Recent Studies in Cuneiform Law," 246; on the Birth Story of Sargon, see Foster, "Birth Legend of Sargon of Akkad," 461, 461n2, but cf. Westenholz, *Legends of the Kings of Akkade*, 38–39, 38n2.

88. Fleming, *Installation of Baal's High Priestess at Emar*, 83, citing Renger, "Untersuchungen zum Priestertum in der altbabylonischen Zeit," 140–41.

remain childless. Mesopotamian *qadištu* women and *sekertu* women were also required to forgo marriage and procreation;[89] in addition, as we have seen, Mesopotamia's *nadītu* women could not have children, even if they, like the *nadītu* of Marduk in Babylon, were allowed to marry.[90] So too, it seems, were the "God's Wives of Amun" required to remain childless, at least by the Third Intermediate Period. As a consequence, all these women, in addition to coming from cultures (at least in the case of Mesopotamia and Egypt) where they were unconstrained by traditions of menstrual impurity, could not incur the impurity—and thus the impediment to cultic service—that their cultures (at least, again, in the case of Mesopotamia and Egypt) associated with childbirth.

The Phoenician priestess Amoashtart likewise could not incur whatever impurities Phoenician tradition might assume are associated with childbirth. Or at least Amoashtart could not incur childbirth impurities at the time when the one text we have about her (*KAI* 14) was written, given that it is the presumption of this inscription that she is a widow (her husband, the old king, had died, and her young son Eshmunazor had come to the throne). In this respect, it may be of note that the woman within Israelite tradition who most expressly acts as a religious functionary—Ma'acah, who commissions a cult image of the goddess Asherah and then has it placed, I have argued elsewhere, within the precincts of the Jerusalem temple[91]—is, like Amoashtart, a widow of a deceased king who served in the royal court as queen mother once her son and then grandson assumed the throne after her husband's death.[92] Can queen mothers, we might thus ask, take on roles as cultic agents, even in Israel, that are barred to other women: first, because they present no risk of introducing into the temple complex the pollution of parturition and, also, if we assume a fairly typical passing of the generations, because they present no risk of introducing the pollution of menstruation (as these queen mothers would generally have been of an age that would render them postmenopausal)?

One wonders likewise if the designation of the frame-drumming women of Ps 68:26(25) as *'ălāmôt*, "young maids," identifies them as young women who

89. Westenholz, "Religious Personnel: Mesopotamia," 294.

90. Harris, *Ancient Sippar*, 303, 317; Harris, "Hierodulen," 392; Harris, "Independent Women in Ancient Mesopotamia?," 151; Harris, "The *nadītu* Woman," 108; Jeyes, "The *Nadītu* Women of Sippar," 267; Stol, "Women in Mesopotamia," 139.

91. Ackerman, "The Queen Mother and the Cult in Ancient Israel," 390, reprinted in this volume at p. 159.

92. That Ma'acah served in the Jerusalem royal court in an official role as a queen mother, or *gĕbîrâ*, is indicated by the fact that her grandson Asa, angered by her having made a cult image of Asherah, removed her (*sûr*) from her position (see 1 Kgs 15:13; 2 Chr 15:16).

are prepubescent and so able to access Yahweh's *qōdeš*, or sanctuary space, in a way that might not have been possible for women who had reached puberty and so had begun to menstruate. Could it conversely be that women during their reproductive years—even when able to access spaces such as the Jerusalem temple compound—were kept at the compound's periphery: quartered within (outlying?) houses assigned to certain of the temple's cult functionaries, as in 2 Kgs 23:7, or restricted to the temple's gateway spaces, as in Ezek 8:14? Note similarly Exod 38:8, which stations women only at the *entrance* to the tent of meeting.

I offer these suggestions only tentatively, as our lack of evidence makes them quite speculative, and I freely admit there is a fair amount of speculation entailed more generally in my remarks here. Nevertheless, it does seem clear that unlike the ancient Israelites, many ancient Near Eastern communities did admit the possibility that women could serve as priests. While I can think of potential reasons for this other than what I have suggested here—for example, did predominantly urban civilizations offer women possibilities for cultic service that predominantly rural cultures like Israel did not?—the stress on childlessness as a common attribute of many women's priesthoods in the ancient Near Eastern sphere suggests to me that ancient Near Eastern cultures shared generally a sense that the impurity of parturition had to be avoided if women were to function as cultic servitors. Conversely, the fact that other ancient Levantine and Near Eastern cultures seem—and I stress the "seem"—not to have associated menstruation as strongly with impurity as did Israel may have given nonchildbearing women elsewhere in the ancient Near East access to cultic spaces and so access to cultic service during their reproductive years that was precluded for their Israelite counterparts.

PART 3

Queen Mothers

❧

CHAPTER 7

The Queen Mother and the Cult in Ancient Israel

❧

In the previous chapter, "Priestesses, Purity, and Parturition," I outlined the preeminent reason that (in my opinion) precluded women from serving as priestesses in ancient Israel: namely, the Israelite conviction that during their reproductive years, women were rendered impure relatively frequently, both during their menses and after parturition, and during these periods of impurity, they, like all persons who were impure, were excluded from cultic settings—and consequently from any possibility of serving in these settings as priestesses or as any other sort of religious functionary. Nevertheless, I argued at the very end of that chapter that Israelite women who were prepubescent or postmenopausal, and so not subject to regulations of menstrual and childbirth impurity, might have had opportunities to act as cultic servitors in the Israelite cult in ways that women of reproductive age did not. In particular, I mentioned the queen mother Ma'acah and the fact that she was both a widow and, arguably, postmenopausal and proposed that this could have facilitated her ability to commission a cult image of Asherah, the great mother goddess of Canaanite tradition, and have it placed, as "I have argued elsewhere," within the precincts of the Jerusalem temple.

The "elsewhere" is the chapter that follows. In it, I propose not only that Ma'acah placed her Asherah image within the precincts of the Jerusalem temple but that queen mothers like Ma'acah—which is to say, the queen mothers in the Judean royal court throughout the preexilic period—devoted themselves to the goddess Asherah as part of their official duties. Indeed, in this chapter I suggest that Judean queen mothers' devotion to Asherah was primary among their official duties and that other responsibilities they

An earlier version of this chapter appeared in *JBL* 112 (1993): 385–401. Used here by permission of the Society of Biblical Literature.

assumed within the royal court—for example, helping determine the royal
succession—stemmed from their role as Asherah devotees.

    This conclusion, which I first published in 1993, subsequently stimulated
me to think further about queen mothers elsewhere in the ancient Near East.
Thus, following immediately after this chapter is a companion chapter, "The
Queen Mother and the Cult in the Ancient Near East." This second chapter,
it is worth noting, was, like its companion, originally published in the mid-
1990s, or some fifteen to twenty years prior to the 2012 essay "Priestesses,
Purity, and Parturition" from which I quoted above and in which I returned,
at least briefly, to the topic of queen mothers as religious functionaries. Not
surprisingly, my thinking about queen mothers matured during those fifteen
to twenty years, and although I remain convinced regarding my central thesis
regarding queen mothers' religious roles, I have revised and refined some
of my arguments in both the "queen mother" chapters that follow to reflect
developments in my understanding. It is a pleasure to have the opportunity
to present these updated analyses here.

1. By Way of Background:
Previous Discussions of the Ancient Israelite Queen Mother

In the 1991 issue of the *Journal of Biblical Literature*,[1] Zafira Ben-Barak published an article on the status and rights of the *gĕbîrâ*, or queen mother, in
ancient Israel.[2] In it, Ben-Barak argued that the *gĕbîrâ* was not an official functionary within the Israelite or Judean monarchy; that is, the *gĕbîrâ* did not lay
claim to privilege in either the Northern or Southern royal court by virtue
of an institutionalized position. To be sure, Ben-Barak noted that there were
gĕbîrôt, or queen mothers, who, according to the Hebrew Bible, did rise to
places of prominence and influence during their sons' reigns, but she suggested
this was effected only by a few authoritative and powerful women through
the force of their own personalities. Such authoritative and powerful women

    1. Ben-Barak, "Status and Right of the *Gĕbîrâ*," 23–34; see also Ben-Barak's earlier article,
"Queen Consort and the Struggle for Succession," 33–40.
    2. The term *gĕbîrâ/gĕberet* is used fifteen times in the Hebrew Bible. In Gen 16:4, 8, and
9, it means "mistress" (describing Sarah's relationship with Hagar), and this translation is
also required in 2 Kgs 5:3; Isa 24:2; 47:5, 7; Ps 123:2; and Prov 30:23. In 1 Kgs 11:19, *gĕbîrâ*
should be translated "queen," referring to the wife of the Egyptian pharaoh. Elsewhere in
Kings, and also in Jeremiah and Chronicles (1 Kgs 15:13; 2 Kgs 10:13; Jer 13:18; 29:2; 2 Chr
15:16), the term means "queen mother."

included, in particular, queen mothers who exerted themselves in the matter of succession upon the death of their husbands, typically by promoting a younger son as heir to his father's throne in defiance of the generally acknowledged claim of the firstborn (or the oldest surviving son if the eldest had died or become unable to rule). Bathsheba, in advocating Solomon's claim to kingship over that of Adonijah at the time of the death of her husband David, is the paradigmatic exemplar of the *gĕbîrâ* who helped engineer the succession of a younger son (1 Kgs 1:5–40); elsewhere in the Hebrew Bible, Ben-Barak cites Maʿacah, the queen mother of Abijam/Abijah (a younger son according to 2 Chr 11:18–23);[3] Hamutal, the queen mother of Jehoahaz (the younger brother of Jehoiakim according to the date formulae found in 2 Kgs 23:31, 36); and Nehushta, the queen mother of Jehoiachin (the younger brother of Zedekiah according to 2 Chr 36:9–11; but cf. 2 Kgs 24:17, where Jehoiachin is identified as Zedekiah's nephew). Further afield, Ben-Barak notes examples of the same phenomenon from Ugarit, from the Hittite Empire, from Assyria, from Yʾdy (Yaʾdiya?) Šamʾal, from Babylon, and from Persia. Ben-Barak stresses that in all these examples, there was no official role for the queen mother in the standard succession to the throne. It was only ambitious *gĕbîrôt*—those who sought the highest office in the land for their sons—who used their influence to determine their husbands' heirs.

In advancing this thesis that the *gĕbîrâ* in the Hebrew Bible had no official position, Ben-Barak was arguing, albeit not explicitly, against a somewhat earlier article on the queen mother, published by Niels-Erik A. Andreasen in 1983 in the *Catholic Biblical Quarterly*.[4] In that article, Andreasen quickly rejects the argument that the queen mother had no institutionalized status. He writes instead that "it soon becomes obvious from the text that the queen mother was not merely treated with deference by the monarch, but that she held a significant official position superseded only by that of the king himself."[5] Andreasen describes this official position as that of "lady counsellor," with counsel being sought especially in regard to the royal succession and also, at least in the case of Bathsheba, in matters judicial and in mediations between political factions (1 Kgs 2:13–25). Andreasen, along with many other commentators,[6] sees the roots of this institutionalized role for the queen mother in second-millennium

---

3. The variant names Abijam and Abijah are most probably the result of textual confusion; see Noth, *Die israelitischen Personennamen*, 234 (no. 117).

4. Andreasen, "Role of the Queen Mother," 179–94.

5. Andreasen, "Role of the Queen Mother," 180.

6. Donner, "Art und Herkunft," 105–45; Molin, "Die Stellung der Gᵉbira im Staate Juda," 161–75; de Vaux, *Ancient Israel*, 118.

BCE Hittite culture, where the queen mother or *tawananna* had significant responsibilities within the social and political affairs of the king's court.

The Hittite *tawananna*, moreover, had responsibilities within the cultic life of Hittite society. Indeed, Shoshana R. Bin-Nun, in a comprehensive study of the *tawananna*, has argued that in the earliest periods of the Hittite Old Kingdom (ca. 1650–1500 BCE), and in pre-Hittite Anatolia as well, the title *tawananna* referred *exclusively* to a religious functionary. Only secondarily, she suggests, in the period of the Hittite Empire (ca. 1400–1180 BCE), does the *tawananna* assume responsibilities within Hittite social, political, and economic spheres. Yet even then, her cultic obligations persist.[7] Despite, however, this primacy of religious function in the duties of the Hittite queen mother, Andreasen argues that when the office was borrowed into Israel, the cultic role of the *gĕbîrâ* was eliminated.[8] On this point, then, Andreasen is in agreement with Ben-Barak, as both of them suggest that there was no official position for the queen mother within institutionalized Israelite religion.

In fact, as Andreasen points out, only a few scholars have advanced arguments supporting an official role for the Israelite queen mother in the religious sphere. In 1970, Samuel Terrien proposed that the queen mother was a functionary within a constellation of religious beliefs and practices—the Jerusalem temple as the *omphalos mundi*, or the "navel" of the world; serpent worship; chthonian divination; a solar cult; and male prostitution involving homosexual and bisexual intercourse—all of which played a role "in the mystical or sacramental aspect of the principle of monarchic succession."[9] But Terrien has found little support for his reconstructions among historians of Israelite religion. The notion of cultic prostitution in Israel and throughout the ancient Near East, whether male or female, has been widely discredited,[10] for

---

7. Bin-Nun, *Tawananna*, 34–50, 107–59.

8. Clearly, we cannot speak of direct borrowing, given the time gap between the fall of the Hittite Empire and the rise of the Israelite monarchy. Still, Herbert Donner has argued that the political structures of second-millennium BCE Hittite society survived in first-millennium BCE Syria and Canaan and from there came to influence the Israelite monarchy in Jerusalem. See Donner, "Art und Herkunft," 123–30; also Andreasen, "Role of the Queen Mother," 181; Naʿaman, "Queen Mothers and Ancestors Cult," 484–86.

9. Terrien, "Omphalos Myth," 331.

10. A pioneering study was published in 1973 by Arnaud, "La prostitution sacrée en Mésopotamie," 111–15. Key foundational studies that followed include Barstad, *Religious Polemics of Amos*, 21–34; Bird, "'To Play the Harlot,'" 85–89; E. J. Fisher, "Cultic Prostitution?," 225–36; Frevel, *Aschera und der Ausschliesslichkeitsanspruch YHWHs*, 2:629–737; Frymer-Kensky, *In the Wake of the Goddesses*, 199–202; Oden, *Bible without Theology*, 131–53; Westenholz, "Tamar, *Qĕdēšā, Qadištu*," 245–65; and U. Winter, *Frau und Göttin*, 334–42.

example, and fully developed solar worship such as Terrien describes seems to have come to Israelite religion only relatively late and from the east: in the eighth and seventh centuries BCE, through increasing Aramaean and even Assyrian influence.[11] Also garnering only minimal scholarly support today is the 1963 proposal of Gösta W. Ahlström, who suggested that the cultic responsibility of the queen mother in ancient Israelite religion was to play the role of the bride in the *hieros gamos*, or sacred marriage, engaged in by the king and some female religious functionary who represented a goddess and who, through her sexual union with the king, somehow secured divine blessings for him and his domain.[12] Currently, however, few historians of religion endorse any reconstruction involving a *hieros gamos* in Israel, and any who do cannot agree with Ahlström's contention that the queen mother (and not the queen or some cultic servitor) functioned as the king's ritual consort.[13]

Still, despite the failure of Terrien and Ahlström to articulate a convincing role for the queen mother in Israelite religion and also despite the conclusions of Ben-Barak and Andreasen that the *gĕbîrâ* had no official cultic function, I believe that the issue is far from settled. Moreover, I propose that the time is ripe to consider the question of the queen mother and the cult anew. The time is ripe because our understanding of what comprised cult in ancient Israel has changed considerably in the last decades. Since the late 1970s, that is, there have been multiple attempts to redefine the nature of Israelite religion in the light of both new archaeological discoveries and more nuanced exegeses of the biblical text. What we have learned from these numerous redefinitions is that the ancient cult allowed a far greater latitude in religious beliefs and practices than the exilic and postexilic editors of the biblical text would admit. We have thus come to doubt the rather homogeneous picture presented by the biblical writers of Israelite religion. Instead, we have increasingly broadened our parameters in describing what the Israelite cult encompassed. In this chapter, I propose to seek evidence amid these broadened parameters that suggests that the queen mother did play some role in Israelite religion.

To be sure, the data that will guide this exploration are sparse, since the male-dominated culture that gave us the Bible, still our primary piece of evidence concerning the Israelite cult, tended not to include significant information concerning women's religious activities. Those female acts of devotion that are described, moreover, are more often than not denigrated (women's

---

11. See Cogan, *Imperialism and Religion*, 84–87.
12. Ahlström, *Aspects of Syncretism*, 57–88.
13. See the criticisms of Andreasen, "Role of the Queen Mother," 182.

worship of the Queen of Heaven in Jer 7 and 44, for example, or their wailing over Tammuz in Ezek 8). Comparative evidence from elsewhere in the ancient Near East, while essential, cannot truly compensate for this deficit in the biblical text, as the comparative material also typically stems from patriarchal societies that overlooked or devalued women's cult activities. From the start, then, I must admit that the reconstruction offered here is speculative. Still, while caution is advisable, I do hope to demonstrate that the queen mother did have an official responsibility in Israelite religion: it was to devote herself to the cult of the mother goddess Asherah within the king's court. I will also suggest that this cultic role was primary among other obligations required of the *gĕbîrâ*. Ultimately, I conclude, with Andreasen and against Ben-Barak, that the queen mother did have sociopolitical responsibilities in ancient Israel, particularly with regard to succession upon the old king's death. But unlike Andreasen, I believe that these sociopolitical functions cannot be divorced from a cultic role. In fact, I will propose that the queen mother's devotions to Asherah stand behind and are fundamental to the role accorded her in matters of succession.

II. Queen Mothers and the Cult of Asherah

The biblical text that most explicitly links an Israelite *gĕbîrâ* with the worship of Asherah (or with a cultic activity of any sort) is 1 Kgs 15:2, 9–13. This text (along with its parallel found in 2 Chr 11:20–22; 15:16) describes the activities of Ma'acah, the queen mother of a king called Abijam (in Kings) or Abijah (in Chronicles),[14] who ruled for three years in Jerusalem (r. 915–913 BCE). Subsequently, Ma'acah served as queen mother for her grandson Asa, who had a forty-one year reign (r. 913–873 BCE). This very fact—that Ma'acah was able to continue to serve Asa as queen mother after her son Abijam/Abijah had died—indicates that, at a minimum, Ma'acah commanded a semi-independent position in the Jerusalem court that was not exclusively dependent on her maternal relationship with her son, the king. Indeed, the fact that Ma'acah was able somehow to claim the title of *gĕbîrâ* in Asa's court, instead of the title going to Asa's actual mother, suggests Ma'acah held a position of some power. To be sure, Ma'acah may have been aided by other factors in claiming the title of *gĕbîrâ* in Asa's royal court: perhaps, for example, Asa's mother suffered a premature death. Nevertheless, Ma'acah's ability to retain the position of queen

14. Above, n. 3.

mother after her own son had died suggests she commanded at least some degree of authority independent of the authority she derived by virtue of her relationship to her son, thereby anticipating my conclusion that the queen mother did have an institutionalized position in the ancient Israelite monarchy.

Still, the authority of Ma'acah as queen mother is not completely independent, as can be seen in 1 Kgs 15:13 and 2 Chr 15:16, which describe how Asa becomes angry at Ma'acah and removes her from the office of queen mother—although the very fact that Ma'acah can be deposed (*sûr*) as *gĕbîrâ* again anticipates my conclusion that the queen mother did hold some sort of official position within the court. The act that angers Asa is that Ma'acah has made what is called in 1 Kgs 15:13 a *mipleset lā'ăšērâ*,[15] to be translated either "an abominable image for Asherah/*'ăšērâ* [the goddess]" or "an abominable image of the asherah/*'ăšērâ* [the stylized tree that symbolized the goddess Asherah in the cult]."[16] The former translation, "an abominable image for Asherah/ *'ăšērâ* [the goddess]," is in my mind preferable. The definite article prefixed to *'ăšērâ* need not preclude our understanding of *'ăšērâ* as a proper name since it is easily explained as appellative, as elsewhere in Deuteronomistic prose (Judg 2:11, 13; 3:7; 10:6). The interpretation of 1 Kgs 15:13 put forward in 2 Chr 15:16, moreover, certainly understands *'ăšērâ* to be a proper name, given that the Chronicles text transposes *mipleset* and *'ăšērâ* (*'āśĕtâ la'ăšērâ mipleset*), leaving us no option but to translate "she [Ma'acah] made for Asherah/*'ăšērâ* [the goddess] an abominable image."[17] In addition, the alternate translation of the Kings text, "she made an abominable image of the asherah/*'ăšērâ* [the stylized cult symbol]" borders on the nonsensical: what does it mean, after all, to make an image of an image? Indeed, elsewhere in Deuteronomistic prose when *'ăšērâ*, the image, is referred to, the noun *'ăšērâ* stands alone without *mipleset* or similar modifier: see, for example, 1 Kgs 16:33, *wayyaʿaś 'aḥ'āb 'et-hā'ăšērâ*, "and Ahab made the asherah/*'ăšērâ*." (Note the similar use of

15. The noun *mipleset*, which occurs only in 1 Kgs 15:13 and in the Chronicles parallel, derives from the verb *plṣ*, "to shudder." Presumably it means "a thing to be shuddered at," "a horrid thing," or, as here, "an abominable image."

16. I take the biblical tradition to be emphatic in its understanding of the *'ăšērâ* as a stylized wooden tree. Deuteronomy 16:21 speaks of "planting" (*nāṭaʿ*) the *'ăšērâ*; elsewhere in the Bible (e.g., 1 Kgs 14:15, 23; 16:33; 2 Kgs 17:10, 16; 21:3; 2 Chr 33:3), the *'ăšērâ* cult object is "made" (*'āśâ*), "built" (*bānâ*), "stood up" (*'āmad*), or "erected" (*hiṣṣîb*). If destroyed, the *'ăšērâ* is "burned" (*bîʿēr* or *śārap*), "cut down" (*kārat*), "hewn down" (*gādaʿ*), "uprooted" (*nātaš*), or "broken" (*šibbēr*). As indicated here, I also, along with most commentators, presume the *'ăšērâ* cult object represented the goddess Asherah and so was called by her name. See further below, n. 19.

17. The LXX of 2 Chr 15:16 reads *tē Astartē* for MT *lā'ăšērâ*. The MT is clearly primitive.

the verb 'ŝh, "to make," in both this passage and 1 Kgs 15:13 while contrasting the treatment of 'ăŝērâ as the verb's object.)[18] Ma'acah, the queen mother, I conclude, is described in 1 Kgs 15:13 as worshipping the goddess Asherah by making a cult image or cult statue dedicated to her.[19]

Asa, who deposes Ma'acah, clearly does not see her action as one that is religiously appropriate, and the biblical authors agree, lauding Asa as one who was "faithful to Yahweh all his days" (1 Kgs 15:14). Many modern commentators have also assumed that Ma'acah's worship of Asherah was heterodox, arguing that it was an alien element introduced by her from Canaanite culture and into the Jerusalem cult.[20] The primary piece of evidence supporting this claim is Ma'acah's presumed foreign ancestry, since elsewhere in the Hebrew Bible the personal name ma'ăkâ does appear as the name of a non-Israelite: Ma'acah, the daughter of King Talmai of Geshur and mother of Absalom (2 Sam 3:3 and 1 Chr 3:2). This Ma'acah of Geshur, moreover, is apparently the grandmother of the Ma'acah of 1 Kgs 15:13, who is identified in 1 Kgs 15:2 and 2 Chr 11:20–22 as the daughter of Absalom.

Ma'acah's foreign heritage, however, need not predicate the conclusion that the Asherah cult Ma'acah promoted was foreign; nor does the fact that King Asa regarded Ma'acah's worship as heterodox necessarily imply such. Rather, certain biblical and archaeological evidence suggests Asa's opinion was not normative in Judah. A case can instead be made that Asherah worship was

18. I understand 2 Kgs 21:7, pesel hā'ăŝērâ, in the same way I have analyzed 1 Kgs 15:13 and thus would translate "an image of Asherah."

19. To be sure, to argue about translating "asherah/'ăŝērâ [the cult symbol]" or "Asherah/'ăŝērâ [the goddess]" is, in a certain sense, to quibble over semantics. As I have suggested above in n. 16, most practitioners of ancient Israelite religion would have interpreted the 'ăŝērâ cult object as something that is a symbol of the goddess Asherah/'ăŝērâ and is in effect synonymous with her. One has only to compare the ancient Israelite understanding of the ark, Yahweh's primary symbol in the Jerusalem temple and in texts that purport to describe the premonarchic period, to see how close the relationship was in Israelite religion between cult object and deity. Numbers 10:35–36, the so-called "Song of the Ark," illustrates perfectly the simultaneity of symbol and god in Israelite imagination: "Whenever *the ark* set out, Moses said, 'Arise, O Yahweh'"; similarly, "when *it* [the ark] rested, he [Moses] said, 'Return, O Yahweh'" (emphasis mine). We would likewise expect that the 'ăŝērâ, the cult symbol, and Asherah/'ăŝērâ, the goddess, were understood by the ancient Israelites as one and the same.

20. See Spanier, "Queen Mother in the Judaean Royal Court," 186–95; also, Ahlström, *Aspects of Syncretism*, 59, 61, who cites Albright, *Archaeology and the Religion of Israel*, 157–59, and Yeivin, "Social, Religious, and Cultural Trends in Judaism," 162–64. See too the remarks of Ackroyd, "Goddesses, Women, and Jezebel," 255, although note that Ackroyd does not agree with the conclusions of Ahlström, Albright, Spanier, and Yeivin.

customary among the populace. Saul M. Olyan has even argued that the worship of Asherah may have been part of the normative Jerusalem cult; Asherah may have been worshipped, that is, along with Yahweh in official Judahite and Jerusalemite religion.[21] Note in this regard that Maʿacah's image devoted to Asherah stood in all likelihood in Yahweh's temple in Jerusalem, as the Jerusalem temple is at least the logical place for a member of the royal family to erect a cult statue: first, for reasons of proximity, as temple and palace stood side by side in Jerusalem, and second, because the temple essentially functioned as the private chapel for the monarch. Kings of the Southern Kingdom of Judah were even considered to be the titular heads of the Jerusalem temple, reserving for themselves the right to appoint temple personnel and to determine the temple's appropriate furnishings,[22] and other members of the royal court—including queen mothers—likely exerted themselves as well in matters concerning cult officials and cult paraphernalia.[23] It follows that when Maʿacah dedicated her cult statue to Asherah, she would have erected it in the Jerusalem temple.

Moreover, we would be wrong were we to assume that Maʿacah's worship of Asherah in Yahweh's temple was an anomaly, eliminated when Asa destroyed the cult statue that Maʿacah had made. Rather, by all indications Maʿacah's cult statue of Asherah was replaced in the Jerusalem temple after Asa's reforms. Such is at least suggested by 2 Kgs 18:4, in which Hezekiah removes an *ʾăšērâ* from Jerusalem as part of his own reforms; this *ʾăšērâ*, like Maʿacah's and for the same reasons, presumably stood in Yahweh's temple. The biblical text is indeed explicit that a third *ʾăšērâ*, the one that replaced the statue Hezekiah destroyed, stood in the Jerusalem temple. Thus 2 Kgs 21:7 describes how Manasseh erected an *ʾăšērâ* in Yahweh's temple in Jerusalem. This *ʾăšērâ* stood there until destroyed by yet another reformer, Josiah (2 Kgs 23:6). Josiah also removed from the Jerusalem temple the vessels made for Asherah as part of her offerings cult (2 Kgs 23:4) and tore down the structures within the temple compound where women wove garments to be draped as clothing over Asherah's cult statue (2 Kgs 23:7).

21. Olyan, *Asherah and the Cult of Yahweh*, 9.

22. David, for example, appoints the two high priests Zadok and Abiathar, who minister to the ark in Jerusalem. See further Cross, *Canaanite Myth and Hebrew Epic*, 208, 215n74, 232. First Kings 2:26–27, which describes Solomon's expulsion of Abiathar from the Jerusalem priesthood, also attests to the king's right to appoint, or in this case depose, temple personnel. See in addition my discussion just following regarding Kings Hezekiah's, Manasseh's, and Josiah's acts regarding the temple's cult furnishings.

23. I have discussed this more thoroughly in Ackerman, "The Queen Mother and the Cult in the Ancient Near East," 194–95, reprinted in this volume at pp. 183–84.

These multiple texts suggest that it was the norm in the Southern Kingdom in the ninth, eighth, and seventh centuries BCE to worship both Yahweh and Asherah in the state temple in Jerusalem. The zeal of the reformer kings, Asa, Hezekiah, and Josiah, to remove the Asherah cult was the exception. This conclusion is supported by archaeological evidence—namely, by the much discussed eighth-century BCE inscription from Khirbet el-Qôm, some ten km east-southeast of Lachish.[24] While this inscription has proven difficult to read, commentators do agree that we find paired in it, from a Judahite provenance, the cult of Yahweh and some allusion to the cult of Asherah.[25] The most satisfying attempt at translation is Patrick D. Miller's:

24. The editio princeps was by Dever, "Iron Age Epigraphic Material from the Area of Khirbet el-Kôm," 158–89. The inscription was restudied by Lemaire, "Date et origine des inscriptiones hébraïques et pheniciennes de Kuntillet 'Ajrud," 131–43; Lemaire, "Les inscriptions de Khirbet el-Qôm," 597–608; and Lemaire, "Who or What Was Yahweh's Asherah?," 42–51. In his reassessment, Lemaire proposed reading a reference to Asherah in the second and third lines of the el-Qôm text—a reading Dever subsequently came to accept: see Dever, "Asherah, Consort of Yahweh?," 22; less completely, Dever, "Material Remains and the Cult," 570, 583n17; Dever, "Recent Archaeological Confirmation of the Cult of Asherah," 40. Other studies of the el-Qôm material include Hadley, "Khirbet el-Qom Inscription" 50–62; Jaroš, "Zur Inschrift Nr. 3 von Ḥirbet el-Qôm," 31–40; Margalit, "Some Observations on the Inscription and Drawing from Khirbet el-Qôm," 371–78; Miller, "Psalms and Inscriptions," 311–32; Mittman, "Die Grabinschrift des Sängers Uriahu," 139–52; Naveh, "Graffiti and Dedications," 27–30; O'Connor, "Poetic Inscription from Khirbet el-Qôm," 224–29; Olyan, *Asherah and the Cult of Yahweh*, 23–25; and Zevit, "Khirbet el-Qôm Inscription," 39–47.

25. There have been four main proposals on how to understand the crucial reading 'šrt at Khirbet el-Qôm and also in the closely related inscriptions from Kuntillet 'Ajrûd. The first, to understand 'šrt as "shrine," cognate with Phoenician 'šrt, Aramaic 'trt', and Akkadian aširtu, as proposed by Lipiński, "The Goddess Aṭirat," 101–19, is unviable; see particularly Emerton, "New Light on Israelite Religion," 2–20, who points out that 'ăšērâ never means "shrine" in the Hebrew of the Bible and thus should not have such a meaning in the Hebrew epigraphic corpus. Emerton and others discuss instead two options: (1) to read 'šrt as "asherah," i.e., the cult object sacred to the goddess Asherah, or (2) to read 'šrt as "Asherah," the divine name. P. Kyle McCarter, "Aspects of the Religion of the Israelite Monarchy," 149, and Patrick D. Miller, "Absence of the Goddess," 246, have further suggested that 'šrt should be understood as a hypostatized aspect of the female side of Yahweh. To choose between these options, while an important task for those concerned with the morphology of the el-Qôm and 'Ajrûd inscriptions, need not overly concern us here. For the historian of religion, the attempt to differentiate between asherah, a sacred symbol, Asherah, the goddess, or Asherah, a female hypostasis of Yahweh, is again, as in n. 19, to quibble over semantics. In the ancient Israelite imagination, the cult symbol of the goddess or a female hypostasis would have been perceived as Asherah herself.

brk 'ryhw lyhwh
wmṣryh l'šrth hwš' lh

Blessed is Uriyahu by Yahweh;
Yea from his adversaries by his asherah he has saved him.[26]

Despite Asa's censure, then, we cannot conclude that the *gĕbîrâ* Ma'acah introduced a foreign cult into the Jerusalem court. Nor, I would argue, should Jezebel, another queen mother who is often regarded by commentators as introducing a foreign cult of Asherah into Israel, be so accused. Instead, I suggest that she, like Ma'acah, worshipped Asherah while *gĕbîrâ* as part of the state cult of the Northern Kingdom.

Here, however, the data are somewhat ambiguous: first because we tend to think of Jezebel only as queen, the wife of Ahab, rather than assigning to her the title of queen mother. But in fact, in 2 Kgs 10:13, she is labeled *gĕbîrâ* after Ahab's death by relatives of King Ahaziah of Judah. At a minimum, then, Jezebel filled the role of *gĕbîrâ* in the minds of the editors who included 2 Kgs 10:13 in the biblical text. If, moreover, 2 Kgs 10:13 is historically reliable, she was considered *gĕbîrâ* by members of the Southern royal family.

Whether though Jezebel as queen mother devoted herself to the cult of Asherah as Ma'acah did is a second ambiguity. Indeed, scholars disagree on whether Jezebel, even when queen, worshipped Asherah in addition to her well-attested allegiance to Baal. The crux of the matter is 1 Kgs 18:19, where Elijah summons to his contest on Mount Carmel the "four hundred and fifty prophets of Baal and the four hundred prophets of Asherah who eat at Jezebel's table." This text seemingly does associate Jezebel with the cult of Asherah; however, subsequent to this passage, the four hundred prophets of Asherah do not again appear, at least in the Masoretic tradition. They do appear in v. 22 of the LXX, but as several commentators have noted, the phrase *hoi prophētai tou alsous* is marked by an asterisk in Origen's Hexapla,[27] indicating a secondary addition in the Greek.[28]

But this evidence simply means that *nĕbî'ê hā'ăšērâ*, "the prophets of Asherah," in 1 Kgs 18:19 is most probably a gloss; it need not mean that Queen Jeze-

---

26. Miller, "Psalms and Inscriptions," 317.

27. The Greek text almost always renders Hebrew *'ăšērâ* as *alsos*, "grove," evidence that supports an understanding of the *'ăšērâ* or cult symbol as a stylized tree (above, n. 16).

28. Day, "Asherah in the Hebrew Bible," 400–401; Emerton, "New Light on Israelite Religion," 16; Lipiński, "The Goddess Aṭirat," 114; these references are pointed out by Olyan, *Asherah and the Cult of Yahweh*, 8n24.

bel did not worship the goddess Asherah. Certainly there were opportunities in Samaria for her to do so. As I have already noted, 1 Kgs 16:33 reports that Ahab erected an *'ăšērâ* in Samaria. Moreover, since 1 Kgs 16:33 occurs at the beginning of the long cycle of narratives concerning Ahab, we can presume that he erected the *'ăšērâ* early in his reign. There was, that is, an Asherah cult of some sort in Samaria during the bulk of Ahab's monarchy, and the king participated in it. Jezebel as Ahab's wife may well have also participated in it as part of her obligations of marriage.

The inscriptional evidence from Kuntillet ʿAjrûd in the eastern Sinai, fifty km south of Kadesh Barnea, also locates a cult of Asherah roughly contemporaneous with Ahab's reign in Samaria (Ahab reigned from ca. 869–850 BCE; the inscriptions date from the beginning of the eighth century BCE).[29] An Asherah cult in the Northern capital is at least strongly implied by the inclusion of the geographical name Samaria in one of the inscriptions found on the site: *brkt 'tkm lyhwh šmrn wl'šrth*, "I bless you by Yahweh of Samaria and by his Asherah/asherah."[30] This inscription, so like the Khirbet el-Qôm material, has also suggested to many that, at least among certain religious circles in Samaria, the cult of Yahweh and the cult of Asherah were paired. This pairing is also suggested by three other inscriptions found at Kuntillet ʿAjrûd: *lyhwh*

29. The bibliography is vast. Key references include the 2012 publication volume, Meshel, *Kuntillet ʿAjrud*, as well as Becking, ed., *Only One God?*; Dever, "Asherah, Consort of Yahweh?," 21–37; Dever, *Did God Have a Wife?*, 160–67, 197–208; Dever, "Recent Archaeological Confirmation of the Cult of Asherah," 37–43; Emerton, "New Light on Israelite Religion," 2–20; Freedman, "Yahweh of Samaria and His Asherah," 241–49; Hadley, *Cult of Asherah*; Lemaire, "Date et origine des inscriptiones hébraiques et pheniciennes de Kuntillet ʿAjrud," 131–43; Lemaire, "Who or What Was Yahweh's Asherah?," 42–51; Lipiński, "The Goddess Aṭirat," 101–19; McCarter, "Aspects of the Religion of the Israelite Monarchy," 137–49; Miller, "Absence of the Goddess," 239–49; Olyan, *Asherah and the Cult of Yahweh*, 25–37; Smith, *Early History of God*, 118–25; and Weinfeld, "Kuntillet ʿAjrud Inscriptions," 121–30.

30. In the original announcements of the ʿAjrûd materials, the excavator, Zeʾev Meshel, understood *yhwh šmrn* as "Yahweh our guardian" (*šōmĕrēnû*); see Meshel, "Kuntillet ʿAjrûd—An Israelite Religious Center," 50–54; Meshel, "Kuntillet ʿAjrûd—An Israelite Site," 118–24; and Meshel, *Kuntillet ʿAjrûd: A Religious Center*. But in 1979, Mordechai Gilula, "To Yahweh Shomron," 129–37, proposed reading instead "Yahweh of Samaria" (*šōmĕrōn*), and almost all commentators, including ultimately Meshel, now prefer this translation (see Meshel, "Did Yahweh Have a Consort?," 31; Aḥituv, Eshel, and Meshel, "The Inscriptions," 86–91). As Emerton, "New Light on Israelite Religion," 3, points out, three other ʿAjrûd inscriptions reading *yhwh tmn* (below, n. 31), which can only be translated "Yahweh of Teman," or "Yahweh of the South," give credence to the translation "Yahweh of Samaria." Emerton also assembles other evidence suggesting that our traditional understanding of Hebrew grammar, which would not permit proper names such as Yahweh to serve as the *nomen regens* in a construct phrase, is flawed.

htmn wl'šrth, "to/by Yahweh of Teman and by his Asherah/asherah" (a phrase found in two different inscriptions) and *brktk lyhwh tmn wl'šrth ybrk wyšmrk wyhy 'm 'dny*, "I bless you by Yahweh of Teman and by his Asherah/asherah. May he bless and keep you and may he be with my lord."[31]

Again, moreover, Olyan has argued that this pairing of Yahweh and Asherah at Kuntillet 'Ajrûd and in Samaria should not be regarded as an alien element introduced by foreigners into Israelite religion; he proposes instead that the worship of Asherah was a part of the normative religion of the Northern Kingdom.[32] Olyan notes several data in support of this conclusion: first, that the reformer king Jehu, is his purge of certain religious images within Samaria and the Northern Kingdom, is not described as destroying the *'ăšērâ* that Ahab had previously erected; indeed, according to 2 Kgs 13:6, this *'ăšērâ* remained standing in Samaria after Jehu's death. Since Jehu's targets in his reform were non-Yahwistic elements in the cult, the fact that the *'ăšērâ* was allowed to survive suggests it was perceived as appropriate within the Northern Kingdom's Yahwistic cult.[33] That there was an *'ăšērâ* in the Northern Kingdom state temple devoted to Yahweh at Bethel, according to 2 Kgs 23:15, likewise suggests the *'ăšērâ* was considered legitimate in the Yahwism of the Northern monarchy.[34] Olyan also suggests that despite the virulent attacks on non-Yahwistic cult elements in the oracles of the Northern prophet Hosea, the cult of Asherah is never condemned, implying that the prophet had no objections to an Asherah cult as part of the official religion of the North.[35] Olyan argues that the silence of another prophet of the North, Amos, regarding Asherah worship is equally of significance.[36] He concludes, "Based only on an examination of the biblical sources, we argue that the asherah was a legitimate part of the cult of Yahweh . . . in the north . . . in state religion and in popular religion."[37]

If Olyan is correct that the biblical evidence does suggest the cult of Asherah was paired with the cult of Yahweh in the state religion of the Northern

31. See Aḥituv, Eshel, and Meshel, "The Inscriptions," 94–100, 105–7. The translations here are my own.

32. Olyan, *Asherah and the Cult of Yahweh*, passim.

33. See also on this point Ackroyd, "Goddesses, Women, and Jezebel," 255–56; Ahlström, *Aspects of Syncretism*, 51; and Freedman, "Yahweh of Samaria and his Asherah," 248.

34. In Amos 7:13, Ahaziah calls the Bethel temple "a king's sanctuary" and "a dynastic temple" (for notes on translation, see Albright, *Archaeology and the Religion of Israel*, 139).

35. Hosea 4:13 does describe the Israelites engaging in what the prophet considers to be illicit worship "under evergreen oak, styrax tree, and terebinth," but the *'ăšērâ* is not explicitly mentioned.

36. Olyan, *Asherah and the Cult of Yahweh*, 6–8.

37. Olyan, *Asherah and the Cult of Yahweh*, 13.

Kingdom, and if in particular the cults of Asherah and Yahweh were paired in Ahab's Samaria, as indicated by the Kuntillet ʿAjrûd material in addition to the biblical text, then Jezebel may well have participated in the cult of Asherah as part of her obligations to state Yahwism. Note here that despite the Deuteronomistic condemnations of Ahab's state cult as syncretistic or even non-Yahwistic because it incorporated Jezebel's worship of Baal, the state religion of Ahab's monarchy in fact remained Yahwism: the sons of Jezebel and Ahab, Ahaziah and Jehoram, both bore Yahwistic names (*ʾăhazyāhû*, "Yahweh has grasped"; *yĕhôrām*, "Yahweh is exalted"), as did their daughter,[38] Athaliah (*ʿătalyāh*, "Yahweh is great"),[39] Athaliah's son Ahaziah, her daughter Jehosheba (*yĕhôšebaʿ*, "Yahweh is abundance"),[40] and her grandson Joash (*yôʾāš*, "Yahweh has given").

There is every possibility, in short, that Jezebel participated in an Asherah cult during her tenure as Ahab's queen, both as part of her marital responsibilities and as part of her obligations of state. Moreover, although we can only speculate, I would argue it is not unlikely that Jezebel continued to participate in an Asherah cult after Ahab's death when she assumed the role of queen mother. To be sure, the only narrative in Kings that describes the widowed Jezebel is the story of her death in 2 Kgs 9. But it may be significant for our purposes that Jezebel is lodged during that scene in her royal residence in Jezreel (1 Kgs 18:45–46) and not in Samaria. She is distanced, that is, from the Baal temple in Samaria most typically associated with her religious allegiances.[41] Her cultic attentions in Jezreel thus may have been focused on the state religion of the Northern Kingdom that paired the cult of Yahweh and the cult of Asherah. It is at least possible, I conclude, that Jezebel as *gĕbîrâ* participated in the worship of Asherah.

It is also possible that one of the most memorable *gĕbîrôt* described in the Hebrew Bible, Athaliah, the daughter of Jezebel and Ahab, participated in the

---

38. There has been some debate on the relationship of Athaliah to Ahab and Jezebel; in 2 Kgs 8:26 and 2 Chr 22:2, Athaliah is called *bat-ʿomrî*, "the daughter of Omri," whereas in 2 Kgs 8:18 and 2 Chr 21:6, she is called *bat-ʾahāb*, "the daughter of Ahab." It is generally conceded that *bat* in *bat-ʿomrî* should be understood in a more general sense of female descendent; the New Revised Standard Version, in fact, translates "granddaughter." But cf. Katzenstein, "Who Were the Parents of Athaliah?," 194–97.

39. This meaning is based on Akkadian *etellu*, "to be great, exalted"; the root *ʿtl* is otherwise unknown in Hebrew.

40. Jehosheba is the daughter of Joram, Athaliah's husband, according to 2 Kgs 11:2. Her mother's name is not given. But since the names of no other wives of Joram are known, it is reasonable to presume that Jehosheba was Athaliah's daughter.

41. But cf. Yadin, "'House of Baʿal,'" 127–29.

cult of Asherah. Athaliah was given by her parents to Jehoram, the king of Judah, as wife, presumably as part of a treaty between the Northern and Southern Kingdoms (2 Kgs 8:18). She became *gĕbîrâ* to their son Ahaziah after Jehoram was killed in battle against the Edomites (2 Kgs 8:20–24), but this arrangement was short lived since Ahaziah was killed as part of Jehu's bloody coup while on a visit to Jezreel (2 Kgs 9:27–28). Athaliah then assumed the throne of Judah for six years until she was deposed as part of a popular uprising led by the high priest Jehoiada (2 Kgs 11:1–20).

Part of Jehoiada's popular uprising involved destroying the Baal temple that was in Jerusalem and killing its priesthood.[42] Although the text does not specify that it was in fact Athaliah who was responsible for having this temple built, commentators unanimously assign it to her reign and are also unanimous in suggesting that Athaliah promoted the Baal cult in Judah under the influence of Jezebel and her patronage of the Baal cult in the North. If this is indeed the case, then we might also expect that Athaliah allied herself with other cults favored by her mother. If, moreover, I have been correct in my assumption above that Jezebel both as queen and queen mother participated in the cult of Asherah, I can suggest that Athaliah would have done the same. Indeed, I would expect as much, given my earlier conclusion that devotion to Asherah was a normative aspect of Yahwistic religion in the South. Note in this regard that, as in the case of Jezebel, the Yahwistic names of Athaliah's descendants prove she participated as required in the state cult.

III. Judean Kingship Ideology and the Queen Mother

In addition to Maʿacah, Jezebel, and Athaliah, the Bible records the names of another sixteen queen mothers. Of this total of nineteen, one, Bathsheba, comes from the period of Israel's united monarchy; the other eighteen come from the period of the divided monarchy. Of these eighteen queen mothers of the divided monarchy, moreover, seventeen come from the Southern Kingdom of Judah, as documented within the Judean royal archives. These queen mothers' names, that is, are included in the formulaic notices that begin the description of the reign of each king of Judah. For kings who reigned before the fall of Samaria, the standard pattern reads, "In the XX year of King PN of Israel, PN began to rule over Judah. He reigned for XX years in Jerusalem; his

---

42. The temple could possibly have been located in Jerusalem's outskirts; see Yadin, "'House of Baʿal,'" 130–32.

mother's name was PN, daughter of PN" (1 Kgs 15:1–2, 9–10; 22:41–42; 2 Kgs 8:25–26; 12:2 [in most English translations, 12:1]; 14:1–2; 15:1–2, 32–33; 18:1–2; similarly, 1 Kgs 14:21). After the fall of Samaria, the basic pattern remains, although the synchronization with the king of Israel is obviously eliminated (2 Kgs 21:1, 19; 22:1; 23:31, 36; 24:8, 18). We should compare to these texts the archival notices for the kings of the Northern Kingdom (1 Kgs 14:20; 15:25, 33; 16:8, 15, 23, 29; 22:52(51); 2 Kgs 3:1; 10:36; 13:1, 10; 14:23; 15:8, 13, 17, 23, 27; 17:1), which in the main parallel their Southern counterparts but fail to name an Is-raelite queen mother. It is also important to recall that the one Northern queen mother whose name we do know, Jezebel, is only assigned the title *gĕbîrâ* in a passage that records the words of Southern visitors who have come to the North (2 Kgs 10:13). There is no text that describes her as being called "queen mother" by native Northerners.

Also significant in this regard is that Jezebel reigns in a court much more characterized by a "Southern" style of kingship than by typical "Northern" custom.[43] For example, while in the South, kingship from the time of David on was determined through a principle of dynastic succession, succession in the North tended to be much more volatile, with the mantle of kingship often falling on nonroyals who laid claim to the office solely because of their skills in charismatic leadership. Jezebel's father-in-law Omri, however, was able to establish a Southern-style dynasty that controlled the throne of Israel through three generations (four kings). Another accomplishment of Omri and his descendants is that they established the city of Samaria as the capital of the Northern Kingdom, and notably, in doing so, they modeled their capital after the Southern capital in Jerusalem. One of the reasons, for example, that the Omride dynasty sought to move the Northern capital from its previous location in Tirzah to Samaria is that Samaria lies in a spot that is less moun-tainous and that is near major trade routes. This location allowed Omri and his descendants to establish alliances with their neighbors—especially their Phoenician neighbors to the north—an act that is highly reminiscent of the alliances Solomon's court in Jerusalem established with its foreign neighbors (1 Kgs 3:1; 5:12). Also like the Solomonic monarchy (1 Kgs 3:1), the Omride court cemented its foreign alliances with foreign marriages, including the mar-riage of Omri's son Ahab to the Phoenician princess Jezebel. Omri's court also followed Solomon's lead in persecuting dissenters. According to 1 Kgs 2:23–35, after Solomon was crowned king, he managed to have his rival, Adonijah, and Adonijah's chief military supporter, Joab, put to death. Adonijah's chief reli-

43. See Alt, "Monarchy in the Kingdoms of Israel and Judah," 321–26.

gious supporter, Abiathar, was also threatened with death, but ultimately was exiled from Jerusalem and sent to his ancestral home in Anathoth. In 1 Kgs 19:1–9, Queen Jezebel similarly threatens the life of her main religious critic, the prophet Elijah, and Elijah responds by fleeing the Northern Kingdom and descending into Judah and eventually into the wilderness of Sinai.

As many commentators have noted, these data imply that while the office of the queen mother does not generally seem to find a home in the traditional court life of the Northern Kingdom, it does appear to be an integral part of the Southern monarchy and of the Southern-styled monarchy of Omri. To explain, I propose to explore further the differing ideologies of kingship found in Israel, on the one hand, and in Judah, on the other, to which I have alluded just above, especially these differing ideologies as initially described by Albrecht Alt in his article "The Monarchy in the Kingdoms of Israel and Judah."[44]

To be sure, in the decades since Alt's article first appeared, there have been modifications and refinements of his thesis. Of particular interest to us is the way in which Frank Moore Cross has built on Alt's work by arguing that one of the features that distinguishes Alt's contrasting ideologies of Northern and Southern kingship is the notion of sacral kingship.[45] As Cross explains, sacral kingship is a doctrine that characterizes only the Southern monarchy. Its tenets suggest that even though the Southern king cannot really be described as a god, nor can he be considered to be in any way divine, it is nevertheless true that a Southern monarch is thought to have a kind of filial relationship with Yahweh.[46] In describing this relationship, the Bible most frequently uses the language of adoption, suggesting that upon assuming office, the king becomes regarded as the metaphorical son of Yahweh, who is accordingly described as the king's

---

44. This essay was originally published in 1951 as Alt, "Das Königtum in der Reichen Israel und Juda," 2–22; for the English translation, see n. 43 above.

45. Cross, *Canaanite Myth and Hebrew Epic*, 241–65.

46. The debate concerning the "divine" versus the "sacral" character of Judean kingship is an extensive one. The most radical position is that advanced by British and Scandinavian proponents of the "myth and ritual" school, who have argued for a Jerusalem ideology of a "god-king" and for associated cultic rituals involving the king's symbolic death and rebirth, followed by his sacred marriage, or *hieros gamos*, to a priestess representing her patron goddess. Most scholars, however, while acknowledging that the British and Scandinavian schools have correctly drawn our attention to the special place of the king in the Jerusalem cult, tend to prefer a more moderate description of the Judean monarchy, one which would characterize Jerusalem kingship not so much as "divine" but rather as "sacral." For bibliography and for the history of the debate on "divine" versus "sacral," see Miller, "Israelite Religion," 218–20; also, the surveys of A. R. Johnson, "Hebrew Conceptions of Kingship," 204–35, and A. R. Johnson, "Living Issues in Biblical Scholarship," 36–42.

divine father. The pertinent texts, all of which Cross assigns to a Jerusalem provenance, are well-known: 2 Sam 7:14; Isa 9:5(6); Pss 2:7; 89:20–38(19–37); and 110:1–7. Here, I quote only the adoption formula of Ps 89:27–28(26–27), to Cross the "ultimate statement" of the Judean royal ideology:[47]

> He [the king] will cry out to me [Yahweh], "You are my father,
>   My god and the rock of my salvation."
> I [Yahweh] surely will make him my first-born,
>   the highest of the kings of the earth.

It is this motif of divine sonship in Judean royal ideology that I believe can provide a clue for understanding the role of the queen mother in the Southern monarchy. For if the Judean royal ideology holds that Yahweh is the adopted father of the king, then it follows that the adopted mother of the king is understood to be Asherah, given, as noted above, that Asherah was seen by many— in both the state and popular cult—as the consort of Yahweh. The language of divine adoption, that is, implies not only Yahweh, the male god, as surrogate father, but also Asherah, the female consort, as surrogate mother.

If this is so, the implications for the Judean queen mother are enormous. As the human mother of the king, the queen mother could be perceived as the earthly counterpart of Asherah, the king's heavenly mother. The queen mother might even be considered the human representative, even surrogate, of Asherah. Assuming such a correspondence would explain why those queen mothers for whom cultic allegiances are described or hinted at in the Bible are depicted as patrons of the goddess Asherah. Indeed, according to the logic I have described, it is nothing but appropriate that these women direct their homage to their divine alter-ego. To do so could in fact be construed, within the royal ideology of Judah, as their cultic obligation.

In addition, I would argue that if my hypothesis is correct, we should see the cultic functions undertaken by the Judean queen mothers on behalf of the goddess Asherah as standing in close relationship to the political responsibilities assigned to the gĕbîrôt within their sons' courts. As I have already indicated, I do agree with Andreasen, against Ben-Barak, that the queen mother in Judah did have an official position within the palace, and I would further agree with Andreasen's description of that position as "lady counsellor." I would, however, differ with Andreasen by suggesting that one reason the queen mother can fulfill this official role of counselor may stem from the belief that

---

47. Cross, *Canaanite Myth and Hebrew Epic*, 258.

she represents the goddess Asherah within the monarchy. An identification of the queen mother with Asherah, that is, could give to the *gĕbîrâ* power and authority which, like the king's, originate in the world of the divine. Such a divine legitimization would then allow the queen mother to function as the second-most powerful figure in the royal court, superseded only by her son, the king. Consider in this regard the issue concerning which the queen mother most often exercises her authority: the matter of the royal succession. Here, the crucial role the *gĕbîrâ* sometimes plays in this transition of power can be intimately connected to the cultic function I have proposed for the queen mother as devotee of Asherah. More specifically, if the queen mother is considered the human representative of Asherah in the royal court, she should be able to legitimate her son's claim to be the adopted son of Yahweh. Indeed, the queen mother, assuming she speaks as the goddess and thus as Yahweh's consort, is uniquely qualified to attest to her son's divine adoption. Thus the right to determine the succession would most naturally and properly fall to her.

I conclude, then, that it is artificial to seek to divorce the political role of the Judean queen mother from a cultic function. I also suggest it is artificial to deny the primacy of the queen mother's cultic responsibilities.

CHAPTER 8

The Queen Mother and the Cult
in the Ancient Near East

꙰

1. Introduction: The Queen Mother and the Cult in Ancient Israel

Among biblical scholars, debate regarding the function of the queen mother, or *gĕbîrâ*, in ancient Israel has generated a steady stream of discussion over the past decades.[1] Primarily, studies have discussed what social and political role the queen mother might have played in the Israelite and/or Judean monarchies,[2] with most concluding that the queen mother had an official position as counselor in her son's court, her advice being sought especially in matters concerning the royal

---

An earlier version of this chapter appeared in Karen L. King, ed., *Women and Goddess Traditions: In Antiquity and Today*, Studies in Antiquity and Christianity (Minneapolis: Fortress, 1997), 179–209. Used here by permission.

1. The term *gĕbîrâ/gĕberet* is used fifteen times in the Hebrew Bible. In Gen 16:4, 8, and 9, it means "mistress" (describing Sarah's relationship with Hagar), and this translation is also required in 2 Kgs 5:3; Isa 24:2; 47:5, 7; Ps 123:2; and Prov 30:23. In 1 Kgs 11:19, *gĕbîrâ* should be translated "queen," referring to the wife of the Egyptian pharaoh. Elsewhere in Kings, and also in Jeremiah and Chronicles (1 Kgs 15:13; 2 Kgs 10:13; Jer 13:18; 29:2; 2 Chr 15:16), the term means "queen mother."

2. Major articles include Andreasen, "Role of the Queen Mother," 179–94; Ben-Barak, "Status and Right of the *Gĕbîrâ*," 23–34; Ben-Barak, "Queen Consort and the Struggle for Succession," 33–40; Bowen, "Quest for the Historical *Gĕbîrâ*," 597–618; Donner, "Art und Herkunft," 105–45; Molin, "Die Stellung der Gᵉbira im Staate Juda," 161–75; and Naʿaman, "Queen Mothers and Ancestors Cult," 479–90. Discussions in monographs include Ahlström, *Aspects of Syncretism*, 57–88; Ishida, *Royal Dynasties in Ancient Israel*, 155–60; Marsman, *Women in Ugarit and Israel*, 345–70; and de Vaux, *Ancient Israel*, 117–19. See also Brewer-Boydston, *Good Queen Mothers, Bad Queen Mothers*, passim.

succession.[3] Conversely, relatively few commentators have considered whether there might also have been a religious role within the state cult for the *gĕbîrâ*, and those who have addressed this issue either have rejected the notion that the queen mother could have had an official place within the state religion or have proposed theories that have proven unconvincing to the scholarly community as a whole.[4] But in a 1993 article, I proposed that we address the question of the *gĕbîrâ* and the cult anew. My conclusion there was that, contrary to the majority of commentators, the queen mother, especially in the Southern Kingdom of Judah, did play an official role in Israelite religion: that role was to devote herself to the worship of the great mother goddess of the Canaanite world, Asherah.[5]

Several pieces of evidence converged to support this determination. Particularly crucial was the fact that in the royal ideology of Judah, the king was viewed both as the biological son of the previous king, his earthly father, and also as the adopted son of Yahweh, his divine father (2 Sam 7:14; Isa 9:5 [in most English translations, 9:6]; Pss 2:7; 89:20–38[19–37]; and 110:1–7).[6] It further seems to be the case that at many points in its history, the Judean royal cult subscribed to the belief that the father god Yahweh should be worshipped alongside a consort, Asherah. I thus proposed that within the Judean royal court, because it held both that the king was the adopted son of Yahweh, the divine father, and that Yahweh had as a consort Asherah, the divine mother, an understanding would have readily developed that the king was the adopted son not only of Yahweh as father but also of Asherah as mother. Yet while the king had by definition no living biological father at the point when he became the adopted son of Yahweh and Asherah (since his biological father, the old king, must necessarily have died in order for the son to assume the throne), Judahite kings typically did have within their courts a biological mother or someone who fulfilled this role as queen mother (as did Ma'acah for her grandson Asa).[7] This biological

3. See, however, Ben-Barak, "Status and Right of the *Gĕbîrâ*," 23–34; less emphatically, Marsman, *Women in Ugarit and Israel*, 362.

4. E.g., Andreasen, "Role of the Queen Mother," 186–88, holds there is no official position for the queen mother within institutionalized Israelite religion, while Ahlström, *Aspects of Syncretism*, 57–88, and Terrien, "Omphalos Myth," 315–38, have proposed theories regarding a religious role for the queen mother that have failed to garner scholarly support.

5. Ackerman, "The Queen Mother and the Cult in Ancient Israel," 385–401, reprinted in this volume at pp. 151–69.

6. Cross, *Canaanite Myth and Hebrew Epic*, 241–65.

7. See 1 Kgs 15:9–10 and my discussion in Ackerman, "The Queen Mother and the Cult in Ancient Israel," 389n14, reprinted in this volume at pp. 156–57.

or queen mother, I suggest, would have easily become identified with Asherah, the king's divine mother, so much so that the queen mother would have been perceived as the human representative or even the earthly counterpart of Asherah within the royal court.

II. The Queen Mother and the Cult in West Semitic Tradition

As I admitted in my 1993 article, the conclusion I offered there was necessarily speculative,[8] hampered by the lack of evidence, both textual and archaeological, that so often plagues historians of Israelite religion. Nor is there significant comparative material from elsewhere in the ancient Near East that can prove conclusively the validity of my reconstruction. Still, I intend to suggest below that if the thesis that the Judean queen mother served in her son's court as the human surrogate of Asherah were adopted, it would help explain certain biblical texts that have heretofore been imperfectly understood by scholars. Similarly, I intend to argue that the Judean paradigm of queen mother as devotee of Asherah held in other monarchies in the West Semitic world, especially the monarchy of the Late Bronze Age city-state of Ugarit. Moreover, I will propose that certain evidence from Ugarit, both written and iconographical, is better illuminated if my thesis is accepted.

Let us turn first to this evidence from Late Bronze Age Ugarit. I begin by recalling what many studies have already shown: that Ugarit does share with the Southern Kingdom of Judah an ideology of sacral kingship.[9] This is most thoroughly indicated in a literary composition, the Kirta epic (*KTU* 1.14–16).[10] In that epic, language identifying King Kirta as the adopted son of the Canaanite high god El is frequent: in the first two tablets of the text, Kirta is repeatedly called the "lad of El" (*ǵlm il*, *KTU* 1.14.1.40–41; 14.2.8–9; 14.6.41 [restored]; 15.2.20), and El (referred to using the epithet "Bull") is almost as often referred to as Kirta's father (*tr abh il*, "the Bull, his father, El," *KTU* 1.14.2.6; 14.4.6; *tr abh*, "the Bull, his father," *KTU* 1.14.1.41; and *tr abk il*, "the Bull, your father, El," *KTU* 1.14.2.23–24). Even more telling is the scene with which the third tablet

8. Ackerman, "The Queen Mother and the Cult in Ancient Israel," 388; see in this volume at p. 156.

9. To be sure, it is crucial not to overstate the nature of the "divinity" ascribed to Ugaritic kings: see the cautions of Merrill, "House of Keret," 5, 7.

10. For sacral kingship in Kirta, see Gray, "Canaanite Kingship," 193–220; Gray, *The KRT Text*, 5–9; Gray, "Sacral Kingship in Ugarit," 289–302; and Merrill, "House of Keret," 5–6.

of the Kirta Epic opens. There, Kirta has been struck by some unspecified illness, and his family gathers around him. Their reaction to his sickness can only be described as one of shock, as they cannot believe that Kirta might die as mortals do. "Shall gods die?" his son Ilihu asks,[11] "Shall the offspring of the Kindly One [a well-known epithet of El] not live?" (*u ilm tmtn // šph lṭpn lyḥ*, *KTU* 1.16.1.22–23; see also 16.2.43–44). Ilihu also, in the same speech, refers to his father's immortality (*lmtk*, literally "your not dying," *KTU* 1.16.1.15). What seems assumed here is an ideology of divine sonship through which Kirta has been adopted into the family of the immortal gods. Not insignificantly, it is in this part of the epic that Kirta is explicitly called the "son of El" (*bn il* and *bnm il*, *KTU* 1.16.1.10, 20, and 16.2.48 [restored]).

The Kirta Epic, however, is a mythological text, and it thus can be questioned whether it reflects accurately the actual royal ideology of Ugarit. Evidence demonstrating that it does includes the verso of the so-called "Ugaritic King List" (*KTU* 1.113), where a list of fourteen royal names appears, with each king's name preceded by the divine determinative (the *il* sign). To be sure, all the kings named are deceased—probably an indication that a monarch could assume the title *ilu*, "divine one," only upon his death.[12] Still, I would argue that in order to be given the title "divine one" at death, the recipient most likely had some extraordinary relationship with the divine during life. Thus, the fact that dead Ugaritic kings are called "divine one" after their deaths suggests that an ideology of sacral kingship similar to that found in first-millennium BCE Judah did function in Late Bronze Age Ugarit.

The presence of this type of royal ideology, of course, was crucial to my earlier proposals concerning the cultic role of the queen mother in the Judean court. This suggests that inherent in the Ugaritic monarchy is the same potential I found in Judah for the queen mother to function in the court as the earthly representative of Asherah. Equally significant in this regard is evidence suggesting that the city-state of Ugarit is willing to ascribe to its queen mothers the same kind of political power that previous commentators have described for the queen mothers of Judah. For example, a letter (RS 11.872; *KTU* 2.13) originally published in 1940 by Charles Virolleaud and then subsequently discussed by H. Neil Richardson contains the words of a king who pays homage to the authority and power of his queen mother by bowing at her feet (*lpʿn*

---

11. For the identity of the speaker, see S. B. Parker, *Pre-Biblical Narrative Tradition*, 179.
12. Lewis, *Cults of the Dead*, 49–52.

umy qlt, lines 5–6) and by invoking the gods, asking them to guard (*nġr*) his mother and bring her peace (*šlm*, lines 7–8).[13]

As both Virolleaud and Richardson point out, the language of this letter closely parallels that of two other letters from Ugarit published in 1938.[14] The first (RS 9.479; *KTU* 2.12), like the Virolleaud/Richardson letter, is addressed *lmlkt*, "to the queen" (line 1); unlike the Virolleaud/Richardson letter, however, the sender here is not specifically identified as the son of the queen, but only by the name *tlmyn*, described further as "your servant" (*'bdk*).[15] This means it is impossible to determine from this letter alone whether the "queen" addressed is the royal wife or the royal mother. The second letter of comparison, however (RS 8.315; *KTU* 2.11), makes clear that the "queen" in question is in fact the queen mother.[16] That letter is also written by *tlmyn*, although this time in conjunction with *aḫtmlk*, who is probably *tlmyn*'s wife. Moreover, the recipient, the "queen" of the previous letter, is specifically called *umy*, "my mother." The addressee of the two letters, therefore, is both a "queen" and a "mother." She is the queen mother.[17] From *KTU* 2.16 (RS 15.09), another letter from *tlmyn* to his queen mother, we learn that the mother's name is *ṯryl*; any doubts that remain concerning *ṯryl*'s status as queen mother are assuaged by a fourth letter, *KTU* 2.34 (RS 17.139), addressed to *ṯryl*, "my mother," from her son, the "king" (*mlk*, line 1).

Several data within this collection of "queen mother" letters are significant. First, in both *KTU* 2.11 and 2.12, as in *KTU* 2.13, the first letter discussed above, the writers acknowledge the queen mother's authority and power by bowing at her feet; in *KTU* 2.12, indeed, *tlmyn* describes prostrating himself some fourteen times before his mother (*šb'd wšb'id*, lines 8–9). This motif is also found in three other "queen mother" letters from Ugarit that I have not yet had occasion to mention: *KTU* 2.24.5–7 (RS 16.137), a letter to "the queen" (to be understood as the queen mother, based on the parallels presented above) from *illdr*, "your servant" (*l mlkt . . . rgm ṯm illdr 'bdk*, lines 1–4); *KTU* 2.33.3–4 (RS 16.402), a letter to "the queen" (again, surely, to be understood as the queen mother) from *irrṯrm*, "your servant" (*l mlkt . . . rgm ṯm irrṯrm 'bdk*, lines 1–2); and *KTU* 2.30.4–5 (RS 16.379), a letter to "the queen, my mother" (*l mlkt umy*,

---

13. Virolleaud, "Lettres et documents," 250–53; Richardson, "Ugaritic Letter," 321–24.

14. Virolleaud, "Lettres et documents," 251; Richardson, "Ugaritic Letter," 322, note on lines 1–2.

15. Virolleaud, "Textes alphabétiques de Ras-Shamra," 127–31.

16. Dhorme, "Nouvelle lettre d'Ugarit," 142–46.

17. See further C. H. Gordon, "Ugaritic *RBT/RABÎTU*," 127; Molin, "Die Stellung der Geḇira im Staate Juda," 168.

line 1) from "the king, your son" (*mlk bnk*, line 3; there can be no doubt here that the "queen" in question is the queen mother).

In addition to paying homage to their queen mothers by bowing before them, reigning kings also, in four of the letters cited above (*KTU* 2.11, 2.12, 2.24, and 2.33), acknowledge the queen mother's authority by repeatedly addressing her as *adt* (*KTU* 2.11.1, 5, 15; *KTU* 2.12.2, 7, 12; *KTU* 2.24.2, 5, 10; and *KTU* 2.33.1, 3, 4), best analyzed as a feminine form of *adn*, "lord."[18] Of further note is an argument advanced by Michael Heltzer, who has proposed that these various "queen mother" letters were missives concerning administrative and political issues, sent by the king when he was absent from Ugarit to the queen mother, who had remained behind at the palace.[19] Thus, when the king was away, the responsibility concerning the day-to-day functioning of the Ugaritic court seems to have resided in the hands of the queen mother.

Another political responsibility the Ugaritic queen mother seems to have assumed is a role in determining the royal succession, as is indicated in a text concerning Aḫatmilki, wife of King Niqmepa and queen mother of their son, Ammištamru II.[20] Ammištamru II was a younger son of Niqmepa, yet his mother exerted enough authority to have him crowned king after the death of his father. She also seems to have served as regent on behalf of Ammištamru, who, it appears, ascended the throne while still a minor.

An Akkadian text that describes the terms of a divorce between the same Ammištamru II and the daughter of Benteśina, king of Amurru, further attests to the political powers of the queen mother at Ugarit.[21] As in modern divorce cases, much of the settlement concerned the custody of the children, especially the crown prince Utriśarruma. Utriśarruma is told that he will remain his father's heir after the divorce only if he allies himself with his father; if he sides with his soon-to-be-divorced mother, the king, Ammištamru, will appoint an alternate heir. Moreover, according to the agreement, even after Utriśarruma becomes king subsequent to his father's death, he cannot reestablish ties with his mother. More specifically, under the terms of the divorce, the son is told

18. So Aistleitner, *Wörterbuch der ugaritischen Sprache*, 8, s.v. *'dn*; see, however, C. H. Gordon, *Ugaritic Textbook*, 351, s.v. *ad* (no. 71).

19. Heltzer, *Internal Organization of the Kingdom of Ugarit*, 182.

20. RS 17.352; *PRU* 4:121–22. For discussion, see Lipiński, "Aḫat-milki, reine d'Ugarit," 79–115; also Ben-Barak, "Queen Consort and the Struggle for Succession," 34, 37; Drower, "Ugarit," 141–42; Ishida, *Royal Dynasties in Ancient Israel*, 155; and Seibert, *Women in the Ancient Near East*, 48.

21. RS 17.159; *PRU* 4:126–27. For discussion, see Yaron, "A Royal Divorce," 21–31; also Seibert, *Women in the Ancient Near East*, 15.

that should he bring his mother back to Ugarit as queen mother (*SAL.LUGAL-ut-ti*), he will be forced to abdicate. What is crucial to note for our purposes is the implicit assumption that the queen mother holds a position of power within the royal court.

Finally, Heltzer has assembled data attesting to the economic power of the Ugaritic queen mother.[22] She owned land and also was able to buy property throughout her tenure in order to supplement her holdings.[23] She, in addition, had her own storage facilities: Heltzer cites *KTU* 4.143, lines 1–2, which speaks of the 250 measures of oil housed in the queen mother's *gt*, a warehouse used for agricultural products. These land holdings, warehouses, and agricultural products seem to have been managed by administrative personnel under the authority of the queen mother: Heltzer notes that she counted among her household a *šākinu*, who served as a chief administrative official; a *mudu*, a sort of chief counselor; and several *mārê šarrati*, an Akkadian term that literally means "sons of the queen" but in reality refers to certain officials of high rank rather than actual biological descendants. Also in the queen mother's entourage were the *bunušū* (Akkadian) or *bnšm* (Ugaritic), her "dependents."

Certain biblical materials are strikingly similar to these Ugaritic data. In 1 Kgs 2:13–25, for example, Bathsheba, now after David's death the queen mother of Solomon, approaches her son bearing a petition from the recently deposed Adonijah. Solomon, to be sure, hardly receives this petition with favor, as it asks for David's concubine (tantamount to asking for David's kingdom; see 2 Sam 3:6–11). But this does not affect the respect the king accords Bathsheba as queen mother. He rises and, as in *KTU* 2.11, 2.12, 2.13, 2.24, 2.30, and 2.33, bows down to her (*wayyištaḥû*), then has a seat placed for her at his right hand (1 Kgs 2:19). A comparison with Ps 80:18(17) and Ps 110:1, where the king is described as sitting at the right hand of God, even suggests that after the throne of the monarch himself, the chair assigned to Bathsheba is the place of highest honor on the royal dais.[24]

This text in 1 Kgs 2:13–25 thus attests to an exalted position for Bathsheba, the queen mother, in Jerusalem, similar to the exalted position held by queen mother in Ugarit; it also demonstrates that one of Bathsheba's chief responsibilities within this exalted position is to serve as an advisor to her son Solomon, bringing to him requests from supplicants like Adonijah and counseling

22. Heltzer, *Internal Organization of the Kingdom of Ugarit*, 182–83.

23. Nougayrol, Laroche, Virolleaud, and Schaeffer, et al., *Ugaritica V*, nos. 159–161 (RS 17.86 + 241 + 208; 17.102; 17.325).

24. Gray, *I & II Kings*, 104.

the king concerning his response. But this was not the only responsibility, it seems, of Bathsheba: equally or perhaps more important was securing for Solomon the throne at the time of David's death. That story, as told in 1 Kgs 1:5–40, describes how the prophet Nathan wanted David to name Solomon as his heir rather than Adonijah, who was the oldest surviving son. To effect this, Nathan went to Bathsheba, who in turn persuaded the king to declare Solomon his successor. The final decree, to be sure, is David's. But it is Bathsheba who, practically speaking, determines the royal succession. Her power in deciding the king's heir is further alluded to in Cant 3:11:

> Look, O daughters of Zion,
> At King Solomon,
> At the crown with which his mother crowned him
> On the day of his wedding,
> On the day of the gladness of his heart.

We may compare to 1 Kgs 1:5–40 and Cant 3:11 the role of the Ugaritic queen mother Aḥatmilki and the part she played in promoting the succession of her son, Ammištamru II. Overall, moreover, we may conclude that as Ugarit and Judah share an ideology of sacral kingship, they also demonstrate a shared understanding concerning the rights and responsibilities of the queen mother in the royal court. If, then, my thesis stated earlier concerning the queen mother and the cult in Judah is correct, we should similarly expect to find the queen mother in Ugarit associated with the cult of Asherah.

Three pieces of evidence, two literary and the other artistic, are particularly suggestive in this regard. The first is an episode, again from the Kirta Epic, that has caused much confusion among scholars. As the epic opens, King Kirta is depicted as bewailing the fact that he has lost his wife and all his children through a series of disasters (childbirth, disease, plague, drowning, and war). In despair, Kirta undertakes a series of ritual preparations designed to induce the god El to appear to him in a dream.[25] Once El appears and learns the cause of Kirta's grief, he provides Kirta with a list of instructions that, if followed, are designed to secure the noble maiden Ḥurriya as Kirta's new wife. When Kirta awakens, he proceeds to follow El's instructions, offering sacrifices, mustering an army, and marching forth to do battle with King Pabil of Udm, Ḥurriya's father. Kirta, however, deviates in one significant aspect from El's instructions.

---

25. I have discussed Kirta's incubation more thoroughly in Ackerman, "Deception of Isaac," 110–11.

On the third day of his march, he and his forces come to a shrine of Asherah, and there Kirta makes a vow to the goddess: that he will dedicate gold and silver to her if he is successful in his quest for Ḫurriya (*KTU* 1.14.4.31–43).

Critics have puzzled over this vow.[26] It appears unnecessary, indeed superfluous, for Kirta to seek divine succor from Asherah since success in his mission has already been promised by El. In fact, although the text becomes fragmentary at a crucial point, it seems that Kirta's vow ultimately brings him harm rather than good. After securing Ḫurriya, the king fails to dedicate the promised riches to Asherah, and, at the end of *KTU* 1.15.3, she pledges to exact revenge. The next complete scene in the epic describes Kirta's seemingly fatal illness—the result, most commentators presume, of Asherah's curse.[27]

Why, then, does Kirta enter into this unnecessary and even foolish vow? I propose that the context of his mission provides a clue. Kirta has presented himself to El as one desperate for an heir: "Grant that sons I might acquire," Kirta begs El. "Grant that children I might multiply" ([*tn b*]*nm aqny* // [*tn n‘*]*rm amid*, *KTU* 1.14.2.4–5). For Kirta, the important point in his marriage to Ḫurriya is not so much the fact that she will serve him as queen but that she will become mother and eventually, upon Kirta's death, queen mother to their royal son. When she becomes queen mother, moreover, my thesis proposes, she will devote herself to the worship of Asherah within her son's court and will even be considered the earthly counterpart of the goddess. This is why Kirta is described in the epic tradition as deviating from El's instructions. Even though, as high god of the pantheon, El's decrees normally are binding, matters concerning queen mothers—even queen-mothers-to-be—appropriately fall within the province of Asherah. Kirta, in seeking a mother for his royal heir, dare not ignore the mother goddess. Kirta's otherwise puzzling vow thus becomes a perfectly comprehensible part of the epic's plot.

Another potentially significant scene is found later in the Kirta Epic, after Ḫurriya has been secured as Kirta's wife. There, at a banquet that celebrates the marriage, El appears and blesses Kirta and especially the son Yaṣṣib whom El

26. Representative are the comments of S. B. Parker, *Pre-Biblical Narrative Tradition*, 159: "This raises the question in the mind of the audience, why, in a long narrative in which Keret is clearly acting out El's instructions to the letter, he should now initiate this unanticipated act with reference to another deity?"; and 172: "The vow is intrusive in the account of Keret's expedition. . . . The vow actually has no function in the tale of El's response to Keret's need of a family."

27. See e.g., S. B. Parker, "Historical Composition of KRT," 163; S. B. Parker, *Pre-Biblical Narrative Tradition*, 176.

predicts Ḥurriya will bear. According to many commentators,[28] this blessing reads (*KTU* 1.15.2.26–28):

> *ynq ḥlb a[t]rt*
> *mṣṣ ṯd btlt ['nt]*
> *mšnq[t ilm]*

> He [Yaṣṣib] will suckle the milk of Asherah,
> Suck at the breasts of Virgin Anat,
> The two wet nurses of the gods.

Commentators in addition have noted parallel traditions from elsewhere in the ancient Near East that describe a royal child being suckled by a goddess: thus John Gray points out that "the Sumerian King Lugalzaggisi was also said to be 'fed with holy milk by Ninḥarsag'"; J. C. L. Gibson and H. L. Ginsberg draw attention to Enuma Elish 1.85, where Marduk nurses at the breasts of goddesses; and Simon B. Parker writes, "Rulers claim to have been suckled by a goddess as early as the presargonic royal inscriptions from Lagash."[29] However, while I agree with Gray, Gibson, Ginsberg, and Parker concerning the stereotypical nature of language describing the divine wet nurses of royal sucklings, I am not convinced that reference only to other ancient Near Eastern comparative material fully explicates the Kirta passage. More specifically, I suggest that the naming of Anat and, in particular, Asherah as wet nurses in the cliché is not accidental. Elsewhere in the Kirta Epic, it is the goddess Astarte who is more typically paired with Anat (*KTU* 1.14.3.41–42; 14.6.26–28). Why here do we find Asherah instead? I have argued that a Ugaritic audience would expect Ḥurriya as queen mother to serve as an earthly surrogate of Asherah. That same audience should then find it appropriate that Yaṣṣib's metaphorical nurse be none other than the mother goddess. The language of the poetry, that is, alludes to the Ugaritic belief

---

28. According to Greenstein, "Kirta," 45n66, the text—although originally read as here, with a reference to Asherah (*aṯrt*)—actually refers to Astarte ('*ṯtrt*). But, as Theodore J. Lewis points out in *Origin and Character of God*, 837n192, Greenstein's reading has not necessarily carried the day: Pardee, "Kirta Epic," 337, reads *aṯrt*, "Asherah," although in "On the Edge," 184–88, Pardee reads *nrt*, "the Luminary," i.e., the sun goddess Šapšu. Lewis himself is noncommittal, although he does point out in *Origin and Character of God*, 475, that Asherah is depicted as suckling newborn gods in *KTU* 1.23.24, 59, and 61.

29. Gray, *KRT Text*, 59; also Gray, "Sacral Kingship in Ugarit," 295–96; Gibson, *Canaanite Myths and Legends*, 91n7; Ginsberg, *Legend of King Keret*, 41; and S. B. Parker, *Pre-Biblical Narrative Tradition*, 162.

that Yaṣṣib's mother, Ḥurriya, the queen at whose breasts the child will actually suck (or the queen who, more realistically speaking, will designate a wet nurse to suckle Yaṣṣib), is the earthly designate of Asherah in the royal court.

Gray, among others, has compared the poetic allusion to Asherah as a divine wet nurse to an ivory relief found by excavators at Ugarit and first published by Claude F. A. Schaeffer.[30] The plaque, which according to the excavators dates from ca. 1350 BCE, shows a woman suckling two male children, one at each breast. There can be no question that the nurse is divine: she has two pairs of wings, one extending upward from her shoulders and the other downward from her waist; from her forehead sprout two horns. I would argue further that this goddess is Asherah, for she wears the Egyptian Hathor-style headdress that Ruth Hestrin has demonstrated is often found in representations of Asherah from throughout the ancient world.[31]

Less definite, but I think still probable, is that the two male children the goddess suckles are meant to be human. Certainly there is nothing in the representation of the two that suggests divinity. Moreover, I believe it can be argued that these two human children are royal.[32] The context of the find is pertinent here; the relief was carved as a decorative panel for the headboard of a bed. At a minimum, this ivory bed would have belonged to an aristocratic family, and more likely to a royal one. One is reminded here of the ivory furniture that decorated Ahab's palace in Samaria (1 Kgs 22:39; see also Amos 3:15; 6:4).[33] That the panel depicts a suckling motif may further indicate that this royal bed was meant for a child, and I would be so bold as to suggest that the royal child whose bed would have merited such an elaborate and exquisitely carved panel would have been the crown prince.[34] And if my thesis concerning the queen mother and Asherah at Ugarit is correct, what more appropriate decoration could there be for the bed of the Ugaritic heir presumptive?[35] Ashe-

30. Gray, KRT Text, 59, commenting on the relief published by Schaeffer, "Les fouilles de Ras Shamra-Ugarit," 54–56, and Pl. VIII; also Schaeffer, Reprise des fouilles de Ras Shamra-Ugarit, Pl. VIII. The relief is held in the Damascus National Museum, Damascus Museum 3599; a photograph is easily accessible in ANEP, Pl. 829.

31. Hestrin, "Lachish Ewer," 215–20; see, however, Schaeffer, "Les fouilles de Ras Shamra-Ugarit," 54–55, and Ward, "La déesse nourricière," 229–30, who argue that the goddess is Anat.

32. Similarly, see the suggestion of René Dussaud, as reported in Schaeffer, "Les fouilles de Ras Shamra-Ugarit," 55 (Schaeffer, on the other hand, considers the sucklers to be divine); also see Ward, "La déesse nourricière," 230–31.

33. See J. W. Crowfoot and G. M. Crowfoot, Early Ivories from Samaria.

34. Similarly, see Gray, "Sacral Kingship in Ugarit," 296n31.

35. Eleanor F. Beach has pointed out to me (private communication) that the ivory beds

rah, the divine mother, is depicted here as fulfilling the duties of her alter-ego, the queen mother, in giving suck to the royal son.[36]

III. The Queen Mother and the Cult of Asherah: More Data from the Bible

Let us turn now to consider certain data from the Bible: one piece of evidence from the Hebrew Bible and the rest from the New Testament. The Hebrew text in question is short: 2 Kgs 23:7, which describes how Josiah, as part of his massive program of religious reformation, "broke down the houses of the *qĕdēšîm* that were in the temple of Yahweh where the women wove garments (*btm*) for the *'ăšērâ.*"[37] Commentators have generally focused here on two points: the translation of *btm* as "garments" and the reference to the *qĕdēšîm*, traditionally understood as male cult prostitutes.

While Hebrew *btm* was vocalized by the Masoretes as *bāttîm*, the plural of *bayit*, "house,"[38] many scholars propose, following A. Šanda and G. R. Driver, that we should revocalize to read *battîm*, cognate with Arabic *batt*, "woven garment."[39] This revocalization is supported by the Lucianic recension of the

---

attested at many West Semitic sites may never have been intended for sleeping but used only for ritual feasting and other ceremonial purposes. Beach's point is compelling, although my thesis about the special iconography of the crown prince's bed holds, I think, regardless of whether the couch is one upon which the child actually slept. Beach also has suggested to me the intriguing possibility that the king's bride, the queen mother-to-be, may have brought such an ivory bed as part of her dowry. The iconography the queen brings with her to her husband's court, that is, might suggest already at the time of marriage the woman's eventual identification with the winged, horned goddess of the Hathor headdress, Asherah.

36. Steve A. Wiggins, in *Reassessment of 'Asherah'*, 63–66, has pointed out two other pieces of evidence from Ugarit that suggest a connection between the earthly queen mother and the goddess Asherah. The first is an incident from the Baal cycle, *KTU* 1.6.1.39–55, where the goddess Asherah, at the request of El, proposes in the face of Baal's death to make Attar, her son, king on Mount Saphon. Asherah, that is, undertakes the responsibility in El's heavenly court for determining the royal succession, a responsibility that is assumed on earth by Ugaritic queen mothers. Wiggins further notes that the title that seems to be used for queen mothers at Ugarit, *rbt* (see further C. H. Gordon, "Ugaritic *RBT/RABÎTU*," 127–32), is also a title used of Asherah in her standard Ugaritic epithet *rbt atrt ym*, "Lady Asherah of the Sea."

37. For MT "houses," the LXX reads *oikon* (singular).

38. See, e.g., BDB, 109, s.v. *bayit*, which understands the verse as referring to tent-shrines woven for Asherah.

39. Šanda, *Die Bücher der Könige*, 2:344 (pointed out by Day, "Asherah in the Hebrew Bible," 407), and Driver, "Supposed Arabisms in the Old Testament," 107 (pointed out by Gray, *I & II Kings*, 664n[b], and by Cogan and Tadmor, *II Kings*, 286).

LXX, which reads *stolas*, "garment, robe."[40] As for the nature of the garments woven for the *'ăšērâ*, there is general consensus that the referent is to clothing that would have been draped over a cult statue dedicated to the goddess Asherah. The practice of clothing cult statues is known from the Bible (Jer 10:9; Ezek 16:18) and throughout the Semitic and eastern Mediterranean worlds.[41]

The problem of the *qĕdēšîm* in 2 Kgs 23:7 is somewhat more complex. In the past, it was assumed that some forms of Israelite religion, under the influence of Canaanite and Babylonian customs, included a form of sacred prostitution in which participants engaged in sexual intercourse with certain cultic personnel (*qĕdēšîm, qĕdēšôt*) in order to "emulate and stimulate the deities who bestowed fertility" and thereby to ensure fruitfulness in the land.[42] More and more scholars, however, have questioned this traditional assumption.[43] Joan Goodnick Westenholz, for example, has suggested that while the *qĕdēšîm* and *qĕdēšôt* are certainly depicted in the Bible as cultic functionaries, there is no firm evidence that their cultic function was sacred sexual intercourse.[44] Nor is there conclusive evidence from Canaanite (Ugaritic) or Mesopotamian (Sumerian, Akkadian, and Assyrian) sources that the role of the *qdšm* and *qdšt* (Ugaritic) or the *qadištu* (Akkadian) was sexual. Indeed, only the Greek historian Herodotus presents a picture of Mesopotamian sacred prostitution, but as Westenholz, Eugene J. Fisher, and, especially, Robert A. Oden cogently argue, Herodotus as a source is on this issue tendentious and therefore unreliable.[45]

It has thus become increasingly difficult to understand the *qĕdēšîm* of 2 Kgs 23:7 as male cult prostitutes; instead, they seem simply to be some class of cultic personnel who are housed in and presumably supported by the temple. This last datum is significant, for their presence in Yahweh's temple sug-

40. Beyond the Lucianic recension, the Greek has become corrupt, reading *chettiein* or *chettieim*, possibly an error for *bettieim*, a transliteration of the original Hebrew *battîm* (so Day, "Asherah in the Hebrew Bible," 407; Montgomery, *Critical and Exegetical Commentary on the Books of Kings*, 539), or possibly a Greek attempt to reflect Hebrew **kuttōnîm*, "tunics" (so Gray, *I & II Kings*, 664n[b]). But, as Day notes, in "Asherah in the Hebrew Bible," 407, this latter suggestion is unlikely, given that the attested plural forms of *kuttōnet/kĕtōnet*, "tunic," are feminine: *kuttōnôt* and *kotnôt*.

41. Gressmann, "Josia und das Deuteronomium," 325–26; Oppenheim, "Golden Garments of the Gods," 172–93 (as pointed out by Cogan and Tadmor, *II Kings*, 286).

42. The quote here comes from Pope, "Fertility Cults," 265.

43. For a good summary of the traditional view, see Oden, *Bible without Theology*, 131, although note that Oden himself provides this summary only to critique it.

44. Westenholz, "Tamar, *Qĕdēšā, Qadištu*," 245–65.

45. Westenholz, "Tamar, *Qĕdēšā, Qadištu*," 261–63; E. J. Fisher, "Cultic Prostitution?," 225–26; and Oden, *Bible without Theology*, 144–47.

gests a group perceived in at least some periods as an accepted part of the Yahwistic cult.[46] Josiah, to be sure, like the Deuteronomistic agenda that inspires him (Deut 23:18[17]), rejects the *qĕdēšîm* (and, presumably, the *qĕdēšôt*) as inappropriate in Yahwism. But evidently there had previously been those within the state cult who felt differently.

Who were those who had thought otherwise? Biblical evidence suggests that among them were Josiah's royal predecessors. The temple stood adjacent to the palace in Jerusalem and essentially functioned as a private chapel for the court.[47] Kings of Judah were the titular heads and chief patrons of the temple cult and as such reserved for themselves the right to appoint temple personnel, as David had appointed Abiathar and Zadok to minister to the ark in its tent shrine when it was brought to Jerusalem and as Josiah himself had attempted to establish the Levitical priests whom he had removed from the outlying *bāmôt* as cult functionaries in the Jerusalem sanctuary (2 Kgs 23:8–9).[48] Similarly, the *qĕdēšîm* of 2 Kgs 23:7, while they clearly did not have the support of the reformer king Josiah, at some point must have been introduced into the temple under royal patronage.

This brings us to the women who wove garments for Asherah in the houses of the *qĕdēšîm*. The text, unfortunately, does not assign a title to these women, although they may well have been *qĕdēšôt*, the female equivalents of the male cult functionaries in whose houses they wove. Certainly, however, even if not *qĕdēšôt*, we can assume the women were some sort of religious personnel: that they could spend their days weaving on behalf of the goddess Asherah must indicate that the temple economy was providing their support. In addition, as religious personnel, we can assume that they, like their male counterparts, were appointed, either directly or indirectly, by the crown. Is it too far-fetched to suggest that the royal patron of these women cult officials would have been female? Moreover, if male cult functionaries were appointed by the most powerful male in the royal court, the king, is it not likely that female cult functionaries would have been appointed by the most powerful female within the monarchy, the queen mother? And, finally, if these female cult personnel were appointed by the queen mother, then is it not significant for my thesis that

46. See Bird, "Place of Women," 419n41.

47. See Albright, *Archaeology and the Religion of Israel*, 139, and the references there; also Pedersen, *Israel*, 3–4:429.

48. On David's "choice" of Zadok and Abiathar, see Cross, *Canaanite Myth and Hebrew Epic*, 208, 215n74, 232. First Kings 2:26–27, which describes Solomon's expulsion of Abiathar from the Jerusalem priesthood, further attests to the king's right to appoint, or in this case depose, temple personnel.

the women religious functionaries the queen mother chose to appoint were dedicated to the service of Asherah, the goddess I have posited was identified in ancient Judah with the queen mother?

To be sure, such a proposal is highly conjectural. But there are supporting data that suggest that Judean queen mothers did have some influence in the disposition of temple accouterments and personnel. Most significant is the fact that the 'ăšērâ image that the queen mother Ma'acah is said to have made (1 Kgs 15:13) stood in all likelihood in the Jerusalem temple, since the temple, as noted above, is in essence a private chapel for the monarchy and thus is the obvious place for a member of the royal family to erect a religious icon. Also of importance is the fact that Ma'acah as queen mother, when she chooses to assert herself in matters concerning the temple cult, asserts herself on behalf of the worship of Asherah. I propose that some unnamed queen mother asserted herself in a similar fashion to appoint the women devotees of Asherah described in 2 Kgs 23:7.

I submit, in short, that as queen mothers like Ma'acah would devote themselves to the goddess Asherah by erecting her cult statue in the Jerusalem temple, they would also see to the maintenance of that cult statue by appointing cult functionaries to weave garments for it and also, possibly, to make offerings on the goddess's behalf (note that the reference in 2 Kgs 23:4 to vessels made for Asherah indicates that the goddess was the beneficiary of libation offerings). Second Kings 23:7, that is, may indicate again the intimate link I have posited between the queen mother and the mother goddess in Judean religion.

After the Jerusalem monarchy fell to the Babylonians in 586 BCE, the Judean royal ideology that I have argued fueled the cultic association of the queen mother with Asherah—namely, the belief that the king was the adopted son of Yahweh, the divine father, and Asherah, the divine mother—ceased to function in the political life of the nation. But even though this ideology ceased to have meaning in the historical present after 586 BCE, exalted notions of kingship remained a vibrant aspect of some Israelites' hoped-for future, in the form of an eschatological vision of an ideal king, descended from David, who would rule in a new age in a new Jerusalem. Such a vision is found already in the proto-apocalyptic works of the exilic and postexilic periods (e.g., Ezek 37:24–25; Zech 9:9–10); in the full-blown apocalypticism of Qumran (e.g., 1QS 9.11; 1QSa 2.11, 14, 20; 1QSb 5.20–29; CD 12.23; 14.19; 19.10; 20.1; 1QM 5.1; 4QCommGenA 6.2–4; 4QFlor 1.11–13); elsewhere in Second Temple period apocalyptic texts (Dan 9:25; *Pss. Sol.* 17:21–44; 18:6–9); and in certain eschatological tradents of the New Testament, especially in the Gospels of Matthew and Luke.

That Matthew's Christology has as an essential component an understanding of Jesus as the new David, the fulfillment of Jewish messianic hopes, is made evident already in the first verse of the gospel, where Matthew introduces Jesus's genealogy by announcing that Jesus is the "son of David, son of Abraham" (Matt 1:1). The genealogy follows, tracing three periods in Jesus's family tree: from Abraham to David (1:2–6a), from Solomon to Jechoniah (1:6b–11), and from Shealtiel to Jesus (1:12–16). The first and second of these periods consist of fourteen generations each, as the gospel itself points out (1:17); Matt 1:17 erroneously counts fourteen generations (instead of thirteen) in the third period as well. From a historical point of view, however, such a tripartite chronology is highly problematic, which suggests that the primary meaning of the genealogy's structure is not historical, but symbolic. Several scholars have noted in this regard that the numerical value of *dwd*, the name of David in Hebrew, is fourteen ($d = 4$; $w = 6$; $d = 4$).[49] The very structuring by "fourteens" in the genealogy thus may reflect Matthew's overarching concern to portray Jesus as the new David.

Matthew's understanding of Jesus as the new David manifests itself also in 2:2–6, where the evangelist insists on Jesus's birth in Bethlehem, the town where David was born (1 Sam 17:12) and also the town from which, according to Mic 5:1(2), the ideal Davidic ruler will come. Matthew's Jesus fulfills other eschatological expectations associated with the new David, especially in the story of the entry into Jerusalem (Matt 21:1–11; see Zech 9:9). For Matthew, in short, no matter how mockingly Herod (Matt 2:2) and the Romans (Matt 27:11, 29, 37) use the title, Jesus really is the "King of the Jews."

The Gospel of Luke is also rich in the ways it describes Jesus as the new David. Luke 24:21 (see also Acts 1:6) speaks of Jesus as the redeemer of Israel; similarly, in 2:38, Jesus is described as the redeemer of Jerusalem. Like Matthew, Luke insists on Jesus's birth in Bethlehem, "because he was of the house and the lineage of David" (2:4). Luke's description of the annunciation to Mary is particularly replete with language of the Davidic monarchy, especially in 1:32–33, where the angel Gabriel promises to Mary a child who will be called Son of the Most High, who will sit on the throne of David, who will reign over the house of Jacob, and whose kingdom will be without end (see also 2 Sam 7:12–16; Isa 9:5–6[6–7]; Ps 89:27–30[26–29]; Dan 2:44; 7:14, 27). This stress in Luke, as in Matthew, on Jesus as the royal messiah is significant for our purposes because Henri Cazelles has suggested that we posit in these two

---

49. E.g., Brown, *Birth of the Messiah*, 80, 80n38; see further the references listed in M. D. Johnson, *Purpose of the Biblical Genealogies*, 192nn1–8.

gospels a role for Mary, Jesus's mother, that corresponds to that of her son's: if Jesus is characterized as the royal messiah, Israel's new king, then Mary, at least figuratively, is depicted as queen mother.[50]

Certain data, especially in Matt 1:1–25, suggest precisely such an understanding of Mary as a queen mother. For example, as is often noted, a peculiar feature of Matthew's genealogy of Jesus (1:1–17) is the fact that it includes four women: Tamar, Rahab, Ruth, and Bathsheba (called in Matt 1:6 "the wife of Uriah").[51] Commentators usually assume that these four women are included because their characters bear some relation to Mary's: like her, they are all said to participate in some extraordinary or irregular marital union, scandalous in the eyes of outsiders yet essential in the preservation of the messianic line; thus, like Mary, they are instruments through which God works the divine will.[52] I would add that like Mary, they either are queen mothers (Bathsheba) or adumbrate that office in the premonarchic period: thus Tamar bears Perez through Judah, to whom is already assigned, in Gen 49:10, the "scepter" and the "ruler's staff" as emblems of monarchy; Rahab, through Salmon, is the mother of Boaz, and Ruth, through Boaz, is the mother of Obed, both of whom are important in biblical tradition because they are immediate ancestors of David, the founder of the Judean royal dynasty.[53]

Even more notable parallels between Mary and the queen mothers of old are found in Matthew's story of the virgin birth (Matt 1:18–25). As is well known, Matthew in that birth narrative quotes the great Immanuel prophecy of Isa 7:14. Or more specifically, Matthew quotes the LXX translation of Isa 7:14, which uses *parthenos*, "virgin," rather than reflecting Hebrew 'almâ, "young woman" (Matt 1:23). Contrast Luke, who, while he does recount the story of the virgin birth, does not cite the Isaiah passage. As Raymond E. Brown has pointed out, this suggests that the virgin birth narrative did not emerge because of the Isaiah prophecy (the prophecy, that is, as it was understood in its Greek manifestation), but instead the tradition of the virgin birth circulated in early Christianity independent of the Isaianic text.[54] What, then,

50. Cazelles, "La Mere du Roi-Messie," 39.

51. See Brown, *Birth of the Messiah*, 71–74; M. D. Johnson, *Purpose of the Biblical Genealogies*, 152–79.

52. Brown, "Genealogy (Christ)," 354; Brown, *Birth of the Messiah*, 73–74; see also Brown, Donfried, Fitzmyer, and Reumann, eds., *Mary in the New Testament*, 78–93.

53. The Bible itself makes explicit this connection between the royal line as descended from Judah to Perez and as descended from Boaz to Obed and then to Jesse, David's father: see Ruth 4:12, 17–22.

54. See further Brown, Donfried, Fitzmyer, and Reumann, eds., *Mary in the New Testament*, 91–95, 119–25.

inspired Matthew but not Luke to quote the prophecy in order to illustrate the virgin birth narrative?

The answer to this question, of course, could simply be coincidence—Matthew thought to cite the passage, Luke did not—or it could be that we should explain Matthew's quote as yet another example of his propensity to quote the Hebrew Bible whenever any potential parallel, no matter how distant, comes to mind. But I am intrigued by the original context of Isa 7:14. In Isa 7, Isaiah, the prophet, confronts King Ahaz, urging him to resist a foreign alliance with Assyria. The child Immanuel, whose name means "God is with us," is to be for Ahaz a sign that foreign alliances are unnecessary and that Israel should rely on God alone. The child is born to an ʿalmâ, a "young woman," whom most commentators now understand to be Ahaz's wife.[55] The child in question is thus Hezekiah, the royal heir, and the child-bearing woman of 7:14 should therefore be Abi, Hezekiah's queen mother (2 Kgs 18:2).[56] It is, of course, impossible to say whether Matthew realized that the original prophecy applied to a queen mother. But if he did, this may explain why he, given his concern to portray Jesus as the new David, chose to quote Isa 7:14.

What, finally, of Mary as queen mother and the thesis that is our concern: that the queen mother served as the earthly representative of Asherah or, to speak in post-Canaanite terms more appropriate to the period of early Christianity, that Mary as the figurative queen mother of Jesus would have been perceived within the cult as the earthly representative of the mother goddess? Certainly, in the rather unrelenting patriarchy of the New Testament, there is no suggestion of this. But can we see in later Mariology the tendency that we found already in second-millennium BCE Ugarit to identify queen mother and a mother goddess? Note in this regard that in the earliest attestation of an emerging cult of Mary, the second-century CE *Infancy Gospel* or *Protevangelium of James*, Mary is said to be dedicated by her parents to a life of service in the temple and, as part of her service, she is chosen to be one of seven virgins who weaves a new curtain for the sanctuary.[57] It is not hard here to hear echoes

55. E.g., Cazelles, "La Mere du Roi-Messie," 40, 51–53; Hayes and Irvine, *Isaiah*, 132, 135–36. Cf., however, Gottwald, "Immanuel as the Prophet's Son," 36–47; Roberts, "Isaiah and His Children," 198.

56. Vawter, "The Ugaritic Use of GLMT," 319, and, later, Wyatt, "'Araunah the Jebusite,'" 45, point out that in *KTU* 1.14.4.41, the term ǵlmt, the Ugaritic cognate of ʿalmâ, is used of Ḥurriya, Kirta's prospective wife and, as I have discussed above, the eventual queen mother in Kirta's royal court.

57. *Prot. Jas.* 10.1–2; for the text, see Cullmann, "Protevangelium of James," 430; for discussion, see Brown, Donfried, Fitzmyer, and Reumann, eds., *Mary in the New Testament*, 247–49, 258–60.

of the weaving women of 2 Kgs 23:7, which describes, I argued above, women appointed to cultic service by the queen mother in order that they might tend to the cult statue of the queen mother's divine patron, Asherah. Mary, that is, within a century of Jesus's death, is described by the author of the *Infancy Gospel* or *Protevangelium of James* as participating in a type of temple service that, in an earlier period in Israel's history, was a part of the cult of Asherah. Also worthy of mention is the *Gospel of Philip*, a collection of Valentinian Gnostic meditations with its roots in the second century CE,[58] in which Mary is interpreted simultaneously both as Jesus's mother and as a female heavenly power, the Holy Spirit (55:23; 59:6; see also *Gos. Thom.*, logion 99).[59] Mary, in short, is said to correspond to a mother figure in the heavens—a mother figure who, again, in an earlier period was the goddess Asherah.

I conclude, then, with this possibility: that even within the radical religious transformation that was early Christianity, the old mythic paradigm that linked the queen mother and the mother goddess still reverberated in the emerging Marian cult.

58. Brown, Donfried, Fitzmyer, and Reumann, eds., *Mary in the New Testament*, 245, 269–70.

59. Isenberg, "Gospel of Philip," 134–36; on the *Gospel of Thomas*, see Brown, Donfried, Fitzmyer, and Reumann, eds., *Mary in the New Testament*, 265, and the references there; for the text, see Lambdin, "Gospel of Thomas," 128.

PART 4

Women and Worship

CHAPTER 9

At Home with the Goddess

In my introductory comments to the first chapter in this volume, "'And the Women Knead Dough': The Worship of the Queen of Heaven in Sixth-Century Judah," I noted that my interest in the cult of the Queen of Heaven had grown over the years from my initial focus—which was on the identity of the Queen of Heaven and why ancient Israelite women may have been particularly interested in devoting themselves to her—to include the question of where in ancient Israel the goddess was primarily worshipped. In this chapter, I address this issue. But more importantly, in this chapter, I pull together threads from several other chapters that appear in this volume to consider other "where" questions: for example, the homes in the courtyard of the Jerusalem temple that housed the weaving women of 2 Kgs 23:7 whom I discussed in chapter 2, "Asherah, the West Semitic Goddess of Spinning and Weaving?" I also consider here the royal palace, where queen mothers made Asherah worship a part of their religious devotions, as I argued in chapters 7 and 8, "The Queen Mother and the Cult in Ancient Israel" and "The Queen Mother and the Cult in the Ancient Near East."

To put the matter another way, the previous chapters in this volume have tended to focus on a specific goddess (for example, the Queen of Heaven or Asherah) or have tended to focus on specific women functionaries within Israelite religion (for example, women who wove cultic cloth or queen mothers). This chapter brings some of those disparate analyses together in order to consider how the insights I have put forward in these previous chapters might be understood in relation to one another—and especially how they

An earlier version of this chapter appeared in William G. Dever and Seymour Gitin, eds., *Symbiosis, Symbolism, and the Power of the Past: Canaan, Ancient Israel, and Their Neighbors from the Late Bronze Age through Roman Palaestina* (Winona Lake, IN: Eisenbrauns, 2003), 455–68. Used here by permission.

might be understood in spatial relation to one another. In the chapter that follows, "Women and the Worship of Yahweh in Ancient Israel," I continue this effort at synthesis by focusing on temporal considerations, asking how women's participation in various goddesses' cults may have been driven by changes over time within Yahwistic religion.

For most English speakers, the word "home"—although it can mean a dwelling of any sort—typically has connotations more intimate and familial: "home" is the residence that houses our closest relatives and where we keep our most important possessions; the shelter that serves us as a refuge and that can even offer us happiness and love; the place, according to Robert Frost's almost hackneyed description, "where, when you have to go there, they have to take you in."[1] Biblical Hebrew has no precise analog; *bayit*, "house," comes closest, especially in those passages (592 according to the count of BDB) where *bayit* describes a "household" or "family."[2] However, unlike English "home," *bayit* was commonly used by the ancient Israelites to refer also to houses that were not family residences: for example, the temple or "house" of Yahweh in Jerusalem or the palace or "house" of the king. In this chapter on goddess worship in ancient Israel, I propose to take my cue from this Hebrew usage and survey our evidence both for goddess worship in family domiciles and for goddess worship in more public "homes," such as Yahweh's Jerusalem temple and also Yahweh's Northern Kingdom shrines, as well as the royal palaces of Jerusalem and Samaria. I undertake this multi-dimensional review because I believe there are some continuities worth considering between our evidence for goddess worship in temple and palace locations, on the one hand, and in familial settings, on the other. Thus, after discussing, respectively, temple-based goddess worship, goddess worship in royal palaces, and goddess cults in family homes, I will conclude with some remarks on the interrelationship between the three.

1. At Home with the Goddess in the Temple

For students of ancient Israelite religion, the 1975–76 discoveries at the northeastern Sinai site of Kuntillet 'Ajrûd, of inscriptions and also perhaps iconography that paired the Israelite god Yahweh with "his *'ăšērâ*," were nothing

1. Frost, "The Death of the Hired Man," 43.
2. BDB, 109, s.v. *bayit*.

less than astonishing.[3] But I have come to think that equally astonishing was the way in which those discoveries caused both archaeologists and biblical scholars to return to and rethink data that were already in our possession. For archaeologists, this primarily meant returning to the eighth-century BCE inscription that William G. Dever had published in 1969–70 from the Judean site of Khirbet el-Qôm and rereading that inscription so that it, too, contained a reference to Yahweh and "his *ăšērâ*."[4] For biblical scholars, the process of reevaluation required returning to the biblical text and rethinking the significance of the forty some occurrences of the term *ăšērâ* (and the related terms *ăšērîm* and *ăšērôt*) found within the Bible's pages. More specifically, biblical scholars found themselves reassessing whether the biblical descriptions of cult activities involving this term *ăšērâ*—descriptions that had generally been taken as evidence of foreign and therefore heterodox beliefs and practices that had been imported into Israel—might instead signify that at least for some ancient Israelites, during at least some points in Israelite history, worship involving this *ăšērâ* was a perfectly appropriate part of the Yahwistic cult. Especially relevant to my discussion in this chapter's first section are biblical passages that might suggest that worship involving this *ăšērâ* was for some ancient Israelites, during at least some points in ancient Israelite history, a perfectly appropriate part of the Yahwistic *temple* cult.

Before turning to these texts, however, a comment on the translation of Hebrew *ăšērâ*: as is well known, there is no consensus among scholars on this matter. For example, while many students of the Kuntillet ʿAjrûd and Khirbet el-Qôm materials have argued that the description of Yahweh's *ăšērâ* in those inscriptions is to be taken as a reference to Yahweh alongside his goddess consort, Asherah, others—concerned about the grammatical improbability of a pronominal suffix on a proper name ("his *ăšērâ*")—have insisted that

3. For the original announcements of these discoveries, see Meshel, "Kuntillet ʿAjrûd—An Israelite Religious Center," 50–54; Meshel, "Kuntillet ʿAjrûd—An Israelite Site," 118–24; Meshel, *Kuntillet ʿAjrud: A Religious Center*; and Meshel and Meyers, "The Name of God in the Wilderness of Zin," 6–10. The official publication volume, Meshel, *Kuntillet ʿAjrud*, appeared in 2012.

4. For the original publication, see Dever, "Iron Age Epigraphic Material from the Area of Khirbet el-Kôm," 158–89; revised studies were published by Lemaire, "Date et origine des inscriptiones hébraïques et pheniciennes de Kuntillet ʿAjrud," 131–43; Lemaire, "Les inscriptions de Khirbet el-Qôm," 597–608; and Lemaire, "Who or What Was Yahweh's Asherah?," 42–51. In his reassessment, Lemaire proposed reading a reference to Yahweh and "his *ăšērâ*" in the second and third lines of the text, a reading Dever subsequently came to accept; see Dever, "Asherah, Consort of Yahweh?," 22; less completely, Dever, "Material Remains and the Cult," 570, 582n17; Dever, "Recent Archaeological Confirmation of the Cult of Asherah," 40.

'ăšērâ in the inscriptions must be taken as a common noun. But a common noun with what meaning? "Shrine," as originally proposed by Edward Lip-iński?[5] "The female aspect of Yahweh," reified and given a separate identity, as suggested by both P. Kyle McCarter and Patrick D. Miller?[6] A cult object called the 'ăšērâ, which is the meaning of the term 'ăšērâ that is found most frequently in the Hebrew Bible? My own preference is for either the first or fourth of these alternatives: to understand Yahweh's 'ăšērâ at 'Ajrûd and el-Qôm either as a reference to Yahweh's goddess consort Asherah or to the cult object known from the Hebrew Bible as the 'ăšērâ. I would also follow the biblical witness in describing this cult object as an image that was in the shape of a stylized wooden pole or tree. Deuteronomy 16:21 speaks of "planting" (nāṭaʿ) the 'ăšērâ; elsewhere in the Bible, the 'ăšērâ cult object is "made" (ʿāśâ), "built" (bānâ), "stood up" (ʿāmad), or "erected" (hiṣṣîb). When destroyed, the 'ăšērâ is "burned" (bīʿēr or śārap), "cut down" (kārat), "hewn down" (gādaʿ), "uprooted" (nātaš), or "broken" (šibbēr).[7]

Moreover, while we have to acknowledge that the image of the sacred tree is nigh on ubiquitous in Semitic art and thus admit that it is often difficult to identify such trees with one particular god or goddess, it is nevertheless the case that our West Semitic evidence more often than not argues for an association of sacred trees with the Canaanite mother goddess Asherah. Ruth Hestrin has perhaps advanced the most persuasive arguments in support of this position, in her descriptions of (1) the late thirteenth-century BCE Lachish Ewer, (2) the several Late Bronze Age gold and electrum pendants depicting a naked female that come from Ugarit and other sites in the northern Levant, and (3) the tenth-century BCE Taʿanach cult stand.[8] Regarding the ewer, Hestrin points out the way in which it pairs sacred tree iconography with a dedicatory inscription addressed to Elat, an epithet of Asherah well known from both Ugaritic and Phoenician sources. Regarding the gold and electrum pendants, she argues that because many of the images found upon them—especially lions, snakes, and the female figure's Hathor headdress—are frequently associated with Asherah,[9] we should conclude that the pendants are depictions

---

5. Lipiński, "The Goddess Aṯirat," 101–19.

6. McCarter, "Aspects of the Religion of the Israelite Monarchy," 149; Miller, "Absence of the Goddess," 246.

7. The LXX, moreover, most commonly translates Hebrew 'ăšērâ by alsos, "grove," and twice by dendra, "trees"; the Latin similarly reads lucus, "grove," or nemus, "wood," "grove," for Hebrew 'ăšērâ.

8. Hestrin, "Cult Stand from Taʿanach," 61–77; Hestrin, "Lachish Ewer," 212–23.

9. On Asherah's association with lions, see, e.g., KTU 1.3.5.37; 1.4.1.8; and 1.4.2.25–26,

of that goddess and should further understand that the stylized branch or tree that is often etched in the figure's navel is a representation of Asherah's sacred tree. Regarding the Ta'anach cult stand (see fig. 2.12), Hestrin suggests that the nude female of the bottom register is Asherah, given that this figure is flanked by the lions characteristically associated with the goddess, and that therefore in register 3 (counting from the bottom), where we again have the flanking lions, we should also read the central figure as a representation of Asherah, although this time depicted in the form of the sacred tree.[10]

Not to belabor the obvious: what all these data suggest to me, and I believe to the majority of commentators, is that the ancient Israelites understood the term *'ăšērâ* both as a proper name, the name of the Canaanite mother goddess Asherah, and as a common noun that described an object in the shape of a wooden pole or tree that represented the goddess Asherah in the cult.[11] Indeed, I believe that the ancient Israelites would have made little differentiation between these two meanings, which is to say that in ancient Israelite religion, the cult symbol of the goddess would have readily been perceived as the goddess herself. As John Day has pointed out, this strategy of designating a cult object by the name of the deity it represents is attested elsewhere in West Semitic religion:[12] thus Philo of Byblos reports that the Phoenicians "consecrated steles and staves" in the names of their deities.[13] Within Israelite religion, we can compare the ancient Israelite understanding of the ark, Yahweh's primary symbol according to Pentateuchal traditions and according to the Bible's descriptions of the Jerusalem temple, in order to see how close the relationship was between cult object and deity. Numbers 10:35–36, the so-called "Song of the Ark," illustrates perfectly the simultaneity of symbol and god in Israelite imagination: "Whenever *the ark* set out, Moses said, 'Arise, O Yahweh'"; similarly, "When *it* [the ark] rested, he [Moses] said, 'Return,

---

where the children of Asherah are called her "pride of lions," *ṣbrt ary*. On the goddess's association with snakes, see, e.g., *KAI* 89, a Punic devotional tablet on which Asherah bears the epithet *ḥwt*, an epithet which may mean "serpent," cognate with Old Aramaic *ḥwh* (Sefire I, A, 31), later Aramaic *ḥiwâ, ḥiwyā', ḥewyā'*, and Arabic *ḥayya*.

10. Robert A. Oden, *Studies in Lucian's De Syria Dea*, 149–55, has further proposed that the caduceus imagery associated in a later period with Phoenician-Punic Tannit, whom Oden identifies primarily with Asherah, had its origins in a depiction of a date palm tree that, over time, became increasingly stylized and abstracted.

11. See also the useful survey of scholarly positions found in Day, "Asherah in the Hebrew Bible," 398–404.

12. Day, "Asherah," 486.

13. Philo of Byblos, *Phoenician History*, as quoted in Eusebius, *Praeparatio evangelica* 1.9.29; trans. Attridge and Oden, *Philo of Byblos*, 33.

O Yahweh'" (emphasis mine). Note, too, 1 Kgs 12:28, where Jeroboam is likewise described as identifying cult symbols with the deity the symbols represent
when he says of the bull *images* of Dan and Bethel that they are "your *gods*,
O Israel, who brought you out of Egypt" (emphasis mine). We would likewise
expect that the *'ăšērâ*, the cult symbol, and Asherah, the goddess, would have
been understood by the ancient Israelites as essentially one and the same.[14]
I noted above that I would favor a translation of the phrase "Yahweh's *'ăšērâ*"
at Kuntillet 'Ajrûd and Khirbet el-Qôm that took the reference to be *either*
to Yahweh's goddess consort Asherah *or* to the cult object known from the
Hebrew Bible as the *'ăšērâ*, but it would perhaps be more accurate for me to
suggest that my preference is for *both/and*, taking the meanings "Asherah the
goddess" and "'*ăšērâ*, the cult object" to be embedded in one another.

It is Saul M. Olyan, writing in the light of the Kuntillet 'Ajrûd and Khirbet
el-Qôm discoveries, who has most persuasively and thoroughly argued for the
presence of the cult object of the *'ăšērâ* in Yahweh's Jerusalem temple.[15] Olyan
in particular points out that each of Judah's reformer kings, Asa, Hezekiah,
and Josiah, is said to have removed an *'ăšērâ* image from Jerusalem, which
suggests to him that in times other than these moments of reformation—that
is, throughout most of the ninth, eighth, and seventh centuries BCE—Asherah's cult object stood uncontested in Yahweh's *cult city* of Jerusalem. We are,
moreover, explicitly told that the seventh-century BCE *'ăšērâ*, the one that
Josiah removed, stood in Yahweh's *temple* in Jerusalem; we are also told that
the temple furnishings of Josiah's day included vessels made for Asherah and
that the temple held within its walls houses,[16] in which women wove garments[17] for Asherah (which I, along with most commentators, take to mean
that these women wove clothing that would have been draped over a cult statue
dedicated to the goddess Asherah).[18] This evidence of Asherah's presence in

14. See similarly the discussion of Olyan, *Asherah and the Cult of Yahweh*, 31–32, regarding the bull iconography in Near Eastern religion and this iconography's ability to function
as both the symbol of deity and the deity (Baal Haddu, El, Yahweh) himself.

15. Olyan, *Asherah and the Cult of Yahweh*, passim.

16. The LXX reads *oikon* (singular).

17. Reading *battîm*, cognate with Arabic *batt*, "woven garment," for the MT *bāttîm*,
the plural of *bayit*, "house," as originally proposed by Šanda, *Die Bücher der Könige*, 2:344
(pointed out by Day, "Asherah in the Hebrew Bible," 407), and Driver, "Supposed Arabisms
in the Old Testament," 107 (pointed out by Gray, *I & II Kings*, 664n[b], and by Cogan and
Tadmor, *II Kings*, 286). This revocalization is supported by the Lucianic recension of the
LXX, which reads *stolas*, "garment, robe."

18. The practice of clothing cult statues is known from the Bible (Jer 10:9; Ezek 16:18; Gressmann, "Josia und das Deuteronomium," 325–26, as pointed out by Cogan and Tadmor, *II Kings*,

the seventh-century BCE temple of Josiah's day leads Olyan to suggest, and I agree, that the eighth-century BCE *'ăšērâ* that Hezekiah is said to remove from Jerusalem also stood in Yahweh's temple. I have similarly argued elsewhere that the ninth-century BCE *'ăšērâ* that Asa destroyed stood in Yahweh's temple,[19] this because that *'ăšērâ* was said to have been made by Asa's queen mother Ma'acah, and where would Ma'acah, as a member of the royal court, most naturally place her *'ăšērâ* but in the temple that was immediately proximate to the family's palace? Thus, while our evidence for the ninth and eighth centuries BCE is not as conclusive as it is for the seventh century BCE, the data still suggest that at several points during the Iron Age II period (ca. 1000–586 BCE), Yahweh shared his "home" in Jerusalem with the goddess Asherah.

In general, the biblical record, given its Judahite bias and perspective, tells us comparatively little about religious practices in Israel's Northern Kingdom, which means we can say comparatively less about Asherah's presence at Yahweh's two Northern "homes" of Dan and Bethel. Only for Bethel do we have any specific evidence, and only for Bethel in the seventh century BCE, one hundred years after the fall of the Northern Kingdom: thus 2 Kgs 23:15 reports that the Southern king Josiah, as part of his sweeping reforms, crossed the old Northern-Southern boundary line to destroy the *'ăšērâ* that stood in the Bethel sanctuary. Still, Olyan has again led the way in suggesting that Asherah worship was, for many, an accepted part of the Yahwism of the Northern Kingdom throughout its existence and that an *'ăšērâ* image would therefore have been expected at Yahweh's Northern temples. Olyan particularly notes the way that Yahweh worship seems paired with Asherah worship in the Northern capital city of Samaria, as is suggested, first, by the Kuntillet 'Ajrûd inscription dedicated to "Yahweh of Samaria and his *'ăšērâ*" and, second, by the fact that the zealous Yahwistic reformer king of the North, Jehu, allowed the *'ăšērâ* that had previously been erected by King Ahab in Samaria to remain standing, this despite Jehu's pains otherwise to remove all non-Yahwistic imagery from the Northern cult. Indeed, Olyan uses the Kuntillet 'Ajrûd evocation of "Yahweh of Samaria" to buttress older theories that had argued for the presence of a Yahwistic shrine in Samaria (even though one is never explicitly referred to in the biblical text); in his words, "the inscriptions mentioning Yahweh *šōměrôn* ["Yahweh of Samaria"] now make it clear that a Yahwistic sanctuary existed in

---

286). It is also attested elsewhere in the Semitic and eastern Mediterranean worlds (Oppenheim, "Golden Garments of the Gods," 172–93, as pointed out by Cogan and Tadmor, *II Kings*, 286).

19. Ackerman, "The Queen Mother and the Cult in Ancient Israel," 390, reprinted in this volume at p. 159; also Ackerman, *Warrior, Dancer, Seductress, Queen*, 144.

Samaria." He then adds, "And . . . the asherah stood in it."[20] If Olyan is correct, then Samaria offers, along with Jerusalem and Bethel, yet another example of Yahweh in his temple "at home with the goddess."

11. At Home with the Goddess in the Palace

I have already mentioned briefly the biblical text that most clearly locates goddess worship in the royal palace in Jerusalem, namely 1 Kgs 15:13 (paralleled by 2 Chr 15:16), which describes how Ma'acah, the queen mother, or *gĕbîrâ*, of King Asa (r. 913–873 BCE), was removed from her position by the king because "'āśĕtâ mipleṣet lā'ăšērâ," which I would translate as "she made an abominable image for Asherah [the goddess]" or, alternatively, as "she made an abominable image of the asherah [the cult image]."[21] In my opinion, this second translation is less satisfactory, since the reading "she made an abominable image of the asherah [the cult image]" borders on the nonsensical: what does it mean, after all, to make an image of an image?[22] Yet whichever of the two translations is preferred, I would nevertheless maintain, as above, that the sense is the same: Ma'acah made a stylized wooden pole or tree that symbolized the Canaanite mother goddess Asherah and was consecrated to her worship.

Asa, in deposing Ma'acah from her position as queen mother, clearly indicates that he does not see the *'ăšērâ* image or the worship of Asherah more gen-

20. Olyan, *Asherah and the Cult of Yahweh*, 35.

21. The specifics of the translation have been debated because the definite article prefixed to *'ăšērâ* can be taken to preclude the understanding of *'ăšērâ* as a proper name. But this argument is not conclusive, as the definite article can be explained as appellative, as elsewhere in Deuteronomistic prose (Judg 2:11, 13; 3:7; 10:6). Indeed, the Chronicler (2 Chr 15:16), by transposing the two words in question in order to read *'āśĕtâ la'ăšērâ mipleṣet*, which can only be translated "she made for Asherah an abominable image," clearly suggests that his Deuteronomistic antecedent intends for *'ăšērâ* to be read as a proper name. A second problem, the meaning of *mipleṣet*, which occurs only in 1 Kgs 15:13 and in the Chronicles parallel, is more easily addressed: the root meaning of *plṣ*, "to shudder," readily suggests that this verb's nominal form should mean something like "a thing to be shuddered at"; "a horrid thing"; or, as here, "an abominable image."

22. Note, in fact, that elsewhere in Deuteronomistic prose, when *'ăšērâ*, the image, is referred to, the noun *'ăšērâ* typically stands alone without *mipleṣet* or similar modifier: e.g., 1 Kgs 16:33, *wayya'aś 'aḥ'āb 'et-hā'ăšērâ*, "and Ahab made the asherah" (note the similar use of *'śh*, "to make," in both this passage and 1 Kgs 15:13 while contrasting the treatment of *'ăšērâ* as object). I understand 2 Kgs 21:7, *pesel hā'ăšērâ*, in the same way I have analyzed 1 Kgs 15:13 and thus would translate "an image of Asherah."

erally as appropriate within the royal cult, and his biblical biographers agree, lauding him as one who was "faithful to Yahweh all of his days" (1 Kgs 15:14, paralleled in 2 Chr 15:17). Many modern commentators have also followed suit, arguing that Ma'acah's worship of Asherah was a foreign and therefore heterodox element introduced by her into the Jerusalem court.[23] The crucial piece of evidence most of these commentators adduce is Ma'acah's presumed foreign ancestry, since she is apparently the granddaughter of another Ma'acah who was brought from the court of King Talmai of Geshur to be married to King David (2 Sam 3:3, paralleled in 1 Chr 3:2). But just as we can no longer presume that the worship of Asherah was foreign to Yahwism in general, we can no longer presume it was foreign to the royal cult in particular. Indeed, given the fact that Asherah worship may have been incorporated into the temple cult of Jerusalem at several points during the Iron II period, and given that the Jerusalem temple cult and the Jerusalem royal cult were integrally linked (through both geographical proximity and ideological confession), we might well suppose that Asherah worship would be as integrated into the religion of the palace as it was integrated into the religion of the temple.

In fact, I have elsewhere argued that there are compelling reasons why a queen mother like Ma'acah would devote herself to the worship of Asherah within the Jerusalem court:[24] this because of the well-known Jerusalem royal ideology that conceives of the king as the metaphorical son of Yahweh (as, for example, in Ps 89:27–28 [in most English translations, 89:26–27], where the king cries out to Yahweh, "You are my father, my God and the rock of my salvation," and Yahweh replies, "I surely will make him my firstborn, the highest of the kings of the earth"). What I have suggested is that if we pair this notion of metaphorical sonship with the notion that during at least several points in the ninth, eighth, and seventh centuries BCE, Yahweh's cult in Jerusalem incorporated the worship of his goddess consort Asherah, then we might well suppose that as Yahweh was understood as the metaphorical father of the Jerusalemite king, Asherah the consort would likewise have been understood as the king's metaphorical mother. And would it thus not follow that the king's actual mother, his queen mother, would associate herself with the cult of this metaphorical mother, the goddess Asherah, as does Ma'acah? Indeed, is it not

23. E.g., Spanier, "Queen Mother in the Judaean Royal Court," 194; also, Ahlström, *Aspects of Syncretism*, 59, 61, who cites Albright, *Archaeology and the Religion of Israel*, 157–59, and Yeivin, "Social, Religious, and Cultural Trends in Judaism," 162–64; cf. Ackroyd, "Goddesses, Women, and Jezebel," 255.

24. Ackerman, "The Queen Mother and the Cult in Ancient Israel," 385–401, reprinted in this volume at pp. 151–69; also Ackerman, *Warrior, Dancer, Seductress, Queen*, 142–54.

likely that the queen mother, as the human counterpart of the king's goddess mother, even represents Asherah in the Jerusalem court?

In the Northern Kingdom, the office of queen mother is not nearly so well represented as is the office of queen mother in the South; thus, of the eighteen queen mothers whose names are preserved in the Bible from the period of the divided monarchy, seventeen come from the Southern Kingdom of Judah. To me, this evidence stands in support of the hypothesis I have just proposed: that there is something about the Southern royal ideology of metaphorical sonship that necessitates an important role in the court for Southern queen mother, whereas the ideology of a more charismatic kingship that Albrecht Alt long ago described for the North does not entail a position of great consequence for the Northern queen mother.[25] I suggest, moreover, that it cannot be a coincidence that the one woman who is assigned the title "queen mother" in the North—Jezebel—holds this office during a period in the history of the Northern Kingdom when Northern kingship most closely resembled the institution of kingship in the South (for example, the Northern monarchy of Jezebel's day operated according to the more typically Southern principle of dynastic succession rather than adhering to a charismatic model; this so-called Omride dynasty conceived of its capital city of Samaria much as an analog to the Southern capital city of Jerusalem; and Omride policies establishing foreign alliances cemented by foreign marriages mimicked similar alliances in the South). I also do not regard it as coincidence that Jezebel, in addition to being the one Northern woman said to hold the more typically Southern office of queen mother, is the one royal woman of the Northern Kingdom said to be associated with the worship of Asherah, in 1 Kgs 18:19 (although I admit that this reference may be a secondary addition).[26]

In short, what I am suggesting in general terms is that a certain ideology of monarchy—an ideology based in dynastic succession where the king is understood as the metaphorical son of Yahweh—drives a certain understanding of the role of the queen mother in the royal court, an understanding that conceives of the queen mother as associated with the cult of Yahweh's consort Asherah, devoting herself to the worship of the goddess and even functioning as Asherah's earthly representative in the palace. More specifically, in Jezebel's case, I am arguing that the prevailing consensus of a generation ago is wrong, and the worship of Asherah that the Bible associates with Jezebel is not to

25. Alt, "Das Königtum in der Reichen Israel und Juda," 2–22.
26. See my discussion in Ackerman, "The Queen Mother and the Cult in Ancient Israel," 392–93; reprinted in this volume at p. 161.

be taken as evidence of a foreign and therefore heterodox cult Jezebel brings with her from her Phoenician homeland. Rather, the Asherah worship associated with Jezebel is appropriately adopted by her within the context of the Southern-style monarchy instituted in the Northern Kingdom by her father-in-law Omri. In a palace conceived of in this particular way, members of the royal court—and especially the king's mother—are comfortably "at home with the goddess."

III. At Home with the Goddess in Family Residences

There are two major bodies of evidence that address the question of goddess worship in noncultic and nonroyal "homes"—that is, in the family residences of non-elite Israelites. These are, first, the biblical texts found in Jer 7 and 44 that allude to families among Judah's population in the late seventh and early sixth centuries BCE who worshipped a goddess known by the epithet "Queen of Heaven," and, second, the numerous so-called pillar figurines, often taken to be images of goddesses, that have been found by archaeologists in Iron II domestic contexts. Two questions about these two bodies of evidence particularly interest me. One, do these bodies of evidence indicate a cult of Asherah located in non-elite domestic contexts that is cognate with the temple- and palace-centered cults of Asherah that seem to be attested, especially in Judah, at points during the ninth, eighth, and seventh centuries BCE? Two, is there any basis for the frequently assumed correlation between family-based goddess worship and women's religious activities?

In the case of the two Jeremiah passages that allude to the worship of the Queen of Heaven, my answer to my first question must be no; I do not believe the goddess called the "Queen of Heaven" is Asherah. Rather, I would identify the "Queen of Heaven" as a composite deity who incorporates elements of West Semitic Astarte and East Semitic Ishtar.[27] Both Astarte and Ishtar, associated with the planet Venus, embody the astral characteristics that the epithet "Queen of *Heaven*" implies; in extrabiblical sources, both are called by the title "Lady of Heaven," which is, obviously, closely related to the Bible's "Queen of Heaven" epithet;[28] and both are associated with agricultural fertility, as is

27. Ackerman, "'And the Women Knead Dough,'" 109–24, reprinted in this volume at pp. 3–18; also Ackerman, *Under Every Green Tree*, 5–35.

28. For the title "Lady of Heaven" used of Astarte, see, from New Kingdom Egypt, an Eighteenth Dynasty stone bowl of Horemheb's reign (r. 1319–1292 BCE) on which Astarte is

Jeremiah's "Queen of Heaven" according to Jer 44:17–18 (in which the Queen's devotees report to Jeremiah that when they worshipped the Queen of Heaven, they had "plenty of food and it went well with us," but when they neglected her cult, they were "consumed . . . by famine").[29] Both Astarte and Ishtar, in addition, have associations with war, as may the Queen of Heaven (the people report to Jeremiah that to leave off her worship means to be consumed not only by famine but also by the sword [Jer 44:18]);[30] also, the cults of both Astarte and Ishtar had as a crucial element the offering of cakes, as, according to Jer 7:18 and 44:19, does the cult of the Queen of Heaven.[31] Ishtar, moreover, is

---

called "Lady of Heaven" (Redford, "New Light on the Asiatic Campaigning of Horemheb," 37); a stele from Memphis dating from the time of Merenptah (r. 1213–1204 BCE), which calls Astarte "Lady of Heaven, Mistress of all the Gods" (Petrie, *Memphis 1*, 19); and a late Nineteenth Dynasty stele of Pharaoh Siptah (r. 1198–1193 BCE), from Abu Simbel, which names Astarte "Lady of Heaven" (Maspero, "Notes de Voyage," 131–32). For this title used of Ishtar, see Edzard, "Inanna, Ištar," 81; Falkenstein, *Inschriften Gudeas von Lagaš 1: Einleitung*, 78–79; Helck, *Betrachtungen zur grossen Göttin*, 73; and Held, "Studies in Biblical Lexicography," 80n24.

29. In Biblical Hebrew, the noun ʿaštārôt, derived from the divine name ʿaštart, means "issue, progeny" and refers specifically to the bounteous issue or progeny of the flocks. The ancient identification of Mesopotamian Ishtar with the storehouse likewise demonstrates that goddess's associations with agricultural bounty.

30. The stele of Merenptah from Memphis (above, n. 28) that identifies Astarte as "Lady of Heaven" depicts the goddess with shield and spear. Other Egyptian representations of Astarte show her on horseback carrying weapons of war (Leclant, "Astarté à cheval," 1–67). Egyptian texts also describe Astarte as a war goddess in both the second and first millennia BCE. In addition, Thutmose IV (r. 1400–1390 BCE) is described as being mighty in the chariot like Astarte (J. A. Wilson, "Egyptians and the Gods of Asia," 250, 250n16), and Astarte is called a shield to Pharaoh Rameses III (r. 1187–1156 BCE) and a part of a thirteenth-century BCE king's war chariot (J. A. Wilson, "Egyptians and the Gods of Asia," 250, 250nn17–18). In the second millennium BCE, moreover, Astarte carries the epithet "Lady of Combat" (Leclant, "Astarté à cheval," 25); a text from the Ptolemaic period (305–30 BCE) similarly describes her as "Astarte, Mistress of Horses, Lady of the Chariot" (Leclant, "Astarté à cheval," 54–58; J. A. Wilson, "Egyptians and the Gods of Asia," 250n16). In the Canaanite realm, Astarte acts as a war goddess in concert with Ḥoron in Ugaritic mythology (*KTU* 1.2.1.7–8; 1.16.6.54–57), and Wolfram Herrmann has pointed out that the obverse of *PRU* 5.1 (19.39) also describes Ugaritic Astarte as a war goddess (Herrmann, "Aštart," 7–16). See too, on the evidence from Ugarit, Schmitt, "Astarte, Mistress of Horses," 215–16; Smith, *Poetic Heroes*, 195–208. Ishtar's associations with war, especially during the Akkadian period, are so well-known that one example can suffice: her epithet as "the Lady of the Battle and of the Fight" in the Code of Hammurapi (col. 50 [rs. 27], 92–93).

31. Regarding Astarte, see the Kition Tariff inscription, which lists the monthly expenditures for the temple of Astarte at Kition and which reads in line 10, *l'pm // 'š'p'yt tn' ḥlt lmlkt*, "for the two bakers who baked the basket of cakes for the Queen [i.e., for Queen

often explicitly called in Akkadian by the precise epithet "Queen of Heaven," and *kawwānîm*, the Hebrew term that is used to describe the bread cakes said to be baked as an offering for the biblical Queen of Heaven (Jer 7:18; 44:19), is usually taken by lexicographers as a loan word from Akkadian *kamānu*, which generically means "cake" but is often more specifically used to refer to cakes baked in honor of Ishtar.[32]

To be sure, some of these same parallels can also be cited with regard to the goddess Asherah; she, too, for example, can be called "Lady" and "Queen"; she, too, can be associated with fertility; her cult, too, surely could include offering cakes (as could the cults of most, if not all, ancient Near Eastern deities). But Asherah, although she can be addressed as "Queen" or "Lady," does not possess the astral characteristics the title "Queen of *Heaven*" implies; her associations with fertility concern more human fecundity than the sort of agricultural bounty that seems to be associated with the cult of the Queen of Heaven; and nowhere, to my knowledge, is the Ishtar-related vocabulary of *kamānu/ kawwānîm* used to describe cakes offered as a part of Asherah's cult. Thus the "Queen of Heaven," while a fascinating example concerning family-based goddess worship (and an example to which I will return below), cannot be taken as an example of family-based *Asherah* worship in Iron II Israel cognate with the Asherah worship I have previously located in temple and palace.[33]

Establishing the identity of the pillar figurines so ubiquitously found in Iron II domestic contexts is an extremely complex (and contested) matter. On one side of the debate, we can locate someone like Carol Meyers, who argues that because images of deities are typically made of precious metals or stones and because such images normally exhibit some symbols of divine identity (e.g., divine headdresses, divine garb, a typical deific pose, or an attached object typically associated with deity), we cannot take the rather plain and humble pillar figurines and related terra-cottas as goddess images. Rather, according to Meyers, they represent votive objects used within household religion to express the quest for female fecundity.[34] The converse position, of

---

Astarte]" (as translated by Peckham, "Notes on a Fifth–Century Phoenician Inscription from Kition," 305–6).

32. Ackerman, "And the Women Knead Dough,'" 115, reprinted in this volume at pp. 14–15; also Ackerman, *Under Every Green Tree*, 30–31.

33. Note that I do presume here, contrary to some commentators, that the goddesses we know as distinct beings from earlier Canaanite sources, most notably from the Late Bronze Age archives of Ugarit, remain more or less distinct in the Iron II period. See Olyan, *Asherah and the Cult of Yahweh*, 19–40, and contrast Dever, "Asherah, Consort of Yahweh?," 28–29.

34. Meyers, *Discovering Eve*, 162.

course, believes that the figures do represent a goddess, and the most common identification proposed is Asherah. Ruth Hestrin suggests, for example, that because the pillar and breasts are made by hand (versus the head, which could either be shaped by hand or made in a mold), we should take the pillar and breasts as the more significant parts of the figure and should see both as symbolizing Asherah, the pillar representing the trunk of Asherah's sacred tree and the breasts representing the life-giving and nurturing attributes of the mother goddess.[35]

William G. Dever arrives at this same conclusion, although by a somewhat different route, by arguing that the discovery of the Kuntillet 'Ajrûd and Khirbet el-Qôm inscriptions, when coupled with the sorts of reassessments of the biblical text I have previously described, point to a worship of Asherah that is so widespread in Israel that the pillar figurines most logically should be taken as a part of this goddess's cult.[36] Othmar Keel's and Christoph Uehlinger's exhaustive *Gods, Goddesses, and Images of God in Ancient Israel* likewise identifies the subject of the pillar figurines as the goddess Asherah, although in Keel's and Uehlinger's case, this is because they see continuities between the pillar figurines and what they call the "Branch Goddess" representations of Asherah from the Bronze Age; also because they feel the El-like character described for Yahweh in, especially, Judah would most naturally be associated with El's Canaanite consort, Asherah.[37] For my own part, I find Keel's and Uehlinger's reminder that the pillar figurines are predominantly attested in Judah to be of particular importance, given that the evidence for Asherah worship I have already surveyed may suggest that the goddess's cult is somewhat more prevalent in Judah than in Israel, especially the goddess's cult as practiced within the royal palace. Still, whatever evidence one takes as primary, I think it is generally fair to say that the majority position would accept the identification of the pillar figurines with Asherah and thus see in them a rich body of evidence suggesting many non-elite Israelites were "at home with the goddess."

And so to my second question: Is there any basis for the correlation that is often assumed between the worship of the goddess Asherah in a familial context and women's religious activities?

My response would be a partial yes. Certainly as I see it, we cannot speak of Asherah worship in the family-based context as the *exclusive* province of ancient Israelite women. Although, as I have earlier argued, they concern a

35. Hestrin, "Lachish Ewer," 222.
36. Dever, *Recent Archaeological Discoveries*, 158.
37. Keel and Uehlinger, *Gods, Goddesses, and Images of God*, 335.

different goddess, the Jeremiah materials regarding the worship of the Queen of Heaven nonetheless strike me as significant here, for according to these portraits of family-based goddess worship, the whole family—or at least the whole nuclear family—is involved: "the *sons* gather wood, the *fathers* kindle fire, and the *women* knead dough to make cakes for the Queen of Heaven" (Jer 7:18).[38] Still, despite this depiction of the whole family's involvement, I think it is fair to say that the women's contribution—the actual making of the offering cakes—is the most religiously significant, and thus it is reasonable to see these women as somehow *especially* involved in the goddess's worship. Indeed, in Jeremiah's polemic against the Queen of Heaven cult in Jer 44, he seems to make exactly this point, as it is *women* who are specifically identified in Jer 44:19 as those who have "burned incense to the Queen of Heaven and poured out libations to her . . . and made for her cakes in her image." It is thus *women*, in the culmination of Jeremiah's fulminations (v. 25), who are singled out for the prophet's special scorn.

Carol Meyers, moreover, has pointed out that it only makes sense that women would be especially associated with rituals like libation offerings and the making of offering cakes within the household sphere; this "because in the household context the female controlled food preparation."[39] To be sure, Meyers is not speaking specifically here of *goddess* worship but more generically about household cult activities; nevertheless, if we do reconstruct an Israelite domestic environment in which Asherah worship was present, then Meyers's comments about the crucial role women would play in any household cult should be evidence for their crucial role in the cult of Asherah. I also believe that some of the data I mentioned earlier regarding the role of women in Asherah worship in Yahweh's Jerusalem temple and in the royal court, especially the Judahite royal court, are relevant. With regard to the role of women in Asherah worship in Yahweh's Jerusalem temple, recall the report of 2 Kgs 23:7 that at least in the seventh century BCE, there were women who were housed within the temple compound who wove garments that were to be draped over the goddess's cult statue. Now, surely, these women were not the *sole* devotees of Asherah within the temple cult, as it must have been the temple's male priesthood that oversaw the erecting of the cult icon of the *'ăšērâ*

---

38. Jeremiah 7:18 is usually translated "the children gather wood," rendering the Hebrew *bānîm* (the plural of *bēn*, "son") as a generic rather than as gender specific. But a comparison with Lam 5:13, a composition closely related to the book of Jeremiah that describes young boys (*nĕʿārîm*) carrying loads of wood, suggests that wood-gathering was a task more typically assigned to males.

39. Meyers, *Discovering Eve*, 163.

in the temple in the first place and that assumed the responsibility for making offerings using the goddess's cult vessels that are mentioned in 2 Kgs 23:4. As with the worship of the Queen of Heaven as described in Jeremiah, that is, we cannot speak of Asherah worship in the Jerusalem temple as the *exclusive* province of women. Yet we can still note that women seem to play a *significant* role in the goddess's cult. Indeed, the description in 2 Kgs 23:7 of women within the temple compound who weave garments for Asherah is the *only* text in the entire Hebrew Bible that describes an actual cultic role for women within the temple's ritual life.

Likewise, the *only* biblical text that speaks explicitly to the ritual life of ancient Israelite queen mothers is the text in 1 Kgs 15:13 that describes Ma'acah's devotions regarding Asherah. Again, we cannot claim from this that Asherah worship in the royal court was the *exclusive* province of women; rather, the fact that the Southern king Manasseh and the Northern king Ahab are each said to have erected an *'ăšērâ* in his capital city suggests royal men, too, could be Asherah devotees. Still, Asherah worship, as I have argued, does seem to have been *especially important* to royal women, the queen mothers of Judah in particular. And hence my partial yes in answer to my question regarding women's role in the worship of the goddess Asherah in a family-based context: over and over, it seems to me, our evidence suggests that goddess worship can have an important place in women's religious lives, both generally (as in the case of the Queen of Heaven) and concerning Asherah worship in particular (as in the case of the women weaving in Yahweh's temple and in the case of the queen mothers' cultic activities).

IV. Conclusions: At Home with the Goddess in Ancient Israelite Religion

Let me end by teasing out some more general implications that I think are embedded in my just-concluded discussion of the role of women in the family-based, royal, and temple worship of Asherah, namely, implications regarding the nature of the phenomenon we often call Israelite "popular" religion. My concern here is particularly with those who would see the term "popular religion" as connoting the religious beliefs and practices of the populace writ large and who, moreover, would see the religious beliefs and practices of this populace writ large as somehow standing in opposition to the religious beliefs and practices of the religious elite, whose religious traditions are represented within the state and temple cult. My arguments here, however, suggest that Asherah worship—which is frequently described using this rubric of "popular religion"—is hardly restricted to the non-elite; indeed, I have proposed that at least one aspect of Asherah worship, the important role of women within Asherah's cult, is best understood by seeing a close interrelationship between the Asherah cult as it was practiced in the temple, as it was practiced in the palace, and as it was practiced in Israelite households. "Popular religion," that is—at least in this one case—needs to be understood as transcending any elite versus non-elite divide; rather the divide here seems to be between a significant cross-section of the Israelite population on the one hand, and, on the other hand, certain biblical authors (especially the prophets Isaiah, Jeremiah, and Micah and the spokespersons of the Deuteronomistic school) who regard the worship of Asherah in Israel as wrong. Again, Jeremiah's descriptions of the worship of the "Queen of Heaven" provide a useful analogy, as at one point those accused by Jeremiah of devoting themselves to the Queen respond by claiming that Jeremiah represents a minoritarian point of view when compared to those across the spectrum of the population—"we, our ancestors, our kings, and our princes" (Jer 44:17)—who engaged in the Queen's worship.

In short, however uneasy at least some spokespersons of the biblical point of view may have found themselves when confronted with Israelite worship of Asherah, I believe our evidence increasingly suggests that during at least some points in Israelite history, some significant cross-section of the population—temple personnel, royal personnel, and non-elite Israelites, including women—found themselves comfortably "at home with the goddess."

CHAPTER 10

Women and the Worship of Yahweh in Ancient Israel

*As I noted in my introductory comments to the previous chapter, the ma-
terials presented in this chapter, "Women and the Worship of Yahweh in
Ancient Israel," expand the focus of chapter 9, "At Home with the Goddess,"
to consider how women's participation in various goddesses' cults may have
changed over time, especially in relationship to women's engagement with
the cult of Yahweh. To address this question, this chapter, like the one that
precedes it, pulls together threads from many of the other chapters found
in this volume. Indeed, although not cited specifically in "Women and the
Worship of Yahweh in Ancient Israel," this chapter's inspiration might be
said to lie in chapter 4, "Why Is Miriam Also among the Prophets? (And Is
Zipporah among the Priests?)" There, I discussed the four women who, by
my reckoning, served as prophets according to biblical tradition (Miriam,
Deborah, Hulda, and Noadiah), and I also briefly mentioned the anonymous "daughters who prophesy" of Ezek 13:17-23 who arguably (at least as
I would interpret) performed medico-magical rituals on behalf of pregnant
and parturient women. What I did not stress in that chapter, however, is that
the biblical tradition can offer markedly different evaluations of these women
prophets. Deborah, Hulda, and Miriam in Exod 15:20 (Num 12:1-15 is a
different matter) are treated as women of note and deserving of honor. Noadiah, however, is portrayed negatively in Neh 6:14 because of her opposition to
Nehemiah, and Ezekiel excoriates the "daughters who prophesy" for, among
other things, "prophesying according to their own imagination" (as opposed,
presumably, to prophesying according to the messages they receive from God).*

An earlier version of this chapter appeared in Seymour Gitin, J. Edward Wright, and J. P.
Dessel, eds., *Confronting the Past: Archaeological and Historical Essays on Ancient Israel
in Honor of William G. Dever* (Winona Lake, IN: Eisenbrauns, 2006), 189–97. Used here
by permission.

Interestingly, moreover, Ezekiel's denunciation and the negative portrayal of Noadiah found in Neh 6:14 come, respectively, from the exilic and postexilic periods (the sixth and fifth centuries BCE), while I would identify the texts that concern Deborah, Hulda, and Miriam as preexilic in date.

Is this difference in date merely coincidence? "Women and the Worship of Yahweh in Ancient Israel" argues no, suggesting instead that the undertaking that the Bible identifies as the major religious event of the late seventh century BCE—the religious reformation efforts in which Judah's King Josiah (r. 640–609 BCE) engaged—had significant (and harmful) ramifications for women's engagement in the cult of Yahweh. To put the matter another way: I have titled this volume Gods, Goddesses, and the Women Who Serve Them, *and this chapter tries to probe the relationship between that title's three elements by asking when and how women could find fulfillment as cultic servitors within the cult of the Israelite god Yahweh, and what happened if they could not.*

According to both the books of Kings and Chronicles, a seminal event in the history of Israelite religion was the reformation movement promulgated by Judah's King Josiah during the last third of the seventh century BCE.[1] Although modern scholars have cautioned that Josiah's reform efforts may have been neither as sweeping nor as lasting as our texts suggest,[2] they have generally tended to agree with the biblical accounts' overall assessment. Mordechai Cogan and Hayim Tadmor, for example, characterize features of the Josianic reform as marking "a new departure in the history of Judah."[3] My purpose in the remarks that follow is to examine what effects this "new departure" may have had on the participation of women in the cult of the Israelite national god, Yahweh.

---

1. The dates associated with Josiah's reformation program are reported differently in Kings and Chronicles. According to 2 Kings, Josiah's reformation program began with the finding of the "book of the law" in the eighteenth year of his reign (i.e., 622 BCE) and culminated with the great Passover celebration held later that same year (2 Kgs 22:3, 8; 23:22–23). According to 2 Chr 34:3, Josiah began his reformation efforts already in ca. 628 BCE, six years prior to the finding of the "book of the law" in 622 BCE and the great Passover celebration held in that same year (2 Chr 34:8, 14; 35:1–19). Scholars often assume the Chronicles chronology is the more reliable, although parts of it may be tendentiously shaped. See Cogan and Tadmor, *II Kings*, 298; also, as there, Cogan, "Tendentious Chronology in the Book of Chronicles," 165–72.

2. See Lohfink, "Cult Reform of Josiah," 459–75, and the references collected in Albertz, *History of Israelite Religion in the Old Testament Period*, 1:345n5.

3. Cogan and Tadmor, *II Kings*, 296.

1. Women and the Production of Cultic Textiles

Women are explicitly mentioned only once in the accounts of Josiah's reforms found in 2 Kgs 23:4–25 and 2 Chr 34:3–7: in 2 Kgs 23:7, where we are told that as part of his efforts to purge forms of worship that he found apostate from the Jerusalem temple, Josiah destroyed the houses that were within the temple compound "where the women wove garments for Asherah"[4]—houses, that is, where women wove clothing to drape over a cult statue dedicated to the goddess Asherah that stood somewhere within the temple complex. I do take MT *l'šrh* to be the proper name of the ancient Canaanite mother goddess Asherah in this verse; the alternative is to read, as the Masoretic pointing (which includes the definite article) suggests, a reference to the cult object known as the *'ăšērâ*. But because I maintain, along with most commentators, that Asherah's adherents understood this cult object, which was in the shape of a stylized wooden pole or tree (Deut 16:21; 1 Kgs 14:15, 23; 16:33; 2 Kgs 17:10, 16; 21:3; 2 Chr 33:3), to represent the goddess in the cult, and because I further maintain that most ancient Israelites made little differentiation between a deity's cultic representation and the actual deity,[5] I hold that even if one were to follow the Masoretic pointing and read 2 Kgs 23:7 as referring to the *'ăšērâ* cult object, the text's reference is ultimately to a statue representing Asherah herself.

I count myself among those scholars, moreover, who claim that Asherah's cult image was being adorned—and therefore the goddess Asherah was being worshipped—in the Jerusalem temple during Josiah's reign because many in ancient Israel, including, presumably, the temple's priests, understood this goddess to be the consort of the Israelite national god Yahweh, who was therefore to receive devotions along with Yahweh in Yahweh's national sanctuary. Like many colleagues who have reached this same conclusion, I have found the inscriptional evidence pairing Yahweh with Asherah that comes from the sites of Kuntillet ʿAjrûd and Khirbet el-Qôm to be particularly significant.[6]

---

4. I read here *battîm*, cognate with Arabic *batt*, "woven garment," for the MT *bāttîm*, the plural of *bayit*, "house," as originally proposed by Šanda, *Die Bücher der Könige*, 2:344 (pointed out by Day, "Asherah in the Hebrew Bible," 407), and Driver, "Supposed Arabisms in the Old Testament," 107 (pointed out by Gray, *I & II Kings*, 664n[b], and by Cogan and Tadmor, *II Kings*, 286). This revocalization is supported by the Lucianic recension of the LXX, which reads *stolas*, "garment, robe."

5. See Ackerman, "At Home with the Goddess," 457–58, reprinted in this volume at pp. 194–96; also, Dever, "Archaeology and the Ancient Israelite Cult," 11*; Olyan, *Asherah and the Cult of Yahweh*, 31–32.

6. For the original announcements of the Kuntillet ʿAjrûd discoveries, see Meshel, "Kun-

Equally significant, I have found, are the many reevaluations of the forty or so biblical texts mentioning the *'ăšērâ* cult object or the goddess Asherah that have been inspired by the Kuntillet ʿAjrûd and Khirbet el-Qôm discoveries. Saul M. Olyan has argued, for example, that while older interpretations of texts that mention Asherah worship in Jerusalem (e.g., 1 Kgs 15:13; 2 Kgs 18:4; 23:4, 6–7, 14) saw in these passages evidence of aberrant and heterodox religious practices imported into Judah from elsewhere, the Kuntillet ʿAjrûd and Khirbet el-Qôm evidence suggests instead that for some ancient Israelites, during at least some points in ancient Israelite history, Asherah worship was a perfectly appropriate part of the Yahwistic cult, including the Yahwistic cult as observed in Jerusalem and in the Jerusalem temple.[7]

Olyan similarly proposes that a reevaluation of the biblical record suggests that for many, Asherah worship was a perfectly appropriate part of the Yahwistic cult as practiced in Northern Kingdom shrines. He argues, for example, that the pairing of Asherah with "Yahweh of Samaria" in one of the Kuntillet ʿAjrûd inscriptions, together with the biblical texts that attest that an *'ăšērâ* cult object stood in Samaria, demonstrates that Asherah was worshipped alongside Yahweh in a Yahwistic temple in the Northern capital city. As in the South, moreover, this seems to have been considered a perfectly appropriate part of

---

tillet ʿAjrûd—An Israelite Religious Center," 50–54; Meshel, "Kuntillet ʿAjrûd—An Israelite Site," 118–24; Meshel, *Kuntillet ʿAjrûd: A Religious Center*; and Meshel and Meyers, "The Name of God in the Wilderness of Zin," 6–10, subsequently followed in 2012 by the official publication volume, Meshel, *Kuntillet ʿAjrud*. For the initial publication of the Khirbet el-Qôm inscription, see Dever, "Iron Age Epigraphic Material from the Area of Khirbet el-Kôm," 158–89; revised studies were published by Lemaire, "Date et origine des inscriptiones hébraïques et pheniciennes de Kuntillet ʿAjrud," 131–43; Lemaire, "Les inscriptions de Khirbet el-Qôm," 597–608; and Lemaire, "Who or What Was Yahweh's Asherah?," 42–51. To be sure, one must admit that the phrase "his [Yahweh's] *'ăšērâ*" found in these corpora is grammatically difficult, and for some, the solution has been to understand *'ăšērâ* in the inscriptions as a common noun rather than the divine appellation Asherah so as to avoid the grammatical improbability of a pronominal suffix being affixed to a proper name. Commentators have thus proposed translating *'ăšērâ* as "shrine" (Lipiński, "The Goddess Atirat," 101–19); as "the female aspect of Yahweh," reified and given a separate identity (McCarter, "Aspects of the Religion of the Israelite Monarchy," 149; Miller, "Absence of the Goddess," 246); or as the *'ăšērâ* cult object. Because "cult object" is the most commonly attested meaning for *'ăšērâ* in the Hebrew Bible, this translation would be my preference among these three alternatives, but I would again argue that because the ancient Israelites understood a deity's cult symbol and the deity to be essentially the same, we can and should understand the Kuntillet ʿAjrûd and Khirbet el-Qôm inscriptions as ultimately speaking of Yahweh's goddess consort.

7. Olyan, *Asherah and the Cult of Yahweh*, 9.

Yahwistic tradition, acceptable, indeed, to even the most zealous of Yahwistic worshippers: for example, the reformer king Jehu, who allowed the 'ăšērâ cult object to remain standing in Samaria while otherwise purging all non-Yahwistic worship from the city.[8] In Yahweh's shrine at Bethel as well, there seems to have been an 'ăšērâ (at least there was in the late seventh century BCE, according to 2 Kgs 23:15), indicating that both Bethel's Yahwistic priests and the Yahwists who worshipped at that sanctuary found Asherah's presence alongside Yahweh acceptable. Moreover, the Northern prophets Amos and Hosea, who otherwise deride many aspects of the Bethel cult (e.g., Hos 8:5–6; 10:5–6; 13:2; Amos 3:13–15; 4:4–5; 5:4–5; 7:10–13), make no complaint about Bethel's 'ăšērâ, which at least "indirectly suggests approval and legitimacy."[9]

Unfortunately, none of these biblical texts, other than 2 Kgs 23:7, makes any mention of the practice of clothing the 'ăšērâ cult statue. Still, there are grounds for assuming that this was a typical aspect of Asherah worship. The clothing of cult statues is mentioned again in the Bible in Jer 10:9,[10] and Jeremiah gives no indication that he sees this as anything but normal in cults that use divine images. Ezekiel implies much the same in Ezek 16:18.[11] Indeed, the making of garments for divine images is a well-known practice in other ancient Near Eastern and eastern Mediterranean communities, attested in sources from Mesopotamia, Egypt, and Greece.[12] At least one set of our materials, moreover, indicates that, as in 2 Kgs 23:7, it was women who undertook the responsibility for producing a cult statue's garments; these are the many records from classical Greece that document how select Athenian women wove and offered to the goddess Athena the new robe or peplos that was draped over her cult statue as the central event of the annual Panathenaia celebration.[13] Marilyn A. Katz further notes that as part of the Panathenaia, "the girls and women of Athens . . . undertook the ceremonial cleansing of the goddess's cult statue,"[14] and we might thus speculate that the women who

8. Olyan, *Asherah and the Cult of Yahweh*, 6–7, 32–35.

9. Olyan, *Asherah and the Cult of Yahweh*, 7.

10. Gressmann, "Josia und das Deuteronomium," 325–26, as pointed out by Cogan and Tadmor, *II Kings*, 286.

11. Dick, "Prophetic Parodies of Making the Cult Image," 19n(j).

12. See, e.g., for Mesopotamia: Matsushima, "Divine Statues in Ancient Mesopotamia," 211–18, and Oppenheim, "Golden Garments of the Gods," 172 (pointed out by Cogan and Tadmor, *II Kings*, 286); for Egypt: Lorton, "Theology of Cult Statues in Ancient Egypt," 133–45; and for Greece: Barber, "Peplos of Athena," 106, citing Mansfield, "Robe of Athena," 443.

13. Barber, "Peplos of Athena," 112–17; Katz, "Sappho and Her Sisters," 515; Lefkowitz, "Women in the Panathenaic and Other Festivals," 79. See also above, figs. 2.8 and 2.9.

14. Katz, "Sappho and Her Sisters," 515.

served Asherah in the Jerusalem temple similarly gave ritual baths to Asherah's cult image. Certainly, the tradition of bathing cult statues, like the tradition of clothing them, is well known from elsewhere in the ancient Near East. Our ancient Near Eastern sources, as well as those from Greece, in addition make clear that the role of those who bathe and clothe the cult image, like the role of the priests who take responsibility for the feeding of the gods, is of major significance within a deity's religious community.[15] Indeed, in Athens, "the *arrhephoroi* [the young girls chosen to help set the warp of Athena's peplos] were considered sufficiently important to be housed, during the term of their service, near the temple of Athena Polias on the Acropolis."[16] The parallel with 2 Kgs 23:7 is striking.

So what, then, is the effect of Josiah's decision in 2 Kgs 23:7 that the houses within the temple's grounds where women wove garments for Asherah's cult statue must be destroyed? At a minimum, obviously, Josiah displaces these women and their work from what I think we must assume was an important and honored location within the temple compound. More significantly, however, Josiah's actions have the effect of prohibiting women from performing a cultic function within the Jerusalem temple that our comparative evidence suggests was an important and honored task within Israelite religion. More significantly still, Josiah's reforms work to remove women from the religiously important and honored positions they may have assumed as Asherah's cultic weavers elsewhere in the land of Israel, and, most significant of all, Josiah's efforts ultimately have the effect of removing ancient Israelite women from their positions as Asherah's weavers both in Jerusalem and elsewhere in the land of Israel for good. For not only is Josiah described in 2 Kgs 23 as displacing Asherah's women weavers from their houses within the temple complex; he is described as acting aggressively to remove any trace of Asherah worship from the temple, from Jerusalem, and throughout Israelite territory. Thus Josiah is said to have removed the cult image of Asherah from the temple and to have burned it at the Wadi Kidron (2 Kgs 23:6), to have removed from the temple all the vessels that would have been used to make offerings to Asherah (2 Kgs 23:4), and to have torn down the sacred images of Asherah that stood east of Jerusalem, just south of the Mount of Olives (2 Kgs 23:14).

So zealously, in fact, does Josiah seek to eliminate Asherah worship throughout Israel that he is described as crossing over the border of Judah to go to the old Northern Kingdom shrine of Bethel to destroy the *'ăšērâ* cult

---

15. Matsushima, "Divine Statues in Ancient Mesopotamia," 216–18.
16. Lefkowitz, "Women in the Panathenaic and Other Festivals," 79.

object that stood there (2 Kgs 23:15). Moreover, while I believe we have some evidence that Asherah worship survived Josiah's reformation efforts and so reemerged after his death,[17] this evidence is sporadic and sparse, and it completely disappears by the early postexilic period. Josiah, that is, may not have been as immediately successful in eradicating Asherah worship among the Israelites as he would have wished, but his goal was certainly realized within the span of two or three generations. By the last quarter of the sixth century BCE, no opportunities remained for ancient Israelite women to serve Asherah as weavers or to serve her in any other capacity.

To be sure, no opportunities remained for men to serve Asherah either: to serve, for example, as the priests who presumably would have made the offerings to Asherah in the Jerusalem temple that are alluded to in 2 Kgs 23:4. Such men, however, should still have been able to serve as priests in the absence of an Asherah cult because of the Israelites' understanding that Asherah was Yahweh's consort and thus was worshipped in conjunction with the male god. The priests, that is, who served Asherah would of necessity also have been servants of her divine husband Yahweh and so, with the elimination of the goddess's cult, would simply have begun to offer their religious service to Yahweh alone. Note in this regard that while Josiah is said in 2 Kgs 23:5 to have deposed the priests of the god Baal and also those priests who made offerings to the sun, the moon, the constellations, and all the host of heaven, there is no mention of his deposing the priests of Asherah when her cult was removed from the Jerusalem temple. Rather, I would suggest, the priests who served Yahweh's female *consort*, as opposed to the priests who served Baal and other gods who were Yahweh's *rivals*, were readily able to transfer their service from Asherah's cult to the cult of Yahweh. But because of the aniconic traditions of Yahwism, which are insisted upon in the biblical text and seem generally to be confirmed by the absence of identifiable Yahweh images in the archaeological record,[18] the work done by the women weavers who served Asherah could not as easily be relocated within Yahwistic tradition. In the Yahwism without Asherah that Josiah promoted, no cult statue remained to be clothed.

The Yahwistic cult did, however, use woven goods and additional kinds of textiles for many other purposes: for example, for priestly vestments, for

17. See, e.g., Jer 17:2; Ezek 8:3–5; and Isa 65:3; I have discussed the latter two of these texts in Ackerman, *Under Every Green Tree*, 55–66, 185–94.

18. See Dever, review of *No Graven Image*, 94; Hendel, "Social Origins of the Aniconic Tradition," 366–68; Hendel, "Aniconism and Anthropomorphism," 205–28; Mettinger, *No Graven Image?*; and Sasson, "On the Use of Images," 63–70. Cf. Schmidt, "The Aniconic Tradition," 75–105, and van der Toorn, "Israelite Figurines," 47–51.

the curtains and other types of draperies that hung in and around Yahweh's sanctuary, and to cover the table of the bread of presence. We have some evidence, moreover, that women may have participated in the production of these cultic fabrics. In Exod 35:25–26, every "skillful woman" (*kol-'iššâ ḥakmat-lēb*) among those encamped at the base of Mount Sinai is said to have brought the colored yarns, fine linen, and spun goats' hair she had produced as offerings to be used in the making of "the tent of meeting, and for all its service, and for the sacred vestments" (Exod 35:21).[19] In Exod 36:1, moreover, we are told that *kol 'îš ḥăkam-lēb* "to whom Yahweh has given skill and understanding to know how to do all the work in the making of the sanctuary shall work in accordance with all that Yahweh has commanded." Although the Hebrew here means literally "every skillful man . . . shall work," we might also translate "every skillful individual," which would suggest this verse alludes back to the "skillful women" mentioned in Exod 35:25–26, who are seen as capable of producing the various textile products for the tabernacle and its service that Yahweh has commissioned. Similarly, in Exod 36:8, we are told that "all those with skill among the workers made the tabernacle with ten curtains," which can be interpreted to mean that the women described in Exod 35:25–26 as skilled in textile production were envisioned as helping to make the tabernacle's elaborate collection of draperies.

The fact remains, however, that in the Exodus accounts of the construction of the tabernacle and all its furnishings, the only explicit mention of women's participation in the creation of cultic textiles is the description in Exod 35:25–26 of them bringing what we might think of as "raw materials" as offerings for other fabricators to use. When the actual making of the tabernacle's textile inventory is described, it is men who are more readily cited as doing this work. We have just seen, for example, that Exod 36:1, if translated literally, refers only to skilled *men* in designating those who shall do the work of constructing Yahweh's sanctuary. Then, once the construction begins, it is Bezalel, the chief of the two main craftsmen in charge of the construction, who is said to make curtains of goats' hair that comprise the tent that was draped over the tabernacle's wooden frame (Exod 36:14) and who likewise, in Exod 36:35, is said to make an elaborately decorated curtain that seems meant to be hung at the entrance of the inner sanctum of the tabernacle in which the ark was housed. Similarly, in Exod 36:37, Bezalel makes an elaborate cloth screen that is to stand at the entrance of the tabernacle's outer chamber. Also, according to Exod 39:2, 8, and 22, he makes the priestly ephod, breastplate,

19. Meyers, "Skilled Women (and Men)," 201–2.

and robe of the ephod using colored yarns and fine linen. He is said to have made as well, along with the sanctuary's other master craftsman, Oholiab, the linen tunics, turbans, headdresses, undergarments, and sashes worn by Aaron and his priestly descendants (Exod 39:27–29). Both Bezalel (in Exod 35:35) and Oholiab (in Exod 35:35 and again in 38:23) are moreover lauded as skilled in doing embroidery work in colored yarns and in fine linen and (in Exod 35:35) in doing the work of weaving.

All of these Exodus materials come, as is well known, from the Pentateuch's P or Priestly source that, most scholars agree, reached its final form in the sixth or fifth century BCE, and it may well be that in stressing Bezalel's and Oholiab's skill in textile work, these P texts signal—in seeming contrast to the preexilic evidence found in 2 Kgs 23:7—a postexilic bias for having men assume the primary and perhaps ultimately the exclusive responsibility for cultic weaving and other types of cultic textile production. In the postexilic books of Chronicles, too, cultic textile production is depicted as a responsibility assumed by men, with the Phoenician artisan Hurum-abi, who has been sent from Tyre to aid in Solomon's temple-building project, described as able to "work . . . in purple, blue, and crimson fabrics and fine linen" (2 Chr 2:13 [in most English translations, 2:14]; see also 2 Chr 2:6[7]). The actual creation of cultic fabrics in the 2 Chronicles temple-building account, however, is ascribed to Solomon himself (3:14). There are no counterparts to these verses in the older Kings temple-building account, which makes no mention of any fabrics at all. As commentators have pointed out, the Chronicles text has added these details, among others, so as to suggest parallels between Solomon's temple and Exodus's description of the tabernacle sanctuary.[20] But what we have to ask for our purposes is whether Chronicles, by stressing, like Exodus's P materials, the role of men in cultic textile production, indicates it shares P's seeming bias that it is men who should properly and perhaps exclusively assume responsibility for the fabrication of cultic cloth. Indeed, does Chronicles, by ignoring the Exodus account's preliminary mention of women's role in generating the raw materials used for cultic fabric, suggest an even stronger bias than Exodus's P materials that cultic textile production should be a responsibility assumed exclusively by men?

In the same vein, we also must ask why Chronicles, in its revisions of the 2 Kings account of Josiah's reform, omits any mention of Josiah's deposing of the women who wove cultic garments for Asherah, even though Chronicles otherwise cites liberally Josiah's attempts to eradicate Asherah worship

20. Japhet, *I and II Chronicles*, 545.

in Israel (2 Chr 34:3, 4, 7). Is this omission coincidence? Is it explained by
Chronicles' general tendency to see Josiah's reforms as concerned only with
a purge of those cults considered non-Yahwistic that were found outside of
the temple, the temple having already been purified, according to Chronicles' chronology, in Manasseh's reign?[21] Or might we again be seeing in the
Chronicles' omission a postexilic bias—in seeming contrast to the preexilic
evidence of 2 Kgs 23:7—that men should assume the primary and perhaps
ultimately the exclusive responsibility for cultic weaving and other types of
cultic textile production? It is, unfortunately, impossible to say for sure, and
arguments from silence are of course notoriously weak. Still, if the latter of
the explanations I have just advanced has any merit, then we have again to ask
about the effects that certain aspects of Josiah's reform efforts had on women's
participation in the cult of Yahweh. If one of the effects of the reform was to
displace women from their service as weavers in the cult of Asherah, and if
there was a roughly concurrent tendency to assign the primary and perhaps
the exclusive responsibility for textile production to men in the associated
cult of Yahweh, then what is ultimately lost to women through the agency of
Josiah's reform is an important and honored role as fabricators of cultic cloth
within ancient Israelite religion.

ii. Women and Music

Athenian women, in addition to weaving the peplos for the annual Panathenaia festival and undertaking the ceremonial cleansing of the goddess's
cult statue, participated in dances in Athena's honor during the course of the
Panathenaic celebration.[22] I and others have similarly documented women's
roles in festal dancing and, more generally, music-making within the cult of
Yahweh. I have described, for example, the special role women seem to play
as dancers and more generally music-makers during the fall harvest festival
of Sukkot.[23] Eunice B. Poethig, followed by Carol Meyers, has likewise described the special role of women in performing the victory songs that celebrate Yahweh's triumphs in holy war (Exod 15:20–21; Judg 5:1–31; 11:34; 1 Sam

---

21. Second Chronicles 33:15–16; for discussion, see Japhet, *I and II Chronicles*, 1019.

22. Katz, "Sappho and Her Sisters," 515; Lefkowitz, "Women in the Panathenaic and
Other Festivals," 79.

23. Ackerman, *Warrior, Dancer, Seductress, Queen*, 253–87.

18:6–7).[24] Meyers has also noted that in Ps 68:25–26(24–25), women playing frame drums are among those musicians who participate in a procession into Yahweh's sanctuary in order to celebrate God as a divine warrior who has vanquished Israel's enemies,[25] and she further argues that because frame drums are an instrument characteristically played by women,[26] their mention in Ps 81:3(2), in the context of an exhortation to make music at the festivals of the new moon, the full moon, and other festal days, demonstrates as well women's role as music-makers within the Yahwistic cult. The mention of frame drums again, along with other musical instruments, in Pss 149:3 and 150:3–5, both of which are hymns urging that praise be sung to God, provides yet more evidence suggesting women's participation in Yahwistic musical performances, and Ps 150, moreover, like Ps 68:25–26(24–25), explicitly places its musicians, including, by implication, its women musicians, within Yahweh's temple compound.[27] We can finally note that, while not as explicitly cultic, women's musical performance is well attested as a part of certain life-cycle rituals, especially weddings, funerals, and other occasions of lamentation (Judg 11:37–40; 2 Sam 1:24; Jer 9:16–20[17–21]; Ezek 32:16; Ps 78:63; and 2 Chr 35:25).[28]

It is striking, however, from the point of view of our inquiry, that almost all of the texts attesting to women's cultic musicianship that I have just cited come from the preexilic or early exilic period (although the Psalms, it must be granted, are notoriously difficult to date). When we turn to look for evidence of women's role as cultic musicians in the late exilic or postexilic period, it is much more difficult to find. We do still find one text that attests to women's participation in rituals of lamentation, although even this text, 2 Chr 35:25, seems to stress women's role as mourners less than does its preexilic counterparts by describing how both "the singing men and the singing women" chanted the laments sung upon the death of King Josiah; contrast Jer 9:16(17), in which only "mourning women" are summoned to come to sing a dirge over the destruction of Jerusalem. Meyers speculates that the addition of men to the retinue of mourners in Chronicles is due to the fact that "the mourning for Josiah, one of the few kings considered a righteous ruler, called for an extraordinary outpouring of mourning, which would have involved profes-

24. Poethig, "Victory Song Tradition"; Meyers, "Mother to Muse," 50–77; Meyers, "Of Drums and Damsels," 16–27; and Meyers, "Women with Hand-Drums, Dancing," 189–91.

25. Meyers, "Women with Hand-Drums, Dancing," 190.

26. Meyers, "Of Drums and Damsels," 19, 21; Meyers, "Women with Hand-Drums, Dancing," 190.

27. Meyers, "Women with Hand-Drums, Dancing," 190.

28. On lamentation, see further Bird, "Israelite Religion," 106.

sional singers of both genders."[29] My own sense, though, is that what may have happened to women's roles as cultic weavers in the aftermath of the Josianic reform also happened with regard to women's roles as cultic and quasi-cultic musicians: that a responsibility assumed by women in the prereformation period became primarily and perhaps even exclusively available to men.

More specifically, according, at least, to the books of Chronicles, the responsibility for music-making in the Yahwistic cult lies solely with the male members of certain clans of the tribe of Levi (e.g., 1 Chr 15:16–24; 16:4, 41–42). The kindred books of Ezra and Nehemiah also seem to describe the temple's singers as men from various Levite clans, although these texts are not unambiguous (cf., e.g., Ezra 2:41, 70). Ezekiel apparently believes as well that the singers in the temple are to be male Levites (Ezek 40:44–46), although he, in contrast to Chronicles and the admittedly ambiguous books of Ezra and Nehemiah, envisions the temple's Levitical musicians as tracing their ancestry back both to the Solomonic-era priest Zadok and to other ancestors within the Levitical line. Chronicles, conversely, along with multiple texts in Ezra and Nehemiah, suggests that the temple's musicians are drawn solely from the Levites' non-Zadokite lineages. Particularly noteworthy according to the Ezra-Nehemiah-Chronicles tradition is the line of Asaph (see, e.g., Ezra 2:41; Neh 7:44; 11:22; 1 Chr 16:7; 2 Chr 35:15), and, consequently, a significant corpus of hymns within the Psalter (Pss 50, 73–83) becomes attributed to him.

Determining the preexilic history of the Levites has proven a daunting task for scholars. Nevertheless, there seems to have emerged a consensus that the "priests of the towns of Judah" mentioned in 2 Kgs 23:8 are members of a non-Zadokite line or lines of Levites who had been serving in shrines in the Judean countryside while priests who traced their descent back to Zadok (and ultimately to Aaron) had, since the time of Solomon, been serving in the temple in Jerusalem.[30] Josiah, though, whose reforms, all scholars agree, were associated in some way with the discovery in the temple of a version of the book of Deuteronomy (called in both Kings and Chronicles the "book of the law"),[31] follows the dictates of Deuteronomy (e.g., Deut 12:2–28) in promoting

---

29. Meyers, "Singing Women (and Men) Who Lament," 284.

30. Cross, *Canaanite Myth and Hebrew Epic*, 195–215, 237–38.

31. The exact relationship between the finding of the "book of the law" and Josiah's program of reform is described differently in Kings and Chronicles. In Kings, some fairly modest attempts at religious rejuvenation seem to have been underway before the reform (i.e., a series of repairs to the temple had begun), but the full-scale reform—the community's making of a covenant that committed them to obeying the terms of the newly discovered law book; the purging of the cult to bring it into accord with Josiah's/Deuteronomy's vision of what Yahwism should be; and the celebration of a great Passover—occurs only after the

the centralization of Yahwistic worship in a place God has chosen "for the dwelling of his name"—that place being, for Josiah, the temple in Jerusalem. Josiah, therefore, according at least to 2 Kgs 23:8 (this material is not paralleled in Chronicles), "brought all of the priests out of the towns of Judah" and to the temple in Jerusalem. Deuteronomy further mandates that a Levite who leaves "wherever he has been residing in Israel and comes to the place that Yahweh will choose . . . may minister in the name of Yahweh his God, like all his fellow Levites who stand there before Yahweh" (Deut 18:6–7), which is to say, in the language of Deuteronomy, that any Levite may serve Yahweh in God's central sanctuary in the same way that all his fellow Levites serve, whether these Levites be of the line of the priest Zadok or not. According to 2 Kgs 23:9, however, the non-Zadokite Levites who were brought by Josiah to Jerusalem "did not come up to the altar of Yahweh"; they were, that is, not consecrated to offer the animal sacrifices to God that were the centerpiece of Yahwistic ritual. Instead, according to 2 Kgs 23:9, they "ate unleavened bread among their kindred," which may mean they were allowed to make grain offerings as part of the temple ritual, along with other non-Zadokite Levites, or that they, along with these non-Zadokite Levites and other temple personnel, consumed unleavened cakes during the great Passover celebration held in Jerusalem as a part of Josiah's reformation efforts.[32]

Yet however we interpret the specifics of 2 Kgs 23:9, the fact remains that according to this text, a substantial number of Levites were brought to the Jerusalem temple as a result of Josiah's reformation efforts but there were deemed unable to perform the central ritual of Yahwistic animal sacrifice for which they had previously taken responsibility in countryside shrines. They thus found themselves in want of something to do, as also the temple's more established priesthood found itself in want of something to do with them. Although our sources are limited, I think we must presume that the origins of the traditions that see the Levites as a class of second-order temple functionaries lie in this period. Certainly, within fifty years of the Josianic reforms, in 573 BCE (Ezek 40:1), Ezekiel envisions the non-Zadokite Levites as responsible for only

---

finding of the "book of the law" and is inspired by it. In Chronicles, the beginning of the reformation efforts date back even before the time of Josiah, to the final years of the reign of his grandfather Manasseh (2 Chr 33:15–16), and many of Josiah's own efforts to eliminate from Israelite religion all types of worship he sees as non-Yahwistic, as well as his efforts to repair and restore the temple complex, predate the finding of the book as well (2 Chr 34:3–13). For Chronicles, what the book inspires is only a ceremony of covenant affirmation and an enormous celebration of the Passover in Jerusalem. See further n. 1 above.

32. Cogan and Tadmor, *II Kings*, 287.

secondary temple rituals. They may not approach Yahweh's altar or come near to anything that has been consecrated to Yahweh: that privilege is reserved for Zadokite descendants alone (Ezek 44:13, 15–16). Instead, the Levites serve as gatekeepers, they slaughter sacrificial animals, and they stand before the people to serve them (Ezek 44:11). Moreover, they serve as singers, although in Ezekiel, as I have already noted, both non-Zadokite Levites and the Zadokites assume this function (Ezek 40:44–46). Still, from Ezekiel's preliminary attempts at status differentiation, it is but a short jump to the hierarchy that is established in Ezra and Nehemiah, in Chronicles, and somewhat in certain P materials in the Pentateuch (e.g., Num 3–4), whereby Zadokite priests take responsibility for the central rituals of Yahwistic faith while the non-Zadokite Levites serve as the temple's gatekeepers, musicians, and temple servants.

Yet if Josiah's reforms establish a trajectory that culminates by the fifth and fourth centuries BCE in the conviction that it is the men of certain Levitical lineages who are responsible for musical performance in the Yahwistic cult, then what of the earlier traditions that assigned to women important roles as music-makers within Yahwistic ritual? Our answer must be that women's ability to participate in the cult as musicians is greatly diminished by the time of the postexilic period. In some cases, as I have already suggested, this may mean that the rituals of music-making associated with mourning that were previously the responsibility primarily or perhaps even exclusively of women were reconceptualized so as to include both men and women (2 Chr 35:25).

In other cases, I suggest, older traditions that described women as the actual makers of music at the time of certain cultic celebrations came to be rendered in far more metaphorical language. For example, in Jer 30:23–24, amid a series of oracles (Jer 30:1–31:40) that almost all commentators date, at least in the form in which they have come down to us, to the early exilic period,[33] Jeremiah speaks of how Yahweh, although now requiring that God's people endure suffering, will eventually come like a storm against the Israelites' enemies and destroy them. Following this triumph of Yahweh, the divine warrior, comes the same sort of victory celebration I have already noted is described in older traditions—the celebration where women, accompanying themselves on frame drums, dance and sing hymns praising Yahweh's saving acts (Exod 15:20–21; Judg 5:1–31; 11:34; 1 Sam 18:6–7). Still, Jeremiah, in drawing on these earlier traditions of women's music-making after a victory in holy war, changes them not insignificantly by suggesting that the celebratory music is no

33. While an older source, we may still see as representative the comments of Bright, *Jeremiah*, 284–87.

longer made by actual women but by the nation Israel, personified as a woman (31:4). Thus, while the notion of women as the ones who take responsibility for the musical performance that follows a holy war is retained, the idea that it is real women who would actually go forth to sing and dance is eroded. To put the matter another way, we might ask of Jeremiah what is left, according to his vision, for the actual women of ancient Israel who would make the ritual music that celebrates Yahweh's triumphs in battle? In the same vein, we might ask of Ezekiel, the Priestly tradition, and the Ezra-Nehemiah-Chronicles corpus what is left, according to their vision, for the women of ancient Israel who would render service as musicians as a part of Yahwistic worship? Our evidence may well suggest that the opportunities available to such women in the aftermath of Josiah's reforms were relatively few.

III. Concluding Reflections

In the biblical text, especially in the prophetic books, women are often derided as responsible for behaviors the prophets deem apostate in the religion of Israel (e.g., Isa 3:16–24; 4:1; 32:9–14; Hosea 1–3; 4:13; Amos 4:1–3). A variant motif personifies Jerusalem, also called Zion, as a female apostate or "harlot" who represents the failure of the entire Yahwistic community to live up to the religious standards the prophets required (Isa 1:21–23; 3:25–26; 57:3, 6–13; Jer 4:30; 13:20–27; 22:20–23; Ezek 16:1–63; 23:1–4, 11–49; Lam 1:8–9). In particular, these texts tend to condemn women, or the woman Jerusalem, for worshipping gods other than the Israelite national god, Yahweh.

Ironically, however, when we look beyond this corpus of prophetic diatribe, which dates from the eighth to the sixth centuries BCE, for actual descriptions of women worshipping gods other than Yahweh, we find only three sets of materials: (1) descriptions of women who served the goddess Asherah (e.g., 1 Kgs 15:13; 2 Kgs 23:7); (2) descriptions of women who participated in the cult of a goddess known only as the Queen of Heaven (Jer 7:16–20; 44:15–19, 25), probably a syncretistic deity who incorporates elements of both East Semitic Ishtar and West Semitic Astarte;[34] and (3) descriptions of women who sat at the northern entrance of the Jerusalem temple's inner courtyard to mourn the death of the god Tammuz that is described in Mesopotamian myth (Ezek 8:14). The first of these three traditions, I have intimated above, should be under-

---

34. Ackerman, "'And the Women Knead Dough,'" 109–24, reprinted in this volume at pp. 3–18; Ackerman, *Under Every Green Tree*, 5–35.

stood as categorically different from the latter two, as women who worshipped Asherah did so as part of their devotion to the Israelite national god, Yahweh. The women who worshipped the Queen of Heaven, conversely, explicitly describe themselves as abandoning the worship of Yahweh in favor of this goddess whom they perceive to be more powerful (Jer 44:15–19), and I think we must presume that the women who devote themselves to Tammuz worship also see themselves as abandoning Yahweh in favor of a rival deity.[35] Quite commonly, this movement away from Yahwistic worship as described in the late seventh-century/early sixth-century BCE texts of Jeremiah and the early sixth-century BCE text of Ezekiel is understood as a response to the growing Babylonian threat faced by Judah from ca. 605 BCE onward: as Judah became more and more endangered by Babylonian military might, the people sought more and more to protect themselves by offering their devotions to gods either wholly (in the case of Tammuz) or partially (in the case of the Queen of Heaven) of Babylonian provenance.

I do not necessarily mean to disagree with this explanation here, but I nevertheless find it quite curious that it is women who are especially described in the late seventh and early sixth centuries BCE as abandoning the worship of Yahweh in the favor of other deities (although cf. Ezek 8:16). I also find it quite curious that, despite the two centuries of prophetic hyperbole condemning women as apostate that I cited above, it is only in the late seventh and early sixth centuries BCE that we have solid evidence of women worshipping other gods instead of Yahweh. In the light of the analysis I have offered in this chapter, I am moved to ask whether the devotions offered to other gods by these late seventh- and early sixth-century BCE women, in addition (perhaps) to being inspired by the threat of the Babylonian invasion, were a response to certain aspects of Josiah's reformation efforts. If the Josianic reform ultimately did have the effect of distancing or even removing women from some important and honored functions they had earlier performed within the cult of Yahweh—the manufacture of cultic textiles for Yahweh's goddess consort and/or the making of cultic music as part of Yahwistic ritual celebrations —then the women of the post-Josianic era may well have felt themselves compelled to abandon Yahwistic worship and find more meaningful venues for religious expression elsewhere.

---

35. Ackerman, *Under Every Green Tree*, 91.

Bibliography

Abbot, Nabia. "Pre-Islamic Arab Queens." *American Journal of Semitic Languages and Literature* 58 (1941): 1–22.

Abousamra, Gaby, and André Lemaire. "Astarte in Tyre According to New Iron Age Funerary Stelae." *WdO* 43 (2013): 153–57.

Ackerman, Susan. "'And the Women Knead Dough': The Worship of the Queen of Heaven in Sixth-Century Judah." Pages 109–24 in *Gender and Difference in Ancient Israel*. Edited by Peggy L. Day. Minneapolis: Fortress, 1989.

———. "At Home with the Goddess." Pages 455–68 in *Symbiosis, Symbolism, and the Power of the Past: Canaan, Ancient Israel, and Their Neighbors from the Late Bronze Age through Roman Palaestina*. Edited by William G. Dever and Seymour Gitin. Winona Lake, IN: Eisenbrauns, 2003.

———. "The Deception of Isaac, Jacob's Dream at Bethel, and Incubation on an Animal Skin." Pages 92–120 in *Priesthood and Cult in Ancient Israel*. Edited by Gary A. Anderson and Saul M. Olyan. JSOTSup 125. Sheffield: JSOT Press, 1991.

———. "Digging Up Deborah: Recent Hebrew Bible Scholarship on Gender and the Contribution of Archaeology." *NEA* 66 (2003): 172–84.

———. "Moses' Death." Pages 103–17 in *Myth and Scripture: Contemporary Perspectives on Religion, Language, and Imagination*. Edited by Dexter E. Callender, Jr. SBLRBS 78. Atlanta: Society of Biblical Literature, 2014.

———. "The Mother of Eshmunazor, Priest of Astarte: A Study of Her Cultic Role." *WdO* 43 (2013): 158–78.

———. "The Queen Mother and the Cult in Ancient Israel." *JBL* 112 (1993): 385–401.

———. "The Queen Mother and the Cult in the Ancient Near East." Pages 179–209 in *Women and Goddess Traditions: In Antiquity and Today*. Edited by Karen L. King. Studies in Antiquity and Christianity. Minneapolis: Fortress, 1997.

———. *Under Every Green Tree: Popular Religion in Sixth-Century Judah*. HSM 46. Atlanta: Scholars Press, 1992.

———. *Warrior, Dancer, Seductress, Queen: Women in Judges and Biblical Israel.* AYBRL. New York: Doubleday, 1998.

———. *When Heroes Love: The Ambiguity of Eros in the Stories of Gilgamesh and David.* Gender, Theory, and Religion 2. New York: Columbia University Press, 2005.

———. "Women and the Worship of Yahweh in Ancient Israel." Pages 189–97 in *Confronting the Past: Archaeological and Historical Essays on Ancient Israel in Honor of William G. Dever.* Edited by Seymour Gitin, J. Edward Wright, and J. P. Dessel. Winona Lake, IN: Eisenbrauns, 2006.

———. "Women's Rites of Passage in Ancient Israel: Three Case Studies (Birth, Coming of Age, and Death)." Pages 1–32 in *Family and Household Religion— Toward a Synthesis of Old Testament Studies, Archaeology, Epigraphy, and Cultural Studies.* Edited by Rainer Albertz, Beth Alpert Nakhai, Saul M. Olyan, and Rüdiger Schmitt. Winona Lake, IN: Eisenbrauns, 2014.

Ackroyd, Peter R. "Goddesses, Women, and Jezebel." Pages 245–59 in *Images of Women in Antiquity.* Edited by Averil Cameron and Amélie Kuhrt. London: Routledge, 1983.

Ahituv, Shmuel, Esther Eshel, and Ze'ev Meshel. "The Inscriptions." Pages 73–142 in *Kuntillet ʿAjrud (Ḥorvat Teman): An Iron Age II Religious Site on the Judah-Sinai Border.* By Ze'ev Meshel. Edited by Liora Freud. Jerusalem: Israel Exploration Society, 2012.

Ahlström, Gösta W. *Aspects of Syncretism in Israelite Religion.* Horae Soederblomianae 5. Lund: C. W. K. Gleerup, 1963.

Aistleitner, Joseph. *Wörterbuch der ugaritischen Sprache.* Berlin: Akademie Verlag, 1974.

Albertz, Rainer. *A History of Israelite Religion in the Old Testament Period.* 2 vols. OTL. Louisville: Westminster John Knox, 1994.

Albright, William F. *Archaeology and the Religion of Israel.* 2nd ed. Baltimore: Johns Hopkins University Press, 1946.

———. "A Catalogue of Early Hebrew Lyric Poems (Psalm LVIII)." *HUCA* 23 (1950–1951): 1–39.

———. *Yahweh and the Gods of Canaan: A Historical Analysis of Two Contrasting Faiths.* Winona Lake, IN: Eisenbrauns, 1968.

Allen, L. C. "More Cuckoos in the Textual Nest: At 2 Kings XXIII.5; Jeremiah XVII.3, 4; Micah III.3; VI.16 (LXX); 2 Chronicles XX.25 (LXX)." *Journal of Theological Studies* 24 (1973): 69–73.

Alster, Bendt, and Herman Vanstiphout. "Lahar and Ashnan: Presentation and Analysis of a Sumerian Disputation." *Acta Sumerologica* 9 (1987): 1–43.

Alt, Albrecht. "Das Königtum in der Reichen Israel und Juda." *VT* 1 (1951): 2–22.

———. "The Monarchy in the Kingdoms of Israel and Judah." Pages 313–35 in *Essays on Old Testament History and Religion*. Garden City, NY: Doubleday, 1967.

Amit, Yairah. "Literature in the Service of Politics: Studies in Judges 19–21." Pages 28–40 in *Politics and Theopolitics in the Bible and Postbiblical Literature*. Edited by Henning Graf Reventlow, Yair Hoffman, and Benjamin Uffenheimer. JSOTSup 171. Sheffield: JSOT Press, 1994.

Anderson, Bernhard W. "Miriam's Challenge." *BRev* 10/3 (June 1994): 16, 55.

Andreasen, Niels-Erik A. "The Role of the Queen Mother in Israelite Society." *CBQ* 45 (1983): 179–94.

Archi, Alfonso. "The high priestess, dam-dingir, at Ebla." Pages 43–53 in *"Und Mose schrieb dieses Lied auf": Studien zum Alten Testament und zum alten Orient: Festschrift für Oswald Loretz zur Vollendung seines 70. Lebensjahres mit Beiträgen von Freunden, Schülern und Kollegen*. Edited by Manfried Dietrich and Ingo Kottsieper. AOAT 250. Münster: Ugarit-Verlag, 1998.

Arnaud, Daniel. "La prostitution sacrée en Mésopotamie, un mythe historiographique." *Revue de l'histoire des religions* 123 (1973): 111–15.

———. *Recherches au pays d'Aštata, Emar VI/3: Textes sumériens et accadiens: texte*. Paris: Éditions Recherche sur les civilisations, 1986.

Ashby, Godfrey W. "The Bloody Bridegroom: The Interpretation of Exodus 4:24–26." *ExpTim* 106 (1995): 203–5.

Attridge, Harry W., and Robert A. Oden. *Philo of Byblos, The Phoenician History: Introduction, Critical Text, Translation, and Notes*. CBQMS 9. Washington, DC: Catholic Biblical Association of America, 1981.

Avaliani, Eka. "Egyptian and Canaanite Religious Convergence: The Mysterious 'Queen of Heaven.'" *Annals of Global History* 2 (2020): 47–51.

———. "Which Goddess Could Be Hidden behind the Title 'Queen of Heaven' in Jeremiah's Prophetic Books?" *Talanta* 39 (2006–7): 239–48.

Ayad, Mariam F. *God's Wife, God's Servant: The God's Wife of Amun (c. 740–525 BC)*. London: Routledge, 2009.

Bachvarova, Mary. "Hurro-Hittite Stories and Hittite Pregnancy and Birth Rituals." Pages 272–306 in *Women in the Ancient Near East*. Edited by Mark W. Chavalas. Routledge Sourcebooks for the Ancient World. London: Routledge, 2014.

Bahrani, Zainab. *Women of Babylon: Gender and Representation in Mesopotamia*. London: Routledge, 2001.

Bal, Mieke. *Death and Dissymmetry: The Politics of Coherence in the Book of Judges*. Chicago: University of Chicago Press, 1988.

Barber, E. J. W. "The Peplos of Athena." Pages 103–17 in *Goddess and Polis: The Panathenaic Festival in Ancient Athens*. Edited by Jenifer Neils. Hanover,

NH: Dartmouth College, Hood Museum of Art; Princeton: Princeton University Press, 1992.

———. *Prehistoric Textiles: The Development of Cloth in the Neolithic and Bronze Ages with Special Reference to the Aegean.* Princeton: Princeton University Press, 1991.

———. "Textiles of the Neolithic through Iron Ages." Pages 191–95 in vol. 5 of *The Oxford Encyclopedia of Archaeology in the Near East.* Edited by Eric M. Meyers. New York: Oxford University Press, 1997.

Barstad, Hans M. *The Religious Polemics of Amos: Studies in the Preaching of Am 2:7b–8, 4:1–13, 5:1–27, 6:4–7, 8:14.* VTSup 34. Leiden: Brill, 1984.

Batten, Loring W. *A Critical and Exegetical Commentary on the Books of Ezra and Nehemiah.* ICC. New York: Scribners, 1913.

Baurain, Claude, Corinne Bonnet, and Véronique Krings, eds. *Phoinikeia grammata: lire et écrire en Méditerranée: actes du colloque de Liège, 15–18 Novembre 1989.* Collection d'études classiques 6. Namur: Société des études classiques, 1991.

Becking, Bob, ed. *Only One God? Monotheism in Ancient Israel and the Veneration of the Goddess Asherah.* London: Sheffield Academic, 2001.

Beckman, Gary. *Hittite Birth Rituals.* 2nd rev. ed. Studien zu den Boğazköy-Texten 29. Wiesbaden: Harrassowitz, 1983.

———. Review of *The Installation of Baal's High Priestess at Emar: A Window on Ancient Syrian Religion,* by Daniel E. Fleming. *BASOR* 293 (1994): 87–88.

Be'er, Ilana. "Blood Discharge: On Female Im/Purity in the Priestly Code and in Biblical Literature." Pages 152–64 in *A Feminist Companion to Exodus to Deuteronomy.* Edited by Athalya Brenner. FCB 6. Sheffield: Sheffield Academic, 1994.

Bell, Catherine. *Ritual: Perspectives and Dimensions.* New York: Oxford University Press, 1997.

Bellis, Alice Ogden. "Feminist Biblical Scholarship." Pages 24–32 in *WIS.*

Beltz, Walter. "Religionsgeschichtliche Marginalie zu Ex 4:24–26." *ZAW* 87 (1975): 209–11.

Ben-Barak, Zafira. "The Queen Consort and the Struggle for Succession to the Throne." Pages 33–40 in *La Femme dans le Proche-Orient Antique: compte rendu de la XXXIIIᵉ Rencontre Assyriologique Internationale (Paris, 7–10 Juillet 1986).* Edited by Jean-Marie Durand. Paris: Éditions Recherche sur les civilisations, 1987.

———. "The Status and Right of the *Gĕbîrâ.*" *JBL* 110 (1991): 23–34.

Bergman, J. "*kōhēn*: Egypt." Pages 61–63 in vol. 7 of *Theological Dictionary of the Old Testament.* Edited by G. Johannes Botterweck, Helmer Ringgren, and Heinz-Josef Fabry. Grand Rapids: Eerdmans, 1995.

Bergmann, Ernst von. "Inschriftliche Denkmäler der Sammlung ägyptischer Alterthümer des österr. Kaiserhauses." *Receuil de travaux* 7 (1886): 177–96.

Berlinerblau, Jacques. *The Vow and the "Popular Religious Groups" of Ancient Israel: A Philological and Sociological Inquiry.* JSOTSup 210. Sheffield: Sheffield Academic, 1996.

Bin-Nun, Shoshana. *The Tawananna in the Hittite Kingdom.* Texte der Hethiter 5. Heidelberg: Carl Winter, 1975.

Bird, Phyllis. "The End of the Male Cult Prostitute: A Literary-Historical and Sociological Analysis of Hebrew *qādēš-qĕdēšîm.*" Pages 37–43 in *Congress Volume: Cambridge 1995.* Edited by J. A. Emerton. VTSup 66. Leiden: Brill, 1997.

———. "Images of Women in the Old Testament." Pages 41–88 in *Religion and Sexism: Images of Women in the Jewish and Christian Traditions.* Edited by Rosemary Radford Ruether. New York: Simon and Schuster, 1974.

———. "Israelite Religion and the Faith of Israel's Daughters: Reflections on Gender and Religious Definition." Pages 97–108 in *The Bible and the Politics of Exegesis: Essays in Honor of Norman K. Gottwald on His Sixty-Fifth Birthday.* Edited by David Jobling, Peggy L. Day, and Gerald T. Sheppard. Cleveland: Pilgrim, 1991.

———. "The Place of Women in the Israelite Cultus." Pages 397–419 in *Ancient Israelite Religion: Essays in Honor of Frank Moore Cross.* Edited by Patrick D. Miller, Paul D. Hanson, and S. Dean McBride. Philadelphia: Fortress, 1987.

———. "Spinning and Weaving." Pages 988–89 in *Harper's Bible Dictionary.* Edited by Paul J. Achtemeier. San Francisco: Harper & Row, 1985.

———. "'To Play the Harlot': An Inquiry into an Old Testament Metaphor." Pages 75–94 in *Gender and Difference in Ancient Israel.* Edited by Peggy L. Day. Minneapolis: Fortress, 1989.

———. "Women in the Ancient Mediterranean World: Ancient Israel." *Biblical Research* 39 (1994): 31–45.

———. "Women (OT)." Pages 951–57 in *ABD* 6.

———. "Women's Religion in Ancient Israel." Pages 283–98 in *Women's Earliest Records from Ancient Egypt and Western Asia.* Edited by Barbara S. Lesko. BJS 166. Atlanta: Scholars Press, 1989.

Black, Jeremy, and Anthony Green. *Gods, Demons, and Symbols of Ancient Mesopotamia.* Austin: University of Texas Press, 1992.

Blau, Joshua (Yehoshua). "Ḥătan Dāmîm." *Tarbiz* 26 (1956): 1–3 (Hebrew).

Blau, Joshua (Yehoshua), and Jonas C. Greenfield. "Ugaritic Glosses." *BASOR* 200 (1970): 11–17.

Bleeker, C. J. "The Goddess Neith." Pages 41–56 in *Studies in Mysticism and Religion Presented to Gershom G. Scholem on His Seventieth Birthday by Pupils,*

Colleagues, and Friends. Edited by Efrain Elimelech Urback, R. J. Zwi Werblowsky, and Chaim Wirszubski. Jerusalem: Magnes, 1967.

Blenkinsopp, Joseph. *Ezra-Nehemiah: A Commentary.* OTL. Philadelphia: Westminster, 1988.

Bloch-Smith, Elizabeth. "Archaeological and Inscriptional Evidence for Phoenician Astarte." Pages 167–94 in *Transformation of a Goddess: Ishtar—Astarte—Aphrodite.* Edited by David T. Sugimoto. OBO 263. Fribourg: Academic Press; Göttingen: Vandenhoeck & Ruprecht, 2014.

Blum, Ruth, and Erhard Blum. "Zippora und ihr ḥtn dmym." Pages 41–54 in *Die Hebraische Bibel und ihre zweifache Nachgeschichte: Festschrift für Rolf Rendtorff zum 65. Geburtstag.* Edited by Erhard Blum, Christian Macholz, and Ekkehard W. Stegemann. Neukirchen-Vluyn: Neukirchener, 1990.

Boedeker, Deborah. "Family Matters: Domestic Religion in Classical Greece." Pages 229–47 in *Household and Family Religion in Antiquity.* Edited by John Bodel and Saul M. Olyan. Oxford: Blackwell, 2008.

Bohmbach, Karla G. "Conventions/Contraventions: The Meanings of Public and Private for the Judges 19 Concubine." *JSOT* 83 (1999): 83–98.

Boling, Robert G. *Judges: A New Translation with Introduction and Commentary.* AYB 6A. Garden City, NY: Doubleday, 1975.

Bonnet, Corinne. *Astarté: dossier documentaire et perspectives historiques.* Collezione di studi fenici 37. Contributi alla storia della religione fenicio-punica 2. Roma: Consiglio nazionale delle ricerche, 1996.

Bordreuil, Pierre. "Astarté, la dame de Byblos." *Comptes-rendus des séances de l'Académie des Inscriptions et Belles-Lettres* 142 (1998): 1153–64.

Bowen, Nancy R. "The Daughters of Your People: Female Prophets in Ezekiel 13:17–23." *JBL* 118 (1999): 417–33.

———. "The Quest for the Historical *Gĕbîrâ*." *CBQ* 63 (2001): 597–618.

Boyd, Mary Petrina. "The House That Wisdom Wove: An Analysis of the Functions of Household in Proverbs 31:10–31." PhD diss., Union Theological Seminary and Presbyterian School of Christian Education, 2001.

Breniquet, Catherine. *Essai sur le tissage en Mésopotamie, des premières communautés sédentaires au milieu du IIIe millénaire avant J.-C.* Traveaux de la Maison René-Ginouvés 5. Paris: de Boccard, 2008.

Breniquet, Catherine, and Cécile Michel. "Wool Economy in the Ancient Near East and the Aegean." Pages 1–11 in *Wool Economy in the Ancient Near East: From the Beginnings of Sheep Husbandry to Institutional Textile Industry.* Edited by Catherine Breniquet and Cécile Michel. Ancient Textile Series 17. Oxford: Oxbow Books, 2014.

Brenner, Athalya. "Introduction." Pages 9–22 in *A Feminist Companion to Judges.* Edited by Athalya Brenner. FCB 4. Sheffield: Sheffield Academic, 1993.

Bresciani, Edda, and Murad Kamil. *Le lettre aramaiche di Hermopoli.* Atti della Accademia Nazionale dei Lincei 8/12. Rome: Accademia Nazionale dei Lincei, 1966.

Brettler, Marc Zvi. *The Book of Judges.* Old Testament Readings. London: Routledge, 2002.

Brewer-Boydston, Ginny. *Good Queen Mothers, Bad Queen Mothers: The Theological Presentation of the Queen Mother in 1 and 2 Kings.* CBQMS 54. Washington, DC: Catholic Biblical Association of America, 2016.

Bright, John. *Jeremiah.* AYB 21. Garden City, NY: Doubleday, 1965.

Brown, Raymond E. *The Birth of the Messiah: A Commentary on the Infancy Narratives in Matthew and Luke.* Garden City, NY: Doubleday, 1977.

———. "Genealogy (Christ)." Page 354 in *The Interpreter's Dictionary of the Bible, Supplementary Volume.* Edited by Keith R. Crim. Nashville: Abingdon, 1976.

Brown, Raymond E., Karl P. Donfried, Joseph A. Fitzmyer, and John Reumann, eds., *Mary in the New Testament.* Philadelphia: Fortress; New York: Paulist, 1978.

Bryan, Betsy M. "In Women Good and Bad Fortune Are on Earth: Status and Roles of Women in Egyptian Culture." Pages 25–46, 189–91 in *Mistress of the House, Mistress of Heaven: Women in Ancient Egypt.* Edited by Anne K. Capel and Glenn E. Markoe. New York: Hudson Hills, in conjunction with the Cincinnati Art Museum, 1996.

Burkert, Walter. *Homo Necans: The Anthropology of Ancient Greek Sacrificial Ritual and Myth.* Berkeley: University of California Press, 1983.

Burnette-Bletsch, Rhonda. "Women after Childbirth." Page 204 in *WIS.*

Burney, C. F. *The Book of Judges, with Introduction and Notes.* 2nd ed. London: Rivington's, 1920.

Burns, Rita J. *Has the Lord Indeed Spoken Only Through Moses? A Study of the Biblical Portrait of Miriam.* SBLDS 84. Atlanta: Scholars Press, 1987.

Bynum, Caroline Walker. "Women's Stories, Women's Symbols: A Critique of Victor Turner's Theory of Liminality." Pages 27–51, 305–18 in *Fragmentation and Redemption: Essays on Gender and the Human Body in Medieval Religion.* New York: Zone Books, 1991.

Cahill, Jane M., and David Tarler. "Ḥammah, Tell el-." Pages 561–66 in vol. 2 of *The New Encyclopedia of Archaeological Excavations in the Holy Land.* Edited by Ephraim Stern. Jerusalem: The Israel Exploration Society, 1993.

Cahill, Jane M., David Tarler, and Gary Lipton (Lipovich). "Tell el-Ḥammah in the Tenth Century B.C.E." *Qad* 22 (1989): 33–38.

Cahill, Jane M., Gary Lipton (Lipovich), and David Tarler. "Tell el-Ḥammah, 1985–1987." *IEJ* 37 (1987): 280–83.

———. "Tell el-Ḥammah, 1988." *IEJ* 38 (1988): 191–94.

Camp, Claudia. "Woman Wisdom as Root Metaphor: A Theological Consideration." Pages 45–75 in *The Listening Heart: Essays in Wisdom and the Psalms in Honor of Roland E. Murphy, O. Carm.* Edited by Kenneth G. Hoglund, Elizabeth F. Huwiler, Jonathan T. Glass, and Roger W. Lee. JSOTSup 58. Sheffield: JSOT Press, 1987.

Campbell, Joseph. *The Hero With a Thousand Faces.* Bollingen Series 17. Princeton: Princeton University Press, 1949.

Capel, Anne K. "Statue of Amenirdas I, God's Wife of Amen." Pages 115–17, 203 in *Mistress of the House, Mistress of Heaven: Women in Ancient Egypt.* Edited by Anne K. Capel and Glenn E. Markoe. New York: Hudson Hills, in conjunction with the Cincinnati Art Museum, 1996.

Carter, Howard, and Percy E. Newberry. *The Tomb of Thoutmosis IV.* Catalogue général des antiquités égyptiennes du Musée du Caire 15. Westminster: Archibald Constable and Co., 1904.

Cazelles, Henri. "La Mere du Roi-Messie dans l'Ancien Testament." Pages 39–56 in *Mariae potestas regalis in ecclesiam.* Vol. 5 of *Maria et ecclesia: Acte Congressus Mariologici-Mariani in civitate Lourdes anno 1958 celebrati.* Rome: Academie Mariana Internationalis, 1959.

Childs, Brevard S. *The Book of Exodus: A Critical, Theological Commentary.* OTL. Philadelphia: Westminster, 1974.

Chisholm, Robert B. "Divine Hardening in the Old Testament." *Bibliotheca sacra* 153 (1996): 410–34.

Clemens, David M. *Sources for Ugaritic Ritual and Sacrifice 1: Ugaritic and Ugarit Akkadian Texts.* AOAT 284/1. Münster: Ugarit-Verlag, 2001.

Clines, David J. A. *Ezra, Nehemiah, Esther.* New Century Bible Commentary. Grand Rapids: Eerdmans; London: Marshall, Morgan & Scott, 1984.

Coats, George W. "Humility and Honor: A Moses Legend in Numbers 12." Pages 97–107 in *Art and Meaning: Rhetoric in Biblical Literature.* Edited by David J. A. Clines, David M. Gunn, and Alan J. Hauser. JSOTSup 19. Sheffield: JSOT Press, 1982.

Cogan, Mordechai (Morton). *Imperialism and Religion: Assyria, Judah and Israel in the Eighth and Seventh Centuries B.C.E.* SBLMS 19. Missoula, MT: Scholars Press, 1974.

———. "Judah under Assyrian Hegemony: A Reexamination of *Imperialism and Religion.*" *JBL* 112 (1993): 403–14.

———. "Tendentious Chronology in the Book of Chronicles." *Zion* 45 (1980): 165–72 (Hebrew).

Cogan, Mordechai, and Hayim Tadmor. *II Kings: A New Translation with Introduction and Commentary.* AYB 11. Garden City, NY: Doubleday, 1988.

Cohn, Robert L. *The Shape of Sacred Space: Four Biblical Studies.* AAR Studies in Religion 23. Chico, CA: Scholars Press, 1981.

Collins, Billie Jean. "Rites of Passage: Anatolia." Page 444 in *Religions of the Ancient World: A Guide*. Edited by Sarah Iles Johnston. Cambridge, MA: Harvard University Press, 2004.

———. "Sin, Pollution, and Purity: Anatolia." Pages 504–5 in *Religions of the Ancient World: A Guide*. Edited by Sarah Iles Johnston. Cambridge, MA: Harvard University Press, 2004.

Collon, Dominique. "Depictions of Priests and Priestesses in the Ancient Near East." Pages 17–46 in *Priests and Officials in the Ancient Near East: Papers of the Second Colloquium on the Ancient Near East—The City and Its Life, Held at the Middle Eastern Culture Center in Japan (Mitaka, Tokyo), March 22–24, 1996*. Edited by Kazuko Watanabe. Heidelberg: C. Winter, 1999.

Coogan, Michael D. "Canaanite Origins and Lineage: Reflections on the Religion of Ancient Israel." Pages 115–24 in *Ancient Israelite Religion: Essays in Honor of Frank Moore Cross*. Edited by Patrick D. Miller, Paul D. Hanson, and S. Dean McBride. Philadelphia: Fortress, 1987.

———. "The Goddess Wisdom—'Where Can She Be Found?' Literary Reflexes of Popular Religion." Pages 203–10 in *Ki Baruch Hu: Ancient Near Eastern, Biblical, and Judaic Studies in Honor of Baruch A. Levine*. Edited by Robert Chazan, William W. Hallo, and Lawrence H. Schiffman. Winona Lake, IN: Eisenbrauns, 1999.

———. "A Structural and Literary Analysis of the Song of Deborah." *CBQ* 40 (1978): 143–66.

Craig, James Alexander. *Assyrian and Babylonian Religious Texts*. 2 vols. Leipzig: J. C. Hinrichs, 1895.

Cross, Frank Moore. *Canaanite Myth and Hebrew Epic: Essays in the History of the Religion of Israel*. Cambridge, MA: Harvard University Press, 1973.

———. "The Old Phoenician Inscription from Spain Dedicated to Hurrian Astarte." *HTR* 64 (1971): 189–95.

Cross, Frank Moore, and David Noel Freedman. *Studies in Ancient Yahwistic Poetry*. SBLDS 21. Missoula, MT: Scholars Press, 1975.

Crowfoot, J. W., and Grace M. Crowfoot. *Early Ivories from Samaria*. London: Palestine Exploration Fund, 1938.

Culican, William. "A Votive Model from the Sea." *Palestine Exploration Quarterly* 108 (1976): 119–23.

Culley, Robert C. "Five Tales of Punishment in the Book of Numbers." Pages 25–34 in *Text and Tradition: The Hebrew Bible and Folklore*. Edited by Susan Niditch. Atlanta: Scholars Press, 1990.

Cullmann, Oscar. "The Protevangelium of James." Pages 421–39 in *Gospels and Related Writings*. Rev. ed. Edited by Wilhelm Schneemelcher. Vol. 1 of *New

Testament Apocrypha. Cambridge, UK: James Clarke & Co.; Louisville: Westminster John Knox, 1991.

Dahood, Mitchell. *Psalms II, 51–100: Introduction, Translation, and Notes.* AYB 17. Garden City, NY: Doubleday, 1968.

———. "La Regina del Cielo in Geremia." *Rivista biblica italiana* 8 (1960): 166–68.

Dalley, Stephanie. *Myths from Mesopotamia: Creation, the Flood, Gilgamesh, and Others.* Rev. ed. Oxford: Oxford University Press, 2008.

David, A. Rosalie. *Religious Ritual at Abydos (c. 1300 BC).* Warminster, UK: Aris & Phillips, 1973.

Dawson, W. R., and T. E. Peet. "The So-Called Poem on the King's Chariot." *JEA* 19 (1933): 167–74.

Day, John. "Asherah." Pages 483–87 in *ABD* 1.

———. "Asherah in the Hebrew Bible and in Northwest Semitic Literature." *JBL* 105 (1986): 385–408.

Delcor, Mathias. "La culte de la 'Reine du Ciel' selon Jer. 7,18; 44,17–19, 25 et ses survivances." Pages 101–22 in *Von Kanaan bis Kerala: Festschrift für Prof. Mag. Dr. J. P. M. van der Ploeg O.P. zur Vollendung des siebzigsten Lebensjahres am 4. Juli 1979 überreicht von Kollegen, Freunden und Schülern.* Edited by W. C. Delsman, J. T. Nelis, J. P. T. M. Peters, et al. AOAT 211. Kevelaer: Butzon & Bercker; Neukirchen-Vluyn: Neukirchener, 1982.

Depla, Annette. "Women in Ancient Egyptian Wisdom Literature." Pages 24–52 in *Women in Ancient Societies: An Illusion of the Night.* Edited by Léonie J. Archer, Susan Fischler, and Maria Wyke. London: Palgrave Macmillan, 1994.

Dever, William G. "Archaeological Data on the Israelite Settlement: A Review of Two Recent Works." *BASOR* 284 (1991): 77–90.

———. "Archaeology and Israelite Origins—A Review Article." *BASOR* 279 (1990): 89–95.

———. "Archaeology and the Ancient Israelite Cult: How the Kh. el-Qôm and Kuntillet 'Ajrûd 'Asherah' Texts Have Changed the Picture." *ErIsr* 26 (1999): 9*–15*.

———. "Asherah, Consort of Yahweh? New Evidence from Kuntillet 'Ajrûd." *BASOR* 255 (1985): 21–37.

———. "Cultural Continuity, Ethnicity in the Archaeological Record, and the Question of Israelite Origins." *ErIsr* 24 (1993): 22*–33*.

———. *Did God Have a Wife? Archaeology and Folk Religion in Ancient Israel.* Grand Rapids: Eerdmans, 2005.

———. "How to Tell a Canaanite from an Israelite." Pages 26–85 in *The Rise of Ancient Israel.* Edited by Hershel S. Shanks. Washington, DC: Biblical Archaeology Society, 1992.

———. "Iron Age Epigraphic Material from the Area of Khirbet el-Kôm." *HUCA* 40/41 (1969–70): 158–89.

———. "Is There Any Archaeological Evidence for the Exodus?" Pages 67–86 in *Exodus: The Egyptian Evidence.* Edited by Ernest S. Frerichs and Leonard H. Lesko. Winona Lake, IN: Eisenbrauns, 1997.

———. "Israel, History of (Archaeology and the 'Conquest')." Pages 545–58 in *ABD* 3.

———. "Material Remains and the Cult in Ancient Israel: An Essay in Archaeological Systematics." Pages 571–87 in *The Word of the Lord Shall Go Forth. Essays in Honor of David Noel Freedman in Celebration of His Sixtieth Birthday.* Edited by Carol L. Meyers and Michael O'Connor. Winona Lake, IN: Eisenbrauns, 1983.

———. "Recent Archaeological Confirmation of the Cult of Asherah in Ancient Israel." *Hebrew Studies* 23 (1982): 37–43.

———. *Recent Archaeological Discoveries and Biblical Research.* Seattle: University of Washington Press, 1990.

———. Review of *No Graven Image: Israelite Aniconism in Its Ancient Near Eastern Context,* by Tryggve N. D. Mettinger. *BASOR* 302 (1996): 93–94.

———. "The Silence of the Text: An Archaeological Commentary on 2 Kings 23." Pages 143–68 in *Scripture and Other Artifacts: Essays on the Bible and Archaeology in Honor of Philip J. King.* Edited by Michael D. Coogan, J. Cheryl Exum, and Lawrence E. Stager. Louisville: Westminster John Knox, 1994.

———. "Unresolved Issues in the Early History of Israel: Toward a Synthesis of Archaeological and Textual Reconstructions." Pages 195–208 in *The Bible and the Politics of Exegesis: Essays in Honor of Norman K. Gottwald on His Sixty-Fifth Birthday.* Edited by David Jobling, Peggy L. Day, and Gerald T. Sheppard. Cleveland: Pilgrim, 1991.

———. *Who Were the Early Israelites and Where Did They Come From?* Grand Rapids: Eerdmans, 2003.

DeVries, Simon J. *Prophet against Prophet: The Role of the Micaiah Narrative in the Development of Early Prophetic Tradition.* Grand Rapids: Eerdmans, 1978.

Dhorme, Édouard. "Nouvelle lettre d'Ugarit en écriture alphabétique." *Syria* 19 (1938): 142–46.

Dick, Michael B. "Prophetic Parodies of Making the Cult Image." Pages 1–53 in *Born in Heaven, Made on Earth: The Making of the Cult Image in the Ancient Near East.* Edited by Michael B. Dick. Winona Lake, IN: Eisenbrauns, 1999.

Dietrich, Manfried. "Das Einsetzungsritual der Entu von Emar (Emar VI/3, 369)." *UF* 21 (1989): 47–100.

Dietrich, Manfried, Oswald Loretz, and Joaquín Sanmartín. "Notizen zum offertext RS 24.260 = Ug. 5, S. 586 NR. 11." *UF* 7 (1975): 543–44.

Dijkstra, Klaas. *Life and Loyalty: A Study in the Socio-Religious Culture of Syria and Mesopotamia in the Graeco-Roman Period Based on Epigraphical Evidence.* Religions in the Graeco-Roman World 128. Leiden: Brill, 1995.

Dodson, Aidan. "The Problem of Amenirdis II and the Heirs to the Office of God's Wife of Amun during the Twenty-Sixth Dynasty." *JEA* 88 (2002): 179–86.

Doniger, Wendy. "Origins of Myth-Making Man." Pages 181–86 in *Paths to the Power of Myth: Joseph Campbell and the Study of Religion.* Edited by Daniel C. Noel. New York: Crossroad, 1990.

Donner, Herbert. "Art und Herkunft des Amtes der Königinmutter im Alten Testament." Pages 105–45 in *Festschrift Johannes Friedrich zum 65. Geburtstag am 27. August gewidmet.* Edited by Richard von Kienle, Anton Moortgat, Hendrik Otten, et al. Heidelberg: Carl Winter, 1959.

Dothan, Trude, and Seymour Gitin. "Miqne, Tel (Ekron)." Pages 1051–59 in vol. 3 of *The New Encyclopedia of Archaeological Excavations in the Holy Land.* Edited by Ephraim Stern. Jerusalem: Israel Exploration Society, 1993.

Driver, G. R. "Supposed Arabisms in the Old Testament." *JBL* 55 (1936): 101–20.

Droogers, André. "Symbols of Marginality in the Biographies of Religious and Secular Innovators." *Numen* 27 (1980): 105–21.

Drower, Margaret S. "Ugarit." Pages 130–60 in *History of the Middle East and the Aegean Region, c. 1380–1000 B.C.* Edited by I. E. S. Edwards, C. J. Gadd, N. G. L. Hammond, and E. Sollberger. 3rd ed. Vol. 2, part 2 of *The Cambridge Ancient History.* Cambridge, UK: Cambridge University Press, 1975.

Dupont-Sommer, André. "Les Phéniciens à Chypre." Pages 75–94 in *Report of the Department of Antiquities, Cyprus, 1974.* Nicosia: Department of Antiquities, Cyprus; Zavallis, 1974.

Ebeling, Erich. *Quellen zur Kenntnis der babylonischen Religion.* 2 vols. Mitteilungen der Vorderasiatisch-ägytischen Gesellschaft 23/1–2. Leipzig: J. C. Hinrichs, 1918–1919.

Edgerton, William F., and John A. Wilson. *Historical Records of Ramses III.* Studies in Ancient Oriental Civilization 12. Chicago: University of Chicago Press, 1936.

Edzard, Dietz Otto. "Inanna, Ištar." Pages 81–89 in *Götter und Mythen im vorderen Orient.* Edited by Hans Wilhelm Haussig. Vol. 1 of *Wörterbuch der Mythologie.* Stuttgart: Ernst Klett, 1965.

Eissfeldt, Otto. "Schamemrumim 'Hoher Himmel,' ein Stadtteil von Gross-Sidon." Pages 62–67 in *Ras Schamra und Sanchunjaton.* Halle: Max Niemeyer, 1939.

Eliade, Mircea. *The Myth of the Eternal Return, or Cosmos and History.* Bollingen Series 46. Princeton: Princeton University Press, 1954.

Elliott, Alison Goddard. *Roads to Paradise: Reading the Lives of the Early Saints.* Hanover, NH: University Press of New England, 1987.

Ellis, Teresa Ann. "Jeremiah 44: What If 'the Queen of Heaven' Is YHWH?" *JSOT* 33 (2009): 465–88.

Emerton, J. A. "New Light on Israelite Religion: The Implications of the Inscriptions from Kuntillet 'Ajrud." *ZAW* 94 (1982): 2–20.

Eskenazi, Tamara. "Out of the Shadows: Biblical Women in the Postexilic Era." *JSOT* 54 (1992): 25–43.

Exum, J. Cheryl. "Feminist Criticism: Whose Interests Are Being Served?" Pages 65–89 in *Judges and Method: New Approaches in Biblical Studies*. 2nd ed. Edited by Gale A. Yee. Minneapolis: Fortress, 2007.

———. *Fragmented Women: Feminist (Sub)versions of Biblical Narratives*. Valley Forge, PA: Trinity Press International, 1993.

———. "Second Thoughts about Secondary Characters: Women in Exodus 1.8–2.10." Pages 75–87 in *A Feminist Companion to Exodus to Deuteronomy*. Edited by Athalya Brenner. FCB 6. Sheffield: Sheffield Academic, 1994.

———. "'You Shall Let Every Daughter Live': A Study of Exodus 1:8–2:10." Pages 63–82 in *The Bible and Feminist Hermeneutics* (= *Semeia* 28). Edited by Mary Ann Tolbert, 1983.

Falkenstein, Adam. "Enheduanna, die Tochter Sargons von Akkade." *RA* 52 (1958): 129–31.

———. *Die Inschriften Gudeas von Lagaš* 1: *Einleitung*. Analecta Orientalia 30. Rome: Pontificium Institutum Biblicum, 1966.

Fewell, Danna Nolan. "Judges." Pages 73–83 in *The Women's Bible Commentary*. Ed. Carol A. Newsom and Sharon H. Ringe. Expanded ed. Louisville: Westminster John Knox, 1998.

Fewell, Danna Nolan, and David M. Gunn. *Gender, Power, and Promise: The Subject of the Bible's First Story*. Nashville: Abingdon, 1993.

Fidler, Ruth. "Writing and Rewriting the History of Israelite Religion: The Controversy Regarding the Queen of Heaven." Pages 141–60 in *Writing and Rewriting History in Ancient Israel and Near Eastern Cultures*. Edited by Isaac Kalimi. Wiesbaden: Harrassowitz, 2000.

Finkelstein, Israel. *The Archaeology of the Israelite Settlement*. Jerusalem: Israel Exploration Society, 1988.

———. *'Izbet Ṣarṭah: An Early Iron Age Site Near Rosh Ha'ayin, Israel*. Oxford: British Archaeological Reports, International Series, 1985.

Finkelstein, J. J. "Review Article: On Some Recent Studies in Cuneiform Law." *JAOS* 90 (1970): 243–56.

Fishbane, Michael. "Exodus 1–4 / The Prologue to the Exodus Cycle." Pages 63–76 in *Text and Texture: Close Readings of Selected Biblical Texts*. New York: Schocken, 1979.

Fisher, Eugene J. "Cultic Prostitution in the Ancient Near East? A Reassessment." *Biblical Theology Bulletin* 5 (1976): 225–36.

Fisher, Loren R., and F. Brent Knutson. "An Enthronement Ritual at Ugarit." *JNES* 28 (1969): 157–67.

Fitzmyer, Joseph A. "The Phoenician Inscription from Pyrgi." *JAOS* 86 (1966): 285–97.

Fleming, Daniel E. *The Installation of Baal's High Priestess at Emar: A Window on Ancient Syrian Religion.* HSS 42. Atlanta: Scholars Press, 1992.

———. "More Help from Syria: Introducing Emar to Biblical Study." *BA* 58 (1995): 139–47.

———. "*Nābû* and *Munabbiātu*: Two New Syrian Religious Personnel." *JAOS* 113 (1993): 175–83.

Foster, Benjamin R. *Before the Muses: An Anthology of Akkadian Literature.* 2 vols. Bethesda, MD: CDL Press, 1993.

———. "The Birth Legend of Sargon of Akkad." Page 461 in *COS* 1.

Frandsen, Paul John. "The Menstrual 'Taboo' in Ancient Egypt." *JNES* 66 (2007): 81–106.

Freedman, David Noel. "Divine Names and Titles in Early Hebrew Poetry." Pages 77–129 in *Poetry, Pottery, and Prophecy: Studies in Early Hebrew Poetry.* Winona Lake, IN: Eisenbrauns, 1980.

———. "Yahweh of Samaria and His Asherah." *BA* 50 (1987): 241–49.

Fretheim, Terence E. *Exodus.* Interpretation. Louisville: John Knox, 1991.

Frevel, Christian. *Aschera und der Ausschliesslichkeitsanspruch YHWHs: Beiträge zu literarischen, religionsgeschichtlichen und ikonographischen Aspekten der Ascheradiskussion.* 2 vols. Bonner biblische Beiträge 94/1–2. Weinheim: Beltz Athenäum, 1995.

Friedman, Richard Elliott. *The Exile and Biblical Narrative: The Formation of the Deuteronomistic and Priestly Works.* HSM 22. Chico, CA: Scholars Press, 1981.

Friend, Glenda. *Tell Taannek 1963–1968 III/2: The Loom Weights.* Edited by Khaled Nashef. Birzeit, Palestine: Palestinian Institute of Archaeology, 1998.

Fritz, Volkmar. "Conquest or Settlement? The Early Iron Age in Palestine." *BA* 50 (1987): 84–100.

Frolov, Serge. "The Hero as Bloody Bridegroom: On the Meaning and Origin of Exodus 4, 26." *Bib* 77 (1996): 520–23.

Frost, Robert. "The Death of the Hired Man." Pages 40–45 in *Collected Poems, Prose, and Plays.* The Library of America 81. New York: Library of America, 1995.

Frymer-Kensky, Tikva. *In the Wake of the Goddesses: Women, Culture, and the Biblical Transformation of Pagan Myth.* New York: Free Press, 1992.

Gal, Zvi. *The Lower Galilee in the Iron Age.* Winona Lake, IN: Eisenbrauns, 1992.

Galpaz-Feller, Pnina. "Pregnancy and Birth in the Bible and Ancient Egypt (Comparative Study)." *BN* 102 (2000): 42–53.

Gaster, Theodore H. *Myth, Legend, and Custom in the Old Testament.* New York: Harper & Row, 1969.

Gelernter, David. "Tsipporah's Bloodgroom: A Biblical Breaking Point." *Orim* 3 (1988): 46–57.

Gennep, Arnold van. *The Rites of Passage.* Translated by Monika B. Vizedom and Gabrielle L. Caffee. 2nd ed. Chicago: University of Chicago Press, 2019. Translation of *Les rites de passage.* Paris: E. Nourry, 1909.

Gibson, John C. L. *Canaanite Myths and Legends.* 2nd ed. Edinburgh: T&T Clark, 1977.

———. *Textbook of Syrian Semitic Inscriptions.* 3 vols. Oxford: Clarendon, 1973–1982.

Gilmour, Garth Hugh. "The Archaeology of Cult in the Southern Levant in the Early Iron Age: An Analytical and Comparative Approach." PhD diss., University of Oxford, 1995.

Gilula, Mordechai. "To Yahweh Shomron and to His Asherah." *Shnaton* 3 (1978/79): 129–37 (Hebrew).

Ginsberg, H. L. "Baʿl and ʿAnat." *Or* 7 (1938): 1–11.

———. *The Legend of King Keret: A Canaanite Epic of the Late Bronze Age.* BASOR Supplementary Studies 2–3. New Haven: American Schools of Oriental Research, 1946.

Gitin, Seymour. "The Four-Horned Altar and Sacred Space: An Archaeological Perspective." Pages 95–123 in *Sacred Time, Sacred Place: Archaeology and the Religion of Israel.* Edited by Barry M. Gittlen. Winona Lake, IN: Eisenbrauns, 2002.

———. "Israelite and Philistine Cult and the Archaeological Record in Iron Age II: The 'Smoking Gun' Phenomenon." Pages 279–96 in *Symbiosis, Symbolism, and the Power of the Past: Canaan, Ancient Israel, and Their Neighbors from the Late Bronze Age through Roman Palaestina.* Edited by William G. Dever and Seymour Gitin. Winona Lake, IN: Eisenbrauns, 2003.

———. "Seventh Century B.C.E. Cultic Elements at Ekron." Pages 248–58 in *Biblical Archaeology Today, 1990: Proceedings of the Second International Congress on Biblical Archaeology, Jerusalem, June-July 1990.* Edited by Avraham Biran and Joseph Aviram. Jerusalem: Israel Exploration Society, 1993.

———. "Tel Miqne-Ekron: A Type-Site for the Inner Coastal Plain in the Iron Age II Period." Pages 23–58 in *Recent Excavations in Israel: Studies in Iron Age Archaeology.* Edited by Seymour Gitin and William G. Dever. Annual of the American Schools of Oriental Research 49. Winona Lake, IN: Eisenbrauns, 1989.

Gitin, Seymour, and Mordechai Cogan. "A New Type of Dedicatory Inscription from Ekron." *IEJ* 49 (1999): 193–202.

Gitin, Seymour, Trude Dothan, and Joseph Naveh. "A Royal Dedicatory Inscription from Ekron." *IEJ* 47 (1997): 1–16.

Goetze, Albrecht. "El, Ashertu, and the Storm-God." Page 519 in *ANET*.

Gordon, Cyrus H. "Ugaritic *RBT/RABÎTU*." Pages 127–32 in *Ascribe to the Lord. Biblical and Other Studies in Memory of Peter C. Craigie*. Edited by Lyle Eslinger and J. Glen Taylor. JSOTSup 67. Sheffield: JSOT Press, 1988.

———. *Ugaritic Textbook*. Rome: Pontifical Biblical Institute, 1965.

Gordon, Edmund I. *Sumerian Proverbs: Glimpses of Everyday Life in Ancient Mesopotamia*. Philadelphia: The University Museum, University of Pennsylvania, 1959.

Gordon, R. P. "Aleph Apologeticum." *Jewish Quarterly Review* 69 (1978–1979): 112–16.

Gottwald, Norman K. "Immanuel as the Prophet's Son." *VT* 8 (1958): 36–47.

———. "Method and Hypothesis in Reconstructing the Social History of Early Israel." *ErIsr* 24 (1993): 77*–82*.

———. *The Tribes of Yahweh: A Sociology of the Religion of Liberated Israel, 1250–1050 B.C.E.* 2nd ed. Maryknoll, NY: Orbis Books, 1981.

Granqvist, Hilma. *Child Problems Among the Arabs*. Helsinki: Söderström, 1950.

Graves-Brown, Carolyn. *Dancing for Hathor: Women in Ancient Egypt*. London: Continuum, 2010.

Gray, John. "Canaanite Kingship in Theory and Practice." *VT* 2 (1952): 193–220.

———. *I & II Kings*. OTL. London: SCM, 1964.

———. *The KRT Text in the Literature of Ras Shamra: A Social Myth of Ancient Canaan*. 2nd ed. Leiden: Brill, 1964.

———. "Queen of Heaven." Page 975 in vol. 3 of *The Interpreter's Dictionary of the Bible*. Edited by George Arthur Buttrick. Nashville: Abingdon, 1962.

———. "Sacral Kingship in Ugarit." Pages 289–302 in *Ugaritica VI: Publié à l'occasion de la XXXe campagne de fouilles à Ras Shamra (1968) sous la direction de Claude F. A. Schaeffer*. Mission de Ras Shamra 17. Bibliothèque archéologique et historique 81. Paris: Mission Archéologique de Ras Shamra; Librairie Orientaliste Paul Geuthner, 1969.

Greenberg, Moshe. *Understanding Exodus*. New York: Behrman House for the Melton Research Center of the Jewish Theological Seminary of America, 1969.

Greenstein, Edward L. "Kirta." Pages 9–48 in *Ugaritic Narrative Poetry*. Edited by Simon B. Parker. SBLWAW 9. Atlanta: Scholars Press, 1997.

Gressman, Hugo. "Josia und das Deuteronomium." *ZAW* 42 (1924): 313–37.

Griffiths, J. Gwyn. "The Egyptian Derivation of the Name Moses." *JNES* 12 (1953): 225–31.

Gruber, Mayer I. "Breast-Feeding Practices in Biblical Israel and in Old Babylonian Mesopotamia." Pages 69–107 in *The Motherhood of God and Other Studies*. South Florida Studies in the History of Judaism 57. Atlanta: Scholars Press, 1992.

———. "Women in the Cult according to the Priestly Code." Pages 49–68 in *The Motherhood of God and Other Studies*. South Florida Studies in the History of Judaism 57. Atlanta: Scholars Press, 1992.

Gubel, E., and P. Bordreuil, eds. "Bulletin d'antiquités archéologiques du Levant inédites ou méconnues VI." *Syria* 67 (1990): 483–520.

Gunn, David M. "The 'Hardening of Pharaoh's Heart': Plot, Character and Theology in Exodus 1–14." Pages 72–96 in *Art and Meaning: Rhetoric in Biblical Literature*. Edited by David J. A. Clines, David M. Gunn, and Alan J. Hauser. JSOTSup 19. Sheffield: JSOT Press, 1982.

Hackett, Jo Ann. *The Balaam Text from Deir ʿAllā*. HSM 31. Chico, CA: Scholars Press, 1984.

———. "In the Days of Jael: Reclaiming the History of Women in Ancient Israel." Pages 15–38 in *Immaculate and Powerful: The Female in Sacred Image and Social Reality*. Edited by Clarissa W. Atkinson, Constance H. Buchanan, and Margaret R. Miles. Boston: Beacon, 1985.

———. "Women's Studies and the Hebrew Bible." Pages 141–64 in *The Future of Biblical Studies: The Hebrew Scriptures*. Edited by Richard Elliott Friedman and H. G. M. Williamson. Atlanta: Scholars Press, 1987.

Hadley, Judith M. *The Cult of Asherah in Ancient Israel and Judah: Evidence for a Hebrew Goddess*. Cambridge, UK: Cambridge University Press, 2000.

———. "The De-Deification of Deities in Deuteronomy." Pages 157–74 in *The God of Israel*. Edited by Robert P. Gordon. Cambridge, UK: Cambridge University Press, 2007.

———. "Fertility of the Flock? The De-Personalization of Astarte in the Old Testament." Pages 115–33 in *On Reading Prophetic Texts: Gender-Specific and Related Studies in Memory of Fokkelien van Dijk-Hemmes*. Edited by Bob Becking and Meindert Dijkstra. Leiden: Brill, 1996.

———. "The Khirbet el-Qom Inscription." *VT* 37 (1987): 50–62.

———. "The Queen of Heaven—Who Is She?" Pages 30–51 in *Prophets and Daniel*. Edited by Athalya Brenner. FCB 2/8. London: Sheffield Academic, 2001.

———. "Wisdom and the Goddess." Pages 234–43 in *Wisdom in Ancient Israel: Essays in Honour of J. A. Emerton*. Edited by John Day, Robert P. Gordon, and H. G. M. Williamson. Cambridge, UK: Cambridge University Press, 1995.

Haldar, Alfred. *The Notion of the Desert in Sumero-Accadian and West-Semitic*

Religions. Uppsala universitets årsskrift 1950: 3. Uppsala: Almqvist & Wiksell, 1950.

Hallo, William W. "Women of Sumer." Pages 23–40 in *The Legacy of Sumer: Invited Lectures on the Middle East at the University of Texas at Austin*. Edited by Denise Schmandt-Besserat. Bibliotheca Mesopotamica 4. Malibu: Undena Publications, 1976.

Hallo, William W., and J. J. A. van Dijk. *The Exaltation of Inanna*. New Haven: Yale University Press, 1968.

Halpern, Baruch. "The Baal (and the Asherah) in Seventh-Century Judah: YHWH's Retainers Retired." Pages 115–54 in *Konsequente Traditionsgeschichte: Festschrift für Klaus Balzer zu seinem 65. Geburtstag*. Edited by Rüdiger Bartelmus, Thomas Krüger, and Helmut Utzschneider. OBO 126. Freiburg: Universitätsverlag Freiburg Schweiz; Göttingen: Vandenhoeck & Ruprecht, 1993.

———. *The First Historians: The Hebrew Bible and History*. San Francisco: Harper & Row, 1988.

———. "The Resourceful Israelite Historian: The Song of Deborah and Israelite Historiography." *HTR* 76 (1983): 379–401.

———. "The Rise of Abimelek Ben-Jerubbaal." *HAR* 2 (1978): 79–100.

Hamori, Esther J. "Childless Female Diviners in the Bible and Beyond." Pages 169–91 in *Prophets Male and Female: Gender and Prophecy in the Hebrew Bible, the Eastern Mediterranean, and the Ancient Near East*. Edited by Jonathan Stökl and Corrine L. Carvalho. Ancient Israel and Its Literature 15. Atlanta: Society of Biblical Literature, 2013.

———. "The Prophet and the Necromancer: Women's Divination for Kings." *JBL* 132 (2013): 827–43.

Harris, Rivkah. *Ancient Sippar: A Demographic Study of an Old Babylonian City (1894–1595 B.C.)*. Uitgaven van het Nederlands historisch-archaeologisch instituut te Istanbul 36. Istanbul: Nederlands Historisch-Archeologisch Instituut, 1975.

———. "Biographical Notes on the *nadītu* Women of Sippar." *Journal of Cuneiform Studies* 16 (1962): 1–12.

———. "Hierodulen." Pages 391–93 in vol. 4 of *Reallexikon der Assyriologie und vorderasiatischen Archäologie*. Edited by Erich Ebeling and Bruno Meissner. Berlin: de Gruyter, 1975.

———. "Independent Women in Ancient Mesopotamia?" Pages 145–56 in *Women's Earliest Records from Ancient Egypt and Western Asia*. Edited by Barbara S. Lesko. BJS 166. Atlanta: Scholars Press, 1989.

———. "The *nadītu* Laws of the Code of Hammurapi in Praxis." *Or* 30 (1961): 163–69.

———. "The *nadītu* Woman." Pages 106–35 in *Studies Presented to A. Leo Oppenheim, June 7, 1964*. Chicago: University of Chicago Press, 1964.

———. "Notes on the Babylonian Cloister and Hearth: A Review Article." *Or* 38 (1969): 133–45.

———. "The Organization and Administration of the Cloister in Ancient Babylonia." *JESHO* 6 (1963): 121–57.

Hart, George. *The Routledge Dictionary of Egyptian Gods and Goddesses*. 2nd ed. London: Routledge, 2005.

Hayes, John H., and Stuart A. Irvine. *Isaiah, the Eighth-Century Prophet: His Times and His Preaching*. Nashville: Abingdon, 1987.

Healey, J. P. "The Kition Tariffs and the Phoenician Cursive Series." *BASOR* 216 (1974): 53–60.

Helck, Wolfgang. *Betrachtungen zur grossen Göttin und den ihr verbundenen Gottheiten*. Religion und Kultur der alten Mittelmeerwelt in Parallelforschungen 2. Munich: R. Oldenbourg, 1971.

———. *Die Beziehungen Ägyptiens zu Vorderasien im 3. und 2. Jahrtausend v. Chr.* 2nd ed. Ägyptologische Abhandlungen 5. Wiesbaden: Harrassowitz, 1971.

Held, Moshe. "Studies in Biblical Lexicography in the Light of Akkadian." *ErIsr* 16 (1982): 76–85 (Hebrew).

Heltzer, Michael. *The Internal Organization of the Kingdom of Ugarit*. Wiesbaden: Reichert, 1982.

Hendel, Ronald S. "Aniconism and Anthropomorphism in Ancient Israel." Pages 205–28 in *The Image and the Book: Iconic Cults, Aniconism, and the Rise of Book Religion in Israel and the Ancient Near East*. Edited by Karel van der Toorn. Leuven: Peeters, 1997

———. *The Epic of the Patriarch: The Jacob Cycle and the Narrative Traditions of Canaan and Israel*. HSM 42. Atlanta: Scholars Press, 1987.

———. "Sacrifice as a Cultural System: The Ritual Symbolism of Exodus 24, 3–8." *ZAW* 101 (1989): 366–90.

———. "The Social Origins of the Aniconic Tradition in Early Israel." *CBQ* 50 (1988): 365–82.

Henshaw, Richard A. *Female and Male: The Cultic Personnel: The Bible and the Rest of the Ancient Near East*. Allison Park, PA: Pickwick Publications, 1994.

Herrmann, Wolfram. "Aštart." *Mitteilungen des Instituts für Orientforschung* 15 (1969): 6–55.

Hestrin, Ruth. "The Cult Stand from Taʿanach and its Religious Background." Pages 61–77 in *Phoenicia and the East Mediterranean in the First Millennium B.C.* Edited by Edward Lipiński. Studia Phoenicia 5. Orientalia lovaniensia analecta 23. Leuven: Peeters, 1987.

———. "The Lachish Ewer and the 'Asherah." *IEJ* 37 (1987): 212–23.

Hoffner, Harry A. "A Canaanite Myth." Pages 90–92 in *Hittite Myths*. 2nd ed. SBLWAW 2. Atlanta: Scholars Press, 1998.

———. "The Elkunirsa Myth Reconsidered." *Revue Hittite et Asianique* 23 (1965): 5–16.

———. "Symbols for Masculinity and Femininity: Their Use in Ancient Near Eastern Sympathetic Magic Rituals." *JBL* 85 (1966): 326–34.

Holladay, William L. *Jeremiah*. 2 vols. Hermeneia. Philadelphia: Fortress, 1986–1989.

Hollis, Susan Tower. "Queens and Goddesses in Ancient Egypt." Pages 210–38 in *Women and Goddess Traditions: In Antiquity and Today*. Edited by Karen L. King. Studies in Antiquity and Christianity. Minneapolis: Fortress, 1997.

Holloway, Steven W. "Distaff, Crutch or Chain Gang: The Curse of the House of Joab in 2 Samuel III 29." *VT* 37 (1987): 370–75.

Houtman, Cornelis. "Exodus 4:24–26 and Its Interpretation." *Journal of Northwest Semitic Languages* 11 (1983): 81–105.

———. "Queen of Heaven *mlkt hšmym*." Pages 678–80 in *Dictionary of Deities and Demons in the Bible*. Edited by Karel van der Toorn, Bob Becking, and Pieter W. van der Horst. 2nd ed. Leiden: Brill, 1999.

Isenberg, Wesley W. "The Gospel of Philip." Pages 131–51 in *The Nag Hammadi Library*. Edited by James M. Robinson. San Francisco: Harper & Row, 1977.

Ishida, Tomoo. *The Royal Dynasties in Ancient Israel: A Study on the Formation and Development of the Royal-Dynastic Ideology*. BZAW 142. Berlin: de Gruyter, 1977.

Jacobsen, Thorkild. "Notes on Selected Sayings." Pages 447–87 in *Sumerian Proverbs: Glimpses of Everyday Life in Ancient Mesopotamia*. Edited by Edmund I. Gordon. Philadelphia: The University Museum, University of Pennsylvania, 1959.

———. *The Treasures of Darkness: A History of Mesopotamian Religion*. New Haven: Yale University Press, 1976.

Janowski, Bernd. "Erwägungen zur vorgeschichte des israelitischen *šelamîm*-Opfers." *UF* 12 (1980): 231–60.

Janssen, Jac. J. "Absence from Work by the Necropolis Workmen of Thebes." *Studien zur Altägyptischen Kultur* 8 (1980): 127–52.

Janssen, Rosalind M., and Jac. J. Janssen. *Growing Up in Ancient Egypt*. London: Rubicon, 1990.

Japhet, Sara. *I and II Chronicles: A Commentary*. OTL. Louisville: Westminster John Knox, 1993.

———. "Sheshbazzar and Zerubbabel—Against the Background of the Historical and Religious Tendencies of Ezra-Nehemiah." *ZAW* 94 (1982): 66–98.

Jaroš, Karl. "Zur Inschrift Nr. 3 von Ḥirbet el-Qōm." *BN* 19 (1982): 31–40.

Jay, Nancy. *Throughout Your Generations Forever: Sacrifice, Religion, and Paternity.* Chicago: University of Chicago Press, 1992.

Jeremias, Alfred. *Das Alte Testament im Lichte des Alten Orients.* 3rd ed. Leipzig: J. C. Hinrichs, 1916.

Jeyes, Ulla. "The Nadītu Women of Sippar." Pages 260–72 in *Images of Women in Antiquity.* Edited by Averil Cameron and Amélie Kuhrt. London: Routledge, 1983.

Jobling, David. "A Structural Analysis of Numbers 11–12." Pages 31–65 in *The Sense of Biblical Narrative: Structural Analyses in the Hebrew Bible.* 2nd ed. Vol. 1. JSOTSup 7. Sheffield: JSOT Press, 1986.

Johnson, Aubrey R. "Hebrew Conceptions of Kingship." Pages 204–35 in *Myth, Ritual, and Kingship: Essays on the Theory and Practice of Kingship in the Ancient Near East and in Israel.* Edited by S. H. Hooke. Oxford: Clarendon, 1958.

———. "Living Issues in Biblical Scholarship: Divine Kingship and the Old Testament." *ExpTim* 62 (1950–51): 36–42.

Johnson, Marshall D. *The Purpose of the Biblical Genealogies with Special Reference to the Setting of the Genealogies of Jesus.* 2nd ed. Society for New Testament Studies Monograph Series 8. Cambridge, UK: Cambridge University Press, 1988.

Jones-Warsaw, Koala. "Toward a Womanist Hermeneutic: A Reading of Judges 19–21." Pages 172–86 in *A Feminist Companion to Judges.* Edited by Athalya Brenner. FCB 4. Sheffield: Sheffield Academic, 1993.

Jongeling, Karel, and Robert M. Kerr, eds. *Late Punic Epigraphy: An Introduction to the Study of Neo-Punic and Latino-Punic Inscriptions.* Tübingen: Mohr Siebeck, 2005.

Kapelrud, Arvid S. *The Violent Goddess: Anat in the Ras Shamra Texts.* Oslo: Universitetsforlaget, 1969.

Kaplan, Lawrence. "'And the Lord Sought to Kill Him' (Exod 4:24): Yet Once Again." *HAR* 5 (1981): 65–74.

Karageorghis, Vassos. "A Cypriot Silver Bowl Reconsidered: 1. The Iconography of the Decoration." *Metropolitan Museum Journal* 34 (1999): 13–20.

———. *Kition: Mycenaean and Phoenician Discoveries in Cyprus.* London: Thames and Hudson, 1976.

Katz, Marilyn A. "Sappho and Her Sisters: Women in Ancient Greece." *Signs* 25 (2000): 505–31.

Katzenstein, Hanna Jacob. "Who Were the Parents of Athaliah?" *IEJ* 5 (1955): 194–97.

Keel, Othmar, and Christoph Uehlinger. *Gods, Goddesses, and Images of God in Ancient Israel*. Minneapolis: Fortress, 1998.

Kellermann, Ulrich. "Erwägungen zum Problem der Esradatierung." *ZAW* 80 (1968): 55–87.

Kemp, Barry J. "Wall Paintings from the Workmen's Village at el-'Amarna." *JEA* 65 (1979): 47–53.

Kerr, Robert M. "Notre-Dame-de-la-Huronie? A Note on *'štrt ḥr*." *WdO* 43 (2013): 206–12.

Koch, Klaus. "Aschera als Himmelskönigin in Jerusalem." *UF* 20 (1988): 97–120.

Kochavi, Moshe. "The Israelite Settlement in Canaan in the Light of Archaeological Surveys." Pages 54–60 in *Biblical Archaeology Today: Proceedings of the International Congress on Biblical Archaeology, Jerusalem, April 1984*. Edited by Janet Amitai. Jerusalem: Israel Exploration Society, 1985.

Kosmala, Hans. "The 'Bloody Husband.'" *VT* 12 (1962): 14–28.

Krahmalkov, Charles R. *Phoenician-Punic Dictionary*. Studia Phoenicia 15. Orientalia lovaniensia analecta 90. Leuven: Uitgeverij Peeters en Departement Oosterse Studies, 2000.

Kramer, Samuel Noah. *Sumerian Mythology: A Study of Spiritual and Literary Achievement in the Third Millennium B.C.* Philadelphia: American Philosophical Society, 1944.

———. *The Sumerians: Their History, Culture, and Character*. Chicago: University of Chicago Press, 1963.

Kramer, Samuel Noah, and John Maier. *Myths of Enki, the Crafty God*. New York: Oxford University Press, 1989.

Kunin, Seth D. "The Bridegroom of Blood: A Structuralist Analysis." *JSOT* 70 (1996): 3–16.

Lafont, Bertrand. "À propos de l'absence cyclique des femmes." *Nouvelles Assyriologiques Brèves et Utilitaire* (1987): no. 45.

Lambdin, Thomas O. "The Gospel of Thomas." Pages 117–30 in *The Nag Hammadi Library*. Edited by James M. Robinson. San Francisco: Harper & Row, 1977.

Lambert, W. G. "Goddesses in the Pantheon: A Reflection of Women in Society?" Pages 125–29 in *La Femme dans le Proche-Orient Antique: compte rendu de la XXXIIIᵉ Rencontre Assyriologique Internationale (Paris, 7–10 Juillet 1986)*. Edited by Jean-Marie Durand. Paris: Éditions Recherche sur les civilisations, 1987.

Lapp, Paul W. "The 1963 Excavation at Ta'annek." *BASOR* 173 (1964): 4–44.

———. "The 1968 Excavations at Tell Ta'annek." *BASOR* 195 (1969): 2–49.

———. "Taanach by the Waters of Megiddo." *BA* 30 (1967): 2–27.

Lasine, Stuart. "Guest and Host in Judges 19: Lot's Hospitality in an Inverted World." *JSOT* 9 (1984): 37–59.

Lattimore, Richmond. *The Odyssey of Homer*. New York: Harper Perennial, 1965.

Leach, Edmund. "Anthropological Approaches to the Study of the Bible During the Twentieth Century." Pages 7–32 in *Structuralist Interpretations of Biblical Myth*. By Edmund Leach and D. Alan Aycock. Cambridge, UK: Cambridge University Press and Royal Anthropological Institutes of Great Britain and Ireland, 1983.

———. "Why Did Moses Have a Sister?" Pages 33–66 in *Structuralist Interpretations of Biblical Myth*. By Edmund Leach and D. Alan Aycock. Cambridge, UK: Cambridge University Press and Royal Anthropological Institutes of Great Britain and Ireland, 1983.

Leclant, Jean. "Astarté à cheval d'après les représéntations égyptiennes." *Syria* 37 (1960): 1–67.

Lefkowitz, Mary. "The Myth of Joseph Campbell." *The American Scholar* 59 (1990): 429–34.

———. "Women in the Panathenaic and Other Festivals." Pages 78–91 in *Worshipping Athena: Panathenaia and Parthenon*. Edited by Jenifer Neils. Madison, WI: University of Wisconsin Press, 1996.

Lemaire, André. "Date et origine des inscriptiones hébraiques et pheniciennes de Kuntillet 'Ajrud." *Studi epigraphici e linguistici* 1 (1984): 131–43.

———. "Les inscriptions de Khirbet el-Qôm et l'Ashérah de Yhwh." *RB* 84 (1977): 597–608.

———. "Who or What Was Yahweh's Asherah?" *BAR* 10/6 (1984): 42–51.

Lesko, Barbara S. "Household and Domestic Religion in Ancient Egypt." Pages 197–209 in *Household and Family Religion in Antiquity*. Edited by John Bodel and Saul M. Olyan. Oxford: Blackwell, 2008.

Lesko, Barbara S., ed. "Responses to Prof. Harris's Paper." Pages 157–65 in *Women's Earliest Records from Ancient Egypt and Western Asia*. Edited by Barbara S. Lesko. BJS 166. Atlanta: Scholars Press, 1989.

Leuchter, Mark. "Cult of Personality: The Eclipse of Pre-Exilic Cultic Structures in the Book of Jeremiah." Pages 95–115 in *Constructs of Prophecy in the Former and Latter Prophets and Other Texts*. Edited by Lester L. Grabbe and Martti Nissinen. Atlanta: Society of Biblical Literature, 2011.

Levine, Baruch A. "The Deir 'Alla Plaster Inscriptions." Pages 140–45 in *COS* 2.

———. *In the Presence of the Lord: A Study of Cult and Some Cultic Terms in Ancient Israel*. Leiden: Brill, 1974.

Levy, Shalom, and Gershon Edelstein. "Cinq années de fouilles à Tel 'Amal (Nir David)." *RB* 79 (1972): 325–67.

Lewis, Theodore J. *Cults of the Dead in Ancient Israel and Ugarit*. HSM 39. Atlanta: Scholars Press, 1989.

————. *The Origin and Character of God: Ancient Israelite Religion through the Lens of Divinity*. Oxford: Oxford University Press, 2020.

————. "Ugaritic Athtartu, Food Production and Textiles: More Data for Reassessing the Biblical Portrayal of Ashtart in Context." Paper presented in the Hebrew Scriptures and Cognate Literature Section of the Annual Meeting of the Society of Biblical Literature, Denver, CO, November 18, 2018. Abstract posted online at https://www.sbl-site.org/meetings/Congresses_Abstracts. aspx?MeetingId=33.

————. "Ugaritic Athtartu Šadi, Food Production, and Textiles: More Data for Reassessing the Biblical Portrayal of Aštart in Context." Pages 138–59 in *Mighty Baal: Essays in Honor of Mark S. Smith*. Edited by Stephen C. Russell and Esther J. Hamori. HSS 66. Leiden: Brill, 2020.

Lichtheim, Miriam. *Ancient Egyptian Literature*. 3 vols. Berkeley: University of California Press, 1975–1980.

Lipiński, Edward. "Aḫat-milki, reine d'Ugarit, et la guerre du Mukiš." *OLP* 12 (1981): 79–115.

————. *The Aramaeans: Their Ancient History, Culture, Religion*. Leuven: Uitgeverij Peeters en Departement Oosterse Studies, 2000.

————. "Fertility Cult in Ancient Ugarit." Pages 207–16 in *Archaeology and Fertility Cult in the Ancient Mediterranean: Papers Presented at the First International Conference on Archaeology of the Ancient Mediterranean, the University of Malta, 2–5 September*. Edited by Anthony Bonanno. Amsterdam: B. R. Grüner, 1986.

————. "The Goddess Aṯirat in Ancient Arabia, in Babylon, and in Ugarit." *OLP* 3 (1972): 101–19.

Lohfink, Norbert. "The Cult Reform of Josiah of Judah: 2 Kings 22–23 as a Source for the History of Israelite Religion." Pages 459–75 in *Ancient Israelite Religion: Essays in Honor of Frank Moore Cross*. Edited by Patrick D. Miller, Paul D. Hanson, and S. Dean McBride. Philadelphia: Fortress, 1987.

Lorton, David. "The Theology of Cult Statues in Ancient Egypt." Pages 123–210 in *Born in Heaven, Made on Earth: The Making of the Cult Image in the Ancient Near East*. Edited by Michael B. Dick. Winona Lake, IN: Eisenbrauns, 1999.

Macalister, R. A. S. *The Philistines: Their History and Civilization*. London: Oxford University Press, 1914.

Madsen, Henry. "Zwei Inschriften in Kopenhagen." *Zeitschrift für Ägyptische Sprache und Altertumskunde* 41 (1904): 114–16.

Malamat, Abraham. "Mari." *BA* 34 (1971): 2–22.

————. "The Proto-History of Israel: A Study in Method." Pages 303–13 in *The Word of the Lord Shall Go Forth: Essays in Honor of David Noel Freedman in*

Celebration of his Sixtieth Birthday. Edited by Carol L. Meyers and Michael O'Connor. Winona Lake, IN: Eisenbrauns, 1983.

Manganaro, Marc. "Joseph Campbell: Authority's Thousand Faces." Pages 151–85 in *Myth, Rhetoric, and the Voice of Authority*. New Haven: Yale University Press, 1992.

Mansfield, John M. "The Robe of Athena and the Panathenaic Peplos." PhD diss., University of California, Berkeley, 1985.

Margalit, Baruch. "Some Observations on the Inscription and Drawing from Khirbet el-Qôm." *VT* 39 (1989): 371–78.

Markoe, Glenn. *Phoenician Bronze and Silver Bowls from Cyprus and the Mediterranean*. Classical Studies 26. Berkeley: University of California Press, 1985.

———. *Phoenicians*. London: British Museum, 2000.

Marsman, Hennie J. *Women in Ugarit and Israel: Their Social and Religious Position in the Context of the Ancient Near East*. Oudtestamentische Studiën/Old Testament Studies 49. Leiden: Brill, 2003.

Martin, James D. *The Book of Judges*. CBC. Cambridge, UK: Cambridge University Press, 1975.

Maspero, M. Gaston. "Notes de Voyage." *Annales du service des antiquités de l'Egypte* 10 (1909): 131–44.

Masson, Olivier, and Maurice Sznycer. *Recherches sur les phéniciens à Chypre*. Hautes Études Orientales 2/3. Geneva: Librairie Droz, 1972.

Matoïan, Valérie, and Juan-Pablo Vita. "Wool Production and Economy at Ugarit." Pages 310–39 in *Wool Economy in the Ancient Near East: From the Beginnings of Sheep Husbandry to Institutional Textile Industry*. Edited by Catherine Breniquet and Cécile Michel. Ancient Textile Series 17. Oxford: Oxbow Books, 2014.

Matsushima, Eiko. "Divine Statues in Ancient Mesopotamia: Their Fashioning and Clothing and Their Interaction with Society." Pages 209–19 in *Official Cult and Popular Religion in the Ancient Near East: Papers of the First Colloquium on the Ancient Near East—the City and its Life, Held at the Middle Eastern Cultural Center in Japan (Mitaka, Tokyo), March 20–22, 1992*. Edited by Eiko Matsushima. Heidelberg: C. Winter, 1993.

Matthews, Victor H. *Judges and Ruth*. New Cambridge Bible Commentary. Cambridge, UK: Cambridge University Press, 2004.

Mazar, Amihai. *Excavations at Tell Qasile, Part 1: The Philistine Sanctuary: Architecture and Cult Objects*. Qedem 12. Jerusalem: The Institute of Archaeology, The Hebrew University of Jerusalem, 1980.

———. *Excavations at Tell Qasile, Part 2: The Philistine Sanctuary: Various Finds, the Pottery, Conclusions, Appendices.* Qedem 20. Jerusalem: The Institute of Archaeology, The Hebrew University of Jerusalem, 1985.

———. "Giloh: An Early Israelite Settlement Site Near Jerusalem." *IEJ* 31 (1981): 1–36.

———. "Iron Age I and II Towers at Giloh and the Israelite Settlement." *IEJ* 40 (1990): 77–101.

McCarter, P. Kyle. "Aspects of the Religion of the Israelite Monarchy: Biblical and Epigraphic Data." Pages 137–55 in *Ancient Israelite Religion: Essays in Honor of Frank Moore Cross.* Edited by Patrick D. Miller, Paul D. Hanson, and S. Dean McBride. Philadelphia: Fortress, 1987.

———. *I Samuel: A New Translation with Introduction and Commentary.* AYB 8. Garden City, NY: Doubleday, 1980.

———. "The Sarcophagus Inscription of 'Eshmun'azor, King of Sidon (2.57)." Pages 182–83 in *COS* 2.

McCreesh, Thomas P. "Wisdom as Wife: Proverbs 31:10–31." *RB* 92 (1985): 25–46.

McGeough, Kevin M. *Ugaritic Economic Tablets: Text, Translation, and Notes.* Ancient Near Eastern Studies 32. Leuven: Peeters, 2011.

McHale-Moore, Rhonda. "The Mystery of Enheduanna's Disk." *Journal of the Ancient Near Eastern Society of Columbia University* 27 (2000): 69–74.

McKay, John. *Religion in Judah under the Assyrians, 739–609 B.C.* Studies in Biblical Theology (Second Series) 26. Naperville, IL: A. R. Allenson, 1973.

McKenzie, Steven L. *The Trouble with Kings: The Composition of the Book of Kings in the Deuteronomistic History.* VTSup 42. Leiden: Brill, 1991.

Mendenhall, George E. "The Hebrew Conquest of Palestine." *BA* 25 (1962): 66–87.

Merlo, Paolo, and Paolo Xella. "The Ugaritic Cultic Texts: The Rituals." Pages 287–304 in *Handbook of Ugaritic Studies.* Edited by Wilfred Watson and Nicolas Wyatt. Handbuch der Orientalistik: Erste Abteilung, Nahe und der Mittlere Osten 39. Leiden: Brill, 1999.

Merrill, Arthur L. "The House of Keret: A Study of the Keret Legend." *Svensk Exegetisk Årsbok* 33 (1968): 5–17.

Meshel, Ze'ev, "Did Yahweh Have a Consort? The New Religious Inscriptions from Sinai." *BAR* 5/2 (1979): 24–35.

———. *Kuntillet 'Ajrûd: A Religious Center from the Time of the Judean Monarchy.* Israel Museum Catalogue 175. Jerusalem: Israel Museum, 1978.

———. "Kuntillet 'Ajrûd—An Israelite Religious Center in Northern Sinai." *Expedition* 20 (1978): 50–54.

———. "Kuntillet 'Ajrûd—An Israelite Site from the Monarchical Period on the Sinai Border." *Qad* 9 (1976): 118–124 (Hebrew).

———. *Kuntillet 'Ajrud (Ḥorvat Teman): An Iron Age II Religious Site on the Judah-*

Sinai Border. Edited by Liora Freud. Jerusalem: Israel Exploration Society, 2012.

Meshel, Ze'ev, and Meyers, Carol. "The Name of God in the Wilderness of Zin." *BA* 39 (1976): 6–10.

Mesnil du Buisson, Robert du. *Études sur les dieux phéniciens hérités par l'Empire Romain.* Leiden: Brill, 1970.

Mettinger, Tryggve N. D. *No Graven Image? Israelite Aniconism in Its Ancient Near Eastern Context.* Stockholm: Almqvist & Wiksell International, 1995.

Meyers, Carol. *Discovering Eve: Ancient Israelite Women in Context.* Oxford: Oxford University Press, 1988.

———. "From Field Crops to Food: Attributing Gender and Meaning to Bread Production in Iron Age Israel." Pages 67–84 in *The Archaeology of Difference: Gender, Ethnicity, Class and the "Other" in Antiquity. Studies in Honor of Eric M. Meyers.* Edited by Douglas R. Edwards and C. Thomas McCullough. Annual of the American Schools of Oriental Research 60/61. Boston: American Schools of Oriental Research, 2007.

———. "Hannah and Her Sacrifice: Reclaiming Female Agency." Pages 93–104 in *A Feminist Companion to Samuel and Kings.* Edited by Athalya Brenner. FCB 5. Sheffield: Sheffield Academic, 1994.

———. "The Hannah Narrative in Feminist Perspective." Pages 117–26 in *Go to the Land I Will Show You: Studies in Honor of Dwight W. Young.* Edited by Joseph E. Coleson and Victor H. Matthews. Winona Lake, IN: Eisenbrauns, 1996.

———. "Material Remains and Social Relations: Women's Culture in Agrarian Households of the Iron Age." Pages 425–44 in *Symbiosis, Symbolism, and the Power of the Past: Canaan, Ancient Israel, and Their Neighbors from the Late Bronze Age through Roman Palaestina.* Edited by William G. Dever and Seymour Gitin. Winona Lake, IN: Eisenbrauns, 2003.

———. "Mother to Muse: An Archaeomusicological Study of Women's Performance in Israel." Pages 50–77 in *Recycling Biblical Figures: Papers Read at a Noster Colloquium in Amsterdam, 12–13 May 1997.* Edited by Athalya Brenner and Jan Willem van Henten. Studies in Theology and Religion 1. Leiden: Deo, 1999.

———. "Of Drums and Damsels: Women's Performance in Ancient Israel." *BA* 54 (1991): 16–27.

———. *Rediscovering Eve: Ancient Israelite Women in Context.* Oxford: Oxford University Press, 2013.

———. "Singing Women (and Men) Who Lament." Pages 284 in *WIS.*

———. "Skilled Women (and Men)." Pages 201–2 in *WIS.*

———. "A Terracotta at the Harvard Semitic Museum and Disc-Holding Female Figurines Reconsidered." *IEJ* (1987): 116–22.

———. "Women with Hand-Drums, Dancing." Pages 189–91 in *WIS*.

Michalowski, Piotr. "Presence at the Creation." Pages 381–96 in *Lingering over Words: Studies in Ancient Near Eastern Literature in Honor of William L. Moran*. Edited by Tzvi Abusch, John Huehnergard, and Piotr Steinkeller. HSS 37. Atlanta: Scholars Press, 1990.

Milanezi, Silvia. "Headaches and Gnawed *Peplos*: Laughing with Athena." Pages 311–29 in *Athena in the Classical World*. Edited by Susan Deacy and Alexandra Willing. Leiden: Brill, 2001.

Milgrom, Jacob. *Leviticus 1–16: A New Translation with Introduction and Commentary*. AYB 3. New York: Doubleday, 1991.

———. *Numbers*. The JPS Torah Commentary. Philadelphia: The Jewish Publication Society, 1990.

Milik, J. T. "Les papyrus araméens d'Hermoupolis et les cultes syro-phéniciens en Egypte perse." *Bib* 48 (1967): 546–622.

Miller, Patrick D. "The Absence of the Goddess in Israelite Religion." *HAR* 10 (1986): 239–48.

———. "Israelite Religion." Pages 201–37 in *The Hebrew Bible and its Modern Interpreters*. Edited by Douglas A. Knight and Gene M. Tucker. Philadelphia: Fortress; Chico, CA: Scholars Press, 1985.

———. "Psalms and Inscriptions." Pages 311–32 in *Congress Volume: Vienna 1980*. Edited by J. A. Emerton. VTSup 32. Leiden: Brill, 1981.

Milne, Pamela J. "Feminist Interpretations of the Bible: Then and Now." *BRev* 8/5 (October 1992): 38–43, 52–55.

Mittman, Siegfried. "Die Grabinschrift des Sängers Uriahu." *Zeitschrift des Deutschen Palästina-Vereins* 97 (1981): 139–52.

Molin, Georg. "Die Stellung der Gᵉbira im Staate Juda." *Theologische Zeitschrift* 10 (1954): 161–75.

Montgomery, James A. *A Critical and Exegetical Commentary on the Books of Kings*. ICC. New York: Scribners, 1951.

Moor, Johannes C. de. "Studies in the New Alphabetic Texts from Ras Shamra II." *UF* 2 (1970): 167–88.

Moore, George F. *A Critical and Exegetical Commentary on Judges*. 2nd ed. ICC 7. Edinburgh: T&T Clark, 1903.

Moran, William L. "Atrahasis: The Babylonian Story of the Flood." *Bib* 52 (1971): 51–61.

Morgenstern, Julian. "The 'Bloody Husband' (?) (Exod 4:24–26) Once Again." *HUCA* 34 (1963): 35–70.

Moscati, Sabatino. "Nuovi studi sull'identità fenicia." *Atti della Accademia Nazionale dei Lincei: Memorie, classe di scienze morali, storiche e filologiche* 9/4 (1993): 3–89.

Müllner, Ilse. "Lethal Differences: Sexual Violence as Violence Against Others in Judges 19." Pages 126–42 in *Judges*. Edited by Athalya Brenner. FCB 2/4. Sheffield: Sheffield Academic, 1999.

Na'aman, Nadav. "Queen Mothers and Ancestors Cult in Judah in the First Temple Period." Pages 479–90 in *Berührungspunkte: Studien zur Sozial- und Religionsgeschichte Israels und seiner Umwelt: Festschrift für Rainer Albertz zu seinem 65 Geburtstag.* Edited by Ruth Ebach, Ingo Kottsieper, Rüdiger Schmitt, and Jacob Wöhrle. Münster: Ugarit-Verlag, 2008.

Nakhai, Beth Alpert. *Archaeology and the Religions of Canaan and Israel.* Boston: American Schools of Oriental Research, 2001.

Naveh, Joseph. "Graffiti and Dedications." *BASOR* 235 (1979): 27–30.

Neils, Jenifer. "Children and Greek Religion." Pages 139–61 in *Coming of Age in Ancient Greece: Images of Childhood from the Classical Past.* Edited by Jenifer Neils and John Howard Oakley. New Haven: Yale University Press, 2003.

———. "The Panathenaia: An Introduction." Pages 13–27 in *Goddess and Polis: The Panathenaic Festival in Ancient Athens.* Edited by Jenifer Neils. Hanover, NH: Dartmouth College, Hood Museum of Art; Princeton: Princeton University Press, 1992.

———. *Women in the Ancient World.* Los Angeles: J. Paul Getty Museum, 2011.

Nelson, Richard D. *The Double Redaction of the Deuteronomistic History.* JSOTSup 18. Sheffield: JSOT Press, 1981.

Niditch, Susan. *Judges: A Commentary,* OTL. Louisville: Westminster John Knox, 2008.

———. "The 'Sodomite' Theme in Judges 19–20: Family, Community, and Social Disintegration." *CBQ* 44 (1982): 365–78.

Noth, Martin. *Die israelitischen Personennamen im Rahmen der gemeinsemitischen Namengebung.* Hildesheim: Georg Olms, 1980.

Nougayrol, Jean, Emmanuel Laroche, Charles Virolleaud, Claude F. A. Schaeffer, et al. *Ugaritica V: Nouveaux textes accadiens, hourrites et ugaritiques des archives et bibliothèques privées d'Ugarit, Commentaires des textes historiques (première partie).* Mission de Ras Shamra 16. Bibliothèque archéologique et historique 80. Paris: Imprimerie Nationale; Librairie orientaliste Paul Geuthner, 1968.

O'Connor, Michael. "The Poetic Inscription from Khirbet el-Qôm." *VT* 37 (1987): 224–29.

Oden, Robert A. *The Bible without Theology: The Theological Tradition and Alternatives to It.* San Francisco: Harper & Row, 1987.

———. *Studies in Lucian's De Syria Dea.* HSM 15. Missoula, MT: Scholars Press, 1977.

Olmo Lete, Gregorio del. *Canaanite Religion: According to the Liturgical Texts of Ugarit.* Winona Lake, IN: Eisenbrauns, 2004.

———. "Religious Personnel: Syria-Canaan." Pages 295–96 in *Religions of the Ancient World: A Guide.* Edited by Sarah Iles Johnston. Cambridge, MA: Harvard University Press, 2004.

Olyan, Saul M. *Asherah and the Cult of Yahweh in Israel.* SBLMS 34. Atlanta: Scholars Press, 1988.

———. *Rites and Rank: Hierarchy in Biblical Representations of Cult.* Princeton: Princeton University Press, 2000.

———. "Sin, Pollution, and Purity: Syria-Canaan." Pages 501–2 in *Religions of the Ancient World: A Guide.* Edited by Sarah Iles Johnston. Cambridge, MA: Harvard University Press, 2004.

———. "Some Observations Concerning the Identity of the Queen of Heaven." *UF* 19 (1987): 161–74.

Onstine, Suzanne. "Gender and the Religion of Ancient Egypt." *Religion Compass* 4 (2010): 1–11.

Oppenheim, A. Leo. "The Golden Garments of the Gods." *JNES* 8 (1949): 172–93.

———. "Mesopotamian Mythology II." *Or* 17 (1948): 17–58.

Pardee, Dennis. "The Kirta Epic." Pages 333–43 in *COS* 1.

———. "On the Edge." Pages 177–96 in *The Perfumes of Seven Tamarisks: Studies in Honour of Wilfred G. E. Watson.* Edited by Gregorio del Olmo Lette, Jordl Vidal, and Nicolas Wyatt. AOAT 394. Münster: Ugarit-Verlag, 2012.

———. *Ritual and Cult at Ugarit.* SBLWAW 10. Atlanta: Society of Biblical Literature, 2002.

———. *Les Textes Rituels.* 2 vols. Ras Shamra-Ougarit 12. Paris: Éditions Recherche sur les civilisations, 2000.

Parker, Robert. *Miasma: Pollution and Purification in Early Greek Religion.* Oxford: Clarendon, 1983.

Parker, Simon B. "The Historical Composition of KRT and the Cult of El." *ZAW* 89 (1977): 161–75.

———. *The Pre-Biblical Narrative Tradition.* SBLRBS 24. Atlanta: Scholars Press, 1989.

Parrot, André. *Mission archéologique de Mari 2: Le palais-documents et monuments.* Paris: Librairie Orientaliste Paul Geuthner, 1959.

Peckham, J. Brian. "Notes on a Fifth-Century Phoenician Inscription from Kition, Cyprus (CIS 86)." *Or* 37 (1968): 304–24.

———. "Phoenicians and Aramaeans: The Literary and Epigraphic Evidence." Pages 19–44 in *The World of the Aramaeans II: Studies in History and Archaeology in Honour of Paul-Eugène Dion*. Edited by P. M. Michèle Daviau, John W. Wevers, and Michael Weigl. JSOTSup 325. Sheffield: Sheffield Academic, 2001.

Pedersen, Johannes. *Israel: Its Life and Culture*. 4 vols. London: Oxford University Press, 1946–1947.

Petrie, W. M. Flinders. *Memphis 1*. London: School of Archaeology in Egypt and Bernard Quaritch, 1909.

Pinch, Geraldine. "Childbirth and Female Figurines at Deir el-Medina and el-Amarna." *Or* 52 (1983): 405–14.

———. "Private Life in Ancient Egypt." Pages 363–81 in *CANE*.

Pitard, Wayne T. *Ancient Damascus: A Historical Study of the Syrian City-State from Earliest Times until Its Fall to the Assyrians in 732 B.C.E.* Winona Lake, IN: Eisenbrauns, 1987.

Poethig, Eunice B. "The Victory Song Tradition of the Women of Israel." PhD diss., Union Theological Seminary, 1985.

Pope, Marvin H. "'Attart, 'Aštart, Astarte." Pages 250–52 in *Götter und Mythen im vorderen Orient*. Edited by Hans Wilhelm Haussig. Vol. 1 of *Wörterbuch der Mythologie*. Stuttgart: Ernst Klett, 1965.

———. "Fertility Cults." Page 265 in vol. 2 of *The Interpreter's Dictionary of the Bible*. Edited by George Arthur Buttrick. Nashville: Abingdon, 1962.

———. *Song of Songs*. AYB 7C. Garden City, NY: Doubleday, 1977.

Porten, Bezalel. *Archives from Elephantine: The Life of an Ancient Jewish Military Colony*. Berkeley: University of California Press, 1968.

Postgate, J. N. Review of *The Installation of Baal's High Priestess at Emar: A Window on Ancient Syrian Religion*, by Daniel E. Fleming. *VT* 43 (1993): 285.

Potts, D. T. *Mesopotamia: The Material Foundations*. Ithaca, NY: Cornell University Press, 1997.

Pressler, Carolyn. *The View of Women Found in Deuteronomic Family Laws*. Berlin: de Gruyter, 1993.

Price, Simon R. F. "Religious Personnel: Greece." Pages 302–5 in *Religions of the Ancient World: A Guide*. Edited by Sarah Iles Johnston. Cambridge, MA: Harvard University Press, 2004.

Pringle, Jackie. "Hittite Birth Rituals." Pages 65–78 in *Images of Women in Antiquity*. Edited by Averil Cameron and Amélie Kuhrt. London: Routledge, 1983.

Propp, William H. C. *Exodus 1–18: A New Translation with Introduction and Commentary.* AYB 2. New York: Doubleday, 1998.

———. "That Bloody Bridegroom (Exodus iv 24–6)." *VT* 43 (1993): 495–518.

———. *Water in the Wilderness: A Biblical Motif and Its Mythological Background.* HSM 40. Atlanta: Scholars Press, 1987.

Puech, Émile. "Un cratère phénicien inscrit: rites et croyances." *Transeuphratène* 8 (1994): 47–73.

Quack, Joachim Friedrich. "Religious Personnel: Egypt." Pages 289–92 in *Religions of the Ancient World: A Guide.* Edited by Sarah Iles Johnston. Cambridge, MA: Harvard University Press, 2004.

Ranke, Hermann. "Ištar als Heilgöttin in Ägypten." Pages 412–18 in *Studies Presented to F. Ll. Griffith.* Ed. S. R. K. Glanville. London: Egypt Exploration Society, 1932.

Rast, Walter E. "Cakes for the Queen of Heaven." Pages 167–80 in *Scripture in History and Theology: Studies in Honor of J. Coert Rylaarsdam.* Edited by Arthur L. Merrill and Thomas W. Overholt. Pittsburgh Theoogical Monograph Series 17. Pittsburgh: Pickwick, 1977.

Redford, Donald B. "New Light on the Asiatic Campaigning of Horemheb." *BASOR* 211 (1973): 36–49.

Reinhartz, Adele. *"Why Ask My Name?" Anonymity and Identity in Biblical Narrative.* Oxford: Oxford University Press, 1998.

Rendsburg, Gary. "Bilingual Wordplay in the Bible." *VT* 38 (1988): 354–57.

———. "Double Polysemy in Proverbs 31:19." Pages 267–74 in *Humanism, Culture, and Language in the Near East: Studies in Honor of Georg Krotkeff.* Edited by Asma Afsaruddin and A. H. Mathias Zahniser. Winona Lake, IN: Eisenbrauns, 1997.

Renger, Johannes. "Untersuchungen zum Priestertum in der altbabylonischen Zeit 1. Teil." *Zeitschrift für Assyriologie und vorderasiatische Archäologie* 58 (1967): 110–88.

Richardson, H. Neil. "A Ugaritic Letter of a King to His Mother." *JBL* 66 (1947): 321–24.

Richter, Hans Friedemann. "Gab es einen 'Blutbräutigam'? Erwägungen zu Exodus 4, 24–26." Pages 433–41 in *Studies in the Book of Exodus: Redaction—Reception—Interpretation.* Edited by Marc Vervenne. Leuven: Leuven University Press, 1996.

Ridgway, Brunilde Sismondo. "Images of Athena on the Akropolis." Pages 119–42 in *Goddess and Polis: The Panathenaic Festival in Ancient Athens.* Edited by Jenifer Neils. Hanover, NH: Dartmouth College, Hood Museum of Art; Princeton: Princeton University Press, 1992.

Ritner, Robert K. "Fictive Adoptions or Celibate Priestesses?" *Göttinger Miszellen: Beiträge zur ägyptologischen Diskussion* 164 (1998): 85–90.

———. "Household Religion in Ancient Egypt." Pages 127–58 in *Household and Family Religion in Antiquity*. Edited by John Bodel and Saul M. Olyan. Oxford: Blackwell, 2008.

Roberts, J. J. M. "Isaiah and His Children." Pages 193–203 in *Biblical and Related Studies Presented to Samuel Iwry*. Edited by Ann Kort and Scott Morschauser. Winona Lake, IN: Eisenbrauns, 1985.

Robins, Gay. "The God's Wife of Amun in the 18th Dynasty in Egypt." Pages 65–78 in *Images of Women in Antiquity*. Edited by Averil Cameron and Amélie Kuhrt. London: Routledge, 1983.

———. *Women in Ancient Egypt*. Cambridge, MA: Harvard University Press, 1993.

Robinson, Bernard P. "Zipporah to the Rescue: A Contextual Study of Exodus IV 24–6." *VT* 36 (1986): 447–61.

Robinson, J. *The Second Book of Kings*. CBC. Cambridge, UK: Cambridge University Press, 1976.

Römer, Thomas. "De l'archaique au subversif: le cas d'Exode 4/24–26." *Études théologiques et religieuses* 69 (1994): 1–12.

Rose, Herbert Jennings, and Charles Martin Robertson. "Athena." Pages 138–39 in *The Oxford Classical Dictionary*. Oxford: Oxford University Press, 1970.

Roth, Martha T. *Law Collections from Mesopotamia and Asia Minor*. 2nd ed. SBLWAW 6. Atlanta: Scholars Press, 1997.

Roussel, Pierre, and Marcel Launey. *Inscriptions de Délos*. Paris: Honoré Champion, 1937.

Rudolph, Wilhelm. *Jeremia*. 3rd ed. Tübingen: Mohr, 1968.

Saady, Hassan el-. "Reflections on the Goddess Tayet." *JEA* 80 (1994): 213–17.

Saggs, H. W. F. *The Greatness That Was Babylon*. New York: Hawthorn, 1962.

Saley, Richard J. "The Date of Nehemiah Reconsidered." Pages 151–65 in *Biblical and Near Eastern Studies: Essays in Honor of William Sanford LaSor*. Edited by Gary A. Tuttle. Grand Rapids: Eerdmans, 1978.

Salles, Jean-François. "Phénicie." Pages 553–82 in *La civilisation phénicienne et punique: Manuel de recherche*. Edited by Véronique Krings. Handbuch der Orientalistik: Erste Abteilung, Nahe und der Mittlere Osten 20. Leiden: Brill, 1995.

Šanda, A. *Die Bücher der Könige übersetzt und erklärt*. 2 vols. Exegetisches Handbuch zum Alten Testament 9. Münster: Aschendorff, 1912.

Sargent, Thelma. *The Homeric Hymns: A Verse Translation*. New York: Norton, 1973.

Sasson, Jack M. *From the Mari Archives: An Anthology of Old Babylonian Letters*. Winona Lake, IN: Eisenbrauns, 2015.

———. "On the Use of Images in Israel and the Ancient Near East: A Response to Karel van der Toorn." Pages 63–70 in *Sacred Time, Sacred Place: Archaeology and the Religion of Israel*. Edited by Barry M. Gittlen. Winona Lake, IN: Eisenbrauns, 2002.

———. "Vile Threat: The Rhetoric of a Marital Spat." Pages 923–41 in *De l'argile au numérique: Mélanges assyriologiques en l'honneur de Dominique Charpin*. Edited by Grégory Chambon, Michaël Guichard, and Anne-Isabelle Langlois. Publications de l'Institut du Proche-Orient Ancien du Collège de France 3. Leuven: Peeters, 2019.

Schaeffer Claude F. A. "Les fouilles de Ras Shamra-Ugarit quinzième, seizième et dix-septième campagnes (1951, 1952 et 1953), Rapport sommaire." *Syria* 31 (1954): 14–67.

———. *Reprise des fouilles de Ras Shamra-Ugarit, campagnes XII à XVII (1948–1953)*. Paris: Librairie orientaliste Paul Geuthner, 1955.

Scheid, John, and Jesper Svenbro. "From the Sixteen Women to the Weaver King: Political Weaving in Greece." Pages 9–34 in *The Craft of Zeus: Myths of Weaving and Fabric*. Cambridge, MA: Harvard University Press, 1996.

Schmidt, Brian B. "The Aniconic Tradition: On Reading Images and Viewing Texts." Pages 75–105 in *The Triumph of Elohim: From Yahwisms to Judaisms*. Edited by Diana V. Edelman. Grand Rapids: Eerdmans, 1995.

Schmitt, Rüdiger. "Astarte, Mistress of Horses, Lady of the Chariot: The Warrior Aspect of Astarte." *WdO* 43 (2013): 213–25.

Schott, Albert, and Wolfram von Soden. *Das Gilgamesch-Epos*. Stuttgart: Reclam, 1977.

Segal, Robert A. *Joseph Campbell: An Introduction*. New York: Garland, 1987.

Seibert, Ilse. *Women in the Ancient Near East*. New York: Abner Schram, 1974.

Shedletsky, Lauren, and Baruch A. Levine. "The *mṣr* of the Sons and Daughters of Ugarit (KTU$_2$ 1.40)." *RB* 106 (1999): 321–44.

Sheffer, Avigail. "Needlework and Sewing in Israel from Prehistoric Times to the Roman Period." Pages 527–59 in *Fortunate the Eyes That See: Essays in Honor of David Noel Freedman in Honor of His Seventieth Birthday*. Edited by Astrid B. Beck, Andrew H. Bartelt, Paul R. Raabe, and Chris A. Franke. Grand Rapids: Eerdmans, 1995.

———. "The Use of Perforated Clay Balls on the Warp-Weighted Loom." *TA* 8 (1981): 81–83.

Sheffer, Avigail, and Amalia Tidhar. "Textiles and Basketry." Pages 289–311 in *Kuntillet ʿAjrud (Ḥorvat Teman): An Iron Age II Religious Site on the Judah-Sinai Border*. By Zeʾev Meshel. Edited by Liora Freud. Jerusalem: Israel Exploration Society, 2012.

———. "Textiles and Basketry at Kuntillet ʿAjrud." *Atiqot* 20 (1991): 1–26.

Silverman, Michael H. *Religious Values in the Jewish Proper Names at Elephantine.* AOAT 217. Kevelaer: Butzon & Bercker; Neukirchen-Vluyn: Neukirchener, 1985.

Smith, Mark S. *The Early History of God: Yahweh and the Other Deities in Israel.* 2nd ed. Grand Rapids: Eerdmans, 2002.

———. "Myth and Mythmaking in Canaan and Israel." Pages 2031–41 in *CANE.*

———. *The Origins of Biblical Monotheism: Israel's Polytheistic Background and the Ugaritic Texts.* New York: Oxford University Press, 2001.

———. *Poetic Heroes: Literary Commemorations of Warriors and Warrior Culture in the Early Biblical World.* Grand Rapids: Eerdmans, 2014.

Smith, Mark S., and Elizabeth Bloch-Smith. *The Pilgrimage Pattern in Exodus.* JSOTSup 239. Sheffield: Sheffield Academic, 1997.

Soggin, J. Alberto. *Judges: A Commentary.* OTL. Philadelphia: Westminster, 1981.

Spanier, Ktziah. "The Queen Mother in the Judaean Royal Court: Maacah—A Case Study." Pages 186–95 in *A Feminist Companion to Samuel and Kings.* Edited by Athalya Brenner. FCB 5. Sheffield: Sheffield Academic, 1994.

Speiser, E. A. "The Epic of Gilgamesh." Pages 72–99 in *ANET.*

Stadelmann, Rainer. *Syrisch-Palästinensische Göttheitin in Ägypten.* Probleme der Ägyptologie 5. Leiden: Brill, 1967.

Stager, Lawrence E. "Archaeology, Ecology and Social History: Background Themes in the Song of Deborah." Pages 221–34 in *Congress Volume: Jerusalem 1986.* Edited by J. A. Emerton. VTSup 40. Leiden: Brill, 1988.

———. "The Archaeology of the Family in Ancient Israel." *BASOR* 260 (1985): 1–35.

———. "The Song of Deborah—Why Some Tribes Answered the Call and Others Did Not." *BAR* 15/1 (January/February 1989): 50–64.

Stern, Ephraim. "A Cypro-Phoenician Dedicatory Offering from Tel Dor Depicting a Maritime Scene." *Qad* 27 (1994): 34–38 (Hebrew).

———. "A Phoenician-Cypriote Votive Scapula from Tel Dor: A Maritime Scene." *IEJ* 44 (1994): 1–12.

———. "Priestly Blessing of a Voyage: Recovery of a Harbor Scene at Dor." *BAR* 21/1 (January/February 1995): 51–55.

Stol, Marten. *Birth in Babylonia and the Bible: Its Mediterranean Setting.* Groningen: Styx, 2000.

———. "Private Life in Ancient Mesopotamia." Pages 485–501 in *CANE.*

———. "Women in Mesopotamia." *JESHO* 38 (1995): 123–44.

———. *Women in the Ancient Near East.* Berlin: de Gruyter, 2016.

Stone, Elizabeth C. "The Social Role of the *Nadītu* Women in Old Babylonian Nippur." *JESHO* 25 (1982): 50–70.

Stone, Ken. "Gender and Homosexuality in Judges 19: Subject-Honor, Object-Shame?" *JSOT* 67 (1995): 87–107.

Szlos, M. Beth. "A Portrait of Power: A Literary-Critical Study of the Depiction of Woman in Proverbs 31:10–31." *Union Seminary Quarterly Review* 54 (2000): 97–103.

Taggar-Cohen, Ada. "Why Are There No Israelite Priestesses?" TheTorah.com. 2016. https://www.thetorah.com/article/why-are-there-no-israelite-priestesses.

Tallqvist, Knut. *Akkadische Götterepitheta*. Studia orientalia 7. Helsinki: Societas Orientalis Fennica, 1938.

Talmon, Shemaryahu. "The 'Desert Motif' in the Bible and in Qumran Literature." Pages 31–63 in *Biblical Motifs: Origins and Transformations*. Edited by Alexander Altmann. Philip W. Lown Institute of Advanced Judaic Studies, Brandeis University, Studies and Texts 3. Cambridge, MA: Harvard University Press, 1966.

Tarragon, Jean-Michel de. *Le Culte à Ugarit, d'après les textes de la pratique en cunéiformes alphabétiques*. Cahiers de la Revue biblique 19. Paris: J. Gabalda, 1980.

———. "Les rituels." Pages 125–238 in *Textes religieux et rituels, correspondance*. By André Caquot and Jean-Michel de Tarragon. Vol. 2 of *Textes Ougaritiques*. Littératures anciennes du Proche-Orient 14. Paris: Éditions du Cerf, 1989.

Taussig, Michael. "Transgression." Pages 349–64 in *Critical Terms for Religious Studies*. Edited by Mark C. Taylor. Chicago: University of Chicago Press, 1998.

Taylor, J. Glen. "The Two Earliest Known Representations of Yahweh." Pages 557–66 in *Ascribe to the Lord: Biblical and Other Studies in Memory of Peter C. Craigie*. Edited by Lyle M. Eslinger and J. Glen Taylor. JSOTSup 67. Sheffield: JSOT Press, 1988.

Teeter, Emily. "Celibacy and Adoption among God's Wives of Amun and Singers in the Temple of Amun: A Re-Examination of the Evidence." Pages 405–14 in *Gold of Praise: Studies on Ancient Egypt in Honor of Edward F. Wente*. Edited by Emily Teeter and John A. Larson. Studies in Ancient Oriental Civilization 58. Chicago: The Oriental Institute of the University of Chicago, 1999.

Teixidor, Javier. *The Pagan God: Popular Religion in the Greco-Roman Near East*. Princeton: Princeton University Press, 1977.

Teppo, Saana. "Women and Their Agency in the Neo-Assyrian Empire." M.A. thesis, University of Helsinki, 2005.

Terrien, Samuel. "The Omphalos Myth and Hebrew Religion." *VT* 20 (1970): 315–38.

Thompson, Wesley. "Weaving: A Man's Work." *Classical World* 75 (1981–82): 217–22.

Throntveit, Mark A. *Ezra-Nehemiah*. Interpretation. Louisville: John Knox, 1992.

Thureau-Dangin, François. "Rituel et Amulettes Contre Labartu." *RA* 18 (1921): 161–98.

Tomback, Richard S. *A Comparative Semitic Lexicon of the Phoenician and Punic Languages*. SBLDS 32. Missoula, MT: Scholars Press, 1974.

Toorn, Karel van der. *Family Religion in Babylonia, Syria, and Israel: Continuity and Change in the Forms of Religious Life*. Studies in the History and Culture of the Ancient Near East 7. Leiden: Brill, 1996.

———. *From Her Cradle to Her Grave: The Role of Religion in the Life of the Israelite and the Babylonian Woman*. Biblical Seminar 23. Sheffield: JSOT Press, 1994.

———. "Goddesses in Early Israelite Religion." Pages 83–97 in *Ancient Goddesses: The Myths and the Evidence*. Edited by Lucy Goodison and Christine Morris. London: British Museum Press, 1998.

———. "Israelite Figurines: A View from the Texts." Pages 45–62 in *Sacred Time, Sacred Place: Archaeology and the Religion of Israel*. Edited by Barry M. Gittlen. Winona Lake, IN: Eisenbrauns, 2002.

———. "Magic at the Cradle: A Reassessment." Pages 139–47 in *Mesopotamian Magic: Textual, Historical, and Interpretative Perspectives*. Edited by Tzvi Abusch and Karel van der Toorn. Groningen: Styx, 1999.

———. *Sin and Sanction in Israel and Mesopotamia: A Comparative Study*. Studia Semitica Needlandica 22. Assen: Van Gorcum, 1985.

Tov, Emmanuel. "Lucian and Proto-Lucian: Toward a New Solution of the Problem." *RB* 79 (1972): 101–13.

Trible, Phyllis. "Bringing Miriam out of the Shadows." *BRev* 5/1 (February 1989): 14–25, 34.

———. "Depatriarchalizing in Biblical Interpretation." *Journal of the American Academy of Religion* 41 (1973): 30–48.

———. "Eve and Miriam: From the Margins to the Center." Pages 15–24 in *Feminist Approaches to the Bible*. Edited by Hershel Shanks. Washington, DC: Biblical Archaeology Society, 1995.

———. "An Unnamed Woman: The Extravagance of Violence." Pages 65–91 in *Texts of Terror: Literary Feminist Readings of Biblical Narratives*. Overtures to Biblical Theology 13. Philadelphia: Fortress, 1984.

Tubb, Jonathan N. "Phoenician Dance." *NEA* 66 (2003): 122–25.

Tufnell, Olga. *Lachish III: The Iron Age, Text*. London: Oxford University Press, 1953.

Turner, Victor. "Betwixt and Between: The Liminal Phase in *Rites de Passage*." Pages 93–111 in *The Forest of Symbols: Aspects of Ndembu Ritual*. Ithaca, NY: Cornell University Press, 1967.

———. *Dramas, Fields, and Metaphors: Symbolic Action in Human Society*. Ithaca, NY: Cornell University Press, 1974.

———. "Liminality and Communitas." Pages 94–130 in *The Ritual Process: Structure and Anti-Structure*. Ithaca, NY: Cornell University Press, 1969.

———. *Process, Performance, and Pilgrimage: A Study in Comparative Symbology*. Ranchi Anthropology Series 1. New Delhi: Concept, 1979.

———. "Social Dramas and the Stories about Them." Pages 137–64 in *On Narrative*. Edited by W. J. T. Mitchell. Chicago: University of Chicago Press, 1981. Reprint of "Social Dramas and the Stories about Them." *Critical Inquiry* 7 (1980): 141–68.

Ussishkin, David. "Excavations at Tel Lachish—1973–1977. Preliminary Report." *TA* 5 (1978): 1–97.

Vanstiphout, H. L. J. "The Disputation between Ewe and Wheat." Pages 575–78 in *COS* 1.

Vaux, Roland de. *Ancient Israel: Its Life and Institutions*. The Biblical Resource Series. Grand Rapids: Eerdmans; Livonia, MI: Dove, 1997.

Vawter, Bruce. "The Ugaritic Use of GLMT." *CBQ* 14 (1952): 319–22.

Virolleaud, Charles. "Lettres et documents administratifs: Provenant des archives d'Ugarit." *Syria* 21 (1940): 247–76.

———. "Les nouveaux textes mythologiques et liturgiques de Ras Shamra (XXIVe Campagne, 1961)." Pages 545–606 in *Ugaritica V: Nouveaux textes accadiens, hourrites et ugaritiques des archives et bibliothèques privées d'Ugarit, Commentaires des textes historiques (première partie)*. Mission de Ras Shamra 16. Bibliothèque archéologique et historique 80. Paris: Imprimerie Nationale; Librairie orientaliste Paul Geuthner, 1968.

———. "Textes alphabétiques de Ras-Shamra provenant de la neuvième campagne." *Syria* 19 (1938): 127–41.

Vriezen, Karel J. H. "Cakes and Figurines: Related Women's Cultic Offerings in Ancient Israel?" Pages 251–63 in *On Reading Prophetic Texts: Gender-Specific and Related Studies in Memory of Fokkelien van Dijk-Hemmes*. Edited by Bob Becking and Meindert Dijkstra. Leiden: Brill, 1996.

Waetzoldt, Hartmut. "Die Situation der Frauen und Kinder anhand ihrer Einkommens-verhältnisse zur Zeit der III. Dynastie von Ur." *Altorientalische Forschungen* 15 (1988): 30–44.

Wallis, Gerhard. "Eine Parallel zu Richter 19:29ff und 1. Sam. 11:5ff." *ZAW* 64 (1952): 57–61.

Waltke, Bruce K. "The Role of the 'Valiant Wife' in the Marketplace." *Crux* 35/3 (Summer 1999): 23–34.

Ward, William A. "La déesse nourricière d'Ugarit." *Syria* 46 (1969): 225–39.

Weadock, Penelope N. "The *Giparu* at Ur." *Iraq* 37 (1975): 101–28.

Weidner, Ernst. "Hof- und Harems-Erlasse assyrischer Könige aus dem 2. Jahrtausend v. Chr." *Archiv für Orientforschung* 17 (1954–56): 257–93.

Weinfeld, Moshe. "Kuntillet 'Ajrud Inscriptions and Their Significance." *Studi epigraphici e linguistici* 1 (1984): 121–30.

———. "The Worship of Molech and the Queen of Heaven and Its Background." *UF* 4 (1972): 133–54.

Weiser, Artur. *Das Buch des Propheten Jeremia.* Das Alte Testament Deutsch 20–21. Göttingen: Vandenhoeck & Ruprecht, 1952.

Wellhausen, Julius. *Die Composition des Hexateuchs und der historischen Bücher des Alten Testaments.* Berlin: G. Reimer, 1899.

Wenham, Gordon J. "*Betûlāh* 'A Girl of Marriageable Age.'" *VT* 22 (1972): 326–48.

Westenholz, Joan Goodnick. "Enheduanna, En-Priestess, Hen of Nanna, Spouse of Nanna." Pages 539–56 in *DUMU-E₂-DUB-BA-A: Studies in Honor of Åke W. Sjöberg.* Edited by Hermann Behrens, Darlene Loding, and Martha T. Roth. Occasional Publications of the Samuel Noah Kramer Fund 11. Philadelphia: Samuel Noah Kramer Fund, University Museum, 1989.

———. *Legends of the Kings of Akkade: The Texts.* Winona Lake, IN: Eisenbrauns, 1997.

———. "Religious Personnel: Mesopotamia." Pages 292–95 in *Religions of the Ancient World: A Guide.* Edited by Sarah Iles Johnston. Cambridge, MA: Harvard University Press, 2004.

———. "Tamar, *Qĕdēšā, Qadištu*, and Sacred Prostitution in Mesopotamia." *HTR* 82 (1989): 245–66.

Whitekettle, Richard. "Leviticus 12 and the Israelite Woman: Ritual Process, Liminality, and the Womb." *ZAW* 107 (1995): 393–408.

Wiggins, Steve A. *A Reassessment of 'Asherah': A Study According to the Textual Sources of the First Two Millennia B.C.E.* AOAT 235. Kevelaer: Butzon & Bercker; Neukirchen-Vluyn: Neukirchener, 1993.

Wijk-Bos, Johanna W. H. van. *Ezra, Nehemiah, and Esther.* Westminster Bible Companion. Louisville: Westminster John Knox Press, 1998.

Wilfong, Terry G. "Menstrual Synchrony and the 'Place of Women' in Ancient Egypt (OIM 13512)." Pages 419–34 in *Gold of Praise: Studies on Ancient Egypt in Honor of Edward F. Wente.* Edited by Emily Teeter and John A. Larson. Studies in Ancient Oriental Civilization 58. Chicago: The Oriental Institute of the University of Chicago, 1999.

Wilkinson, Richard H. *The Complete Gods and Goddesses of Ancient Egypt.* London: Thames and Hudson, 2003.

Willett, Elizabeth A. "Women and Household Shrines in Ancient Israel." PhD diss., University of Arizona, 1999.

Williamson, H. G. M. *Ezra, Nehemiah.* WBC 16. Waco, TX: Word Books, 1985.

Wilson, John A. "The Egyptians and the Gods of Asia." Pages 249–50 in *ANET*.

Wilson, Robert R. "The Hardening of Pharaoh's Heart." *CBQ* 41 (1979): 18–36.

———. *Prophecy and Society in Ancient Israel*. Philadelphia: Fortress, 1980.

Winter, Irene. "Women in Public: The Disk of Enheduanna, the Beginning of the Office of En-Priestess, and the Weight of Visual Evidence." Pages 189–201 in *La Femme dans le Proche-Orient Antique: compte rendu de la XXXIIIᵉ Rencontre Assyriologique Internationale (Paris, 7–10 Juillet 1986)*. Edited by Jean-Marie Durand. Paris: Éditions Recherche sur les civilisations, 1987.

Winter, Urs. *Frau und Göttin: Exegetische und ikonographische Studien zum weiblichen Gottesbild im Alten Israel und in dessen Umwelt*. OBO 53. Freiburg: Universitätsverlag; Göttingen: Vandenhoeck & Ruprecht, 1983.

Wolkstein, Diane, and Samuel Noah Kramer. *Inanna, Queen of Heaven and Earth: Her Stories of Hymns from Sumer*. New York: Harper & Row, 1983.

Wolters, Al. "The Meaning of *Kîśôr* (Prov 31:19)." *HUCA* 65 (1994): 91–104.

———. "Proverbs XXXI 10–31 as Heroic Hymn: A Form-Critical Analysis." *VT* 38 (1988): 446–57.

———. "*Ṣôpiyyâ* (Prov 31:27) as Hymnic Participle and Play on *Sophia*." *JBL* 104 (1985): 577–87.

Wright, David P. "David Autem Remansit in Hierusalem: Felix Coniunctio!" Pages 215–30 in *Pomegranates and Golden Bells: Studies in Biblical, Jewish, and Near Eastern Ritual, Law, and Literature in Honor of Jacob Milgrom*. Edited by David P. Wright, David Noel Freedman, and Avi Hurvitz. Winona Lake, IN: Eisenbrauns, 1995.

Wright, David P., and Richard N. Jones. "Discharge." Pages 204–7 in *ABD* 2.

Wyatt, Nicolas. "'Araunah the Jebusite' and the Throne of David." *Studia theologica* 39 (1985): 39–53.

———. *Religious Texts from Ugarit: The Words of Ilimilku and His Colleagues*. The Biblical Seminar 53. Sheffield: Sheffield Academic, 1998.

Yadin, Yigael. "The 'House of Ba'al' of Ahab and Jezebel in Samaria, and That of Athaliah in Judah." Pages 127–35 in *Archaeology in the Levant: Essays for Kathleen Kenyon*. Edited by P. R. S. Moorey and Peter Parr. Warminster, UK: Aris & Phillips, 1978.

Yaron, Reuven. "A Royal Divorce at Ugarit." *Or* 32 (1963): 21–31.

Yee, Gale A. "Ideological Criticism: Judges 17–21 and the Dismembered Body." Pages 138–60 in *Judges and Method: New Approaches in Biblical Studies*. Edited by Gale A. Yee. 2nd ed. Minneapolis: Fortress, 2007.

Yeivin, Shmuel. "Families and Parties in the Kingdom of Judah." *Tarbiz* 12 (1941): 241–67 (Hebrew).

———. "Social, Religious, and Cultural Trends in Judaism under the Davidic Dynasty." *VT* 3 (1953): 149–66.

Yoder, Christine Roy. *Wisdom as a Woman of Substance: A Socioeconomic Reading of Proverbs 1–9 and 31:10–31.* BZAW 304. Berlin: de Gruyter, 2001.

Young, Rodney. "The 1961 Campaign at Gordion." *American Journal of Archaeology* 66 (1962): 153–68.

Yoyotte, Jean. "The Divine Adoratrices of Amun." Pages 174–82 in *Queens of Egypt: From Hetepheres to Cleopatra.* Edited by Christiane Ziegler. Paris: Somogy; Monaco: Grimaldi Forum, 2008.

Zecchi, Marco. "The God Hedjhotep." *Chronique d'Egypte* 76 (2001): 5–19.

Zertal, Adam. "The Settlement of the Tribes of Israel in the Manasseh Region." PhD diss., Tel Aviv University, 1987 (Hebrew).

Zevit, Ziony. "The Khirbet el-Qôm Inscription Mentioning a Goddess." *BASOR* 255 (1984): 39–47.

———. *The Religions of Ancient Israel: A Synthesis of Parallactic Approaches.* New York: Continuum, 2001.

Zimmern, Heinrich. *Akkadische Fremdwörter.* Leipzig: J. C. Hinrichs, 1915.

Illustration Credits

※

Figure 2.1. Red-figure calyx-krater showing Athena Ergane. Inv. no. 1120, from the collection of the Regional Museum of Ceramics of Caltagirone, Sicily. Reproduced with the authorization of the Regional Museum of Ceramics of Caltagirone; further reproduction and/or duplication by any means is prohibited.

Figure 2.2. Detail of an aryballos painting showing Athena and Arachne. From Gladys Davidson Weinberg and Saul S. Weinberg, "Arachne of Lydia at Corinth," in *The Aegean and the Near East: Studies Presented to Hetty Goldman on the Occasion of Her Seventy-Fifth Birthday*, ed. Saul S. Weinberg (Locust Valley, NY: J. J. Augustin, 1956), 263. Used by permission of the American School of Classical Studies Athens-Corinth Excavations.

Figure 2.3. Loom weight with owl. Bryn Mawr College Library Special Collections, Bryn Mawr College. Gift of Cornelius C. Vermule. Accession no. T.182.

Figure 2.4. Drawing of fifth-century BCE relief showing Athena Ergane (?). From Antonio Di Vita, "Atena Ergane in una terracotta dalla Sicilia ed il culto della dea in Atene," *Annuario della Scuola Archeologica di Atene e delle Missioni Italiane in Oriente* 30–32 (1952–54): 143.

Figure 2.5. Sixth-century BCE statue of Athena. Acr. 625 © Acropolis Museum, 2018. Photo by Yiannis Koulelis.

Figure 2.6. Late fifth- or early fourth-century BCE terra-cotta relief plaque of a mortal woman. Acr. 13055 © Acropolis Museum, 2011. Photo by Vangelis Tsiamis.

Figure 2.7. Late fifth- or early fourth-century BCE terra-cotta relief plaque of Athena. Acr. 13057 © Acropolis Museum, 2011. Photo by Vangelis Tsiamis.

Figure 2.8. Parthenon frieze showing Athena. Image © Trustees of the British Museum.

Figure 2.9. Fifth-century BCE terra-cotta statue of Athena (?). Title: *Statuette of a Seated Woman or Goddess.* Date: 500–470 BCE. Medium: Terracotta with slip and traces of polychrome paint. Dimensions: 7 3/8 x 4 5/8 x 3 5/8 in. (18.7 x 11.7 x 9.2 cm). The Museum of Fine Arts, Houston. Gift of Miss Annette Finnigan, 37.16.

Figure 2.10. Remains from the storage room of the so-called Cultic Structure at Tell Taʿanach. From Paul W. Lapp, "The 1963 Excavation at Taʿannek," *BASOR* 173 (1964): 28; the complete article is available on the online journal platform of the University of Chicago Press.

Figure 2.11. Plan of the Taʿanach cultic structure. From © Ziony Zevit, 2001, *The Religions of Ancient Israel: A Synthesis of Parallactic Approaches,* Continuum, an imprint of Bloomsbury Publishing Plc., p. 236. Used by permission of Continuum.

Figure 2.12. Drawing of the Taʿanach cult stand. From © Ziony Zevit, 2001, *The Religions of Ancient Israel: A Synthesis of Parallactic Approaches,* Continuum, an imprint of Bloomsbury Publishing Plc., p. 319. Used by permission of Continuum.

Figure 2.13. Rolled hem from textiles at Kuntillet ʿAjrûd. From Avigail Sheffer and Amalia Tidhar, "Textiles and Basketry," in *Kuntillet ʿAjrud (Ḥorvat Teman): An Iron Age II Religious Site on the Judah-Sinai Border,* by Zeʾev Meshel, edited by Liora Freud (Jerusalem: Israel Exploration Society, 2012), 298 (fig. 9.11).

Figure 2.14. Linen from Kuntillet ʿAjrûd. From Avigail Sheffer and Amalia Tidhar, "Textiles and Basketry," in *Kuntillet ʿAjrud (Ḥorvat Teman): An Iron Age II Religious Site on the Judah-Sinai Border,* by Zeʾev Meshel, edited by Liora Freud (Jerusalem: Israel Exploration Society, 2012), 301 (fig. 9.16).

Figure 5.1. Bronze bowl in the collection of the Metropolitan Museum of Art (74.51.5700). From Jonathan N. Tubb, "Phoenician Dance," *NEA* 66 (2003): 122; the complete article is available on the online journal platform of the University of Chicago Press.

Figure 5.2. Bronze bowl in the collection of the Louvre (AO 4702). From René Dussaud, "Coupe de Bronze Chypro-Phénicienne Trouvée en Gréce," *Annual of the British School at Athens* 37 (1936/1937): 94.

Figure 5.3. Bronze bowl in the collection of the Iran Bastan Museum (Inv. No. 15198). Drawing by Kristin S. Sullivan.

Figure 5.4. Bronze bowl from Cyprus. The Metropolitan Museum of Art, the Cesnola Collection, purchased by subscription, 1874–76 (74.51.4555). Image © The Metropolitan Museum of Art.

Figure 5.5. Silver bowl from Cyprus. The Metropolitan Museum of Art, the Cesnola Collection, purchased by subscription, 1874–76 (74.51.4557). Image © The Metropolitan Museum of Art.

Index of Authors

✣

Index of Subjects

☙

Aaron and Israel's exodus story, 96, 104–5, 108–9

Abi, queen mother of Hezekiah, 187

Abiathar, 159n22, 167, 183

Abijam/Abijah (son of Ma'acah), 153, 156

Adonijah, 153, 166–67, 176–77

Ahab: and Asherah cult, 157–58, 161–64, 197, 198n22, 206; four hundred prophets of, 77; and Jezebel, 161–64, 166

Ahasuerus, 77

Aḫatmilki, queen mother of Ammištamru II, 175–76, 177

Ahaz, 187

Ahaziah, 161, 164, 165

Ahmose, 134–35

Ahmose-Nefertari, 134

Ammištamru II, 175–76, 177

Ammonites, 60–61

Amoashtart (mother of Eshmunazor), 112–13, 122, 123–26, 128–29, 136, 146

Amon, 85

Amos, 77, 163, 212

Anat, 7, 10–11, 22, 30, 118, 179

Anshar, 67

Anu, 67

Aphrodite: Astarte and, 9–10, 123, 126; Homeric Hymn to, 26. *See also* Astarte

Apsu, 66–69, 70

Arachne, 27–28

ark of the covenant, 38n68, 158, 183, 195–96, 215

Asa (grandson of Ma'acah), 146n92, 156–61, 196–97, 198–99

'ăšērâ: cult object and Asherah worship in Yahweh's temples, 36–38, 157–65, 184, 192–98, 205–6, 210–17; term and translation of, 193–96, 198, 211n6

Asherah: associations with fertility, 203; as consort of Yahweh, 31, 167–69, 171–72, 193–96, 199–201, 210, 214; cult object of the 'ăšērâ and Asherah worship in Jerusalem temple courtyard, 36–38, 157–65, 184, 192–98, 205–6, 210–17; and Hathor headdress, 42, 180, 181n35, 194; and Israelite "popular" religion, 206–7; Josiah's reforms and cult of, 19, 36–37, 159–60, 181, 196, 197, 210–17; Kuntillet 'Ajrûd site in northern Sinai, 46–49, 160n25, 162–64, 192–98, 204, 210–11; and Marian cult in early Christianity, 185–88; Ma'acah's erection of her cult image in the Jerusalem temple, 146, 151, 156–61, 184, 198–99, 206; queen mother Jezebel and the cult in Samaria, 161–65, 166–67, 200–201; queen mothers as human surrogates of, 165–69, 171–81, 187–88, 198–201; and Queen of Heaven worship, 7, 203; sacred tree/tree of life imagery, 31, 42–43, 44n91, 157, 194–95, 204, 210; Tel Miqne-Ekron site, 39, 44–46; Tell Ta'anach site, 40–44, 194–95; as West Semitic patron goddess of spinning and weaving, 29–49; Woman Wisdom, 30–36, 58; the women who wove garments for Asherah in the temple (2 Kgs 23:7), 19–20, 36–38, 159, 183–84, 196,

Index of Scripture and Other Ancient Sources

✢